D0078723

The integration of a
child into a social world

The integration of a child into a social world

EDITED BY

MARTIN P. M. RICHARDS

NORTHWEST MISSOURI STATE
UNIVERSITY LIBRARY
MARYVILLE, MISSOURI 64468

CAMBRIDGE UNIVERSITY PRESS

75-10037

Published by the Syndics of the Cambridge University Press
Bentley House, 200 Euston Road, London NW1 2DB
American Branch: 32 East 57th Street, New York, N.Y.10022

© Cambridge University Press 1974

Library of Congress Catalog Card Number: 73–82464

ISBNs:
0 521 20306 6 hard covers
0 521 09830 0 paperback

First published 1974

Printed in Great Britain by
Cox & Wyman Ltd, London, Fakenham and Reading

301.1572
R 51i

APR. 2 3 1975 /5, 50

For Ana

Contents

Contents

Contributors

MARY D. SALTER AINSWORTH
Department of Psychology, Johns Hopkins University

SILVIA M. BELL
Department of Psychology, Johns Hopkins University

JUDITH F. BERNAL
Unit for Research on the Medical Applications of Psychology,
University of Cambridge

N. G. BLURTON JONES
Department of Growth and Development, Institute of
Child Health, University of London

JEROME S. BRUNER
Institute of Experimental Psychology, University of Oxford

JOAN BUSFIELD
Department of Sociology, University of Essex

ROM HARRÉ
Sub-faculty of Philosophy, University of Oxford

JANE HUBERT
Department of Social Anthropology, London School of Economics

DAVID INGLEBY
Medical Research Council Unit on Environmental Factors in Mental
and Physical Illness, London School of Economics

JOHN and ELIZABETH NEWSON
Child Development Research Unit, Department of Psychology,
University of Nottingham

MARTIN P. M. RICHARDS
Unit for Research on the Medical Applications of Psychology,
University of Cambridge

JOANNA RYAN
Unit for Research on the Medical Applications of Psychology,
University of Cambridge

Contributors

JOHN SHOTTER
Department of Psychology, University of Nottingham

DONELDA J. STAYTON
Department of Psychology, Johns Hopkins University

BARBARA and JACK TIZARD
Institution of Education, University of London

Preface and editorial acknowledgement

The first plans for this book were made about two and a half years ago while I was preparing a new course on the psychology of development for social science students. In that course I wanted to discuss several ongoing research projects, but I realised that this presented a problem for students because much of this work was only available in scattered journal articles or unpublished research reports. From this came the idea of asking these researchers to write essays describing recent developments in their work – stepping back a little from the daily life of detail to pick out the broad trends and patterns. As the book was discussed among the potential contributors, another point emerged. Though there were divergences in theoretical views, several people had a sense that their research was moving in a common direction and was starting to constitute something of a 'new look' in development work. So the book itself, in a small way, became a focus for this movement. This has made my job as editor an easy one because it meant that several of the contributors were involved in theoretical discussions with each other and shared many interests in their work. It was not difficult to bring them together to discuss, criticise and, I think, improve the first drafts of the chapters. These exchanges have not led to a consensus but they have helped to extend points of contact between authors and have clarified the disagreements. I would like to thank all the contributors for the time and trouble they put into these discussions.

Members of the Unit for Research on the Medical Applications of Psychology have assisted in the preparation of the book in many ways and, not least, by providing me with a congenial and stimulating environment in which to work. Bob Phillips read the first drafts of the chapters and provided valuable comments. Moira Steel has exercised skill in improving grammar and style as she types. I should like to express my gratitude to them all.

September 1973

M.P.M.R.

I

Introduction

M. P. M. Richards

The book is a collection of essays about the early development and socialisation of children. It is concerned with the process by which an infant becomes a competent member of his social community and develops the fundamental human attributes of speech, social communication, thought, self-reflection and consciousness. These are not evident at birth but emerge slowly as the child develops and apparently grow out of the relationships he forms with the adults around him. Though in many respects we may regard an infant as a presocial being, he is not fully social as he is not yet a competent member of a social community. Rather, he is a biological organism with biological propensities and organisation who becomes social through his encounters with social adults. So throughout development there is an essential tension between the biological and the social. The infant and his social world are in constant interaction; just as the biological infant structures and modifies his social environment, so he is socially structured by it and his biology is modified. All of this means that the study of development is of its very nature interdisciplinary and will cut across the traditional boundaries that have been used to divide up the subject matter of academic study. We have to look outwards from psychology, both towards biology, and sociology and other disciplines, to obtain a rounded view of the developing infant. It is a belief in this broad interdisciplinary approach that unites the contributors to this volume. Though several theoretical issues divide them, this is overriden by a concern to take a broad view of the process of development and to follow the problems across academic boundaries.

British research has traditionally taken this broad approach and has usually avoided the narrow psychological framework which has characterised some American work in this field, particularly the neo-behavourist research on socialisation. I do not think that the maintenance of this openness in British work has anything to do with any higher intellectual standards or any greater toleration for other people's ideas but rather has been a matter of necessity. Our developmental research community has always been small – sometimes to the point of extinction – and it has never been self-sufficient, so its members have been forced

75-10097

1

to make contacts outside psychology with both biologists and social scientists. In doing this they have learnt much about other facets of their own problems. In addition to the more general influence of contact with work going on in other disciplines, there are some rather specific traditions of research which have served to broaden our frameworks. In this introduction I want to discuss two of these which I shall contrast with some American work on socialisation. This, I hope, will provide a perspective from which to view the chapters which follow.

A longstanding liberal concern with social inequalities in our society which has been so central in British sociology was extended to research on children in the pioneering work of J. W. B. Douglas. In 1946, he began a survey designed to examine the availability and effectiveness of antenatal and maternity services which involved interviewing every woman who gave birth during one week in March. As these data were analysed, the potential value of the sample for a follow-up study was quickly realised and the National Survey, as it came to be known, has continued until the babies reached adulthood. The project has led to four major reports (Douglas and Rowntree, 1948; Douglas and Blomfield, 1958; Douglas, 1964; Douglas, Ross and Simpson, 1968) as well as a wealth of papers which trace in considerable detail the development, health, education and social circumstances of this cohort of children. In addition, the National Survey served as a model for another project which was launched twelve years later, the Perinatal Mortality Survey. Again the first concern was the mothers, their infants and the circumstances of their deliveries (Butler and Bonham, 1963; Butler and Alberman, 1969), but once again the sample has been followed up and is providing valuable psychological and educational information about the progress of the children (Davie, Butler and Goldstein, 1972).

Large-scale surveys of this nature are often criticised because, it is said, they tell us nothing about the process of development. This, of course, is true as all they can give us are correlations between environmental factors and attributes of the children, and both have to be measured in a relatively rough and ready way, given the large size of the samples. However, this by no means exhausts their usefulness for the developmentalist because they do draw attention to the range of factors that must be considered in the analysis of development and firmly locate the process in both the biological and the social world. We have learnt, for example, that not only are premature babies more often born to mothers who are in less privileged social positions but that the developmental outcome of prematurity is closely related to the social class of their families. More detailed analysis of these sorts of problems has been

2

pursued by a lively community of medical sociologists, particularly at Aberdeen. Illsley (1967), whose work has been very influential in the field, describes the scope as follows:

Women begin their preparation for childbearing early in life – indeed, they begin it at the time of their own conception. Adult health, which has so strong a bearing on reproductive functioning, is the end result of a series of social and physical experiences which begin with fetal health or injury and continue throughout childhood and adolescence. The forces that determine childhood growth and adult health are interwoven with social processes which influence value systems and have significant effects on courtship, ages at marriage and conception, attitudes toward intercourse and marriage, toward pregnancy, health and illness, and toward behavior concerning birth control and child spacing. Nutritional habits which affect growth and development and may influence reproductive efficiency themselves have social and economic origins and are linked to value systems.

In this view, the pattern of childbearing, for the individual or the social group, represents the complex outcome of long-term, interacting social and biological experiences. This interplay of forces is relevant not only to the incidence of pregnancy complications but also to the long-term effects of the obstetric process on the functioning of the child. Malfunctioning of the child, although directly associated with obstetric complications, may have its origins in genetic factors or in childhood experience. Obstetric difficulties in the mother and impaired development in the child may have no causal connection, both being independent manifestations of an unhealthy social or physical environment. Disentangling of correlation and cause may therefore demand the study of social processes and their effects on parents, child, and siblings over a long period.

Even this is too narrow a canvas. Geographical and secular variations in pregnancy outcome make it necessary to study the distinctive features of regional, national, ethnic, and cultural groups and to take account of socio-economic change, trends in age and parity, etc. Phenomena loosely given the same name in different places or at different times (e.g., prematurity or pre-eclampsia) may differ in their clinical significance and in their underlying causes as markedly as infant mortality in primitive Africa, Victorian England, and contemporary Sweden (p. 76).

It is this same broad canvas that is required for the analysis of development and we are indeed fortunate in having this research as a foundation for our own studies.

The second tradition I want to mention is not British in origin but is one we have inherited from the Continent. This is animal ethology. My remarks here will be brief as a much fuller discussion by Blurton Jones appears later in the book. Ethological work has been important for developmental studies of children at the level of methodology, theory and for what we might loosely term our frames of mind.

Ethology, through its own development from the earlier interests of naturalists, has always laid great stress on techniques of observation of animals in their natural habitat. These methods had an immediate appeal

3

for psychologists working with children who had many dissatisfactions with their methods of laboratory experiment and indirect interview techniques. They wanted to get out into the child's environment and the ethologists produced techniques that could be adapted for studies of this kind. At the theoretical level, ethology has provided one of the starting points for Bowlby's work (1951, 1958, 1969). By bringing together strands of ethological and Freudian theory Bowlby provided a view of the relationship of mother and infant which has given a focus for British work for the last two decades. Though these theories have been increasingly subject to criticism and modification in recent years, as will be seen in a later chapter of this book (see also Schaffer, 1971; Rutter, 1972), their importance as a stimulus for research cannot be overrated.

As well as by their direct effect, theories modify research and thinking by their more diffuse influence on attitudes and frames of mind and on the general intellectual climate in which research is carried out. In this way too, ethology has played a major role in shaping current developmental studies. Psychologists have come to appreciate the importance of biological structure as well as becoming used to asking evolutionary questions about their own societies.

Early in the preparation of this volume, one of the publishers' representatives suggested that the word 'socialisation' should appear in the title. This was rejected – unanimously, I think – by the contributors. In doing this we were not trying to suggest that socialisation was not a central theme of the book but that the word itself had become associated with theoretical views of the topic which we did not share. In particular, the word has tended to become the property of psychologists who adopt a neo-behaviourist approach to the study of development, and it is this line of American research I want to contrast with the British traditions I have just described. As I have already indicated, the analysis of human social development requires both an adequate notion of what a society is and of a biological individual, as well as of the ways in which an individual lives in his social and environmental space. These are lacking in the neo-behaviourist tradition, where socialisation is seen as a psychological process of learning and of the training of the individual. It is regarded as something that has to be imposed on the child – the child does not become social but is made social by the conscious efforts of various members of society. The difference between becoming and being made is an important one because the neo-behaviourists imply that the child is mere putty to be worked on by external forces. The child's biological structure is played down and he is seen to be entirely passive in his own development. Indeed, the notion of development itself may

4

be lost, and is replaced by a very mechanical idea of change as a response to external pressure.

This can lead to a very one-sided view of the origin of individual differences and Bell (1968) has pointed out how pervasive this has been in American work. A one-way influence of parents on children was assumed. Researchers attempted to relate differences between children to variations among parents and their caretaking techniques without preserving any notion of interaction or the influence of children on parents. A large body of work in this mode searched for relationships between such things as feeding routines and toilet training methods and characteristics of the children. Caldwell's (1964) thorough review shows how little was learnt through these studies. Stable associations were not found, not necessarily because these caretaking practices do not have any effects but because the methodology assumed that they would have the same effects on all children at all times. No allowance was made for the possibility that parents adapted their caretaking styles to the characteristics and demands of their particular children. Subsequent studies which did take account of individual differences between children and allowed for interactive effects and the possibility that different infants might react to the same environmental conditions in varying ways have disclosed some consistent patterns. For example, Moss (1967) was able to relate prenatal assessments of maternal personality and postnatal caretaking measures to the infant's behaviour provided that he took account of the infant's individual level of irritability.

In the analysis of an interactive system, as we have with the child and his environment, it is not only necessary to take account of the roles of both sides of the process but also to use a methodology which allows for the richness of the interaction itself. This cannot always be reduced to simple rules of cause and effect. Some of the complications are well illustrated by an observational study of two children by Escalona and Corman (1971). One of the things that interested these authors was the extent to which the mother's presence or absence influenced the behaviour of their children. Both children showed a marked change in behaviour when their mothers left the room but the direction of the effect was opposite in the two cases. One child became less responsive and activity was reduced, while the other child did exactly the reverse. Results like this do not mean that we cannot find general principles to describe a child's responses to his environment but that our analysis on which generalisations are based must take account of the complexities of interaction and the broader contexts on which it occurs. We must also learn to see the world a little more from the child's point of view. In the case of Escalona and Corman's children, clearly the departure of the mother had a different meaning for the two children. Our problem here is partly one of methodology. The physical sciences have given us methods which are highly efficient for the analysis of simple mechanical systems. The temptation is to use them for complex interactive systems because we have little else to put in their place. In later chapters there are suggestions of where we may look for more appropriate methods; however, we have to recognise that we are severely limited in our abilities to analyse interactive systems. But just because we are limited in our techniques, it does not mean that we should attempt to treat the interactions of the developing child as if they were those of a simple machine.

The process of socialisation has been further obscured by a strongly functionalist view in American sociology which went hand in hand with the neo-behaviourist psychology. As several writers have noted, it is not too surprising that a society that was built by immigrants from diverse cultures should be concerned about how these people will fit in and how they will form a common identity. Furthermore, as that common identity was seen to emerge it was not unnatural that social scientists should be impressed by the apparent effectiveness of schools and other institutions in moulding children to their new life. But such concerns have led to a brand of sociology which has overemphasised the adaptation of individuals to particular styles of life and social roles and has underemphasised the process by which the individual is able to take part in any social life. Adapting to a new job has been put on a par with the process of becoming a social human being. The term socialisation has been used to describe both these processes and in doing so the word has become trivialised. This view of socialisation is adopted by Brim (1966) who states that 'the function of socialization is to transform the human raw material of society into good working members'. Elsewhere he says that the sociological questions are 'how society manages to socialize the individual so the work of society gets done and how individuals manage gradually to transform the social system in which they live'. If one thinks of the history of the various ethnic groups of immigrants that arrived in the States between the two world wars, one can see the pertinence of these questions, but the use of the term 'socialisation' to cover all these issues has led to much confusion and tends to treat as unproblematic the primary concern of this book – the process by which a child develops any kind of social life. This psychological superficiality is indicated by the way this school of sociology regards various groups of people they label as deviant as examples of the 'failure' of socialisation. For the way in which the contributors to this volume would wish to use the term, a failure of socialisation would create a non-human being, if a being at all. It would be a creature lacking in the powers of speech, in consciousness, in the ability to form any social relationships, or to reflect on his own actions. Members of a group which sociologists may describe as deviant do not, of course, fail in these ways. They are simply people who have opted for, or who have been forced to adopt, a moral order which is unacceptable to the majority.

Our task in the analysis of socialisation is to describe, and explain, the process by which the single cell that is formed at conception develops into a recognisable human who can live among and communicate with the fellow members of his society: so we are concerned with the development of the basic human attributes – the skills necessary to take any part in human life. These are acquired, at least in a partial form, relatively early in the long period of human immaturity so that by the time a child is two or three years old he is able to take part effectively in social exchange. His ability to speak is the most obvious indication of his membership of society but this is neither necessary nor sufficient and much else is required. He must be able to assess and use the social context in which he lives so it can give meanings to his actions. He must build an internal picture of this world so he can order it, and reflect on his own actions from the position of others. He needs to understand the meaning of I, me, you and us. He must be able to make public his feelings and his intentions. Motor skills too are required. It is on these kinds of attributes that our adaptations (or lack of them) to varying environments and social roles depend.

To approach this task we must build a holistic view of the developing organism which can include both biological structure and the world in which it lives. A child is born with a biological structure that allows behaviour to be patterned and adapted to the surroundings. Growth and adaptation take place in a social world. A mother is much more than a caretaker, she can and does structure the infant's environment. She and the other people that surround the infant relate their actions to his and so provide him with a means of building connections with their world and an entry to their social culture. They also act as mediators for him of the wider social order and it is through them that the child begins to learn about his place in the world.

The book is divided into three sections. The first deals with the infant's social world and its connections with the wider society; then attention is turned to the infant himself and his acquisition of some of the basic human attributes. The final section is more theoretical and contains a number of diverse views about the nature of development and socialisation and our ways and means of studying it.

The first section begins with an analysis by Joan Busfield of our assumptions about marriage and parenthood. She underlines some of the consequences of more or less universal parenthood in our society and shows how closely a woman's identity is tried to her production of children. Little work of this kind has ever been undertaken but it is essential if we are to understand the ways in which a mother as a member of our society regards her child. This approach is taken a step nearer the infant by Jane Hubert's investigation of preparation for childbirth and mothers' feelings about the experience of pregnancy and delivery. With her anthropological framework, she is able to place our way of doing things in a wider perspective. This demonstrates how fragmented our intergenerational transfer of knowledge has become so that each mother must develop her own way of coming to terms with her child. Seldom are the ways of infants learnt first hand before the event through relatives and friends and so a mother becomes very dependent on the sometimes contradictory advice of professionals. It is the nature of this advice that forms the theme of the Newsons' essay. They trace changes in the professionals' wisdom over the last century and show how it has often reflected our moral concerns about children.

The first chapter of the second section has a dual aim. It both discusses the very early steps in the social development of infants and attempts to relate the earlier chapters on the social environment of infancy to the succeeding ones on the interrelation of mother and child. In the first of these, Mary Ainsworth and her co-workers provide an introduction to attachment theory and describe some of their recent empirical investigations of the connections between styles of maternal response and the growth of the mother–infant relationship. This research follows in the theoretical framework developed by John Bowlby. In a different way the Tizards' chapter also stems from Bowlby's work. Bowlby's influential World Health Organisation report, *Maternal Care and Mental Health* (1951), was concerned with the care of children reared outside families in institutions. The Tizards have investigated what might well be termed post-Bowlby substitute care. They demonstrate that the social structure of an institution has a great deal to do with the ways in which the caretakers relate to the children and so influence their development. Judy Bernal's essay takes a closer look at attachment theory itself and some of the problems in measuring attachment. She suggests that it may underplay some of the particularly human aspects of an infant's development. The two contributions following look at two such aspects: Jerry Bruner discusses motor skills while Joanna Ryan analyses the early stages of the acquisition of language. Both these chapters place the development they discuss firmly in the context of the adult–child interaction. Joanna Ryan shows that it is through his relationship with adults that the child builds meanings

8

for his words and acquires the many paralinguistic skills, apart from speech itself, which are required to use speech for communication. This chapter is unusual in that its author uses recent philosophical work to clarify psychological concepts.

The final section provides some rather diverse theoretical views. Both John Shotter and Rom Harré stress what they regard as the uniquely human nature of our own development. Harré's work extends some of the ideas of the ethno-methodologists to infancy and childhood and in so doing provides another view of attachment theory. Nick Blurton Jones's contribution has quite different roots. He describes the relevance of ethology to our view of socialisation and so pulls the discussion towards zoology and a more evolutionary perspective. The final chapter is intended to serve as a general comment on the rest of the book. In it, David Ingleby looks at the ideological basis of child psychology and so gives us a starting point from which we may build a more reflective attitude to our own work.

REFERENCES

Bell, R. Q. (1968). A re-interpretation of the direction of effects in studies of socialization. *Psychol. Rev.* **75**, 81–95.
Bowlby, J. (1951). *Maternal Care and Mental Health*. Geneva, W.H.O.
Bowlby, J. (1958). The nature of the child's tie to his mother. *Int. J. Psycho-Anal.* **39**, 9–52.
Bowlby, J. (1969). *Attachment and Loss,* Vol. I, *Attachment*. London, Hogarth Press.
Brim, O. G. (1966). Socialization through the life-cycle. In Brim, O. G. and Wheeler, S. (eds.). *Socialization after Childhood*. New York, Wiley.
Butler, N. R. and Bonham, D. G. (1963). *Perinatal Mortality*. Edinburgh, Livingstone.
Butler, N. R. and Alberman, E. D. (eds.) (1969). *Perinatal Problems*, Edinburgh, Livingstone.
Caldwell, B. M. (1964) The effect of infant care. In Hoffman, M. L. and Hoffman, L. N. W. (eds.). *Review of Child Development Research*, Vol. 1. New York, Russell Sage Foundation.
Davie, R., Butler, N. R. and Goldstein, H. (1972). *From Birth to Seven*. London, Longmans.
Douglas, J. W. B. (1964). *The Home and the School*. London, MacGibbon and Kee.
Douglas, J. W. B. and Blomfield, J. M. (1958). *Children under Five*, London, Allen and Unwin.
Douglas, J. W. B. and Rowntree, G. (1948). (Joint Committee of R.C.O.G. and Population Investigation Committee) *Maternity in Great Britain*. London, Oxford Univ. Press.
Douglas, J. W. B., Ross, J. M. and Simpson, H. R. (1968). *All Our Future*. London, Davies.
Escalona, S. K. and Corman, H. H. (1971). The impact of mothers' presence upon behavior: the first year. *Human Development*, **14**, 2–15.

Illsley, R. (1967). The sociological study of reproduction and its outcome. In Richardson, S. A. and A. F. Guttmacher (eds.). *Childbearing – Its Social and Psychological Aspects*. Baltimore, Williams and Wilkins.

Moss, H. A. (1967). Sex, age and state as determinants of mother–infant interaction. *Merrill–Palmer Quart.* **13**, 19–36.

Rutter, M. (1972). *Maternal Deprivation Reassessed*. London, Penguin.

Schaffer, H. R. (1971). *The Growth of Sociability*, London, Penguin.

2

Ideologies and reproduction[1]

Joan Busfield

It is a commonplace that patterns of reproduction in different societies are neither identical nor unchanging. Both levels of fertility and types of fertility control show considerable variation. Whilst in some societies high mortality has been matched by a pattern of virtually unrestricted reproduction, uncontrolled fertility is rare in human populations (Lorimer, 1954), and there is considerable evidence of limitation of fertility below the maximum level not only in pre-industrial Europe (Wrigley, 1969) but also among the so-called primitive populations (Douglas, 1966). In modern industrial societies where mortality is very low, fertility control is also extensive. Control of fertility, whether high or low, has always been achieved by a variety of means, sometimes consciously related to restricting reproduction, sometimes not, and any one level of fertility may be achieved in a large number of ways. All these phenomena have been widely noted and discussed: less marked is the fact that the beliefs surrounding reproduction in different societies likewise vary. A society or a social group's pattern of reproduction occurs in an ideological context where particular beliefs, both those about reproduction *per se* and others that have reproductive consequences, affect, and are affected by, that pattern of reproduction. These beliefs provide a cognitive framework which structures individual action: they constitute the social reality in which reproduction takes place and they offer guidelines for, and justifications of, the actions of members of a society, which in aggregate result in a particular level of fertility. Whether our concern is with the determinants of family size and the spacing of children, or with the nature of social relations within the family, or with childrearing and child development, the beliefs and values that frame the childrearing process are of considerable importance.[2] As I shall discuss below, they may be used, for instance, to legitimate particular childrearing practices.

[1] Plamenatz (1970) in considering the meaning of the word ideology says 'It is used to refer to a set of closely related beliefs or ideas, or even attitudes characteristic of a group or community. This is, as it were, the least that it means, though it often means more besides.' I use the word here in this minimal sense.

[2] It is interesting that the study of fertility has been very separate from the study of the family. Not only has the former tended to be separate from sociological

11

Recent studies of fertility have tended to focus almost exclusively on the economic and social structural determinants of fertility and have ignored the cultural and ideological framework without, however, showing that these factors are unimportant.[3] One notable exception is the work of J. A. Banks (1954) on the decline of family size in Victorian England. Apart from this, the area has been left almost entirely to anthropologists, and even here the volume of work in recent years has not been very great (Lorimer, 1954; Ardener, 1962). Banks suggests that economic factors led to the decline in family size by constraining the realisation of existing values as to the proper time to marry, the necessary style of living and so forth. It was the necessity of conforming to these standards, which were not themselves unchanging, in a new set of economic circumstances that resulted in the alteration in fertility behaviour.

The relationship between ideological and economic factors is a complex one. In the short term, ideologies probably provide a framework within which economic and social structural factors operate, exerting their influence by controlling the conception of possible courses of action, the exact course that is realised depending on the given set of economic and social circumstances. However, in the long term, it may well be that it is economic and structural factors that are of major importance in changing beliefs about reproduction: that they encourage particular patterns of fertility and that existing ideologies adjust to them. If this is so, the ideologies may still, nevertheless, be important factors in maintaining and regulating the fertility behaviour. Moreover, ideological and cultural change will often occur at a different pace from the changes in social and economic conditions. However, as we shall see, the relevant beliefs themselves sometimes have a conditional nature and incorporate references to economic and structural factors.

The aim of this paper is to describe the beliefs surrounding fertility in England at present, contrasting them with those of different times and places.[4] Delineation of the ideological framework of reproduction is the

[3] The exception to this is religion, which is treated as a face-sheet variable and hardly ever as anything more. For a review of much recent work and further references, see Hawthorn (1970).

[4] An important source of data on these and other beliefs is the rationales that people offer to explain their behaviour, often *post hoc*. Such public and everyday rationales (commonsense rationales) have to be distinguished from sociologists' attempts at scientific explanations of both ideal and statistical norms, explanations which may or may not coincide with the rationales (Schutz, 1967).

concerns, but even where a sociology of fertility has been attempted, there has been little effort to use the insights that might be gained from a sociological understanding of family life.

12

essential preliminary to any attempt to elucidate the precise causal role played by the beliefs. I will focus especially on those beliefs that are generally accepted throughout the society rather than on those which differentiate individuals and social groups.[5] In examining the main aspects of the ideological context of reproduction, we will first examine beliefs about parenthood in general and secondly examine beliefs surrounding the specific design and building of the family of procreation.[6]

PARENTHOOD

Perhaps the most significant aspect of current reproductive behaviour in industrial societies, and yet one that is so taken for granted that it is rarely mentioned, is the fact that parenthood remains almost universal. Reproduction is statistically normative for the majority of adults within these societies. Widespread parenthood has remained, despite the extensive control of fertility, and in general changes in the proportions who become parents have played a relatively small part in the control of fertility.

In England and Wales approximately 80 per cent of adults become parents.[7] The fact that such large proportions become parents in industrial societies is perhaps somewhat surprising. Population reproduction could, presumably, be carried out just as efficiently by a smaller proportion of women having larger families. However, restriction of parenthood seems only to arise where there are strong pressures to control fertility and alternative means of control are either inefficient or unacceptable within the existing ideological context (Davis, 1963).

[5] In the study of our own culture it is easier, and more relevant for some explanatory purposes, to study obvious differences in beliefs at one time. However, by adopting a cross-cultural or diachronic comparative perspective we can highlight beliefs that exist in our culture that are accepted by almost all its members. These beliefs tend to be taken for granted yet, taking a broader perspective, they should not be totally ignored. They may well play a major role in determining a particular activity and are ignored at our cost. This is one attempt to remedy this common oversight. The approach is one that has been more often adopted by anthropologists than sociologists. It makes use of general knowledge of the culture obtained by 'participant observation' (in this case by being a member of that culture), as well as data obtained by surveys and so forth.

[6] Much of my evidence about the ideal norms and rationales governing parenthood and family building comes from fifty detailed interviews carried out by the author as an unpublished pilot study for a survey of fertility. The interviews were of fertile married women living in Ipswich and were carried out in the period September 1966 to March 1967. The interviews were relatively unstructured and were tape-recorded. Unattributed quotations in the text are from these interviews and are verbatim.

[7] It may seem surprising that such an apparently obvious statistic is not available. However, the Census only asks questions about the fertility of women who have been married at some time, and it is not possible to make the necessary calculations from the information provided by the Registrar General.

13

Ireland is an example of a country where, at times, relatively large proportions of the population have been excluded from the role of parent when it has been important to control fertility, yet many of the other possible means of control have been unacceptable.

How are strong pressures for parenthood created in English society? What beliefs exist as to the importance and value of having children? In England, the pattern of extensive parenthood occurs in a cultural context that both directly stresses the importance and desirability of becoming a parent and also encourages childbearing in less obvious ideological ways. As I shall show, the direct and indirect pressures are closely inter-linked and together create a situation in which having children is a natural and inevitable event for the majority of individuals.

One major feature of the current ideological framework of reproduction, which plays an essential role in encouraging parenthood, is the existence of a closely defined link between marriage and childbearing. On the one hand it is expected and regarded as desirable that those who marry will have children; and on the other it is expected that those who want to have children will marry.

The connection between marriage and childbearing is obviously a fundamental one. Marriage is often seen as the social institution that legally and publicly arranges childbearing and is sometimes defined in these terms. The most recent edition of *Notes and Queries,* the standard terminological guide for anthropologists, defines marriage as 'a union between a man and a woman such that children born to the woman are legitimate offspring to both partners' (Royal Anthropological Institute, 1951). This definition sees marriage as an agreement that creates legitimate offspring, i.e. offspring who can stand in clearly defined relationships to existing kinship groups, which is important not only for the transmission of property but also for social location and identification. As Lucy Mair (1971, p. 17) puts it when considering the functions of husbands, 'husbands are important mainly as fathers; that is to say, as men who give their name, their status in so far as this is inherited, and the right to inherit their property, to the children of a woman with whom they have made a particular kind of contract'. However, definitions like this ignore other activities which in many societies are arranged through marriage such as the control and regulation of sexual activities, the arrangement of household and economic activities, and the organisation of residential location; and they ignore, too, the fact that the importance of marriage as a way of institutionalising reproduction varies between societies.[8] We should not assume that having children is the only reason for marriage. Nevertheless, in many societies one of the central functions

---

[8]   For discussions of the problem of defining marriage cross-culturally see Goldschmidt (1966) and Harris (1969).

of marriage is the arrangement of childrearing and related activities such as the transmission of property.

It is not surprising, therefore, that in England as in most societies, marriage is regarded as a desirable step in childrearing; that it is held up as an ideal for those who want to have children. In some societies the ideal is not always realised, sometimes because the economic costs of the social conventions surrounding marriage are excessive (Blake, 1961). But this is not generally true in England at present, although the expense of providing living accommodation and household goods is an important reason for deferring marriage, just as it has been in the past, especially amongst certain social groups (Banks, 1954). It is perhaps more surprising that those who do marry, for whatever reason, are usually expected and encouraged to have children. In English society, at least, just as marriage is deemed necessary for those who have children, so having children is deemed necessary for those who marry. In other societies, having a child is even more crucial to marriage. The marriage may not be finalised until a first or even a second child is born, or a marriage becomes void if no children are born within a certain time (Lorimer, 1954). Amongst the Nuer, marriage involves four steps. The first three are the betrothal, wedding and consummation ceremonies, but it is only the fourth, the birth of the first child, that completes the marriage (Evans-Pritchard, 1951).

How are the two aspects of the relationship between marriage and reproduction stressed in English society? First, how is marriage made a necessary condition for reproduction? The main method is the culturally pervasive one of the stigmatisation of illegitimacy. Illegitimacy itself is relatively rare in England and Wales. In 1967 the proportion of illegitimate births of all live births was 84 per 1000 (Registrar General, 1969). Its stigmatisation occurs in a variety of ways. Children born outside marriage are distinguished in law from those born within marriage (or where the parents marry subsequently). They have a specific designation, being referred to as either children born 'out of wedlock' or 'bastards' and are given a different status from other children, primarily *vis-à-vis* rights, of inheritance. More importantly, stigmatisation is also expressed in the everyday societal beliefs that the illegitimate child is disadvantaged. The typical objection to illegitimacy is presented in terms of the consequences for the child who, it is claimed, will suffer from the fact of illegitimacy, both from the label of illegitimate, with the sense it creates of being different from other children, and from the absence of a father to provide guides and models for his or her behaviour and to share with the mother the physical and psychological burdens of childrearing. It is the father's role in facilitating a better emotional environment for childrearing that is given especial prominence in the argument. The current prejudice against 'broken homes', under which homes with unmarried mothers are subsumed, as the cause of all behavioural and psychological abnormalities and difficulties provides a buttress for the arguments.[9] Less attention is paid in the defence of legitimacy to differences in the economic situation of the fatherless child and to the family's disadvantaged material position, which arises from the inferior position of women in society, particularly in the labour market. Yet it is arguable that it is this more than anything else that is the problem for fatherless children (Marsden, 1969).

Given the way in which illegitimacy is stigmatised in England it is not surprising that the stigma of a premarital conception is less than that of an illegitimate birth, for similar arguments and objections cannot be made when the parents do marry at some stage and thereby create this ideal family structure for their child. Although the ideal is still held to be conception within marriage, the proportion of those whose first child is conceived before marriage is now quite large. In 1966–7 in England and Wales, of those with no previous liveborn children, about one in four births were conceived premaritally, and for similar women aged under 20 at marriage, about 40 per cent of births were conceived before marriage (Registrar General, 1969). Moreover, the percentage of extramaritally conceived maternities legitimated by marriage before the birth of the child has declined from 60 per cent in 1950 to 51 per cent in 1967 (*ibid.*). In England and Wales no legal distinction is made between premaritally conceived children and those conceived within marriage. A further factor that may account for the lesser stigmatisation of premarital conception than illegitimacy is that concealment is easier with the former, although rapid adoption makes concealment possible with illegitimate births. There is some evidence that adoption is seen as the socially acceptable way of handling illegitimacy and that those who do not adopt this alternative are more heavily stigmatised than those who do, allowing for the fact that subsequent to adoption the fact of having had an illegitimate birth may be totally concealed. Moreover, where children suitable for adoption are relatively scarce, attitudes to illegitimacy may become somewhat more tolerant (Vincent, 1961).

It is the 'marriage entails childbearing' aspect of the connection between the two that introduces a strong pro-natalist component into

---

[9] The prejudice has been well-documented by Wootton (1959) in her discussion of delinquency. The extent to which it may also be unfounded with respect to other consequences has been carefully examined by Illsley and Thompson (1961), who found in a sample of Aberdeen women that those who had come from homes broken in some way, were on the whole better adjusted to pregnancy and maternity in later life. A study that provides evidence of some negative consequences for the illegitimate child when adoption does not occur, though attributing these in many instances to poorer material circumstances, is that of Eileen Crellin and others (1971).

the ideology. There are a variety of ways in which childbearing is made to seem obligatory for those who marry. First, it is interesting to note that the marriage service itself often expounds that an important reason for marriage is childbearing, creating an expectation that those who marry will have children. In England and Wales in 1973, 45 per cent of marriages were solemnised with Church of England or Church in Wales ceremonies (Registrar General, 1969). The 1928 version of the Church of England prayerbook – the form commonly used in these services – lists three 'causes for which Matrimony was ordained' and states, 'First it was ordained for the procreation of children, to be brought up in the fear and nurture of the Lord and to the praise of His holy name'. In the Roman Catholic marriage ceremony (which accounted for 11 per cent of marriage ceremonies in 1967) there is a similar emphasis on the importance of having children, and this is emphasised throughout the Roman Catholic theology.

More importantly, the connection is stressed in the explicit norm against childlessness, except where it is involuntary, amongst married couples. In 1961, of women aged 30 with uninterrupted first marriages, only 17 per cent had not had at least one live birth, and of similar women aged 40 only 13 per cent had not had at least one live birth (General Register Officer, 1966). There has been some variation in the proportion of married women in the post-war period who have remained childless. As a considerable proportion of these women (probably about 10 per cent of all married women) do not choose to remain childless, the proportion of married women having or wishing to have children is very high. Moreover, the pressure does not simply arise from the statistical norm. First, childbearing is simply assumed. For those who are not already pregnant at marriage, the question is not 'Are you going to have children?' but '*When* are you going to have children?' And for those who appear to be deviating and have not yet had children after a few years of marriage, control is exerted through definitions of selfishness and lack of responsibility. Childless couples are liable to a variety of strictures implicitly condemning their behaviour. One argument uses the idea that children reduce a couple's freedom to suggest that married couples without children cannot cope with such restrictions and are somehow less mature and less adequate than those who can. When a woman becomes pregnant after some years of marriage, comments like, 'You've had your freedom long enough' indicate that willingness to give up that sort of freedom is defined as a virtue rather than a vice. Similarly, spending on consumer durables and evening entertainment, though generally regarded as pleasurable, desirable and a symbol of status, becomes reprehensible if substituted for childbearing. Rainwater (1965), in some preliminary work for his study of family design in American cities, asked respondents to characterise a woman who wants no children and found that 'there was universal rejection of the woman who wants no children as either totally self-involved, childish, neurotic or in poor health'.

Secondly, childbearing is also encouraged by the belief that children help to maintain a marriage: that somehow children ensure stability. Children are seen as providing a shared interest between husband and wife. Where other shared interests are few, this may be particularly important. To quote the study of a mining community: 'Many a mother admits eventually that but for the children she might have found it impossible to maintain the tie with her husband (Dennis, Henriques and Slaughter, 1969). The corollary of this belief is the idea that divorce is more likely amongst childless couples. In fact, the figures are not unambiguous (Chester, 1971) and are difficult to interpret.

With the existence of a strong ideological connection between marriage and childbearing, entry into the parental role is effected either by beliefs that directly stress the desirability of childbearing, or by beliefs that stress the desirability of marriage for reasons other than those of childbearing, since once married these couples will encounter pressures to have children, or by beliefs that stress the desirability of both.

Perhaps the strongest encouragement to the joint role of marriage and childbearing is the idea that it is a married couple with children who constitute a proper, natural and complete family. The idea that it is children who create a family for a married couple is conveyed in expressions such as 'they haven't got a family' or 'their family has left home'. For in the context of a married couple, to talk of the family is to talk of the children. In many ways in the society 'family' equals 'children'. One woman in discussing the importance of children conveys this sense of marriage and childbearing as the essential components of family life this way: 'I think that children make a family and I think that if you get married it is important to have a family.' The nuclear family unit is very heavily emphasised in this society, although not to the exclusion of broader family networks. Society is organised around this basic unit and those who do not conform to this pattern encounter various difficulties, especially in making alternative domestic arrangements.

There are a range of beliefs stressing the importance and desirability of having children, beliefs that constrain and motivate individuals into the parental role by making children highly valued objects in the society. First, children are seen as a source of emotional satisfaction while still dependent, and as providing interest and variety in life. Children are thought to create a range of experiences both emotional and intellectual which are virtually unique. In a recent study in England, respondents with children were asked 'In general, how different do you think your lives would be without children?' The majority not only felt that their lives would be worse rather than better without children, but said that their lives would be less satisfying emotionally and much more dull. Not surprisingly, wives stressed this even more than husbands. They talked of being lonely and miserable without children, and of the emptiness and boredom that would result.[10] Life with children is thought to be richer and more interesting than life without. This expressive value of children must be particularly important in a society that is seen as increasingly instrumental. Of course, there is variation in the precise nature of the interest and variety provided by children. Parents may emphasise the satisfaction they get from companionship, or from watching the children grow up, or from teaching them skills, and so forth.

One overriding idea in the current ideology is that emotional satisfaction derives from doing things for one's children, especially providing them with opportunities that parents have not had for themselves. Again what things or opportunities are provided depends on situational exigencies. Children are often seen as offering a second chance for an individual to achieve the things that he has not managed to achieve himself. 'I want to give my child what I didn't have' is a common cry. Or if the parents have achieved those things for themselves they may want the pleasure of providing them for their children, so that they do not have the same struggle and effort that they themselves experienced. Moreover in their concern for what they can do for their children, parents frequently assert that children make effort and sacrifice worth while. Many men when questioned about their jobs stress that children are an important motivating factor in their striving and sacrifice. 'I do it for my children' or 'I do it for my family' is a common justification of hard work and long hours. If individuals are motivated to endeavour by their children, then parenthood may be an important driving force in occupational effort. Whether it is or not, beliefs of this type seem to provide one way of making everyday activities, both for men and women, meaningful, and this is what makes children a source of emotional satisfaction. The feeling that one's activities are beneficial to one's children provides a sense of purpose, 'a reason for living', that may be particularly important when religious beliefs have declined.

But satisfaction is also thought to derive from one's children's successes: from what they do as well as from what one does for them. The two are by no means always differentiated and the satisfaction from doing things for one's children clearly originates in part from the fact that one's own efforts are likely to affect a child's performance and

---

[10]   This is shown from preliminary analysis of data from a survey of the social determinants of fertility of 290 couples in Ipswich, which was carried out by Geoffrey Hawthorn, Michael Paddon and the author. Interviewing took place from September 1969 to June 1970.

chances of success. How a child appears to others on the dimensions held important by the parents is crucial. Children in this way offer a chance of enhancing status. Dennis and his colleagues have described how this operates for women in a traditional mining community.

Women are denied participation in those activities whereby men achieve success or reprobation. They definitely try to assert their individual worth among other women by doing the job of motherhood as well as or better than their neighbours. In fact this means showing the outward signs – new clothes, new toys, well-fed children. It is by these standards that a mother is immediately judged. The child is in the dangerous position of being a status-object for he mother (Dennis, Henriques and Slaughter, 1969, p. 238).

Children's successes are not only intrinsically satisfying to parents, they are also a mark of successful endeavour on their own part. Sociologists have tended to concentrate on studying the relation between children's performance in the educational sphere and the encouragement provided by parents, and in so doing have found considerable variation between social groups in parental encouragement. They have tended to ignore other possible status dimensions such as those of achievement in sport, physical appearance, personal relations and so forth.

Secondly, there is the belief that having children is one way of ensuring some sort of immortality for oneself or one's family. This is a frequent theme in Shakespeare's sonnets:

> Thou are thy mother's glass, and she in thee
> Calls back the lovely April of her prime;
> So though though windows of thine age shall see,
> Despite of wrinkles, this thy golden time.
> But if thou live, remember'd not to be,
> Die single, and thine image dies with thee.

or,

> And nothing 'gainst Times scythe can make defence
> Save breed, to brave him when he takes thee hence.

Concern for familial similarities is strong, from the initial searching for similarity in the facial and other bodily characteristics of a newborn baby, to later marking of similarities of personality and aptitude. This sense of keeping some part of oneself alive by the passing on of characteristics to one's children appears at present to be based more on a conception of transmission through genetic inheritance than by transmission through education and learning, although the two may not be clearly distinguished. Certainly the language used is more that of the former than the latter: 'she gets that from me' is used interchangeably with 'she's inherited that from me' and genetic inheritance is apparently extended to account for all similarities between parent and child. This sense of familial and personal continuity may be particularly important where belief in one's own direct immortality is no longer generally accepted. It is, however, the least clearly articulated aspect of the value placed on children in the society.

Thirdly, children are seen as offering security and pleasure in later life when they will be living within the nuclear family no longer. Again parents in discussing their children when they are older stress the emotional satisfactions they will offer, especially mentioning companionship. They tend actively to reject the suggestion that they expect any financial support from their offspring in their old age, although a large proportion of old people do receive some sort of transfer of income from their children (Townsend, 1963). Presumably, the idea of financial dependence on their children is unattractive and is no more palatable when it becomes a reality (*ibid.*). This fits into the view that children are conceived of primarily in expressive terms and to introduce instrumental elements conflicts with this conception. The importance of having children and of contact with children in the lives of old people has been well documented (*ibid.*) and young people anticipate this when imagining their lives as old people (Veness, 1962).

This advantage of children is one aspect of the general way in which children are felt to strengthen familial bonds. Not only do they offer a shared interest to husband and wife, but to other family members as well. Grandchildren offer a way of strengthening the bond between grandparents and their children, at a time when other factors are likely to weaken the existing ties, by providing a topic of common interest and an opportunity for a sharing of experience. Grandchildren are often a way the older generation can continue to play an important role in the lives of their own children. This leads them to encourage their children to become parents.

All these ideas about the importance and value of children lead to a situation where those who want to have children yet cannot, suffer from their situation. They are pitied by others and feel frustrated and inadequate themselves (Humphrey, 1969; Klein, 1965). This is especially true of women since, as we shall see, few conceive of alternatives to marriage and childbearing as the central purpose of their lives. In some societies having children may be even more important for women. Infecundity in a woman may, for instance, be sufficient grounds for divorce or deemed the greatest humiliation (Lorimer, 1954). The misery and disappointment that attaches to childlessness is a common feature of the cultural values surrounding reproduction and is evidence of the almost universal emphasis on the importance and desirability of parenthood.

What are the current ideas about the marital state, in addition to being

B

21

deemed the appropriate setting for reproduction, that make it seem desirable to get married? First, marriage publicly confers a variety of status advantages. Those who are married are regarded as being more adult and more mature than those who are not, other things being equal. This is evidenced in a variety of ways. Married children are expected and allowed to be more independent of parental ties. Unless there are housing difficulties they are not expected to live at home and their main focus of emotional attachment will be assumed to be their spouse rather than their parents. Legally their nearest relative becomes their spouse and not their parents. Marriage of a child reduces the parents' responsibility for that child and this could be one factor leading parents to want to see their children married, which they usually do. However, pressure of this nature is not as great as in those societies where an unmarried daughter is regarded as being in grave moral danger: where the loss of her virginity reduces family honour and the chances of a 'good' marriage (Mair, 1971). Marriage, too, is a sign of personal and sexual adequacy, of competence in one's sexual role. Those who are not married are believed to be somehow less competent and successful in their personal relationships, to be less desirable and less attractive. This is true for both men and women, though as we shall see, this type of status disadvantage is probably greater for women than for men. In the past, for some groups, getting married has been a mark of financial status and financial independence. This is relatively unimportant now that getting married itself is thought to require little in the way of financial assets. However, being married for some is a necessary component of a certain style of life that is thought to bring status. Wives with the attendant paraphernalia of houses, children, and consumer durables can be important items of conspicuous consumption. Moreover, a wife who does not work (where working could be interpreted as due to financial pressures) may be an important element in maintaining status.

Secondly, marriage organises role specialisation between a man and a woman and institutionalises a division of labour which is felt to be advantageous to both partners. For a man, marriage provides someone who is expected to cook, do the housework, and look after his children, to generally provide his home comforts. And if a wife does not carry out these tasks herself she is expected to ensure that they are carried out by someone. This is not to say that husbands do not play an important part in carrying out such tasks, but they are not under the same obligation to do so. For a woman, marriage provides someone who is expected to make the necessary financial provision for a place of residence and for the maintenance of herself and her children. The precise nature of the role differentiation varies between social groups, but whatever the specific pattern, marriage is thought to be necessary to such arrangements.

Related to this and to the previous point is the fact that marriage provides a clear-cut role identity, eliminating ambiguity and ambivalence.

Thirdly, marriage is seen as providing companionship and intimacy on a secure basis for both partners. It circumvents the uncertainties of finding emotional and sexual satisfaction and friendship. The notion of marriage as 'settling down' presumably refers to this as well as to the idea of marriage signifying maturity. Marriage is a way of stabilising interpersonal relationships, and must therefore contribute to general social normality and stability: to 'social order'.

In this situation where the desirable features of both marriage and childbearing are generally emphasised it is not difficult to show how almost everyone is drawn into marriage and childbearing. Furthermore, there is especially strong socialisation of women into the necessity and desirability of marriage and childbearing. Young men expect that they will eventually marry and become parents and see some of the advantages of doing so, but women not only expect to do so and see advantages from doing so, but they are socialised to actively seek to attain this goal and, in general, to avoid others. And it is the strength of their motivation for marriage and children that is important in ensuring, given male expectation of these events, the maintenance and near universality within the society of the two institutions of marriage and reproduction.

The major factor in this socialisation of women is that the female role and identity are defined primarily in terms of marriage and motherhood, so that women who do not get married tend to be seen as not properly female and it is assumed they must be inadequate in some way. This is so despite the fact that with family size at an average of two to three children in Western societies and most childbearing occurring within the first ten years of marriage, only about a quarter of women's working lives are spent in childbearing and dealing with preschool children. And even if we allow for child care of school children, not more than half a woman's working life is taken up. Yet there is little preparation for occupational roles after childbearing and little serious consideration of alternative roles to those of wife and mother. In contrast, for men the roles of husband and father are not offered as the sole or even necessarily the most important roles. This differential in the importance of marriage and childbearing to male and female identities is evidenced in the connotations of the terms spinster and bachelor. The term bachelor does not have strong negative connotations. It is assumed that those who are not married, are not married from choice, and we take the term bachelor to imply this. The negative definitions used to encourage marriage are those of selfishness and pleasure-loving. Being a bachelor is usually seen as a transitional state. The term spinster, on the other hand, is a negative one in the society. For women the unmarried state is seen as undesirable

23

and those who remain in it are assumed to do so involuntarily, which the connotations of the term spinster reflect. Few would dare to ask a woman why she was not married: they would fear the embarrassment of arousing feelings of failure and inadequacy. The spinster, unlike the voluntarily childless wife, is not seen as selfish but rather as the victim of misfortune. In contrast to the word bachelor, the term is often not used until it is felt that a woman has little chance of marriage and the state is likely to be permanent.

A woman's status is much more closely linked than a man's to being a spouse; she is trained to expect that as an adult her important and salient roles will be those of wife and mother. Success for a woman becomes, therefore, managing to get married, making it difficult for her to choose not to get married and ensuring that the majority of women enter marriage. Once they have done so, childbearing follows almost inevitably. Men, of course, are socialised into the roles of husband and father by the models they encounter throughout their childhood and adolescence, but prior to the assumption of these roles, little active interest in how to get into them or cope with them is apparent or catered for. Active socialisation for boys concentrates on the occupational role. Girls, on the other hand, are expected to show and do show an active interest in the roles of wife and mother. In adolescence it is getting into them that is treated as problematic, interesting and important, not the subsequent coping with them. Study of teenage magazines read by girls shows that, as in the classic romances, marriage and the assumption of a happy life thereafter is the end of the story. There is no discussion of how to be a good and efficient wife and mother (Gavron, 1966). The sole criterion of eligibility for marriage is that the two partners should be in love, and the only thing that will make a girl more likely to be loved is her physical appearance, which makes her more or less attractive. There is little mention of friendship, domestic abilities or personal qualities, although presumably, in reality, these factors play a larger part. It would be interesting to speculate about how the emphasis on appearance has become established as the important factor affecting a girl's chances of marriage. Perhaps its ready visibility gives it a public quality which makes it suitable for the market transactions of marriage, in a market where the women have to show their desirability since men are defined as making the choice. It may also reflect the belief that all women are capable of successfully carrying out the duties of wife and mother and/or that these tasks are relatively trivial, and be a product of the concern with the wives as objects of conspicuous consumption.

Another aspect of marriage for women, reflecting both their subordinate status within the society and the importance of marriage to them, is that a woman's status tends to be defined in terms of her husband. For a woman, marriage is almost the sole way of achieving social mobility in her own right, whereas for men the possibilities of achieving social mobility through marriage are small. Marrying into a family that provides wealth or a job in a family firm or within the family's patronage provide the only possibilities of mobility.

That women, rather than men, should be particularly anxious to marry, is not inevitable. Lucy Mair (1971) has recently argued that women are the most concerned to marry where the husband is the economic provider in the family. On the other hand, in societies where marriage brings a man considerable advantages, such as providing him with a source of labour in his wife and children, or making him a member of a particular lineage that provides him with support and defence, then it is the men who are most motivated for marriage.

FAMILY DESIGN AND FAMILY BUILDING

I shall now turn to consider the current beliefs about the desirable composition of the family of procreation, and about how this design is to be achieved. Although there is considerable variation in the specific plans (or lack of them) a couple makes in building their family, there is nevertheless a common set of beliefs that can be drawn on within the society to justify and to rationalise particular family designs, and that also limit the nature of the alternatives considered.

First there is the question of family size. In recent years in England and Wales mean family size has been approximately 2.25 children. When asked to state their ideal or desired family size the majority of women give an answer in the range of two to four children (across a range of wordings of the question) (Woolf, 1971). Questions about ideal family size are not without problems of interpretation and almost certainly do not reflect ideals unaffected by expectations relating to the respondents' existing circumstances, and those on desired family size clearly do. Nevertheless, the figures on expressed ideal and desired family size tend to fall almost entirely within this range of two to four and have shown considerable consistency over the past few decades.[11] Any shifts tend to be within this range.

What are the beliefs that legitimate this norm of two to four children? How is the importance attached to having children reconciled with extensive control of fertility and small family sizes? The norm of two to four children occurs in a context of two opposing sets of ideas. On the

[11] The similarity of responses to questions about ideal and desired family size suggests that both reflect the ideal norm, although presumably answers to questions on desired family size take more account of the couple's particular conditions. Recent studies of ideal family size in Europe and the United States are summarised in Hawthorn (1970).

one hand there are the ideas that a larger family size is desirable in that it creates a better family environment for childrearing. Just as I have argued that children are felt to be necessary to the existence of a proper and complete family, so having more children is thought to create more of a real family atmosphere with more of what are seen to be the desirable constituents of family life: more companionship and more giving and sharing by both parents and children. This belief finds clear expression in the fact that the desirable family size is bounded by a lower limit of two children. There is a strong emphasis on the undesirability of having only one child. The recent Family Intentions study of 6306 married women showed that none of them thought that a family size of only one child was ideal for families with 'no particular worries about money or anything like that' (Woolf, 1971). The specific rationales that are offered to back up this ideal are framed in terms of the negative consequences for the only child that draw on ideas about companionship, co-operation and concern for others. It is assumed that the environment of the only child will be one of loneliness and indulgence. 'The only child is a lonely child', 'the only child is a spoilt child' are the common and publicly acceptable objections to the one-child family. The salience of this belief in the society emerges when couples report that they have been especially strict with an only child for fear of spoiling him or her. In addition the parents who choose to have only one child encounter definitions of selfishness comparable to those assigned to couples who choose to have no children at all.

Against this ideology in which children are highly valued and a large family is felt to be more effective in producing the desirable attributes of family life, is the issue of resources, which requires control of family size. Childrearing is thought to demand certain resources that are not limitless and it is felt that higher returns can result from the investment of the available resources in a smaller number of children. Hence there are motivations for restricting family size. The resources that are deemed important are those of finance, time and energy, so that the problem with a large family is giving the children adequate financial support, care and attention. We see here a concern with what has been called the 'quality' of children as opposed to quantity. It is deemed important not just to have children, but to have and create children of a certain kind and to do this requires resources. For as we mentioned above, in the contemporary ideology it is giving things and doing things for one's children that is central to the emotional satisfaction that they provide. And it is just this provision of goods and opportunities that requires these three types of resources.

That children cost money if they are to be brought up satisfactorily is a fundamental aspect of the contemporary ideas about family size. Lee

26

Rainwater (1965) in his study of families in Chicago, Cincinnati and Oklahoma City identifies a norm about family size which he reports as 'one should not have more children than one can support, but one should have as many as one can afford'. Whilst there is no comparable study in this country to allow us to say that this is true here, there is evidence that the central feature of this norm, that choice of an appropriate family size should be conditional on financial resources, is widely accepted in this country. Couples believe that one's financial situation should be taken into consideration in deciding upon a particular family size. What one can afford should be an important consideration in determining one's family size. When asked their reasons for choosing a particular family size, the majority mention financial considerations (Hawthorn and Busfield, 1968). This does not mean that babies are simply consumer durables or are even treated as if they are consumer durables. As Judith Blake (1968) has pointed out, there are many obvious ways in which having a child differs from purchasing some durable item of consumption, which make the consumer durable model in applicable to children and which make it impossible simply to predict fertility differentials by income. Yet, this lack of equivalence between children and consumer durables does not mean that in making decisions about family size, it is not generally believed that issues of cost and of what one can afford should play a part. Hence financial concerns are a dominant feature of the rationales offered to explain particular family sizes. 'That's all we can afford' is a common response to explain a particular choice of family size. However, we cannot assume from this that there is a norm that 'one should have as many children as you can afford'. If there is it would be this feature of the two part norm identified in America that would probably change if fears about negative social consequences of population growth become widespread. It is more likely that the other part of Rainwater's norm – that 'one should not have more children than one can support' – does exist in this country, since this would appear to be the belief implicit in justifications of particular family size by claims that that is all that can be afforded.

An important consequence of the fact that family size is allowed to be conditional on questions of what can be afforded is that couples appear to have some choice within a range of family sizes, and they have the means successfully to legitimate their own particular choice of family size, sometimes even if that family size falls outside the normative range of two to four. For instance, it seems likely that in the 1930s when a family size of one was more common than in either previous or subsequent periods, parents were able to justify having only one child by reference to notions of what could be afforded in the situation. Similarly, the few very wealthy families are probably able to justify having more than four children. However, the circumstances need to be shown to be exceptional for such deviations to be acceptable.

But financial resources are not the only concern: time and energy are also seen to be limited. Children need care and attention and these are not in unlimited supply. For even where financial resources are considerable these cannot readily, if at all, buy some of the aspects of care and attention deemed necessary. This necessary standard is generally thought to involve a certain amount of time and energy that must be parental. And in a climate of opinion where maternal and paternal deprivation are feared, parental substitutes are generally seen as second best, and their use kept to a minimum.

Again this allows some latitude in chosen family sizes, as the amount of resources, actual or perceived, varies from couple to couple, as does the standard of resources that they regard as necessary. Just as some couples think it essential to spend a relatively large amount of money on each child, so some couples think it important to spend a large amount of time and energy on activities with each child.

Secondly, there are ideas and beliefs about the desirable sex composition of the family. The common desire is for a family which includes both boys and girls. Underlying this is some idea of the desirability of a balance of sexes within the family, for where four children are desired, the common preference is for two boys and two girls. The reasons offered for this balancing of the sexes gives us little information about the ideas lying behind the preference. Couples simply talk about this being a 'nice family'. However, as no control can be exerted over the sex of one's children where infanticide is unacceptable, there is little need for much legitimation of the desire. Various possible explanations of the desire suggest themselves: the desire for a balance of the sexes could simply be due to the fact that neither male nor female children seem to offer any particular advantages to parents, which they clearly have done in other societies. Yet if this is so, it is rather surprising as the subsequent social position and social roles of males and females are very different. It is more likely that the rather different characteristics and social roles of males and females in the society are recognised and the desire for a balance of the sexes reflects ideas about the sexes being essentially complementary and therefore necessary to each other, whether for co-operation or competition. Or it may be that the perceived advantages of male and female children though different are of equal weight.

There is a general preference, particularly by husbands, for a boy as the first child, and certainly for at least one boy in the family. The desire for a male child is not surprising, given the slight patrilineal and male bias of the society. Family names are transmitted through male offspring, and although property can pass to females the eldest male has traditionally inherited both the family title and the family house. The degree of emphasis on the need for a male heir is far less than has existed in other societies and is far less important, but the male bias in family composition is still apparent. It has been calculated that in India the desire to have a surviving son requires a family size of four children, because of the relatively high level of mortality (Heer, 1968). American studies of the sex composition of families show that couples are more likely to have a further child at any given parity, when the last child is a female child than when it is a male (Freedman, Freedman and Whelpton, 1960). The fact that this male bias still operates within a general preference for a balance of the sexes may not only be due to the fact that the male bias in inheritance (though not in status) is only slight and the fact that many couples are not much concerned with the transmission of property since they have virtually none to pass on, but also to the fact that there is a general belief that girls are easier to bring up and as children generally produce fewer problems.

A further aspect of family design is that of the desirable timing of childbearing. First there is the issue of the spacing between children. There is a general belief that about two years is the right gap between children. This is supported on the one hand by the idea that a shorter gap produces strain on the mother from such close pregnancies and from trying to cope with a young baby whilst pregnant. As one mother puts it 'We said we didn't want any more say until she could walk and things like that, till I'd got her out of nappies a bit'. On the other hand there is the belief that a longer gap means that the two children are not close enough in age to be companions for each other, and the oldest will be sufficiently old at the birth of the second one to experience considerable jealousy. But there is also the question of the timing of childbearing in relation to other events or benchmarks, which may override the above concerns. One important benchmark that operates here, as elsewhere in our society is age.[12] Just as with other features of the ideological framework surrounding reproduction we find general acceptance of beliefs that encourage opposing tendencies. We find beliefs that if acted upon result in childbearing at a relatively early age alongside those that may lead to later childbearing. Both sets of beliefs have a general legitimacy in the culture and are drawn upon in reproductive decisions. They are belief that relate both to the timing of marriage and to the timing of births within marriage. On the one hand it is felt that childbearing should be commenced fairly early in marriage before a couple have become 'too set in their ways' readily to adapt to the presence of children. The recent Family Intentions survey found that 'those who thought

[12] Philip Aries (1962) discusses how age is not always a salient category for the members of a society.

29

they had married "too old" mentioned most frequently a preference for being younger with their children as a reason for this view' (Woolf, 1971, p. 43). This notion is not only based on the ideas that age brings rigidity and makes people less adaptable, but also on the belief that if a couple has too long a period of the comforts, ease and freedom of life without children they will have too much to lose and so will give up the idea of having them. It is almost as if couples are pressed into having children young before they have sufficient experience fully to realise the costs and consequences of childbearing. It is also generally believed, with of course some justice, that childbearing should not be left till too late an age because of the greater physical difficulties that may be entailed, the increased chance of some deformity of the baby and the reduced possibility of conception. However, the majority of childbearing now occurs well before the ages at which such problems arise. On the other hand, what may encourage an initial deferment of childbearing is the belief that a couple's economic situation should be sound before having children, since once they come along it is much more difficult to realise the desirable pattern of consumption. Often it is felt that separate living accommodation from the couple's own parents is a necessary requisite for starting a family, and that some progress should have been made on the path of acquiring the necessary household goods. Again, this is a complex issue, for where a couple can be certain that the husband's economic situation will improve in future, then childbearing can start before the improvement actually occurs. This belief in the necessary consolidation of one's social and economic position before childbearing has been shown to have some foundation. An American study of couples with premarital pregnancies showed that even when allowance was made for differences in age and educational level, they were economically less well off than other couples, whether measured by occupational status, family income or accumulated assets (Coombs, Freedman, Friedman and Pratt, 1969). However, the relation of these two sets of ideas is such that the latter may be seen as conditional on the former. The ideal is that early childbearing is desirable *if* economic circumstances allow it.

What beliefs frame the achievement of these aspects of family design? Not surprisingly, the main emphasis is on the desirability of planning one's childbearing. This is not to say that families are completely planned, but it is accepted that they should be. Few couples, even if they do not plan the births of their children, fail to attempt to control their fertility consciously and directly during their marriage by using some contraceptive method. A survey in 1967–8 showed that 91 per cent of a sample of English women married before the age of 35 had used some method of birth control (Glass, 1970). This individual effort at fertility control is a necessary concomitant of the use of contraception as a means

30

of fertility control. Where control occurs by a late age at marriage, or by customs such as particular patterns of infanticide, or the regulation of sexual relations, then there may be no awareness by individuals of the negative consequences for fertility of these conventions. Where contraception is used individuals must themselves want to control their fertility and they must therefore perceive advantages from doing so. Of course the available means of contraception are changing as are the beliefs about their advantages and disadvantages. These will not be considered here, although one factor that affects these beliefs should be mentioned. This is the issue of whether contraception is preferably under male or female control. Although many couples believe that fertility control should be a couple's joint responsibility, in practice the method used has to be either a male or female one. As female methods at present are generally more efficient, those who are most concerned about efficiency tend to accept these. Where there is an ideology not simply of male initiation and dominance in sexual relations, which is probably widespread, but of male power, the male methods will tend to be more acceptable. It may therefore be particularly important to have efficient male as well as female methods. The current interest in vasectomy may in part be accounted for in these terms (Cartwright, 1970).

Abortion, although now more easily and publicly available in many industrial societies, is less widely accepted than contraception, except by Roman Catholics. Abortion at present tends to be defined as a method of last resort rather than one suitable for regular use. However, acceptability is always conditional and many women, although generally disliking abortion, are willing to use it as a means of birth control under certain circumstances.

REPRODUCTION AND CHILDREARING PRACTICES

In attempting to describe the key features of the current beliefs surrounding reproduction, we have shown how quite often beliefs about what is desirable for the purposes of childrearing form part of the explicit justification for particular aspects of what is held to be desirable for reproduction: the belief in the need for the father's presence in bringing up a child provides a support for the institution of marriage, and the belief that parents should not be fixed in their ways if they are to be successful in this role encourages childbearing at a young age. In this section I want to speculate briefly on some of the possible consequences of existing reproductive practices and of the supporting ideologies for the process of childrearing. First, there is the fact that the majority of adults become parents. This means there is no real selection in terms of suitability for the important task of childrearing, since childbearing and childrearing are usually associated roles. We do have some evidence about those who fail to become parents. Those with very low I.Q.s and those who are chronically mentally ill from a young age are underrepresented in the category of parents, but so too, but to a lesser extent, are women of higher social origins (and probably education). The idea of imposed selection for parenthood is obviously an invidious one: those in power would select according to their definition of a good parent. Nevertheless, the social consequences of almost universal parenthood must be far reaching, producing great variety in childrearing practices and socialisation, and considerable inefficiency in terms of various criteria (which are regarded as important by some) such as development of linguistic skills, security of family background, educational opportunities, and so forth.

Secondly, the fact that marriage and childrearing are defined as the most important roles for women also has important consequences for childrearing. On the one hand, it encourages women to devote time and energy to the task and should allow for specialised training, on the other hand it cuts down the part played by men in bringing up children, and by reducing a woman's interests and experience may make her a less stimulating parent. The way in which study of the rearing of children in inadequate social environments has been conceptualised in terms of, and focused on, maternal deprivation relates to and is evidence of our cultural emphasis on the maternal role in childrearing. Moreover, the existing ideology that assumes all women are, in some sense innately, capable of parenthood, emphasising appearance as the desirable female characteristic, minimises the training for the maternal role. Likewise, there is little concern for training men into the paternal role. In both cases, simply remembering one's own narrow familial experience and learning on the job are the major ways of acquiring childrearing skills.

Thirdly, there is the emphasis on small family units. This is, as we have said, associated with concern for the quality of children. Clearly, here as elsewhere sorting out the precise causal interplay is nigh impossible. However, there can be little doubt that just as concern for being able to do certain sorts of things for one's children plays a part in restricting family sizes, so small family sizes enable the available resources to be spread less thinly. Certainly the fact that women have been freed from almost continuous pregnancy allows a shift of attention from childbearing to childrearing (Sullerot, 1971). This concentration of resources could account for the well-known correlation between family size and educational achievement, but the two may be spuriously associated through some factor such as planning orientation, which leads to smaller families and greater attention to education (Lane, 1972). Certainly, a child that is positively wanted and planned for is likely to

32

receive more consistent care, affection and attention than one that is just accepted as an uncontrollable necessity. But maternal love can have other consequences: the relationship between mother and child can become one of mutual overdependence, the mother with no alternative roles being unwilling and unable to relinquish tight control over her child, and the child being unable to free himself from her, borne down by feelings of obligation and dependence (Greer, 1971). Presumably, a small family size increases parental power and influence generally, which increases the importance of the role played by the parents in the socialisation process for good or ill.

Finally, early childbearing may produce, as is claimed, more flexible and adaptable parents with more companionship and a less hierarchical relation between parent and child, but it also reduces the time and opportunities for acquiring the resources, experience, and understanding that are deemed beneficial to the childrearing process.

CONCLUSION

The recent interest of sociologists in ideologies has tended to be theoretical rather than empirical, and this attempt to outline the existing ideologies surrounding reproduction has necessarily been somewhat speculative. The attempt has been made in the belief that such ideological factors do play an important causal role. Ideologies play an important part in social control; they constrain individuals by presenting them with a set of expectations for their behaviour and appropriate rationales that support the expectations. These relate to accepted values within the society.

What emerges from our analysis is the importance that is attached to having children in English society. Childbearing is encouraged not only directly by the high value placed on children, but also indirectly by the value attached to marriage, since once married, for whatever reason, couples are subject to strong expectations that they will have children. Children are seen as essential to family life to such an extent that in many ways we equate the family with children. Widespread parenthood is therefore both part of the general emphasis on the importance of the institution of the family in the society, and helps to maintain this emphasis. This fact is of crucial importance. We can speculate that, for instance, it makes the establishment of equality of opportunity more difficult, since, the family plays a major role in the transmission of existing inequalities to the next generation. Widespread parenthood presumably also affects attitudes to work and other non-familial activities, and encourages, given the existing family organisation, family rather than community centredness.

Just as it is deemed necessary for most people to become parents so it is deemed necessary for those who bear children to provide resources, care and attention in bringing them up. In so doing, children not only provide emotional rewards in themselves but they make instrumental activities more rewarding. Moreover, this concern for giving children adequate opportunities and resources may well legitimate greater consumption and consolidation of resources. What is done in the name of one's children in English society is seen to be done not from selfishness but from altruism.

Although a high valuation of children does not require that couples should have *many* children, merely that they should have *some* children, nevertheless the importance attached to children at present introduces, I believe, a strong pro-natalist bias into the society. On the one hand, where most people become parents, then the pressures to control fertility to their desired level are likely to be less than where a larger proportion have decided not to become parents at all. For once a couple has at least one child the difference made by one extra child is likely to be smaller than the addition of a child to a couple with no children at all. On the other hand, if in this situation the main check on family size is one of resources, then an increase of resources, as with growing affluence, may lead to greater family sizes. The increased resources may, of course, be taken up by higher consumption of investment of resources per head, but where children are highly valued this is less likely than it otherwise would be.

ACKNOWLEDGEMENT

I would like to thank Geoffrey Hawthorn, Michael Paddon and Michael Lane for their comments on this paper, and other colleagues at the University of Essex for suggesting relevant empirical data.

REFERENCES

Ardener, E. (1962). *Divorce and Fertility: an African Study*. London, Oxford Univ. Press.
Aries, P. (1962). *Centuries of Childhood*. New York, Knopf.
Banks, J. A. (1954). *Prosperity and Parenthood*. London, Routledge and Kegan Paul.
Blake, J. (1961). *Family Structure in Jamaica*. New York, The Free Press.
Blake, J. (1968). Are babies consumer durables? *Population Studies*, **22**, 5–25.
Cartwright, A. (1970). *Parents and Family Planning Services*. London, Routledge and Kegan Paul.
Chester, R. (1971). The duration of marriage to divorce. *Brit. J. Sociol.* **22**, 172–82.

34

Coombs, L. C., Freedman, R., Friedman, J. and Pratt, W. F. (1969). Premarital pregnancy and status before and after marriage. *Amer. J. Sociol.* **75**, 800–200.

Crellin, E., Kellmer-Pringle, M. L. and West, P. (1971). *Born Illegitimate.* London, National Foundation for Educational Research.

Davis, K. (1963). The theory of change and response in modern demographic history. *Population Index*, **29**, 345–66.

Dennis, N., Henriques, F. and Slaughter, C. (1969). *Coal is Our Life*, London, Tavistock.

Douglas, M. (1966). Population control in primitive groups. *Brit. J. Sociol.* **17**, 263–73.

Evans-Pritchard, E. E. (1951). *Kinship and Marriage among the Nuer.* London, Oxford Univ. Press.

Freedman, D. S., Freedman, R. and Whelpton, P. K. (1960). Size of family and preference for children of each sex. *Amer. J. Sociol.* **66**, 141–6.

Gavron, H. (1966). *The Captive Wife.* London, Penguin.

General Register Office, (1966). *Fertility Tables, Census 1961.* London, H.M.S.O.

Glass, D. V. (1970). The components of natural increase in England and Wales. *Population Studies, Supplement.*

Goldschmidt, W. (1966). *Comparative Functionalism.* Berkeley, Univ. Calif. Press.

Greer, G. (1971). *The Female Eunuch.* London, Paladin.

Harris, C. C. (1969). *The Family.* London, Allen and Unwin.

Hawthorn, G. (1970). *The Sociology of Fertility*, London, Collier-Macmillan.

Hawthorn, G. and Busfield, J. (1968). Some social determinants of family size: report of a pilot study. University of Essex, in mimeo.

Heer, D. M. and Smith, D. O. (1968). Mortality trend, desired family size and population increase. *Demography*, **5**, 104–21.

Humphrey, M. (1969). *The Hostage Seekers.* London, Longmans.

Illsley, R. and Thompson, B. (1961). Women from broken homes. *Sociol. Rev.* **9**, 27–54.

Klein, J. (1965). *Samples from English Cultures*, Vol. 2. London, Routledge and Kegan Paul.

Lane, M. (1972). Explaining educational choice. *Sociol.* **6**, 255–66.

Lorimer, F. (1954). *Culture and Human Fertility.* Paris, U.N.E.S.C.O.

Mair, L. (1971). *Marriage.* London, Penguin.

Marsden, D. (1969). *Mothers Alone.* London, Allen Lane.

Plamenatz, J. (1970). *Ideology.* London, Macmillan.

Rainwater, L. (1965). *Family Design: Marital Sexuality, Family Size and Contraception.* Chicago, Aldine.

Registrar General (1969). *Statistical Review of England and Wales, 1967, Part II.* London, H.M.S.O.

Royal Anthropological Institute (1951). *Notes and Queries on Anthropology* (6th edn.). London, Routledge and Kegan Paul.

Schutz, A. (1967). Common-sense and scientific interpretation of human action. In *Collected Papers, I: The Problem of Social Reality.* The Hague, Nijhoff.

Sullerot, E. (1971). *Woman, Society and Change.* London, Weidenfeld and Nicolson.

Townsend, P. (1963). *The Family Life of Old People.* London, Penguin.

Veness, T. (1962). *School Leavers*, London, Methuen.

Vincent, C. E. (1961). *Unmarried Mothers*. New York, The Free Press.

Woolf, M. (1971). *Family Intentions*. London, H.M.S.O.

Wootton, B. (1959). *Social Science and Social Pathology*. London, Allen and Unwin.

Wrigley, E. A. (1969). *Population and History*. London, Weidenfeld and Nicolson.

3

Belief and reality:
Social factors in pregnancy and childbirth

Jane Hubert

Social anthropology has during its development taken little interest in the problems of socialisation. Most anthropologists, implicitly or explicitly, have subscribed to some sort of *tabula rasa* view of the human species, believing that within fairly broad limits a human society can culturally reproduce itself by the training it gives to its young members. The processes by which this end was achieved were rarely subjected to serious study. The American Culture and Personality school of the thirties, associated particularly with Kardiner (1939), seemed to justify this view in laborious detail, and clearly revealed the circular nature of the argument. Initiation ceremonies widely reported from simpler societies, which were often accompanied by pain, seclusion and instruction, were assumed to cram into weeks or months the transition from child to adult that takes years in our own culture, but anthropologists tended to concentrate on the ceremonies themselves, and their organisation, merely noting that they appeared to have the desired effects upon the initiates. Margaret Mead's work in Samoa (1928) and New Guinea (1930) was an exception, and there were a few other isolated examples of an interest in socialisation, though mainly with a psychological slant (e.g. Meyer Fortes' (1938) work in Taleland). Since the war the Whitings (1963) ambitious Six Cultures project has had virtually no impact, at least not on social anthropology. Similarly, speculations about the effects of the length of the *post-partum* taboo on sexual intercourse on just about every conceivable aspect of the individual personality and social structure have left most anthropologists impressed but somewhat aghast at the crudity of the categories apparently inseparable from such cross-cultural comparisons.

Interest in the ways in which cultures are transmitted cross-generationally has, however, recently revived, principally in detailed studies of specific cultures, the sort of intensive study at which anthropology excels, and this is witnessed in this country by a volume in the A.S.A. Monograph series devoted to socialisation (Mayer, 1971).[1] Part at least of this revival is due to the vast amount of recent work on cognitive

---

[1] This volume contains papers on specific studies as well as an excellent review of anthropological approaches to socialisation, with a bibliography, by A. I. Richards.

systems and patterns of thought in general. Anthropologists have however been successful over the years in collecting ideas and beliefs about such things as conception, pregnancy and birth, and infant and child care, as well as a wealth of data about practices in a wide range of societies (e.g. Ford, 1945). It would not be relevant here to attempt any world-wide survey of beliefs and customs in this field but there is one point of difference relevant to our own culture. Most cultures traditionally studied by anthropologists, i.e. small-scale 'simple' societies, are fairly homogeneous, within each culture, in their views about the role of women, and in their beliefs about the physiological processes involved in conception, pregnancy, birth and infant care. The beliefs and practices vary widely from society to society, as any superficial acquaintance with anthropological literature will show, but each tends to be internally consistent. Within a culture women have a set of socially-accepted expectations about how they conceive, what it is like to be pregnant, how they will give birth to their children, and what it is like to be a mother. In our own society we do not have this satisfyingly consistent pattern. There is a 'scientific' view of all these, but the ideas, beliefs and expectations held by a large proportion of the population not only do not conform to this view, but are also very diverse. Just how little the scientific or medical explanations are accepted or even known about is obviously not comprehended by the people who know and try to communicate them. Even in the most helpful clinical environment, such as antenatal clinics, little is communicated because of a fundamental lack of rapport between educated, informed staff and comparatively uneducated patients. Outside the clinical environment there are still widespread inhibitions in the discussion of sexual and reproductive matters, especially between generations but also within them. Even when inhibitions on discussion between mothers and daughters are overcome, daughters tend to regard with healthy suspicion some of the basic assumptions of their mothers about sex and reproduction. Old wives' tales still abound, and often merge into fact in a most confusing way. The difference between our society and the majority of the societies studied by anthropologists is that in the latter the acquisition of information is not only verbal, but is gained through observation and participation; in our own society nearly all of what a girl knows about childbirth, for example, is obtained from a whole variety of different sources: family, kin, clinics, peers and so on, but not through direct knowledge and experience.

Apart from lack of adequate and effective, society-wide communication about sex and reproduction, which results in a wide diversity of beliefs and attitudes, there is also a lack of homogeneity within our culture over time. For example, over the years in America and Britain attempts have been made to influence child development by laying down new rules for methods of baby care,[2] feeding and toilet training, the most famous in recent generations being Truby King (1924) and Benjamin Spock (1948, 1957). Socialisation is an all-embracing process, not confined to a few particular factors, thus Truby King and Spock babies have grown up, within their respective generations, as adjusted or ill-adjusted as other babies within the society; but the fact that there are different views, different prescriptions for behaviour towards newborn and older babies especially perhaps regarding methods of feeding, means that each individual has to some extent to learn for herself her role as parturient and mother. Women expecting their first babies are, comparatively speaking, even now unprepared for the role they have to undertake, through lack of communication about what to expect, and through the effects of the lack of common rules of behaviour as well as lack of experience. This lack of rules of behaviour applies not only to infant care, but also the processes that have led up to motherhood, that is, adolescent sexual behaviour, methods of birth control, behaviour during pregnancy and so on, all of which are relevant to the behaviour and attitudes that emerge when the infant is born.

The process of socialisation is said to begin, in some aspects, at the birth of an infant. If this is so then the attitudes, expectations and behaviour of the mother are obviously crucial factors affecting this process. What these attitudes, expectations and behaviour patterns are will not only depend on a whole range of social and psychological factors, but also on the series of events that led up to the birth and their effect on the mother including the expectations of pregnancy and childbirth, and their relation to the actual experience. It is suggested that how a woman feels and behaves when presented with a newborn baby is affected by her attitude to and expectations of childbirth, pregnancy and the nature of the original conception, i.e. whether it was desired or not. This chapter, then, is concerned not with the child itself, but with the mother, and with some of the factors that affect her attitude and behaviour towards her child; no attempt will be made to assess the nature of the effects that the particular behaviour differences have on the infant, since this is a quite separate topic.

As already suggested, there is a general state of uncertainty, and varying degrees of ignorance and knowledge about the nature of pregnancy and its symptoms, what to expect of labour, and immediately afterwards. Since almost every first birth is hospitalised and antenatal attention is of a very high standard, one might expect that this would not be so. It is true that the physical health of mother and baby is very adequately provided for, but there is evidence to suggest that the majority of working-

[2]   This topic is discussed at greater length by the Newsons elsewhere in this volume.

39

NORTHWEST MISSOURI STATE
UNIVERSITY LIBRARY
MARYVILLE, MISSOURI 64468

class women do not know what to expect in relation to conception, pregnancy, labour and initial care of a child, especially with regard to breastfeeding. It is important to discover how far experience conforms to expectations, where and how these expectations are acquired and how far they are confirmed by what actually happens, since this affects a new mother's behaviour, her relationship with her baby and fundamental early decisions regarding it.

To illustrate these aspects I shall discuss a piece of research carried out in South London with a sample of working-class women expecting their first babies.[3] It should be emphasised at the outset that the research was not concerned with socialisation, but was an anthropological study basically concerned with kinship attitudes and behaviour in the context of first pregnancy and confinement, and the relative importance of the immediate family, extra-familial kin, friends, neighbours, welfare and medical services both in terms of practical help, and also as sources of advice and information, and the extent to which these might coincide or conflict. The study also aimed at documenting the attitudes and beliefs regarding conception, pregnancy and birth, and the surrounding practices within our own society. An attempt was made to assess the extent to which women accept the information offered by for example their mothers, and by the antenatal clinic, and to what extent their attitudes filtered the information given. Data were collected on prenatal attitudes to breastfeeding and infant care, and these were compared with actual postnatal practices; also on the relation between attitudes and knowledge of the symptoms of pregnancy, and of labour, and the actual experience of them. Subsidiary information was also gathered on how and why the baby was conceived in the first place, methods of birth control, and beliefs about these. Social anthropological methods were used in the study, i.e. intensive interviewing of a relatively small number of informants, to obtain as full information as possible. The women in the sample were talked to, without the use of questionnaires, both before and after the birth of their babies. It is doubtful whether the sort of material gathered at these interviews about beliefs, attitudes and expectations could have been obtained by any less intensive methods, since it was often a lengthy and difficult process extracting the true opinions of the women, and obtaining their confidence was an essential first step. It was also vital in the interview situation to make sure that the interviewer was not seen as a representative in any way of the welfare or hospital services, since this tended to bias the information towards what the informant thought were acceptable attitudes and beliefs, as Newson

[3] This research was financed by the Wenner-Gren foundation for Anthropological Research, New York and the Social Sciences Research Council of Britain to whom I am most grateful.

40

and Newson (1963) discovered in Nottingham. In this type of research, the advantage of being an independent anthropologist, with no apparent connection with hospital or clinic, was immeasurable. The sample was drawn in batches each month for a number of months, from the lists of an antenatal clinic in an offshoot hospital of one of the London teaching hospitals. Being a study of first pregnancies, the sample covered married women, a proportion of whom conceived premaritally, and some unmarried women. In the final sample were thirty-four married women (including eleven premarital conceptions) drawn in a random sample, and twenty unmarried women (who were the total intake over the period).

Discussion of the material will be divided into four sections, covering conception, pregnancy, birth and the period immediately after birth, when crucial decisions are made, particularly with regard to breastfeeding.

CONCEPTION

Although at first sight beliefs about conception may not seem relevant to attitudes to the baby nine months later, they are discussed here for two reasons. The first is that the nature of these ideas illustrates very clearly the ineffectiveness of various campaigns about contraception and sex education even among present-day, urban, young women, and secondly because the material collected among these working-class women in South London suggests that there may be a correlation between whether a pregnancy was planned or not, and the subsequent decision as to whether to breastfeed or not, which will be discussed later.

Among the married women in the sample, it is evident that, even apart from premarital conceptions, a large proportion of babies conceived within the marriage were also unintentional. In fact two-thirds of the pregnancies among married women (both pre and postmarital conceptions) were mistakes, and more than half of these were definitely unwelcome pregnancies. Among the unmarried women only one pregnancy was intentional. Both married and unmarried women had a wide variety of ideas about conception, and methods or reasons for not conceiving. Only three or four had used any sort of effective method of birth control, and these had all stopped specifically to have a child. All the unintentional pregnancies were the result of using no effective method of birth control except the widely practised method of withdrawal. Many theories were expounded, some with elements of practicality but all – in view of the fact that the sample consisted of pregnant women – had failed. Some of these theories are, of course, well-known ones; for example, among the women who had conceived premaritally was one who believed that if she took Beechams Pills after

41

intercourse it would 'clear you all through'. Another thought that merely sitting on the lavatory afterwards was sufficient as 'it would all come out'. Another method used was of sitting up sharply afterwards, which was thought in some way to cut off the relentless flow halfway up. Especially among the single girls there was a touching faith in the speed and efficiency of the man, but again there were myths, one of the most widely believed being that it could not happen the first time a girl had intercourse. On the other hand, one girl said that 'staying together I didn't think it could happen' as she believed that only promiscuous girls got pregnant. What was evident was that there was a real lack of knowledge about birth control methods and about the whole process of conception and reproduction. Sexual intercourse, conception, birth control, etc. were not subjects that were often discussed with their mothers, even after marriage, and this was in spite of the fact that two-thirds of the married girls lived round the corner from their mothers. Apart from this there seemed to be little connection made in the girls' minds, especially among the single girls, between having sexual intercourse and conceiving a baby – until it actually happened. All this is important because this state of ignorance, or at best indifference, when it results in an unwelcome pregnancy (even when this later becomes accepted, and even desired), affects the attitude and behaviour of the young mother towards her child, as will be discussed later. Whatever the reasons for conceiving, or rather, for not avoiding conceiving, it is apparent that the muddling through that seemed to characterise the behaviour of most of the girls through pregnancy and labour and the first weeks of motherhood, is evident at the time of conception as well. There is evidence to suggest, too, that this situation will not be radically changed subsequently, that is, after the first unintentional birth, since many of the women, when interviewed postnatally, stated both that they did not intend to have another baby for a certain length of time, or, in some cases, ever, and also that they were not practising any form of birth control other than the ineffective non-methods used before.

PREGNANCY

In our culture an enormous amount of attention is paid to pregnancy and childbirth. Medical antenatal care is generally of a very high standard, with full regular checks throughout pregnancy, and, usually, some attempt is made to prepare women in their first pregnancy for their labour and for the care of the new infant. In spite of this, however, many women seem to go through pregnancy with little idea of what is happening to them, and with only vague ideas about what it is normal to expect during pregnancy in terms of symptoms, and what can be done to relieve them. This is not the direct fault of the staff in the clinic, who can with all honesty say that a patient has only to ask for advice or information, but it is seldom realised that the comparatively uneducated working-class women such as those in the South London study do not always feel that they can ask questions. Since they do not know whether to vomit daily for three months is normal or not they may not like to ask for relief. There is a fundamental lack of rapport which is not always obvious to the educated, informed staff of the clinic who assume a certain level of knowledge and grasp of the situation in cases where it is not present. Among the sample there were cases of women enduring such symptoms as severe back pains, vomiting throughout pregnancy, etc., who did not think to ask for help, partly because they thought that their symptoms were probably usual and therefore not to be complained about, and partly because they had no idea that anything could be done about them anyway.

There was also to some extent a conflict between the attitude and advice of the antenatal clinic, and those of their mothers and the older generation in general, due partly to the changes that have taken place in attitudes towards pregnancy and confinement in recent years, and partly to the protective feelings of their mothers. While they were pregnant many of the women found that their mothers tended to treat them as though they were marginally ill; they made them put their feet up, and rest a lot; not carry heavy things or do anything strenuous. Sometimes they were advised not to eat certain foods for fear of upsetting themselves or the baby or do certain things like stretch their arms upwards for fear of strangling the baby, and so on; in fact they were given a wide range of both spurious and sensible advice. Advice from the clinic, on the other hand, tended to be brisk and practical, and the emphasis was on treating the pregnant woman as a well person, almost, one might think, as a vessel carrying the expected child. The numbers of women attending each session of the clinic, and the necessarily perfunctory way in which those without any special difficulties were treated, all tended to make the women feel that they were just one of a mass (which in some senses of course they are) and that their problems were not important. There is thus a conflict between the sort of advice and attitudes that a woman gets from various sources. The clinic may stress the normality of the whole process of pregnancy, but to the individual, and often her close kin, the situation is not one of normality, not only in cases where there are symptoms which may be alarming and unpleasant, but also because the whole process is new and sometimes bewildering. Thus even where there is excellent medical supervision, and even serious attempts to communicate knowledge there is in fact a wide gap between the fund of knowledge held by the doctors, midwives, and so on, on which they base their concept of the normality of pregnancy, and the limited and very diverse beliefs and ideas held by many of the women they deal with.

BIRTH

This lack of communication also meant that the majority of these women expecting their first child were ill-prepared for labour when it actually happened, and this sometimes seemed to affect attitudes towards the newborn infant and to correlate with a lack of interest in the first instance, though this was not necessarily so. Again the fault is not entirely with those who were supposed to have given the information, but was due merely to lack of rapport. In no case had any of the women seen a baby being born: thus all their information came from secondary sources and as such was bound to some extent to be inadequate. But the total unexpectedness of labour in so many cases was evident, from the nature of onset, the loneliness of the first stage, the pain, the effects of drugs and the use of the gas-and-air machine, to the initial feeling of indifference towards the baby.

The majority of girls, when interviewed during their pregnancy, showed no real dread of labour. Many were worried that they would not recognise the first signs, or that they would be alone when it started and they would not be able to get to the hospital, but in general the attitude was one of equanimity; there was the feeling that there was nothing that could be done about it, it had to happen, so one might as well not worry. Some would have liked to know more about it, a few were scared at the idea of pain, but the general assumption seemed to be that it would all be quite straightforward. In many cases the onset of labour was, in fact, very unexpected; the symptoms that they had been told to expect were often absent, and since the symptoms that had been described to them meant little to them in terms of what was actually going on inside them, different signs were often ignored because they had not been specifically mentioned. If they had had more sense of what was happening physiologically, what they were experiencing would have made more sense. This ignorance existed even when the girls had attended classes since again, these assumed too high a level of sophistication and knowledge.

In a number of cases the onset of labour began a protracted period of bewilderment and fear. This was often aggravated by the periods of time that many were left alone on their arrival in hospital, sometimes even up to twenty-four hours, with only occasional visits from a nurse or midwife. There tended to be a feeling that everyone was very busy and that requests for help or information would be looked upon as unnecessary fussing. Some women found the loneliness of the first stage of labour worse to endure than the pain that followed. At all stages what most of them wanted was reassurance and understanding. It is significant that many called for their mothers during the most painful times, only one called for her husband, more often they cursed their husbands, and blamed them for what they were suffering. There was a general bewilderment and sense of inability to cope with what was happening; there was occasionally embarrassment too, especially when the birth was induced. Midwives were often seen as bad-tempered and hurried. Of course all this is what the mothers themselves report, and it is true that they are particularly vulnerable at this time, being upset by things that at other times would not affect them at all, but this is their experience of the situation. Looking back at labour, except in the cases of short and easy labour, the whole process was seen as unpleasant and painful, and the feeling in general was that somehow they could have been more prepared for the experience. It was often said that 'no one prepares you', 'people say it's nothing to worry about, but it's the most dreadful experience', and so on. It should perhaps be mentioned that a few of the women whose accounts were gruesome, started off by saying it was not too bad (just as one woman who had described what was obviously to her a dreadful experience said that when her husband asked her how it had been, she had told him it was 'all right'). There is a reluctance in some cases to discuss at first the difficulties of labour, but once it was apparent that the listener was genuinely interested in what it had really been like, the experience was described more realistically, at least in their terms; it is what happens to them as they see it, and how it affects their attitudes and behaviour, that matters here.

It would be true to say that women in our own and similar Western societies get more expert and full medical attention during pregnancy and labour than in less-developed cultures, and the number of deaths in childbirth, and the neonatal mortality rates are lower; nevertheless it is in our society that labour is looked upon as something difficult and painful, with the consequent administration of drugs, anaesthesia and mechanical aids of various kinds. In many primitive societies women work up to the onset of labour, have their baby, and return very soon to work and normal life. Among the Melpa of New Guinea a woman retires quite alone to give birth, digs a hole for the placenta, feeds the baby and then returns to her normal life. This is an extreme, as in most societies female kin are present and may help with the birth (and are thus prepared for the experience themselves when it happens), but the stereotype existing in these societies is of birth as a simple process. In our own culture there is some over-sophistication of childbirth, and regardless of the 'scientific' view, it is considered as an ordeal to be endured, and often becomes one.

MOTHERHOOD

It is partly because of the amount of attention paid in our culture to pregnancy and confinement that it is difficult for women to project themselves during their pregnancy to the time beyond the confinement, the birth being thought of as so overwhelmingly important in itself – an ultimate point forming an almost insurmountable block to a proper vision of the situation and events beyond it. Mothercraft classes may be attended but they are not adequate preparation for what is to come. Various factors are important here. One is that within our society girls and women do not come into close contact with newborn babies. The relative isolation of the nuclear family, at least in terms of dwelling place, means that each woman rears her newborn infant from scratch. Of course there are situations where an elder daughter is living in her parents' house where a much later sibling is born, or a girl may live in the house of a sister who has a baby, but in general women do not live in large kin groups. In societies where large kin groups do live together or in very close proximity babies are regularly produced to whom other females in the group automatically become to some extent substitute, or alternative, mothers. In England, certainly in present-day working-class families, some girls have their first baby never having actually seen anyone breastfeed or otherwise care for a baby. Their experience of newborn babies is often limited to what they see asleep in a pram, and the information they receive from various sources is conflicting and to some extent unconvincing.

Apart from this lack of close contact with other new babies, the emphasis of antenatal care on the confinement does affect expectations and attitudes towards motherhood and the situation that exists after the birth. Of course an enormous amount of nest-building does occur. Pregnant women, and their kin, knit dozens of matinee jackets, collect vests, dresses, nighties and nappies, buy cots, prams, bottles and toys. It is significant that the wide range of female kin, who rally round and provide a wealth of material goods at this time, are of little use as sources of practical advice and information. Their function is seen, apart from contributing the odd old wives' tale, not as advisers or practical helpers, but as suppliers of various articles for the expected child.

In spite of all this nest-building it is largely true to say that the baby itself is not realistically conceptualised. It is often, in effect, thought of as an object, in some sense a new possession, and not as a separate, characterful person in its own right. It is natural to some extent, when the baby is *in utero*, for a woman to think of it as an extension of her

46

own persona, but this in itself does not mean that she should not be able to envisage it as a separate entity. Like the doll in the mothercraft class, the baby is often thought of as something that lies still in the crook of its mother's arm during its bath, and unprotestingly lets itself be dressed up in all the pretty clothing. There was sometimes the explicit idea of the baby as a doll: 'it will be like having a doll again . . . something to dress' one woman thought. Another said that the baby was a terrible shock to her 'always eating or crying' and she too had thought it would be like having a doll. Many mothers expressed similar emotions. Instead of a quiet, undemanding, doll-like baby, the new mother is often presented with a squalling, starving animal whose needs are both unpredictable and apparently insatiable. To make it worse this happens at a time when many women are at their lowest ebb, exhausted by pregnancy and labour, and often in the grip of either mild or severe depression.

The majority of women, on their return from hospital, felt that they just could not cope, and where possible went to stay with their own mothers, mainly, perhaps, for moral support, but also to ease one of the main problems which, with a new baby, was that of getting everything done, since the actual caring for the baby took far longer and was far more wearing than any had anticipated. This is borne out not only by what the women reported, but also in many cases by their own unkempt appearance at this time compared with that at antenatal interviews when they had little else to attend to, and quite often by the state of their homes, which tended to be strewn with washing, washing lines, piles of nappies and so on. Those who were attempting to breastfeed had the worst time, with a very few exceptions, since they found that each feed took ages, and since they did not know how much milk was being taken, they tended to go on and on with each feed, and feed more often than necessary since crying would be attributed to hunger. Apart from feeding, the new mothers were bewildered by the sheer amount there was to do with a baby compared with before it was born, and this was interspersed with either occasional or frequent panics about the baby's health, whether it was choking to death, rupturing itself crying, dying when it held its breath, and so on.

The unexpectedness of the forceful and disruptive presence of a hungry, active baby is obviously a crucial factor affecting the environment in which the baby finds itself. It is important, too, that this environment did not exist until the baby did itself. By its arrival the baby creates for itself an environment which is as totally new to its mother as it is for itself.

The decision whether to breastfeed a baby or not is obviously a very important one. The question here is not whether it is better for the baby or not – and since informed opinion cannot agree it is unlikely that anyone else can feel sure one way or the other – but what the attitude of the mother is, and the behaviour resulting from it. In the earlier discussion of intended and unintended conceptions, it was suggested that the decision whether or not to breastfeed may be related to this. Of the married women, almost two-thirds of their pregnancies were unintentional, and it is significant that of these only 18 per cent breastfed their babies, compared with 42 per cent of the mothers whose babies were planned. The use of the term 'planned' is perhaps too strong; it is used here only to mean that there was some desire to have a baby at that time, as contrasted with unplanned, where there was not the intention to have one. The difference is often only one of attitude, since the women not intending to have one behaved in no effectively different way, in terms of birth control, except in a few cases, from the ones who did. Thus it is apparent that whether a woman intends or does not intend to have a baby seems to influence her behaviour nine months later, at least in respect of feeding practices, and further research might reveal other effects as well. Often attitudes towards the initially unwelcome baby change throughout pregnancy, and in most cases there is in the end at least a conscious acceptance and even welcoming of the pregnancy, but the effect still remains. Which are the crucial factors involved in the correlation obviously requires further investigation.

The actual reasons for not breastfeeding tended to be on two levels. It was often difficult to extract cogent reasons, and in some cases there were obviously not any very explicit ones, merely a feeling against it; but in a large number of cases it was possible after some time to elicit more coherent statements of attitude.

Many of the women said that they would not breastfeed because of the embarrassment of doing it in front of other people, and therefore the inconvenience. In all cases it was thought of as something that was done in private, some even saying that they would not do it in front of their husbands, and in a few cases not in front of their own mothers. It was seen as something that would prevent them from visiting friends when they wanted to, and would mean leaving the room when there were visitors at home. This, in cases where there is only one functional room, is obviously very relevant, although these were certainly not the only conditions in which the inconvenience was mentioned. There are clearly many elements involved in this attitude. One is probably shyness in exposing a part of the body not usually exposed. Another element, which leads on to the second type of reason given for not breastfeeding, is the feeling of revulsion for the whole business. Many girls said they just could not do it, or the idea made them sick, and in many cases this was a revulsion from the animal quality of it. One woman was put off by seeing a West Indian woman feeding her baby because she 'looked like an ape' and the baby made 'slurping' noises as it fed – which the un-favourably impressed woman imitated. Another was put off by a West African woman feeding for similar reasons. It is significant that most girls do not see anyone breastfeeding these days except, as they say, West Indians, Africans or gypsies, who do it in public, and these are all groups with whom they do not want to be identified, as they are looked down upon as of lower social status. It may be relevant here that the location of the research was in one of the areas of London with a high immigrant population. The attitude to the occasional middle-class woman whom they saw happily feeding in public places was one of horror and almost disbelief. It is of course interesting that slightly higher in the social scale some women probably do breastfeed because they wish to be identified with the professional middle-class, among whom breast-feeding is now the fashion.

With some women the desire not to breastfeed was only expressed in rather vague terms, for instance, 'I can't stand (the idea). I know it's natural but it turns me over', or 'I just don't like the idea'. Of the ones who said embarrassment was the problem it was clear that privacy was not necessarily a practical problem but was seen as one, and is therefore significant. Other reasons for not breastfeeding included such things as not knowing how much milk the baby was getting, being messy, incon-venient, bad for the figure, restricting on what one eats, time-consum-ing, embarrassing, 'dead out of fashion', and so on. Reasons for breastfeeding tended to be more concerned with the baby, for example, that it was bette for him, that it makes the relationship closer, provides some immunity to disease and so on.

Whether breastfeeding has any advantages over bottlefeeding or not, the ambiguous attitude towards breastfeeding does imply a conception of a certain separateness between mother and child. It means that what is a natural animal function, in so far as it is part of the relationship between mothers and their young of any mammalian species, can be rejected or accepted, and in many cases it is rejected out of hand, usually early in pregnancy when the question first arises. In primitive societies there is no alternative to breastfeeding, whereas here there is a choice, which implies the possibility of separateness of mother and child, at least in conceptual terms.

In fact, however, it is obviously more detrimental to the relationship between mother and child to try to breastfeed and fail, or feel that it is not adequate, or do it when it is felt to be unpleasant or painful. Of the small proportion of women in this South London sample who did try to breastfeed, the majority gave up very early, some in a few weeks, others after a few days; only two or three persevered and found it satisfying and easy. The women who thought they ought to breastfeed but found it difficult became more hostile to their babies than those who did not try at all. It was these women who felt most acutely that they could not cope on their return from hospital. One woman found that she was feeding for eight hours in the twenty-four, and was worn out and depressed, not having left the house for two weeks. Another found she was feeding nearly all day, and never had time to eat or sleep herself, until late one night her husband found a bottle, and after giving a bottlefeed she had her first night's sleep for two weeks. In these cases any virtues in breast-feeding must be outweighed by the effects of an exhausted mother whose approach to the baby becomes tense and hostile. This may seem a black picture, but again, it is largely the result of lack of adequate preparation for breastfeeding and motherhood in general and also of a lack of sympathetic help at the time; however, it is significant here, perhaps, that one middle-class mother, who was interviewed but was not in the main random sample, found breastfeeding very rewarding despite initial difficulties and considered the nurses at the hospital attentive and helpful, because she was able to communicate with them and felt able to ask for help and advice. She also had scales at home and could test-weigh to check how much milk was being taken at each feed. One of the chief disadvantages seen by those who did try to breastfeed was that it was not possible to tell how much milk the baby had taken.

The picture painted in this chapter of the whole process of pregnancy, childbirth and early motherhood may appear rather gloomy, and I have concentrated largely on the less rewarding aspects in order to stress the lack of communication that exists today. It is not intended to mean that all first pregnancies are a nightmare, but to suggest that certain aspects of the situation may affect the relationship between mother and child.

The 'scientific' view of a set of natural processes is well understood by certain people in our culture, but it is barely communicated at all to a large proportion of the population. Their physical well-being is well cared for, but their ideas and expectations are very confused, and their experience as a result is often surprised and unpleasant. Their attitudes to their babies, and the taking of crucial decisions such as whether to breast or bottlefeed, are seriously influenced by their existing attitudes and earlier experiences.

Although this particular piece of anthropological research was not intended to consider socialisation as such, I think it does show that some very important factors affecting the early relationship between mother and child, and important decisions on the actual treatment of the baby, are to be found in the ideas and beliefs of the mother and her whole attitude to conception, pregnancy and birth. Further, it shows that these ideas and beliefs not only do not correspond to the 'scientific' view, but are not consistent or homogeneous even within one social class. This situation contrasts markedly with that reported from primitive cultures, and it is not impossible that this diversity of beliefs, experience and expectations may be related to the comparatively great difficulties experienced at birth and during the immediate post-partum period in our culture.

REFERENCES

Note. Not all these sources are specifically referred to in this chapter. Some are included because they provide further reading on the topics discussed as well as an introduction to anthropological writing on reproduction.

Ainsworth, M. D. S. (1967). *Infancy in Uganda.* Baltimore, Johns Hopkins Univ. Press.

Bott, E. (1957). *Family and Social Networks.* London, Tavistock.

Cartwright, A. (1970). *Parents and Family Planning Services.* London, Routledge and Kegan Paul.

Devereux, G. (1955). *A Study of Abortion in Primitive Societies.* New York.

Fleury, P. M. (1967). *Maternity Care: Mothers' Experience of Childbirth.* London, Allen and Unwin.

Ford, C. S. (1945). A Comparative Study of Human Reproduction. Yale Univ. Publications in Anthropology No. 32.

Fortes, M. (1938). Social and psychological effects of education in Taleland. *Africa,* **11,** Suppl. part 4.

Goscher-Gottstein, E. R. (1966). *Marriage and First Pregnancy.* London, Tavistock.

Gunther, M. (1970). *Infant Feeding.* London, Methuen.

Kardiner, A. (1939). *The Individual and his Society.* New York, Columbia Univ. Press.

Kitzinger, S. (1967). *The Experience of Childbirth.* London, Penguin.

Mayer, P. (1971) (ed.). *Socialisation. The Approach from Social Anthropology.* A. S. A. Monog. No. 8. London, Tavistock.

Mead, M. (1928). *Coming of Age in Samoa.* New York, Morrow.

Mead, M. (1930). *Growing Up in New Guinea.* New York, Morrow.

Minturn, L. and Lambert, W. W. (1965). *Mothers of Six Cultures: Antecedents of Childrearing.* New York, Wiley.

Newson, J. and Newson, E. (1959). *Patterns of Infant Care in an Urban Community.* London, Allen and Unwin.

Price-Williams, D. R. (1969). *Cross-Cultural Studies.* London, Penguin.

Report of the Maternity Services Committee (1959). (Cranbrook Report). London, H.M.S.O.

Schofield, M. (1967). *The Sexual Behaviour of Young People.* London, Penguin.

Spencer, R. F. (1949–50). Primitive Obstetrics. *CIBA Symposium,* **11,** 1157–88.

Spock, B. (1948, 1957). *Baby and Child Care.* New York, Duell, Sloan and Pearce.

Truby King, F. (1924). *The Expectant Mother and Baby's First Month, for Parents and Nurses.* London, Macmillan.

Whiting, B. B. (1963) (ed.). *Six Cultures: Studies of Child-Rearing.* New York, Wiley.

Wright, E. (1964). *The New Childbirth.* London, Tandem.

4

Cultural aspects of childrearing in the English-speaking world

John and Elizabeth Newson

If anthropologists from centres of learning in New Guinea or the Congo were to turn the tables on us and publish studies of the behaviour patterns found among the English-speaking peoples of Great Britain and the United States, one phenomenon to which they would surely pay special attention would be the cult of Child Psychology. The demand of an ever more literate population for books, pamphlets and magazines on parenthood is met by a stream of material which surpasses itself each year, not only in volume, but in the seductive, indeed sumptuous, way in which it is produced. Commercial firms marketing goods for the infant consumer hand out subsidised baby books as part of their advertising policy; others run advisory services or distribute regular magazines in which child care is discussed. In the publishing world as a whole, periodicals concerned with the family become more and more specialised: quite apart from the dozens of magazines addressed to women generally, we find some catering for the interests of parents in particular, some especially for the 'mother-to-be', and others for parents of individual age-groups or of children with special characteristics or handicaps. Books about childhood appear on every level, from those in which specialist communicates only with specialist, through all types of handbook for readers with a vocational interest in children, to those in which the expert and the less expert, with equal show of authority, make parents the target of their beliefs (substantiated or not) on how children 'should' be brought up. And, in support of the printed word, television and radio move in with their advice and discussion programmes, educational bodies run courses in psychology for parents, parent–teacher associations organise lectures, and one can even learn from a gramophone record how to teach one's children about sex.

Seen in historical and anthropological perspective, perhaps the most interesting aspect of the contemporary preoccupation with childrearing is that today we are self-consciously concerned with the possible *psychological* consequences of the methods which we use in bringing up our children. This attention to the total psychological development of the child is indeed a new phenomenon, in that earlier generations of parents have been chiefly preoccupied by the related themes of physical

c

survival and moral growth, rather than with concepts of mental health or social and emotional adjustment. So massive a change of emphasis must be of fundamental significance, not only to the anthropologist and the social historian, but to the child psychologists, psychiatrists and psychotherapists whose very existence as a group depends upon the climate of opinion which regards their professional skills as valuable and necessary, and which places them on an equal footing in social esteem with the more anciently respected callings of the paediatrician and the pedagogue. In this chapter, we intend briefly to survey some of the cultural and technological correlates of a society's attitudes towards child upbringing generally; and, more specifically, to examine a few of the ways in which the individual methods which parents adopt in the handling of their small children are defined or modified by the intricate pattern of cultural pressures to which they find themselves subject. We would ask the reader to bear in mind from the outset, however, that we write from the viewpoint of the English urban sub-culture, in which we are not only fieldworkers and observers but life members; nevertheless, we believe that the English and American complexes of parental experience show very many points of coincidence, both historically and contemporaneously, both in the things that parents do and in the reasons for which they do them: and that, therefore, a discussion in these terms will have a validity for parent–child behaviour on both sides of the Atlantic.

From the physical point of view, the human child is at its most vulnerable during and just after birth, and it remains 'at risk', in the actuarial sense, throughout early childhood, particularly during what our society thinks of as the preschool years. For the whole of human history up to the turn of the present century, simple physical survival has been the dominant issue in child upbringing: a question not of 'How shall I rear my child?' but of '*Will* I rear him?' In the middle of the eighteenth century, the mortality rate for children under five in England and Wales has been estimated as seventy-five for every hundred births.[1] In 1865, the infant mortality rate was 154 per thousand live births; a hundred years later it is 21.8 per thousand (Registrar General, 1963). Even to-day, of course, whether the child will survive at all is still the overriding consideration for millions of mothers in the underdeveloped areas of the world. There are still countries in which a mother can expect one in three of her children to die before reaching the age of five (U.N.I.C.E.F., 1964). If we take the 'developing countries' as a group, compared with

[1] Sangster (1963) gives this figure, which he obtained from Bready's (1938) history of England 'before and after Wesley'. Sangster points out (private communication) that the Wesleyans were especially interested in death and regularly quoted mortality statistics in their journals. Rousseau in *Emile* (1762, p. 325) more optimistically presumes 50 per cent of persons not living to childbearing age: but he is speaking in the context of people of his own class, not the population as a whole.

54

the 'more developed countries', infant mortality (in the first year) is more than five times as high in the first group as it is in the second; but during the years from one to four – that is, after weaning – the mortality rate in the developing countries is *forty times* as high as elsewhere: forty deaths for every thousand children surviving their first year, compared with one per thousand in the more developed areas (Pate, 1965). These statistics expressed in terms of expectation of life testify even more vividly to the distance Western society has travelled in being able to take the survival of our children almost for granted. At birth, a baby in India has an expectation of life of 32 years; in Mexico, 39 years; in the United Arab Republic, 38 years. The United States baby can expect a life span of 70 years, and in the United Kingdom this rises to 71 years. Once a child has survived his vulnerable first five years, his expectation of life naturally increases, but this increase will vary in direct proportion to the dangers which he has so far evaded: thus the United Kingdom 5-year-old can now expect to live until he is 75, the American until he is 72. The Indian child, however, once he is five, increases his expectation from 32 to 46 years; the Mexican, from 39 to 55 years; and the 5-year-old of the United Arab Republic can now expect to live to the age of 59, having added 21 years to his total expectation of life by virtue of having survived the 'preschool' period (U.N.I.C.E.F., 1964).

The ability to view infant care practices in any other light than whether they help the infant in his basic struggle to live is, then, something peculiar to our own century and, within this century, to the technologically advanced countries in which infant and child mortality rates have now been reduced to comparatively insignificant proportions. Briefly, child psychology is a luxury which only a small section of the world's parents can afford to consider: mothers need a respite from the most urgent problems of hunger, sickness and exposure before they can give much attention to questions of personal adjustment and maladjustment. And this factor of priorities is reflected in the literature directed towards parents, which, though it may often be out of touch with individual parental needs and circumstances, is written within a total social context and expresses closely enough prevailing social trends. Thus what is interesting about the women's magazines in England during the first years of the twentieth century is not the content of the advice given on childrearing, but the fact that so little advice is given at all; sometimes, from one year to the next, children are barely mentioned save for the occasional appealing illustrations, the pattern for a christening bonnet or the recipe for a nursery pudding. For the literate group of women who might be expected to read magazines, this was in fact a transitional period: freed to a greater extent than ever before from the shadow of

55

death, this was not yet the time of the educated lay interest in infant psychology which was soon to be aroused by Montessori, Froebel, Susan Isaacs and the Freudians generally; nor had the hygienist movement yet got under way. Future historians may one day look back on this short period as a golden guilt-free age for parents!

THE RELIGIOUS MORALITY

It is true that much was written about the moral upbringing of children during the eighteenth and nineteenth centuries; but this topic was itself clearly linked with the expectation of death, rather than with the hope of a balanced and integrated life. The Evangelical movement, despite its minority status, cast its influence far more widely than the actual numbers of its adherents might suggest; it is of especial interest to students of childrearing attitudes, in that its followers were so prolific in their writings that their beliefs (or watered-down versions of their beliefs) dominated both the advisory literature available to parents and the children's own reading matter for upwards of two centuries. For the Evangelicals, the prospect of heaven or hell was a major source of motivation in their attempts to 'form the minds' of their children. Susanna Wesley herself, mother of John and Charles, puts this plainly enough in a letter to John:

I insist upon conquering the wills of children betimes; because this is the only foundation for a religious education . . . religion is nothing else but the doing the will of God, and not our own . . . Heaven or hell depends on this alone. So that the parent who studies to subdue (self-will) in his children, works together with God in the saving of a soul: the parent who indulges it does the devil's work; makes religion impracticable, salvation unattainable; and does all that in him lies to damn his child, soul and body, for ever! . . . This, therefore, I cannot but earnestly repeat, – Break their wills betimes; begin this great work before they can run alone, before they can speak plain, or perhaps speak at all. Whatever pains it cost, conquer their stubbornness; break the will, if you would not damn the child. I conjure you not to neglect, not to delay this! Therefore (1) Let a child, from a year old, be taught to fear the rod and to cry softly. In order to do this, (2) Let him have nothing he cries for; absolutely nothing, great or small; else you undo your own work. (3) At all events, from that age, make him do as he is bid, if you whip him ten times running to effect it. Let none persuade you it is cruelty to do this; it is cruelty not to do it. Break his will now, and his soul will live, and he will probably bless you to all eternity. (Wesley, 1872)[2]

'Break the will, if you would not damn the child' – and damnation was a very present and real risk, in an age when most families would have lost at least one infant and often several. Passages from the catechisms devised for small children by the many child-orientated members of this

---

[2] This letter, and the two quotations that follow it, are taken from Sangster (1963), a most useful source-book on the Evangelists.

movement show very clearly the emphasis upon death as a part of normal experience:

Q: When mus you repent and believe, children?
A: Now, Sir, in childhood.
Q: Why must you do it now, children?
A: Because we may soon die, Sir.

The famous and vastly influential *Token for Children* (1753) by John Janeway was even more explicit:

Are you willing to go to hell, to be burned with the devil and his angels? ... O! Hell is a terrible place ... Did you never hear of a little child that died ... and if other children die, why may not you be sick and die? ... How do you know but that you may be the next child that may die? ... Now tell me, my pretty dear child, what will you do?

Isaac Watts' much loved and quoted hymns (1842) include many verses such as these:

Why should I say, ' 'Tis yet too soon
To seek for heav'n, or think of death?'
A flow'r may fade before 'tis noon,
And I this day may lose my breath.
(from Song XIII, *The Danger of Delay*)

There is an hour when I must die,
Nor do I know how soon 'twill come;
A thousand children, young as I,
Are call'd by death to hear their doom.
(from Song X, *Solemn Thoughts of GOD and Death*)

The pious and happy deaths of good little boys and girls, with, for variety, the occasional frightful deaths of irreligious children[3] who were assumed to have passed straight to the eternal fires of hell, are continually described and lingered over in children's books of the eighteenth and nineteenth century, from Janeway onward. The 'Child's Companion' of 1829, a well-illustrated little volume of stories and poems, contains no fewer than thirteen improving deathbed scenes, together with one discourse on death and two poems inspired by gazing on children's graves. The headstone of a 2-year-old moves the poet to observe:

Two years! oh happy little life
We cannot weep its early end;

and he concludes with the familiar warning:

[3] Typical in content, but outstanding in its setting, is the story of the death of Augusta Noble, which forms one chapter ('Fatal Effects of Disobedience to Parents') of Mrs Sherwood's extremely popular *History of the Fairchild Family*, first published in 1818 and reprinted many times throughout the nineteenth century.

The grave may open next for *you*!
You may not see another Spring.
eep death, and *heaven,* and *hell* in view;
Begin the present year, *anew.*

The combined effect of the religious beliefs of the Evangelicals and
the historical facts of childhood mortality upon trends in child upbringing is clear enough. Given a society in which death is a familiar occurrence and in which most children will have experienced the loss of a
sibling through death; given, too, a belief in a highly authoritarian God
with unlimited powers of reward or punishment through heaven or hell:
the logical consequence is to prepare children as carefully for death as
for life, to ensure above all else that the child shall be 'saved' at least
spiritually, if not physically, and indeed to avoid tempting the deity by
any suggestion that life is preferable to a happy death. Charles Wesley
(1868) wrote a number of hymns for the use of parents; he himself lost
his first two children.

I ask as with my parting breath,
To each allotted be
A holy life, or early death;
But which, I leave to thee.

Moreover, the likelihood of death at a tender age leaves no time for a
gentle, patient, permissive approach to child upbringing; the lesson
must be learnt by the child early and certainly: 'Break his will *now,* and
his soul will live'. The all-powerful God is consciously represented[4]
within the family by the almost equally powerful father: 'Vengeance is
mine' saith the Lord, but meanwhile vengeance is Papa's. In the sort of
conflict situation in which Benjamin Spock (1946) would suggest 'dis-
tracting him to something interesting but harmless' or 'give him a grace-

---

[4] The father's situation as God's vicar is explicitly stated in many books. Mrs
Sherwood (1818) gives Mr Fairchild a speech to his 6-year-old son which is worth
quoting in its entirety: the situation is that the child has refused to learn his Latin
grammar, despite punishments so far of bread and water for three meals and a
flogging with a 'small horsewhip'. 'Mr Fairchild got up and walked up and down
the room in great trouble; then turning to Henry, he said "Henry, listen to me;
when wicked men obstinately defy and oppose the power of God, He gives them
up to their own bad hearts; He suffers them to live, perhaps, and partake of the
light of the sun and of the fruits of the earth, but he shows them no marks of his
fatherly love or favour; they have no sweet thoughts, no cheerful hours, no delight-
ful hopes. I stand in the place of God to you, whilst you are a child; and as long
as I do not ask you to do anything wrong, you must obey me; therefore, if you
cast aside my authority and will not obey my commands, I shall not treat you as I
do my other children. From this time forward, Henry, I have nothing to do with
you; I will speak to you no more, neither will your mamma, or sisters, or John, or
Betty. Betty will be allowed to give you bread to eat, and water to drink: and I
shall not hinder you from going to your own bed to sleep at night; but I will have
nothing more to do with you; so go out of my study immediately."' (Mrs Sherwood, 1818).

ful way out' (from a temper tantrum), or where Susan Isaacs in 1932 tells the mother 'not to be too ready to treat any momentary defiance as an immediate occasion for a pitched battle of wills', the Evangelicals and their followers were, on the contrary, eager to seize upon such an opportunity, since their battle was with the devil himself, and the child's spiritual salvation at stake; distraction was the last thing they would have advised, for it was their urgent intention to rouse in the young child a vivid appreciation of his own shortcomings, as being the quickest and most effective means of subjugating his will to higher authority.

THE MEDICAL MORALITY

Curiously enough, the Evangelical concern to eradicate the devil in the child finds many echoes in the hygienist movement which dominated the twenties and thirties of our own century. Martha Wolfenstein (1955) has brilliantly analysed the changing pattern of advice given in succeeding editions of *Infant Care*, the bulletin for parents published by the United States Children's Bureau; a close parallel in the United Kingdom is found in the *Mothercraft Manual* (Liddiard, 1928). Although not a Government publication, this book, first published in 1923, achieved considerable popularity before the Second World War and has run to twelve editions, all revised by the original writer, the most recent being that of 1954; in England it was the main vehicle for the principles of Sir Truby King and his Mothercraft Training Society. The passage that follows (very similar to advice given during this period in *Infant Care*) comes from the 1928 edition, and might well be subscribed to by Susanna Wesley: the emphasis may be different, but the spirit is the same. The italics are ours, and mark the parts which had been deleted by the time the twelfth edition was reached in 1954; the word *trained* was replaced by *rightly guided*. There are several signs in the twelfth edition that the writer still hankers for the old methods, despite the necessity for tempering some of the more repressive advice, and the book remains far more authoritarian in tone than more recently written baby-books.

Self-control, obedience, the recognition of authority, and, later, respect for elders are all the outcome of the first year's training, as emphasised in preceding chapters. The baby who is picked up or fed whenever he cries soon becomes a veritable tyrant, and gives his mother no peace when awake; while, on the other hand, the infant who is fed regularly, put to sleep, and played with at definite times *soon finds that appeals bring no response, and so* learns that most useful of all lessons, self-control, and the recognition of an authority other than his own wishes. If parents and nurses would only realise how much easier it is for the child to bend to the social and moral laws in later life, when *trained* from infancy, how much sorrow might be saved. *To train an infant for the first year is comparatively easy, but after that the child begins to resent authority, and the conscientious mother has to be prepared to fight and win all along the line, in matters small and great.*

In many ways, the hygienists can be seen as the heirs of the Evangelicals; here again, this trend of social attitudes towards infant care must be set in its broader context. In the twenties, both in England and in America, we have a situation in which the infant and child mortality rates are fast declining, mainly owing to new advances in medical knowledge; at the same time, the world's values have been shaken by the First World War, writers and journalists have both more freedom and more inclination than ever before to discuss religion from an agnostic point of view, and the vengeful God of heaven and hell no longer impresses in quite the old way. For middle-class parents at least, however, a new power is taking his place: the equally authoritarian medical expert. The morality of aseptic rationalism has superseded that of spiritual regeneration.

It was indeed clear in the twenties that the medical profession had something important to say to mothers. The infant death rate was still high enough, especially among the poor, for parents not yet to have become complacent; meanwhile, the promise was held out, and for the first time could be kept, that babies could be successfully reared *provided* that medical advice was faithfully followed. This was an inducement not to be ignored; most parents, given the choice, would prefer the expectation of earthly survival for their children to the hope of heavenly reward. The time was in fact ripe, not only for a secession from religion (which, after all, had never given parents anything very tangible), but for a transfer of allegiance from the other traditional reference groups of parents: away from the methods prescribed by folklore, custom and the baby's grandmother, and towards the new blessings held out by scientific mothercraft.

Medical hygienism was quite obviously a necessity, nor is it likely to become completely unfashionable; the consequence of this interest to the student of child care was that the enthusiasm justifiably generated by its successes led to an assumption that *mental* hygiene, applied on the same principles, would be equally beneficial. Without, apparently, a single doubt as to the validity of this premise, the advice was laid down, the warnings given.

The leading authorities of the day – English, foreign and American – all agree that the first thing to establish in life is *regularity of habits*. The mother who 'can't be so cruel' as to wake her sleeping baby if he happens to be asleep at the appointed feeding-time, fails to realize that a few such wakings would be all she would have to resort to . . . The establishment of perfect regularity of habits, initiated by 'feeding and sleeping by the clock', is the ultimate foundation of all-

60

round obedience. Granted good organic foundations, truth and honour can be built into the edifice as it grows. (Truby King, 1937)

Never play with or excite a baby before bedtime . . . Half the irritability and lack of moral control which spoil adult life originate in the first year of existence. The seeds of feebleness and instability sown in infancy bear bitter fruit afterwards. (Truby King, 1937)

Masturbation – This is a bad habit . . . The great thing is to recognise the condition early . . . Untiring zeal on the part of the mother or nurse is the only cure; it may be necessary to put the legs in splints before putting the child to bed. He must never be left in such a position that he can carry on the habit, he must be made to forget it; this sometimes takes three months, or longer in the worst cases . . . This habit, if left unchecked, may develop into a serious vice. The child's moral nature becomes perverted; one such child has been known to upset a whole school. (Liddiard, 1928)

Thumb Sucking – If this is done frequently and perniciously it must be taken in hand and treated as a bad habit. Sometimes it is enough to put on cotton gloves; if not, the best plan is to make a splint of corrugated cardboard [illustrated in original]; this allows free movement of the arm from the shoulder joint but prevents the hand from getting to the mouth. These splints should be taken off twice daily and the arms exercised and rubbed. (Liddiard, 1928)

There is a sensible way of treating children. Treat them as though they were young adults. Dress them, bathe them with care and circumspection. Let your behaviour always be objective and kindly firm. Never hug and kiss them, never let them sit in your lap. If you must, kiss them once on the forehead when they say good night. Shake hands with them in the morning. Give them a pat on the head if they have made an extraordinarily good job of a difficult task. Try it out. In a week's time you will find how easy it is to be perfectly objective with your child and at the same time kindly. You will be utterly ashamed of the mawkish, sentimental way you have been handling it. (Watson, 1928)

It seems extraordinary to today's parents in England and the United States that women of the twenties and thirties should have been prepared to accept either the content of these pronouncements or the authoritarian tone in which they were made; yet accepted they were, in that innumerable women made valiant efforts to stifle their natural desire to cuddle their babies and to feed them when they were hungry, or were wracked with guilt and shame when they 'mawkishly' rocked the child or sentimentally eased his stomach pangs in the small hours with a contraband couple of ounces. For the educated mother in particular, it took a great deal of courage to reject a system of upbringing which combined quasi-religious appeals to 'duty' and 'rightness' and 'goodness'[5]

---

[5] Many examples could be given. One will suffice: 'There is no doubt whatever as to the duty of mother and nurse in this matter' (Truby King, 1937, p. 16). He is referring to the need to wake the infant if he is asleep when the clock says that it is feeding time. He also has a section on 'The Destiny of the Race in the Hands of its Mothers', and refers the reader to the state of motherhood during the decline and fall of the Roman Empire.

with a claim to be based on the rational attitudes which she herself, as a 'modern' woman, was supposed to have embraced. During the last few years, we have begun to learn something of these mothers' true feelings from the women who suffered the regime at first hand: what stands out in such accounts is the emotion which is still generated in the mother by her own memories. The quotations that follow are both from personal letters to the present writers, commenting on a published suggestion that those who give advice to parents often do not pay enough attention to the parents' own views. The first correspondent holds a distinguished position in the highest ranks of the nursing profession; the second is the author of books on social work with children.

I am so in agreement . . . that I feel quite emotional. My daughter was born during the Truby King period, and it took a month of untold agony for myself and the child before I threw every book I had out of the house and all my well meaning and Truby King obsessed relatives with them. From then on, mother and child progressed happily, and since those early and terrible days I have treated advice with cautious courtesy. As for breast feeding, I feel so strongly about this that I can hardly express myself! For the mother who finds breast feeding terribly difficult – and there are so many of these – the solemn pronouncements she will hear from her own parents and from health visitors, obstetricians and other professional people can lead to real emotional and mental suffering. I well remember the long watches of the night when I and my baby struggled to overcome a physical incapability on my part, and I cannot begin to tell you the relief on both sides when I strode out of the house, bought the largest tin of baby food I could find, and gave her the first square meal she had had since birth.

I was caught up in the Truby King Mothercraft doctrine of 1935 . . . The health visitors prated and bullied; one's baby screamed and tears splashed down one's cheeks while milk gushed through one's jersey. But one must *never* pick the baby *up* – it was practically incestuous to *enjoy* one's baby, so I gathered, young, obedient, motherless, indoctrinated mother that I was. I made up my mind then that *next* time I had a baby I would *love* it. But that baby never came . . . In my day, we were instructed that frost never hurt a baby yet, and if the baby cried it must be *mastered*. Working-class women cuddled their babies up in the warm as women had done for millions of years. We, the young graduate law-abiding wives of the thirties, cried *ourselves* as our babies went blue with cold . . . See Mary McCarthy's novel *The Group* . . . She speaks for us all.

'The young, graduate, law-abiding wife' is indeed exemplified in Mary McCarthy's Priss, whose situation is exacerbated by being married to a paediatrician. We cannot quote here more than a short paragraph, but the whole of chapters 10 and 14 of *The Group* should be required reading for those whose profession it is to advise parents (McCarthy, 1963).

The nights were the worst. There were nights when, hearing him start at three or four in the morning, she would have welcomed anything that would let him stop and rest – paregoric, a sugar-tit, any of those wicked things. During her pregnancy, Priss had read a great deal about past mistakes in child rearing; according to the literature, they were the result not only of ignorance, but of sheer selfishness: a nurse or a mother who gave a crying child paregoric usually did it for her own peace of mind, not wanting to be bothered. For the doctors agreed it did not hurt a baby to cry; it only hurt grown-ups to listen to him. She *supposed* this was true. The nurses here wrote down every day on Stephen's chart how many hours he had cried, but neither Sloan nor Dr Turner turned a hair when they looked at that on the chart; all they cared about was the weight curve.

MORALITIES OF NATURAL DEVELOPMENT AND NATURAL NEEDS

Meanwhile, from the direction of the psychoanalysts and the nursery educationalists, another school of thought had been arising. In some ways not altogether opposed to the hygienist school (they did not very much approve of cuddling, although as early as 1932 Ian Suttie had protested against the 'taboo on tenderness'), nevertheless a basic interest in the child's natural intellectual and social development,[6] together with a less inhibited approach to sexual function, opened the door to greater permissiveness generally. In her enlarged edition of *The Nursery Years* (1932), when the Children's Bureau was still advising mechanical restraints for thumbsucking, Susan Isaacs preferred extra play and companionship, and – incredible immorality! – '*substitute pleasure*, in the shape of a good boiled sweet'. Where the Children's Bureau had now advanced from restraint to diversion as a treatment for masturbation, Isaacs was giving a brief account of Oedipal conflict and advising parents that they were 'far more likely to do harm by rushing in to scold or correct than by leaving the child to deal with it himself – in a general atmosphere of calm goodwill', and was citing Dr Ernest Jones in her support. Perhaps of especial importance for the liberating influence of the educationalists was their emphasis upon natural play and its functional status in the child's development.[7] Natural play was good – it was also messy and dirty. It was functional – but it was also enjoyed by the child. And if adults were to learn about child development by observing free play, there must also be free communication. At last, the dirty, happy, noisy child could be accepted as a good child.

[6] Of especial interest in this context are Susan Isaacs' two seminal works (1930, 1933), which recorded at great length the actual play and conversation of children in the nursery environment; the second volume begins uncompromisingly: 'This book is addressed to the scientific public, and in particular to serious students of psychology and education'. Piaget, too, was beginning to arouse interest in young children's conceptual development: *The Child's Conception of the World* was published in England in 1929, and his next two books appeared in 1930 and 1932.

[7] Obviously the roots of these educational ideas go back to Rousseau (1762), but, although a continuous chain of interest can be traced right through the nineteenth century, it was not until the late 1920s that such theories were communicated in practical terms to a substantial body of parents.

63

Martha Wolfenstein (1955) points out the distinction which has long been made 'between what a baby "needs", his legitimate requirements, whatever is essential to his health and well-being, on the one hand, and what the baby "wants", his illegitimate pleasure strivings, on the other'. The hygienists considered only physical needs as legitimate – and even hunger, if expressed at an unsuitable time, was excluded. The wish for companionship was very definitely in the category of illegitimate pleasure strivings: 'We now come to the *treatment*, as it were, for a baby who cries simply because he wants attention, which is: "Baby must cry it out".'[8] In general, the baby's wishes had tended in the past to be suspect, and the mother had been expected to look for some non-permissible motive behind them, in the form either of dangerous (probably erotic) impulses or of a rebellious determination to dominate the mother; in either case, constant control of the child was called for, and only the baby who had submitted himself completely to the mother's control could be called a good baby. Now that virtue could be acknowledged in the toddler as he freely followed his own natural[9] pursuits and interests – not excluding the exploration of his own body – the ground was finally prepared for an acceptance of babies' desires as needs in themselves: 'Babies want attention; they probably need plenty of it' (Children's Bureau, 1945). In Wolfenstein's words (1955), 'What the baby wants for pleasure has thus become as legitimate a demand as what he needs for his physical well-being, and is to be treated in the same way.'

Hygienist theories were in any case too stress-provoking to the mother to have lasted very many years; the only group who did seem to derive satisfaction from them were some who, standing in an advisory role to the parents, found in such an authoritarian regime a source of power. There are still such personalities in advisory positions today; fortunately for parents, as we shall see, this attitude is out of fashion. The final reversal came with the publication of two seminal books, an article and a film; and again it was from the direction of psychoanalysis that the change came. In the United States, Margaret Ribble (1943) published *The Rights of Infants*; in England John Bowlby (1952) followed up his earlier studies of maternal deprivation as an antecedent of what he had called 'the affectionless character' (1946) with his report for the World Health Organisation, *Maternal Care and Mental Health*; and in the opening volume of the journal *Psycho-Analytic Study of the Child*, Rene Spitz (1945) published his paper on hospitalised infants and the effects

8   This statement comes from a work entitled *Cries of the Baby*, by Dr Theron Kilmer, which is quoted by Truby King (1937, revised and enlarged ed.) as being 'full of ripe wisdom'.

9   The history of the cult of 'nature' in all its aspects is itself of great interest to historians of child psychology and child nutrition; we cannot explore this topic here, however.

of lack of mothering, and supported this with the widely circulated documentary film, *Grief: a Peril in Infancy*. All these writers brought dramatic evidence (some of which has since been more critically appraised (Pinneau, 1950; Ainsworth, 1963)), that babies and young children *need* mothering – not only the mother's presence, but the rocking, cuddling and lap play which had been so expressly forbidden – and that to deprive the baby of the natural expression of maternal warmth could prevent normal development of social relationships and permanently mar his personality. According to Margaret Ribble (1943), indeed, for the newborn baby 'the need for contact with the mother is urgent in order to keep the reflex mechanisms connected with breathing in operation as well as to bring the sensory nervous system into functional activity'. While statements such as this invited the charge that factual evidence was becoming confounded with too-hasty interpretation, the basic thesis survived and has been strengthened by other workers not of the psychoanalytic school: notably the ethologists and zoologists, as well as child psychologists (Lorenz, 1952; Harlow, 1961; Schaffer and Emerson, 1964).

The effect of these works can hardly be overestimated: it was immediate, and still continues. Bowlby's report was abridged and published as a paperback (1953), thus becoming widely available to the lay public; in the year of publication and the five years following, more than seventy-five thousand copies were sold, and nearly as many in the next five years: an exceptional sale in Britain for a book not intended as a baby book for parents. Theories of maternal need rapidly found a place in countless training courses for workers with children. In England, James Robertson (1953, 1958), a colleague of Bowlby's at the Tavistock Clinic, started a campaign to persuade children's hospital wards to admit mothers together with their children, or at least not to restrict visiting in any way;[10] some hospitals welcomed the idea, others resisted it, but meanwhile a Government committee was set up which in 1959 published the 'Platt Report' on the welfare of children in hospital, recommending 'that all hospitals where children are treated will adopt the practice of unrestricted visiting, particularly for children below school age', that 'it is particularly valuable for the mother to be able to stay in hospital with her child during the first day or two', and that 'children should not be admitted to hospital if it can possibly be avoided'. Parents themselves thereupon set up a pressure group of their own (*Mother Care for Children in Hospital*, now the *National Association for the Welfare of Children in Hospital*), which, with all the enthusiasm

---

[10] Robertson's scientific film, *A Two-Year-Old goes to Hospital* (1953), was designated by the British Film Institute as a film of national and historic importance, and a print is preserved in the National Archives.

of maternal solicitude that has the acknowledged right on its side, and with the help of a sympathetic press, is gradually altering the atmosphere of children's hospital care. Anna Freud (1943, 1960), who had been one of the first to call attention to the emotional difficulties of small children separated from their mothers, attacked from yet another angle, affirming the emotional need, not only in the baby but in his mother, to be together during the first weeks of the child's life, and criticising maternity hospital practice that separated the two. Clearly, parents generally must welcome the news that cuddling is not only nice but necessary; perhaps, however, we should spare a compassionate thought once more for the intellectual mothers of the thirties, whose sufferings as they tried to be 'good' mothers are now repeated in the knowledge that all their efforts only led them to be 'bad' mothers: as one of our correspondents added, 'Here is Bowlby, still out to make us feel guilty – about our rejection of the children we loved but were not *allowed* to love.'

INDIVIDUALISM AND THE 'FUN MORALITY'

The widespread influence of Ribble, Bowlby and Spitz, although it was supported by new, more permissive baby books such as Benjamin Spock's *Baby and Child Care* (1946), cannot be entirely explained in terms of parents' reaction against the rigours of aseptic mothercraft. Once again the trend must be seen in historical and sociological perspective. Babies were not the only people whose rights were being demanded at the end of the Second World War; other groups, too, submerged in anonymous poverty through years of unemployment, had in wartime received for the first time their fair share both of work and of food, and were now making it clear that neither malnutrition nor the grinding degradation of worklessness could any longer be tolerated by the 'lower classes' of the victorious nations. Perhaps, too, the final horrors of the war – Hiroshima, Nagasaki and the discovery of the concentration camps – shocked ordinary people, for a time at least, into a more humanitarian frame of mind; and perhaps, combined with this, was a determination to enjoy family life after the unhappy experience of war separations and before the more dreadful possibilities with which all mankind now has to live. Both in Britain and in America, especially marked during the later fifties and early sixties, the voices of dissent began to rise – against McCarthyism, against the Bomb, against any established authority that tells individuals what to do and how to do it – voices that said, and continue to say, 'They shan't push us around any longer.' The protest of the human individual against the massive forces which control him is indeed a theme which can be seen in contemporary art, literature, music and drama,[11] in the struggles against racialism, poverty and war, in the popular movements of Western youth and in the renewed campaign for women's emancipation; so we can hardly be surprised if parents too begin to question the authority of the experts.

The beginning of this trend, in which the fundamental need of parents is to be happy in parenthood, can be seen in two ways. In the first place, the tone in which advice is given changes from the strictly authoritarian to the friendly, neighbourly, perhaps big-sisterly approach. The old bullying manner is completely gone; we now find a persuasive, informal atmosphere, supported by illustrations which reflect the text in their message that bringing up babies is hair-raising, maybe, but lots of fun for everyone – just as the clinical photographs and chaste drawings of the old baby books reflect their atmosphere of stern duty.[12] Where in the thirties the mother was given solemn warnings as to what *would* happen if she disobeyed the rules, the mode now is to refer her, with continual reassurances however, to what *might possibly* result from some mistaken handlings: 'Here's what happens once in a while when the needs of the child aren't recognized' (Spock, 1946, chapter on 'The Two Year Old'). Where formerly she was told that 'the leading authorities of the day all agree . . .', now it is no more than suggested that 'many doctors feel . . .'. Spock is the supreme example of the friendly, conversational approach: just paternalistic enough to give confidence and reassurance, he is otherwise prepared to talk to the mother on equal terms. He probably has no serious rival on either side of the Atlantic, though to a much smaller audience of discriminating parents the English psychoanalyst, the late D. W. Winnicott, speaks (1964) with a similar skill (as does Dr Hugh Jolly to readers of *The Times*).

The second way in which this trend can be seen is in the content of advice given. That it is more permissive goes without saying: permissive both to the child and to the parents. But it is changed too in that it is not so much the details of infant care that are laid down as the principles which should be followed in deciding the details. Parents are no longer told what methods to adopt, but rather the *frame of mind* in which to adopt them. Flexibility is the keynote. *Infant Care* (1958 edition) shows many examples. On the baby's sleeping place: 'Do whatever way disturbs your sleep least'; on his clothing: 'Some mothers prefer . . . others

---

11   Some representative names from Great Britain are Francis Bacon for art; Alan Sillitoe for literature (Sillitoe, 1959); Osborne and Beckett, followed by Pinter and Hopkinson for straight drama, and Jonathan Miller and his 'Beyond the Fringe' group paving the way for a whole era of satirical revues; and the folk song–pop movements for music. American readers will easily provide their own examples.

12   In Truby King's *Feeding and Care of Baby* (1937), the only illustration in which anybody seems to be having fun is one entitled chillingly 'Nurse Imitating a Fond Relation' – from which is drawn the moral that babies should not be overstimulated.

think . . .'; on genital play: 'This is a common thing, and can go un-noticed. But sometimes it is disturbing to mothers, so if you feel uncomfortable about it you can try giving him a toy to hold while he's on the toilet seat'; and in general: 'If you take it easy in caring for your baby, you will be doing him a great service.' Flexibility serves one major aim: to allow parents to enjoy their role. 'When you both feel light-hearted enough to enjoy your baby, you are making a good start' says *Infant Care* on its second page, and Spock uses the same injunction, 'Enjoy Your Baby', as a subheading in his chapter 'The Right Start'. In Martha Wolfenstein's words (1955), 'Fun has become not only permissible but required'; the modern mother is already a creature whose 'feelings of inadequacy are matched only by her undying efforts', according to Johnson and Medinnus (1965), and 'fun morality' now ensures that 'her self-evaluation can no longer be based entirely on whether she is doing the right and necessary things but *becomes involved with nuances of feelings which aren ot under voluntary control*' (Wolfenstein, 1955, our italics).

SOCIOLOGICAL CONCOMITANTS OF INDIVIDUAL PRACTICES

A flexible approach to childrearing is not only the result of a favourable conjunction of a reaction against rigidity, a cultural mood of individualism and the 'fun morality'; to be viable, such a trend must be accompanied by a low infant mortality rate, a comparatively high standard of living for the mass of the population, and an appropriate technology. All of these are present in Great Britain and the United States.

The medical expert of the twenties and thirties was a figure of immense prestige because he held out the best chance the infant could have, and at last a good chance, of surviving. At that period, as is still true in many parts of the world, ordinary people were fully aware of how much they owed to specialist medical knowledge. Today, that debt remains; but, in highly developed communities, the constant awareness of it does not. Survival, and healthy survival, is taken for granted; since the antibiotics revolution, the majority of parents have little experience of nursing a child through more than a couple of days' real illness. In England, middle-aged working-class parents sometimes grumble rue-fully that their adolescent children, having been born to the Welfare State and full employment, have no conception of the hardships of working-class life before the war, especially during periods of illness; in the same way, young mothers are barely aware of the old horror of tuberculosis, diphtheria, smallpox and rickets, from which their children are so efficiently protected, and some of the medical profession take hard the passing of the days when the doctor's word was law and his edicts not to be trifled with. The fact that a parent may now be prepared to question a doctor's diagnosis, or even criticise his treatment, can be a painful blow for a profession whose traditions are so deeply authoritarian.

Once the doctor no longer holds the infant's survival in his hand, parents are free to make choices for themselves in the methods they use in rearing the child; but in many of their decisions they are still dependent, more dependent than they realise, upon technological facilities and upon a reasonable standard of living. We may now consider one or two practical examples of the sorts of parental choices which are in fact free only within rather narrow limits.

The issue of breastfeeding versus bottlefeeding is an interesting case because, at first sight simple in the factors involved, it conceals more subtle undercurrents. In the first place, it must be understood that for millions of women there is no such issue. The choice cannot be made, simply because there is no available alternative to human milk.[13] Obviously a basic prerequisite to bottlefeeding is a plentiful supply of fresh or suitably preserved disease-free milk, and the money with which to buy it; beyond this, however, if bottlefeeding is not to involve an immediate rise in infant deaths through gastro-intestinal infections, both sterilisable feeding equipment and the means of sterilisation are necessary. Thus the social conditions in which it is feasible for mothers to choose bottlefeeding on any large scale will include comparatively high material living standards, comprising at least running water, efficient sanitation and convenient cooking arrangements. These are the first pre-conditions of a massive decline in breastfeeding, and it is probably true to say that the addition of the further technological refinements and conveniences which some mothers already begin to regard as necessities – refrigerators, sterilisers, electric bottlewarmers and the like – will probably hasten any move away from breastfeeding.

Given the availability of clean milk, glass or plastic bottles, rubber or plastic nipples, uncontaminated water, and stoves to boil it on, the mother, in order to choose, still has to have some surplus in the family income; for the cheapest artificial formula is more expensive than breast-feeding. Thus, once bottlefeeding becomes feasible at all in a society, we may expect any trend towards this method to start among the wealthier families and spread gradually downward: indeed, at this stage the feeding bottle may become a status symbol, a signal to other mothers that in

[13] F. Le Gros Clark (1953) has pointed out that 'those who are accustomed to see cow's milk as simply a natural "bridge" from the breast to solid foods have not grasped the full extent of the problem. Most of the peoples of the world have still practically no milk but mother's milk; and for several thousand years at least the human stock seems to have had no domesticated milk herds.'

this particular establishment artificial food can be afforded.[14] Class differences of this sort were in fact found by research workers in the United States during the forties (Davis and Havighurst, 1946). And one might go on to predict that, at any given time in a society's development, artificial feeding would be most popular among those women who enjoy the highest material standards of living: not least because these are also the women who are likely to have more of their interests and social contacts outside the home, and who therefore might be less willing than the working-class mother to be restricted by breastfeeding. One would, however, be wrong in such a prediction; for the class trend in terms of money is eventually interrupted by another class trend in terms of beliefs and ideals. As a country's economy improves, there comes a time when *all* mothers, whatever their socio-economic class, can afford financially to make their own choice as to whether or not to breastfeed; and it is at this point that more personal considerations, themselves correlated with social class affiliations, begin to take over. Once this stage is reached, indeed, the class trend is not only halted but reversed. In the United States, it was the middle-class mothers who were found by Sears, Maccoby and Levin (1957) to be most likely to breastfeed.[15] In England this reversed trend is clearer still, in a country where breastfeeding is still much more widely practised and medical opinion much less ready to endorse feeding by formula. The table below shows the proportion of mothers of different social classes in the English Midland city of Nottingham who were breastfeeding their babies at various ages (Newson and Newson, 1963).

Class differences in the proportions of mothers still breastfeeding at different times after birth

N = 709	Professional and managerial	Shop and clerical	Skilled manual	Semi-skilled manual	Un-skilled manual
Percentage still breast feeding at:					
1 month	60	50	50	51	34
3 months	39	34	24	22	12
6 months	20	12	11	11	7

14 Motivation of this sort may, as in other instances of human prestige-seeking, outrun the family's ability to afford the luxury, in this case with more than usually harmful results. The U.N.I.C.E.F. Professor of Child Health at Makerere Medical School writes: 'In Uganda as elsewhere *the advertising of dried milk* is a great menace. The milk is far beyond the price the mothers can afford – a third of the basic monthly wage would have to be used to feed a four-month-old baby . . . The commercial persuaders are apparently winning hands down and, unfortunately, their undoubtedly successful techniques are too costly for health departments' (Jelliffe, 1965).
15 These studies are usefully integrated by Bronfenbrenner (1958).

What are the factors which make such a reversal possible? When we inquire further into the motivation behind the decision not to breast-feed,[16] we find two very distinct patterns of attitude and belief. The wives of professional workers appear to be strongly influenced by considerations of 'duty' and 'principle'; current English baby books often refer to breastfeeding as 'baby's birthright', and professional-class wives seem to accept this extension of the common intellectual assumption that the 'natural' thing is necessarily the 'right' thing. It is not without significance here, perhaps, that while working-class people embrace what used to be the luxuries of civilisation – soft white bread, canned fruit and so on – it is among the professional classes that we find a return *on principle* to the home-baked bread and unrefined foods which were once the necessary economy measure of the low-income family. Thus professional-class mothers very often seem to be firmly committed to natural feeding as a matter of principle; whether or not they find the experience enjoyable (and many do find in it the most intense satisfaction), few seem to doubt that by this means their babies will be given an ideal start, both nutritionally and psychologically, and that artificial feeding, however expensively supervised, is at best an inferior substitute. Failure to breastfeed, other than for the best of medical reasons, is thus likely to result in painful guilt feelings, such as are illustrated in this quotation:

I think I'm inclined to shirk that a little bit, I don't know why; I felt ashamed of myself afterwards. I didn't seem to get the hang of it very well – I don't know if it'd improve as you have more children, I think you get into the swing better . . . He was very slow . . . in that sort of a state you're still a bit low yourself, and I think you're inclined to – you know – take the easiest way out, and as a result I didn't keep it up for very long (one month). I'm afraid to admit it was just plain laziness on my part.

The working-class wife's sense of duty to her family centres far more definitely upon provision of warmth and food – the material comforts of life, rather than the satisfaction of psychological needs. The use of a bottle fits in ideally with this tradition, for in the gradual consumption by her baby of a visible amount of milk, often well sweetened, she has a patent confirmation of her nurturant role. Many working-class mothers complain of having no yardstick by which to measure whether or not the

[16] In a community whose authorities traditionally endorse breastfeeding, it is of course not enough to ask the mother whether she had any reason for changing to bottlefeeding: almost invariably, her first answer will be a respectable medical one, e.g. that the milk was too thin, too thick, too scant, or didn't suit the baby. This answer accepted, the mother may then be asked whether she enjoyed feeding, and whether she would have stopped anyway, even if her milk had been suitable: only at this point can the private attitude, which often underlies the public excuse, be reached.

71

breastfed baby is replete. In the words of a haulier's wife, 'With a bottle you can put 'em down and think, well, you've had your quarter of a pint. You know how much they've had. I couldn't get peace of mind by the breast.' In the same study, the authors found another factor impelling working-class wives away from breastfeeding: the consideration of prudery, a squeamishness about exposing the breast in order to suckle, which was restricted entirely to the wives of manual workers. Not one professional-class mother, even among those who had not enjoyed breastfeeding, suggested that a 'natural' activity like feeding a baby might cause them any embarrassment: but a substantial number of working-class women expressed the shame they felt at feeding in front of their husbands or their other children, or even in front of the baby himself, 'once he began to know'. It is possible that working-class prudery about nudity generally is bound up with deep-seated fears of the breaking of incest taboos, so much more a real possibility in the heavily overcrowded household; and the breast has, through the mass media of the last thirty years, gained such potency as a sex symbol that one would hardly be surprised if the mother regarded its exposure chiefly as a blatant sexual invitation. Once the prudish attitude exists, at all events, overcrowding makes it a powerful force in decision making: few women are prepared to leave the comfortable living-room, and the television set, in order to feed the baby in modest isolation.

In infant feeding, then, we see decisions being taken by mothers within a socio-economic-technological context: once economic and technological factors are reasonably constant for all mothers in the society, we can discern the operation of other class-linked factors, all of which work in the opposite direction from those expected on economic grounds alone, and these factors will, in the absence of strong medical indications either way, remain paramount for the mother over any advice she may be given by doctor or baby clinic.

Many other current trends in the care of small children are still more clearly the product of the material circumstances and socio-economic roles applicable to the individual parent. The mother's ability to be 'relaxed' over toilet training, for instance, may be more dependent than she likes to think upon an efficient hot water supply, automatic washing machine and plastic pants, or upon disposable napkins or a good nappy service – or, alternatively, upon a warm sun and a culture pattern that allows children to run naked! It is not so easy to remain calm and allows children to run naked! It is not so easy to remain calm and accepting as the toddler wets nappy after nappy, if washing them involves a mother be quite so 'friendly and easy-going about the bathroom' (Spock) if the bathroom doesn't exist and the lavatory is the other side of the back yard or down a flight of tenement stairs and shared with three or four other families of careless habits. Again, whether the pre-school child is expected to stand up for himself and hit back when he is among his peers, or whether he is withdrawn from such conflict by his mother, can be seen as partly, though not entirely, a function of the type of housing occupied by the family, according to whether the child can be withdrawn into his own yard or garden and whether neighbouring entrances are separated by fence or hedge (Newson and Newson, 1968). We have quoted elsewhere the comments of a lorry-driver's wife whom we interviewed about her 7-year-old daughter, but they are worth re-peating; this family has lived in terraced housing backed by one com-munal yard for six dwellings, but now lives on a large housing estate, in one of a circle of houses facing each other across a small 'close', each with its own wedge-shaped front garden.

I don't think people do fall out like they used to do. When they lived in *yards* they used to fall out, you know. But while the mums was arguing, the children was friends again! I mean, I sometimes get a bit annoyed, but I never go out and shout about it – I'm annoyed *at home*, if you know what I mean. (You think people fell out a bit more when they lived in yards?) Oh, *definitely*; 'cause you see – now Elaine's friend lives over there, don't she? (across the close). Well, if she does anything that annoys *me*, I'm not right next door so that I *burst* – I mean, you chunter in the house and it's out of you, and you don't *say* anything then, do you? I don't know if you've noticed anybody else say that? (Well, we've been thinking this, as a matter of fact . . .) Yes, well, you see it's these *hedges* that do it. I don't think – mind you, my next-door neighbour and me, we really are friends, for years and years – but I don't think it's so friendly, you know, as we used to be when we had yards. These hedges cut everything off. But, mind you, they cut the quarrels off as well, don't they? So . . . But I try not to fall out over children – I don't think it pays you, you only get resentful, don't you? I mean, there's a *big* lad, thirteen, and he let his dog jump up at her, and I did shout at *him*, and his mother never spoke to me no more – she was really annoyed with me, she was! But we didn't *fall out*, we just *didn't speak*. (It's easier just to stop speaking . . .) When there's hedges – yes!

The sort of questions which it is even appropriate to ask about child upbringing, too, is often decided by technological and economic factors: for instance, television now has its role as a 'pleasure striving' which many parents feel they must control (Sears, Maccoby and Levin, 1957), or as something which a child may be deprived of as a punishment (Newson and Newson, 1968); the affluent society brings with it the anxieties of ownership, and 17 per cent of the offences for which Not-tingham 1-year-olds were smacked concerned destructive behaviour to household property (excluding electrical, and therefore potentially dangerous, equipment), with a further 7 per cent for playing with television knobs; and the second Nottingham study has found that a potent source of conflict between modern mothers and their 4-year-olds is the situation in which the toy pile in the household has reached un-manageable proportions and the mother wishes to throw away some of the more battered remains. The father's place within the family is another example of the operation of socio-economic factors, which we may now examine more closely.

Of recent years the role of the father has received more attention from the baby books, and the trend, both in the advice given and in actual family life, is towards his taking an evermore active part in bringing up his child, from babyhood onward. A number of forces can be seen to be involved; most of them, however, are directly connected with material standards of life both at home and at work. Improvement in conditions of housing is an important consideration; the 'do-it-yourself' revolution in home decoration has made its impact on the majority of families, even in poor areas where the basic fabric of the houses is substandard: with the result that 'home' is much more likely to be a pleasant place to be, father can enjoy being houseproud as well as mother, and outside acti-vities no longer offer the one escape from a sordid family environment. Indeed, as we have pointed out elsewhere (1968), television commercials are at pains to demonstrate that the well-turned-out family and the sprucely decorated home are perfect foils one for the other, and advertis-ing interests give full support to the advisory literature in holding out 'having fun as a family' as the ideal situation for any well-adjusted parent. The increase in the amount of leisure time available to fathers generally must also be important: shorter working hours ensure that the father has more than enough time for mere physical recuperation, and the fact that technological aids make his actual work easier and less exhausting in the first place adds to the surplus time he has in which to enjoy his family. In addition, as primary schools begin to reach parents with the message that there is more to education than the 'three Rs', and particularly as progressive educationalists press for greater involvement of parents, the father begins to feel that he can and should be contributing to his young children's development in more enjoyable and satisfying ways than the traditional disciplinary role: indeed the *only* way in which fathers seem to be diminishing their childrearing activities is in the area of discipline, which many prefer to hand over to the mother.

The long-term study of children in Nottingham, whose findings on breastfeeding were quoted earlier, shows a high degree of father par-ticipation even in the care of the baby. On the basis of specific questions on how often the father would bath the child, play with him, take him out alone, feed him, attend to him in the night, change his napkin and put him to bed, the 709 fathers in this all-class sample were rated as: highly participant (would care for the child as readily as the mother);

moderately participant (inclined to be choosy as to which things he would do, or would look after the baby sometimes but not as a matter of course); and non-participant (would take part only in an emergency such as the mother's illness). Playing with the child, it was found, had to be excluded from consideration, since 99 per cent of the fathers of 1-year-olds were said to do this. In the case of babies of this age, the largest group of fathers (52 per cent) were found to be 'highly participant', 27 per cent were moderately so, and only 21 per cent could be rated as non-participant. Three years later, as the children reached their fourth birthday, much the same proportion of fathers (51 per cent) was taking a highly active part in the children's care; but the proportion taking a moderate share had risen to 43 per cent, and only a tiny group of 6 per cent were now non-participant. In evaluating the social change which has taken place over the years, the reader may reflect that, between the wars, the number of fathers rateable as highly participant by these rather exacting standards would probably have been negligible, particularly with reference to babies of twelve months. A man used to be thought of as being highly participant in his children's upbringing merely on the strength of playing with them often, and perhaps reading to them or telling them stories; as we have seen, paternal playing is now so universal as to have become useless as a criterion.

Again, however, within modes of behaviour which are typical for a given society at a specific time, clear differences can be seen between socio-economic groups. This study found that fathers in the shop and clerical category were more active in baby care than any other occupational group: 61 per cent of them were rated as highly participant, and only 6 per cent were non-participant. On the other hand, unskilled labourers were the least active in this way: only 36 per cent were highly participant, and 36 per cent were non-participant. By the time the children were 4 years old, the professional class fathers had overtaken the non-professional white collar group and were the most participant: 60 per cent were rated as 'high', while the former leaders had dropped to 54 per cent. Although the participation of unskilled workers had greatly increased overall (only 12 per cent were now non-participant), they remained at the bottom of the table.

For some explanation of these social differences, we can look both to the circumstances of work and to the future ambitions of these various economic groups. Manual workers are physically tired when they arrive home; their first need is food and rest, and the manual worker's wife is traditionally and actually prepared to accommodate family demands to this. It is also true that as one descends the social scale – that is to say, as brawn takes precedence over brain – the work roles of men and women in Western culture become more and more separated, and this separation tends to spill over into the home. At the top end of the scale, fathers of professional status are not expected to be quite so physically exhausted at the end of the day; what is more, they are much more likely to be married to wives who themselves have professional qualifications, and who are therefore less prepared to accept an exclusively male right to be freed from domestic responsibilities. However, young professional men also expect to do a certain amount of work at home in the evenings: preparing lessons, doing accounts or other paper-work, or, at this stage in their careers, studying for further qualifications; they thus have a reasonable excuse for not looking after the baby quite so much as might otherwise be expected of them. The shop or clerical worker falls between these two situations: having spent his day in a job no more physically arduous than his wife's, as she well knows, his time once he reaches home is usually his own, and therefore, since he has no valid reason to escape, his family's. The shift towards greater participation by professional-class fathers as the child reaches four probably reflects this group's intellectual interests; while only a few take an active interest in the 1-year-old baby's conceptual development, four is an age which this type of father, with professional ambitions for his child, finds stimulating and challenging, and for this reason he will be beginning to take what he consciously sees as an educational role towards the child.[17] And although we have discussed these differences partly in terms of excuses *not* to participate, such a massive social change in roles could hardly have taken place without a basic willingness on the father's part to involve himself with his young children.

FRIEND OR AUTHORITY: THE PARENTAL DILEMMA

Perhaps the most powerful motivation impelling fathers in general to share in traditional maternal tasks is one aspect of the fun morality: the desire of parents to be the *friends* of their children. The mothers and fathers of today's children, looking back to their own childhoods, often speak regretfully of a relationship with that earlier generation of parents which could have been so much closer had their parents been less authoritarian in outlook: they themselves hope to achieve not merely respectful affection but comradeship from their children. 'We're pals, you know,' says a mother of her 4-year-old. 'Oh, we enjoy each other, her and me.' Clearly, this reflects a new feeling of equality between parents and children which allows the parents even to accept correction from a child, and indeed to take pride in it: and, too, there is the ques-

---

[17]   A fuller discussion of the work and family roles of young parents will be found in Newson and Newson (1963).

tion of frankness: a willingness on the parents' part to answer the child truthfully, without continually taking refuge on the parental pedestal. As a driver's wife in Nottingham put it:

I think there's a much closer relationship between parent and child; I notice it with my older children – they can talk to me a lot easier than ever I could with my mother – even though she was a real good mother, I mean she was a wonderful person really, but you just couldn't get through to them in those days, I don't think, same as mine do to me. I think they're better for it, they want to be able to confide in you now and again; mind you, times have altered – there seems to be a greater pace altogether these days, they grow up very quickly.

What parents of every social class seem ill-prepared for, however, is the fact that a radical change in childrearing principles is likely to produce a radically changed generation of children. In very many mothers (and fathers), from every class group, can be detected an uneasiness, a confusion, as to what they are achieving and what they are trying to achieve. It appears in the Nottingham labourer's wife, who complained:

When they get big they're very difficult, aren't they? They seem to be more full of life than we was, I don't know if it's the war that's done it or what. They seem to like their own way a lot more, don't they? I don't know whether it's us that's doing it or not.

It appears in the professional-class mother who, having committed herself heavily to the theory that friendly verbal explanations will produce rational co-operation in a toddler, finds that he is rationally *unco*-operative and that in practice her careful explanation tends to degenerate into an exasperated scream of 'get on and DO it!'. It appears, too, in adults' ambivalent attitude to the first generation of adolescents who are the product of a *generally accepted* primary school ethic that taught them early on to think for themselves: it seemed a good idea when they were five, but what about when, still thinking for themselves, they reject *our* most cherished values?

If we may quote our own summary of satisfactions and doubts in the parental role:

It is in this confusion that we can discern the major dilemma of contemporary parents, particularly those further up the social scale. On the one hand, they have embraced an egalitarian relationship with their children, and genuinely enjoy and value the friendship that goes with it; as a matter of principle, they reject plain coercion as a method of dealing with children. An outstanding feature in the case of the very young child in particular . . . is that the mother will worry and complain, sometimes for years, over some habit which could easily be suppressed *if she were prepared to do so* – the dummy or the sordid cuddly, for instance (of which she so often feels ashamed), could simply be destroyed – and yet she will go on worrying, and devising endless persuasive methods of changing the child's behaviour, rather than exert the sort of repressive authority which was the approved method of the twenties and thirties. On the other hand, parents cannot entirely divorce themselves from their historical antecedents: no longer believing that children should be seen and not heard, nevertheless they still retain, at the back of the mind as it were, an image of the 'good' child who, while obviously bright and alert, at the same time defers to parental wishes and in general makes a pleasant public impression unmarred by displays of egotism, rowdiness or greed. The attainment of this fleeting vision of 'goodness' by methods more suited to producing an independent spirit, full of Kingsley's 'divine discontent', is the impossible task which parents half-consciously set themselves; inevitably, compromise in aims, means, or both has to be accepted somewhere along the way. In the democratic context, too, antisocial behaviour on the part of the child can be doubly disturbing to the parent: 'naughtiness' under an authoritarian regime can be viewed with equanimity as natural rebellion against what the child does not like, to be met with an extension of the repressive measures; but 'naughtiness' under an egalitarian system involves *a rejection by the child of the parent's proffered friendship*, which he *is* supposed to like – and, so far as the mother can see, eventually has to be met by a change in policy away from the rational permissiveness to which she is ideologically committed and towards the authoritarianism which she had put behind her. (Newson and Newson, 1968)

Doubtless this ambivalence among parents is partly responsible for the most recent modification of the advice given by the more sensitive barometers of parental need such as Spock and the Children's Bureau; a modification which might well be the first sign of a coming trend away from permissiveness, though surely not back to the rigidity of the pre-war years. It is a change which was noted by Martha Wolfenstein as being already detectable in the 1951 edition of *Infant Care*: she quotes the suggestion that the baby may get the parents 'at his mercy by unreasonable demands for attention'. The 1955 edition, approving the term 'self-*regulation*' of feeding, says: 'If we really carried out "self-demand" we could turn a baby into a tyrant' (Children's Bureau, 1955, p. 12). Spock, in the 1957 revised edition of *Baby and Child Care*, tells the reader: 'If an angry parent keeps himself from spanking, he may show his irritation in other ways . . . I'm not particularly advocating spanking, but I think it is less poisonous than lengthy disapproval, because it clears the air, for parent and child'; and in a new section entitled 'Some common misunderstandings about discipline', one misunderstanding is 'that when children misbehave the parents shouldn't become angry or punish them but should try to show more love. All of these misconceptions are unworkable if carried very far' (Spock, 1957, section 473). In other words, just as children's aggressive impulses are natural and acceptable, so too are those of parents, and need not be worried about too much. It is significant that, although the rights of children continue to be championed (A.C.E., 1971; *Children's Rights*, 1971), this concern is paralleled by a growing 'backlash' output (Whiteley and Whiteley, 1964; Manners, 1971); the publication of a book on *The Rights of Parents* would not in the present mood seem odd.

78

What has happened here is that the permissiveness which characterised the fun morality has spilled over to include parents too; while the
flexibility which we have already noted is extended even to tolerance of
impatience and aggressiveness on the part of the parent. We are, in fact,
witnessing what is almost a cult of non-advice. In Nottingham, parents
who seek direction from the welfare clinics on the regulation of feeding
tend to be told 'Do what you find suits you best', 'follow your own
instinct'. In briefing a group of health visitors who were to administer a
questionnaire, and stressing the necessity for their advisory role to be
set aside as far as possible during this, the authors were told 'You are out
of date: health visitors don't give advice nowadays'; the mothers, it may
be added, have not yet caught up with this view. Carl Rogers and the
movement towards non-directive therapy have probably had an indirect
but powerful influence, particularly through social work training courses,
upon the trend which makes 'advisory' an unfashionable word and 'supportive' the only acceptable adjective. However much we may welcome
the principle behind such a change, we may also question how far social
agencies' fond belief in their new role is in fact conveyed to those whose
social deficiency they are trying to make good; conceivably, parents
wanting help may find non-direction as unrealistic in meeting their
immediate practical problems as was rigid authoritarianism.

Perhaps one should add that in one field, at least, there are signs of
new life in the hygienist morality as represented by the behaviourists.
The need for intervention rather than *laissez faire* methods in creating
an improved quality of life for mentally retarded children has stimulated
a growing body of writing on techniques of 'behaviour modification', as
it is euphemistically called. Although basically designed for use where
'ordinary' parental relationships totally break down, some of these techniques now begin to be put forward for use in schools and in family
domestic situations. Is it imagination that suggests, not merely John
Watson, but Susanna Wesley herself dictating this advice?

Wolf, Risley, and Mees (1964) have discussed how a disturbed child's bedtime
problems were solved, by a relatively simple procedure. At bedtime the disturbed
child was placed in his bed with the door of his room left open. If the child got
out of bed, he was instructed to return to bed and go to sleep or the bedroom
door would be closed. If a temper tantrum occurred, the door remained closed
until the child ceased his tantrum. When the child returned to bed, the door
was opened and remained so as long as he complied with the request . . . With a
little ingenuity, this basic procedure can be modified and used with most bedtime problems. While opening and closing a door will work, a light or a child's
favorite blanket may be used. That is, a light in the child's room is either left on
or turned off according to the behaviour he exhibits; or the child's favorite
blanket – or toy or teddy bear – can be removed until he behaves properly. It
can be seen that this method utilizes negative reinforcement as well as response-

contingent withdrawal of reinforcement. An aversive stimulus is removed (the door is opened) when the child exhibits the specified behaviour: negative reinforcement is being used. When a favorite blanket or toy is removed because an undesirable behaviour is exhibited, response-contingent withdrawal of reinforcement is being used. (Blackham and Silberman, 1971)

CONCLUSION

In the foregoing pages, we have tried to make a brief survey both of the broad sociological movements to be discerned in childrearing practices through the past two hundred years and of some more specific issues in child upbringing as they are affected by cultural and subcultural considerations. Over the years, we have seen a deity-centred morality giving way to a science-centred morality, both with curiously similar results in the tone of parental behaviour. Science-become-God is deposed by a new child-centred morality, though still invoked in order to provide evidence for the rightness of the way parents *want* to behave; and this again begins to be modified when parents find permissiveness as demanding as, and more disturbing than, strictness. The response of parents to the far more subtle and complex pressures put upon them by the trend towards non-advice shows some indication that they perhaps find such demands less easy to meet satisfactorily, and moreover less easy to evade, than the earlier clear-cut directives: there is also a good deal of evidence, however, that, far from being permissive in a mindless way, parents are stimulated by flexibility of advice to think for themselves about their actions, and to look critically at their own behaviour, painful though this may be (Newson and Newson, 1968).

As we look ahead, despite a certain mood of reaction against the child-is-always-right school of thought, it is hardly conceivable that children will lose their place well at the centre, nor that the movement back to 'tender loving care' will for many decades be reversed. There are circumstances, however, in which a medical or other autocracy might well usurp present parental rights: in the case of high radiation hazard, for example, when a return to breastfeeding might be no longer a matter of personal choice but of necessity to survival as, for nutritional reasons, it was and is, elsewhere and elsewhen (Widdowson, Slater and Harrison, 1960); or as population growth makes new forms of governmental control necessary and technology makes them possible. Meantime, while society makes progressively fewer demands on its members in terms of physical effort, by giving them education it is enabled to demand more and more of their intelligence. Mothers and fathers have never in history been more conscious either of the complexity of their responsibilities or of the splendour of their rewards.

REFERENCES

A.C.E. (1971). (Advisory Centre for Education) *Where* (journal) throughout this year. Cambridge, England.

Ainsworth, M. D., Andry, R. G., Harlow, R. G., Lebovici, S., Mead, M., Pough Dane, G. and Wootton, B. (1963). *Maternal Deprivation: a Critical Assessment*. Geneva, W.H.O.

Blackham, G. J. and Silberman, A. (1971). *Modification of Child Behaviour*. California, Wadsworth.

Bowlby, J. (1946). *Fourty-Four Juvenile Thieves*. London, Baillière, Tindall and Cox.

Bowlby, J. (1952). *Maternal Care and Mental Health*. Geneva, W.H.O.

Bowlby, J. (1953). *Child Care and the Growth of Love*. London, Penguin.

Bready, J. W. (1938). *England before and after Wesley*.

Bronfenbrenner, U. (1958). Socialization and social class through time and space. In Maccoby, E., Newcomb, T. M. and Howarth, E. L. (eds.). *Readings in Social Psychology* (3rd ed.). New York, Henry Holt.

Children's Bureau, U.S. Department of Health, Education and Welfare (1945, 1958). *Infant Care*.

Children's Rights (1971–2). Bi-monthly magazine. London, Children's Rights Publications.

Davis, A. and Havighurst, R. J. (1946). Social class and color differences in child rearing. *Amer. Sociol. Rev.* **11**, 698–710.

Freud, A. (1943). *Infants without Families*. New York, Internat. Univ. Press.

Freud, A. (1960). Series of four talks for World Mental Health Year on B.B.C. programme *Parents and Children*, May–June.

Harlow, H. (1961). Development of affectional patterns in infant monkeys. In Foss, B. M. (ed.). *Determinants of Infant Behaviour* **1**. London, Methuen.

Isaacs, S. (1929, 1932). *The Nursery Years*. London, Routledge and Kegan Paul.

Isaacs, S. (1930). *Intellectual Growth in Young Children*. London, Routledge and Kegan Paul.

Isaacs, S. (1933). *Social Development of Children*. London, Routledge and Kegan Paul.

Janeway, J. (1753). *A Token for Children*.

Jelliffe, D. B. (1965). The health worker's approach. In Gyorgy, P. and Burgess, A. (eds.). *Protecting the Pre-School Child*. London, Tavistock.

Johnson, R. C. and Medinnus, G. R. (1965). *Child Psychology: Behavior and Development*. New York, Wiley.

Le Gros Clark, F. (1953). The weaning of the human child. *Nutrition* summer.

Liddiard, M. (1928, 1954). *The Mothercraft Manual*. London, Churchill.

Lorenz, K. (1952) *King Solomon's Ring*. London, Methuen.

McCarthy, M. (1963). *The Group*. London, Weidenfeld and Nicolson.

Manners, E. (1971). *The Vulnerable Generation*. London, Cassell.

Ministry of Health Central Health Services Council (1959). Report of Committee (Chairman Sir Harry Platt) on *The Welfare of Children in Hospital*. London, H.M.S.O.

Newson, J. and Newson, E. (1963). *Infant Care in an Urban Community*. London, Allen and Unwin.

Newson, J. and Newson, E. (1968). *Four Years Old in an Urban Community*. London, Allen and Unwin.

Pate, M. (1965). Introduction to Gyorgy, P. and Burgess, A. (eds.). *Protecting the Pre-School Child*. London, Tavistock.

Piaget, J. (1929). *The Child's Conception of the World*. London, Routledge and Kegan Paul.

Pinneau, S. (1950). A critique on the articles by Margaret Ribble. *Child Developm*. **21**, 203–28.

Registrar General (1963). *Statistical Review of England and Wales*. London, H.M.S.O.

Ribble, M. (1943). *The Rights of Infants*. New York, Columbia Univ. Press.

Ribble, M. (1944). Infantile experience in relation to personality development. In Hunt, J. McV. (ed.) *Personality and the Behaviour Disorders* **2**, New York, Ronald Press.

Robertson, J. (1953). *A Two-Year-old Goes to Hospital* (film). London, Tavistock Child Development Research Unit.

Robertson, J. (1958). *Going into Hospital with Mother* (film). London, Tavistock Child Development Research Unit.

Robertson, J. (1958*a*). *Young Children in Hospital*. London, Tavistock.

Robertson, J. (1958*b*). *Hospitals and Children*. London, Gollancz.

Rousseau, J. (1762). *Emile* (Everyman ed.). London, Dent.

Sangster, P. (1963). *Pity My Simplicity*. London, Epworth Press.

Schaffer, H. R. and Emerson, P. (1964). Development of social attachments in infancy. *Monogr. Soc. Res. Child. Developm*. **29**, No. 3, 1–77.

Sears, R. R., Maccoby, E. and Levin, H. (1957). *Patterns of Child Rearing*. Evanston, Ill., Row Peterson.

Sherwood, Mrs M. (1818). *The History of the Fairchild Family*, London, Ward Lock.

Sillitoe, A. (1959). *The Loneliness of the Long-Distance Runner*. London, Allen.

Spitz, R. (1945). Hospitalism. *Psychoanal. Study Child*, **1**, 53–74.

Spock, B. (1946, 1957). *Baby and Child Care*. New York, Duell, Sloan and Pearce.

Spock, B. (1970). *Decent and Indecent*. London, Bodley Head.

Suttie, I. (1935). *The Origins of Love and Hate*. London, Routledge and Kegan Paul.

Truby King, F. (1937). *Feeding and Care of Baby* (revised ed.). London, Oxford Univ. Press.

U.N.I.C.E.F. (1964). *Children of the Developing Countries*. London, Nelson.

Watson, J. B. (1928). *Psychological Care of Infant and Child*. New York, W. W. Norton.

Watts, I. (1842). *Divine Songs, attempted in easy language for the use of children*. 'New Edition', London, S.P.C.K.

Wesley, J. (1872). *Works*. London, Wesleyan Conference Office.

Wesley, J. and Wesley, C. (1868). *Poetical Works* (ed. G. Osborn).

Whiteley, C. H. and Whiteley, W. (1964). *The Permissive Morality*. London. Methuen.

Widdowson, E., Slater, J. and Harrison, G. E. (1960). Absorption, excretion and retention of strontium by breast-fed and bottle-fed babies. *Lancet*, **2**, 1960.

Winnicott, D. W. (1964). *The Child, the Family and the Outside World*. London, Penguin.

Wolfenstein, M. (1955). Fun morality: an analysis of recent American child-training literature. In Mead, M. and Wolfenstein, M. (eds.) *Childhood in Contemporary Cultures*. Chicago, Univ. Chicago Press.

5

First steps in becoming social

M. P. M. Richatds

INTRODUCTION

In this chapter I have two aims. I want to describe some of the first steps in the process by which the infant becomes social and, at the same time, I hope to provide an introduction to the following chapters which deal with various aspects of the child's relationships with adults and to show some of the ways in which these link with the earlier discussions of the social context of development.

As most observers of infants have noticed, there is an enormous gap between the simplicity of available social developmental psychological theory and the complexity and richness of what we can see. All too often, psychological theory is a very pale shadow or no shadow at all of the world we see around ourselves. In so far as there has been theoretical direction for the natural history sorts of studies of mother and child, it has come directly or indirectly from the participants in the series of conferences which were organised jointly by the Tavistock Clinic and the Ciba Foundation (Foss, 1961, 1963, 1965, 1969). These brought together not only ethologists, who had long been committed to observational studies, and psychologists with their experience of laboratory situations, but also clinicians with varied interests and approaches. The mixture proved to be fruitful and these meetings not only stimulated new research but they also served to bring the problem of the origins of social behaviour to the attention of many people who were not primarily concerned with early infancy.

The major guiding framework which has dominated this group of researchers is John Bowlby's theory of attachment (1958, 1969). This theory is essentially an attempt to look at the relationship of mother and child in terms of physical distance. Bowlby began with a concern for the effects of separation on infants placed in institutions away from their mothers (1951) and for the permanent separation of adults through death and the ensuing grief and mourning (1961). The same theme of physical space between individuals plays an important part in his theory of the attachment of child to mother. As a first step this idea was helpful and it appeared to unify some of the animal studies with some human observation. However, more recently, it has been criticised on several grounds (see, for example, Bernal, chapter 8 in this volume, and Kohlberg, 1969). I do not wish to continue this debate here but I will make two points.

Over the years since Bowlby's work was first published there has been a shift in research interest. His own primary concern was the growth of the relationship between mother and child and the influence of the quality of this relationship (attachment) on the child's subsequent development. Now the central question tends to be the growth of social behaviour itself. This is, of course, a much broader question and in answering it there is no reason to restrict consideration of the social context to the mother alone (Richards, 1971*b*). Indeed, as some have pointed out (e.g. Wortis, 1972) to do so is to adopt a particular political position. However, Bowlby cannot be criticised for producing a theory that is deliberately confined to one question and some of the fault seems to lie with those of his critics who have taken the child's tie with his mother to be synonymous with the growth of sociability.

In recent years, encouraged by the changes in linguistic theory, psychologists have become more concerned with the human aspects of human development. This has led to a more cautious view of the relevance of animal studies (e.g. Bernal and Richards, 1973) and to a much more general dissatisfaction with traditions of psychology that are modelled on physical science and do not draw a sharp distinction between people and things (see Shotter, chapter 11 in this volume). This shift in ideological emphasis has made many people suspicious of a theory that does not pick out the especially human aspects of development, which leans so heavily on evidence from animal species and that uses physical distance as a core concept. One would have to take an ultraconservative view of the philosophy of science to believe that this is simply an argument that could be settled by any appeal to 'evidence'. One's position is largely determined by a general ideological stand and by what one believes that psychology is to be used for (the relationship of ideology to the practice of psychology is discussed in detail by Ingleby in chapter 14 in this volume). I should make it clear that my interest in this chapter is in the development of *human* social life. Given this concern with human socialisation which only partially overlaps with Bowlby's theoretical interests and the lack of other detailed theory which could be used to guide our discussion, I shall be stressing the theoretical aspects of the problems and attempting to provide some framework in which future observational studies may proceed. I shall assume that the infant is predisposed to become both adult (Trevarthen, 1973) and social (Berger and Luckman, 1967). Just as food is required to nurture a body and to allow the development of an adult form, so the infant needs a social environment to develop social skills. But the social environment is not alone sufficient, the developmental process also involves the biological nature of the neonate.

During the first year of postnatal development an infant is transformed from a social incompetent, totally dependent on the goodwill of adults, to a skilled social operator who is well able to hold his (or her) own in a wide variety of social situations. I will be describing some of the early stages of this process of transformation or socialisation. Unlike Ainsworth and her co-workers (chapter 6 in this volume), I do not regard the infant as a social creature. He has the potentiality of a social being but this requires development in a social world for its expression. As Becker (1972) has said, socialisation 'means the formation of *human beings* out of helpless, dependent *animal matter* . . . it explains the original formation of the social self' (author's italics, p. 51).

THE CARETAKER'S FIRST RESPONSES

I first want to consider some aspects of the infant's immediate environment. As Hubert shows in chapter 3, our culture provides for very little direct transmission of knowledge about infants and reproduction to pass from generation to generation. This picture is strongly supported by our studies in Cambridge (Richards and Bernal, 1972). We found that very few primiparous mothers had had any significant previous contact with young infants. It was rare to find a mother who had bottle-fed a baby, and even rarer to find out who had seen a baby breast-fed. As for actually attending a birth, this was unheard-of except for those who belonged to one of the professions that maintain a monopoly over this experience.

In the absence of direct knowledge, the mother is free to fantasise about what her child will be like. Few mothers seem able to extend the feeling of having a living being within themselves to the baby they are presented with after birth. Her first reaction is usually to a thing, an object to be examined and explored. She shows interest in what he does but seldom makes any immediate attempt to respond to him as a person. This seems particularly marked when the birth takes place in a hospital as is almost universal in our culture. Here the event is defined almost exclusively as a medical and technical situation. This may lead the mother to feel that any human response to her infant in inappropriate and she is unlikely to see any such reaction from any of the people who attend the birth. At home deliveries midwives do not seem to find it necessary to construct such an exclusively clinical atmosphere and they lack the props of the hospital delivery room furnishings. Often they show signs of human recognition and greeting of the infant and will kiss, rock, touch and talk to newborns and encourage the mother and other adults to do the same.[1]

During the first week or so of life the infant and parents often reach their first confrontation (later if the infant is being cared for by professionals in a hospital). The infant makes a demand, perhaps by crying for a long period, which the parents either do not know how to meet or do not wish to meet. For the first time the child is demonstrating his autonomy and independence and the way in which his parents will have to modify their life in order to cope with him. So the brief initial phase when the parents are spectators of their child's actions moves on to a stage where there is active negotiation; though, of course, it is a somewhat limited negotiation, as most of the power resides with one of the parties. To parents in our culture, the issue of power is a real one and it seems very important that they can feel in control of their children. When a mother cannot pacify her child her feelings of panic may, in part, stem from the knowledge that she is powerless and has lost power over her infant. Notions of power also enter into the first social encounters where the all-important definition of what constitutes a social act is controlled by adults. The parents treat as social those actions of the baby that they believe they have caused. Early 'spontaneous' smiles are usually dismissed as mere physiological 'wind', whilst those that the parent can evoke become social events which are built into sequences of mutual social acknowledgement. This point will be further discussed below.

So far I have emphasised the parents' lack of direct knowledge about infants and the ways in which they must often discover for themselves means of caretaking and building social relations with their infants. However, it must not be thought that parents start entirely from scratch. Adults and children possess biological pre-adaptations as well as conscious intentions that lead them to infants and provide them with a basic vocabulary of actions appropriate to interaction with infants. These are evident right from the moment of delivery. As Klaus and his co-workers (1970) and others have noticed, a mother's greeting of her infant at the birth involves a relatively stereotyped set of responses. There is a characteristic pattern of exploration in which the mother first uses her finger tips and later employs the palms of her hands. Also there is a universal tendency to align the face so that it is in the mirror plane of the baby's. Adults with no previous experience of infants tend to hold a newborn across their body, often with the baby's head towards their

[1] A classic study of the definitions of social reality in the management of women's reproductive functions is given by Emerson (1970). Evidence of the way in which birth has become a technical process organised for the benefit of the technicians may be found in Haire (1972).

left so that their right (dominant) hand is free to touch the infant. It might be objected that there was not much freedom about these matters as there are not many positions in which an infant can be held. But this rather misses the point that the constraints are biological ones which introduce a good deal of predictability into the situation, particularly from the infant's point of view. When held in this position the infant's limited powers of accommodation mean that his eyes will be focused on the adult's face (White, 1967), and an infant in this position is most likely to be visually alert (Korner and Grobstein, 1966; Korner and Thoman, 1972) so that active visual contact between the two partners is very likely to occur.

THE PATTERNING OF INFANT BEHAVIOUR

From early in foetal development, an infant's behaviour is patterned in both space and time. Many configurations of behaviour or action patterns not only make units which are functional and are recognisable in form (such as sucking, crying or smiling) but they also occur with highly structured temporal patterns (Wolff, 1967; Richards, 1971). Adult caretakers recognise these patterns and assume that some of them provide indications of what is occurring inside the infant. They assume that smiling represents a state of contentment or stability and that crying is related to hunger or some other discomfort. By such recognition they confer the status of social actions upon these behaviour patterns. But it must be stressed that this recognition involves cultural assumptions and is not simply a matter of putting inevitable labels on the behaviour. Meanings given by adults to infant patterns also vary with and are dependent on the contexts in which these occur. This, of course, is obvious in the behaviour of adults for whom we no more expect a one-to-one association of gesture and meaning than we do for sound patterns and meaning in language (Leach, 1972). Take the example of the gesture of holding up a hand, palm forward. What does this mean? We can give an answer if we know that it is given by a policeman standing in the middle of a street, a priest facing a congregation, or someone about to go through a swing door. But the gesture alone is ambiguous. A rather different view is held by some human ethologists (e.g. Eibl-Eiberfeldt, 1970) who argue for a direct and universal correspondence between action pattern and meaning. To them a smile is a smile in all cultures at all times. Their main evidence for this contention are photographs from many different cultures showing the same action pattern in both adults and children. This does confirm the universality of biological patterns but it tells us nothing about the meaning that they may be given at various times and places. For that we need some analysis of

87

the dynamics of social interaction in these situations and this we are not given.

Some of these points can be further illustrated by taking the example of crying. To some attachment theorists, crying is an attachment behaviour because it serves as a signal to the mother that the infant requires attention. So to them the crying is assumed to have a universal meaning. This, however, is an ethnocentric view because in many cultures the newborn spends the first few months of his life in constant contact with the mother's body so that signals that have a routine function of bringing mother to baby would have no role. It is also often assumed that in our own culture crying is the major signal that the infant uses to indicate his hunger to his mother and so regulate the pattern of feeds. Again, even if this can be shown to be true in Europe and America, it is not universal. Among the ! Kung bushmen where infants are carried on the mother's body, the infant's movements seem to be the usual indication to the mother that the infant requires access to the breast. Crying is used to signal emergencies (Konner, 1972 and in preparation).

Whether or not patterns such as crying have universal meaning is not merely an academic quibble. If one does assume they do, a mother who does not respond to her infant's crying is failing to conform to a biological requirement and is therefore in some way insensitive, pathological or otherwise perverse. However, if one looks at the meaning of a cry as a matter of cultural definition which is negotiated between mother and child (within biological limits), a failure to respond is not a failure at all but simply one step in the socialisation of the child. This and related questions are discussed by Bernal in chapter 8 and Ingleby in chapter 14, while a rather different view is given in chapter 6 by Ainsworth, Bell and Stayton.

But if we do accept that cultural conventions do determine meanings of gestures in different situations we have hardly solved a problem, indeed we have raised a whole series of new ones. How does an infant discover what his smile means to other people in different situations? How do adults interpret these kinds of gestures in infants? Do they understand them to mean the same things at different ages? How much individual variation is there in these matters? What does that depend on? Should we expect that differences are related to social class in the same way as for speech? We cannot answer any of these questions, mostly because the necessary investigation has not been undertaken. A start has been made in the observations of Spitz (1965), Wolff (1963, 1969) and others but much more work is required.

The studies that have been done on crying at least indicate the complexity of some of these questions. It has been shown that infants produce three cry-types which can be recognised with sound spectrographic analysis (Wass Höckett *et al.*, 1968) and by caretakers in some situations (Wolff, 1969). These are usually called the 'hunger' cry, the 'mad' cry and the 'pain' cry. The first and second may not be very fundamentally different because in many situations, if the infant is ignored, a 'hunger' cry changes into a 'mad' cry. So the difference may simply be one of intensity. However, to show that these cries can be distinguished is not the same as showing that they are used differentially by mothers or what meaning they are given in interaction and how this may (or may not) change with age.

Moss's (1967) observational study showed clearly that crying bouts in the early months of life were very likely to be followed by maternal contact though they were seldom preceded by social interaction. But studies like this do not provide evidence about the kind of cry the infant was making nor do they make clear the exact relationship between the infant's crying and the caretakers' interventions. Sander's (Sander *et al.*, 1970) studies have demonstrated that social situations influence the amount of crying in the newborn period. Using automatic recorders for crying and caretaker interventions, it was found that crying scores were much higher in a nursery (with many infants and several caretakers) than with rooming-in. As might be expected, the delay time (time from onset of crying to intervention by caretaker) was much longer in the nursery than in the one-to-one caretaking situation. So it is tempting to conclude that the long latency might lead to the higher crying rate. However, another part of this study showed that this was not the reason. Babies that had spent the first ten days in the nursery were transferred to one of two nurses on an individual basis for the next sixteen days before they were fostered. Infants with nurse B all showed a drop in crying after day 10 while those with nurse A all continued to cry at the same rate. Comparisons of the delay times for the two nurses showed that nurse A was *quicker* than nurse B. Total caretaking time was the same for both the nurses (and in the rooming-in situation) but nurse B's interventions were each longer on average. The authors suggest a major factor may be the quality of what goes on during caretaking. But even this does not exhaust the complexities of this study. Some babies were cared for by nurses A or B right from birth but on the tenth day were changed from one nurse to the other. Under these conditions none of the infants showed any marked changes in crying rates on day ten. Here nurse B seemed unable to exercise her pacifying effect. Though we must be cautious with these results because they involve a small number of infants and a very limited number of caretakers and caretaking situations, I think they do serve to illustrate how little we know about the effects of caretakers even at the grossest levels.

Our own studies in Cambridge suggest that the likelihood of a mother picking up her baby to feed it in the first ten days is not primarily regulated by crying but also involves the context of the baby's behaviour (Bernal, 1972). Here the time since the last feed was the most important determinant of the mother's intervention. Local professional wisdom suggests a four-hourly interval between feeds and it is not until at least three hours after a feed that an infant's cry is likely to be answered by a mother. In this situation the context seems more important than what the infant is doing (at least at this age). The important lesson for the infant is how little effect his crying has on his caretakers.[2]

I have gone into crying in a little detail because it does illustrate how misleading any simple idea of a link between a signal and response may be. Perhaps we have made rather heavy weather of trying to understand the nature of these interactions by presupposing a signal–response relationship and so paying too little attention to the broader context in which these exchanges occur. But our methods for analysing situations like this in ways that take full account of the social realities involved are primitive, to say the least, and so we are always tempted to take a rather mechanical view of what occurs. But I think the time has come to abandon the apparent security of recording those rather external things that are easy to measure, and try to put themselves in the position of the participants in the action. Clearly there are connections between the infant's internal state, his action in the social world (e.g. his crying) and the meaning accorded to that action by a caretaker but they are tenuous and, initially at least, they may vary widely from individual to individual. We need a series of very detailed developmental studies before we can be more specific.

CHANNELS OF COMMUNICATION

The infant's predispositions to social life do not simply consist of action patterns to which caretakers can give meaning. They also include the baby's selective attention to the world around him. These operate in such a way that he selectively attends to features that form part of adult communication modes and so allow the formation of agreed channels for communication between adult and infant. From a very early age one can observe rudimentary dialogues between infant and adult in which there seems to be agreement about how communication is to be effected even if the nature of what has to be communicated is little more than a mutual

---

[2] In chapter 6 Ainsworth, Stayton and Bell also discuss the influence of caretaking styles on crying. It should be noted that their study concerns older children than those described here.

90

acknowledgement that there is another person there. We know almost nothing about how the infant comes selectively to attend to the 'right' features but there is plenty of observational evidence about the predictability of the process. Infants attend to faces. This seems so natural to us adults who do the same and assume (correctly) that a face is the richest source of information about a person's state that we do not perhaps appreciate what a feat it is for an infant and how greatly it simplifies his making sense of the social world. Of course, adults are always thrusting their faces at infants but they also thrust bottles and breasts and, as Spitz (1965) has pointed out, infants do not make the mistake of trying to converse with these sources of food. But seeing the advantages for the infant of being able to structure the world in this way does not explain how he does it. In spite of a long series of investigations it is not clear why infants find faces so attractive (this work and other studies related to the problems discussed in this chapter are described by Schaffer, 1971).

Another example of this kind of selection is the well-demonstrated preference of infants for speech-like sounds (Hutt *et al.*, 1968; Eisenberg, 1969; Freidlander, 1970; Eimas *et al.*, 1971; Trehub and Robinovitch, 1972). Again, from the infant's point of view, an ability of this nature means that he has a handle on the world. He does not begin from scratch, trying to make sense of the pet canary's song and the squeaking of his bedroom door along with the lullabies his mother sings to him. He has a preadaptation which will lead him into the channel of communication which will eventually allow the acquisition of language. This process is discussed in detail by Ryan in chapter 10, but it is worth noting here that the beginnings of language acquisition may fairly be said to be observable in the first days of extra-uterine life. A further spin-off from this process is that it will also lead infants to look at faces because infants often turn towards the source of sounds which catch their interest.

Social communication involves rather precise temporal sequences of actions. One has to both speak and listen. Social communication itself is much more than a simple mutual responsiveness to signals and it involves notions of mutuality, reciprocity and intersubjectivity. One of the greatest problems in attempting to trace the development of this process in the pre-verbal infant is that all the concepts that have proved so useful in the analysis of adult communication are essentially linguistic. Notions such as intention and intersubjectivity are defined in the framework of speech among members of a linguistic community. We have the same problem when we consider the content of the messages that may pass between an adult and a pre-verbal infant. Often there is every impression of an interaction sequence of the intersubjectivity that can be understood from the conversations of adults but nothing is said, at least, by the infant. We have no direct or even fairly indirect ways of knowing what he has understood. On the other hand, observations of these early social exchanges do not suggest any quantum leap in their quality of communication with the development of speech. The outside observer is usually impressed by the steady increase in understanding that occurs from a point long before the infant produces any speech through the early stages of language acquisition.

Furthermore, the early development of social communication gives every impression of being a generative process. An infant does not appear to be learning a series of discrete signals which can be used to express a series of separate meanings but rather that he is developing general rules or underlying structures which can be elaborated to become more inclusive and differentiated so that both a wider range and subtlety and greater specificity of communication becomes possible. This generative quality also implies a degree of independence from the immediate situation so that this non-verbal communication shares a measure of the detachment from the here and now which is common to language. Though it is fairly easy to sketch out some of the broad features of this prelinguistic social communication, a more thorough analysis is limited by the extreme crudity of our methods of investigation and our lack of a conceptual vocabulary which does not imply full membership of a linguistic community.

One of the first things that is required in social communication is for you to be sure that your partner is actually attending to you and is involved in communication with you. Are you listening? Do you see what I see? Do you see what I mean? Clearly this degree of inter-subjectivity is not present in the newborn and will take many months to develop. But within weeks of birth one can observe its beginnings. There are long sequences of interaction where the first fumbling links of inter-subjectivity are made. The infant looks at the caretaker's face. The caretaker looks back into the eyes of the infant. A smile moves on the infant's face. The adult responds with a vocal greeting and a smile. There is mutual social acknowledgement. The 'meaning' of this exchange does not simply depend on the action patterns employed by the two participants. Each must fit his sequence of actions with that of the other; if this is not done, the exchange may well become meaningless. An important means of knowing that a message is intended for you is that it follows an alternating sequence with yours.

After the first few weeks, the interaction sequences and their mutual timing patterns become more complex. The following is an account from an earlier study carried out in conjunction with Dr C. Trevarthen:

After eight weeks or so when social smiling is well established, the mother may spend long periods eliciting smiling in her infant. During such periods the infant is held on the mother's lap facing her and supported by her arms or is placed in an infant seat. The mother smiles and vocalises to the infant and moves her head rhythmically towards and away from his face. The infant first responds by rapt attention, with a widening of his eyes and a stilling of his body movements. Then his excitement increases, body movements begin again, he may vocalise and eventually a smile spreads over his face. At this point he turns away from his mother before beginning the whole cycle once again. Throughout this sequence the mother's actions are carefully phased with those of the infant. During the infant's attention phase the mother's behaviour is restrained but as his excitement increases she vocalises more rapidly and the pitch of her voice rises. At the point when he is about to smile her movements are suddenly reduced, as if she was allowing him time to reply. However, not all mothers behave in this way. Some subject their infants to a constant and unphased barrage of stimulation. The infant is given no pauses in which to reply and he seems totally overwhelmed by his mother. Instead of playing this game for long periods, he is quickly reduced to fussing and crying and shows sustained and prolonged turning away from the mother's face. (Richards, 1971a, pp. 37–8)

The infant also has to develop the ability to phase his actions with those of his adult caretaker over much longer periods of time. He must learn that there is a time and a place for everything, or, rather, that there are few times and places for most things. Sander's study which was mentioned above suggests that at some feeding times infants are 'prepared' to stay awake for much longer periods of time than at others. Often regular 'play times' or periods in which there is intense social interaction are set up. Fathers may have play sessions with the baby in the evening when they return home from work. Through the patterning of these activities the infant gradually discovers about the wider social world. He has to learn that adults are not always willing to participate in social exchanges and that there are many other calls on their time. Many of these are directly controlled by factors outside the home – the father's pattern of work, for example – and so provide a rather direct link between the child's immediate experience of the world and his position in the social structure.

PEOPLE AND THINGS

Some preliminary observations have suggested that in the newborn period infants may employ different modes of behaviour when relating to people or to things (Trevarthen and Richards, in preparation). If later work confirms this finding it will provide another example of a pre-adaptation to social life. As adults, we have quite different expectations and means of relating to people and things. If infants begin extra-uterine development with dichotomous modes of responding in these two fundamentally different situations, it would provide an important way of structuring the environment. These first observations indicate that when infants are given an interesting thing to look at they concentrate attention on it. The eyes narrow and scan over the object. The body posture seems tense. The arms, hands and fingers are orientated towards the object in incipient pointing gestures. With social situations the infant seems to 'sit back'. The body is loose and the hands and arms drop. The eyes widen and attention appears less focused. The face is more mobile with many mouth movements, and, of course, smiling is common.

The feedback loops which describe these two situations are quite different. If something is done to a thing, we expect a reaction. We expect something that is a fairly direct consequence of what we have done and follows on immediately after our action. People are different because they do not react in a simple way. The simple loop of action and reaction become complex because it includes another mind. If we say something to someone the last thing we expect is for them to repeat back our own words. What is returned is some complement or alternation to what we have done. The problems raised here have been much simplified, but I hope enough has been said to indicate how helpful it might be to an infant if he always 'knew' when he was communicating with a person rather than doing something with a thing.

There is another piece of evidence that is perhaps relevant here. This is a study by Weisberg (1963) which demonstrated that the vocal responses of three-month-olds could be much more effectively conditioned with social than with non-social reinforcement. To have any effect on the infant's behaviour, an adult had to join in a sequence that had been initiated by the infant; a mechanical intervention by a buzzer was ineffective.

This section has been speculative, but I have tried to indicate some ways in which one can analyse early social encounters. Most of the observational work remains to be done.

CONCLUSION

In this chapter I have tried to show that the beginning of socialisation involves the giving of social meaning to the actions of the infant. This is a very different view from that of the stimulus–response psychologists who assume that the infant is in some way forced into a social world. I have pointed to some of the ways in which the infant is preadapted to social life so that he can construct his social world out of the social encounters that occur with adults. The infant takes an active part in the process – he must, for development is not possible without a developing organism. But in doing so he is formed as a social individual.

Perhaps the most impressive thing about the infant's social development is our ignorance of the processes involved. In saying this I am not trying to underestimate the research that has been done but rather to emphasise the complexity of the problem with which we have to deal. In trying to sketch out some of the processes involved I am attempting to build up a framework, a point of view, which can be used as the basis of further observational work.

ACKNOWLEDGEMENT

Our research on mothers and infants is supported by grants from the Nuffield Foundation and the Mental Health Research Fund. I should like to express our thanks to these bodies, and to all the mothers and infants who have co-operated in our studies.

REFERENCES

Becker, E. (1972). *The Birth and Death of Meaning* (2nd ed.). London, Penguin.

Berger, P. L. and Luckman, T. (1967). *The Social Construction of Reality*. London, Allen Lane.

Bernal, J. F. (1972). Crying during the first ten days of life, and maternal responses. *Developm. Med. Child Neurol.* **14**, 362–72.

Bernal, J. F. and Richards, M. P. M. (1973). What can the zoologist tell us about human development? In Barnett, A. S. (ed.) *Ethology and Development*. Little Club Clinics in Developm. Med. London, S.I.M.P. with Heinemann.

Bowlby, J. (1951). *Maternal Care and Mental Health*. London, H.M.S.O.

Bowlby, J. (1958). The nature of the child's tie to his mother. *Int. J. Psychoanal.* **39**, 350–73.

Bowlby, J. (1961). Processes of mourning. *Int. J. Psycho-anal.* **42**, 317–40.

Bowlby, J. (1969). *Attachment and Loss,* Vol. 1, *Attachment*. London, Hogarth Press.

Eibl-Eiberfeldt, I. E. (1970). *Ethology: The Biology of Behavior*. New York, Holt, Rinehart and Winston.

Eimas, P. D., Siqueland, E. R., Jusczyk, P. and Vigorito, J. (1971). Speech perception in infants. *Science*, **171**, 303–6.

Eisenberg, R. B. (1969). Auditory behaviour in the human neonate. *Internat. Audiol.* **8**, 34–45.

Emerson, J. (1970). Behaviour in private places: sustaining definitions of reality in gynaecological examinations. In Dreitzel, H. P. (ed.) *Recent Sociology*, Vol. 2. London, Collier-Macmillan.

Foss, B. M. (1961, 1963, 1965, 1969) (ed.). *The Determinants of Infant Behaviour*, Vols. 1–4. London, Methuen.

Freidlander, B. Z. (1970). Receptive language development in infancy: issues and problems. *Merrill-Palmer Quart.* **16**, 7–15.

Haire, J. R. (1972). *The Cultural Warping of Childbirth*. Milwaukee, International Childbirth Education Association.

Hutt, S. J., Hutt, C., Lenard, H. G., Bernuth, H. V. and Muntjewcuff, W. J. (1968). Auditory responsivity in the human neonate. *Nature*, 218, 888–90.

Klaus, H. M., Kennell, J. H., Plumb, N. and Zuehlke, S. (1970). Human maternal behaviour at the first contact with her young. *Pediat.* 46, 187–92.

Kohlberg, L. (1969). Stage and sequence: the cognitive–developmental approach to socialisation. In Goslin, D. A. (ed.) *Handbook of Socialisation: Theory and Research*. Chicago, Rand-McNally.

Konner, M. J. (1972). Aspects of the developmental ethology of a foraging people. In Blurton Jones, N. J. (ed.) *Ethological Studies of Child Behaviour*. London, Cambridge Univ. Press.

Korner, A. F. and Grobstein, R. (1966). Visual alertness in neonates; implications for maternal stimulation and early deprivation. *Child Development*, 37, 867–76.

Korner, A. F. and Thoman, E. B. (1972). Visual alertness in neonates as evoked by maternal care. *J. exp. Child Psychol.* 10, 67–78.

Leach, E. (1972). The influence of cultural context on non-verbal communication in man. In Hinde, R. A. (ed.) *Non-Verbal Communication*. London, Cambridge Univ. Press.

Moss, H. A. (1967). Sex, age and state as determinants of mother–infant interaction. *Merrill-Palmer Quart.* 13, 19–36.

Richards, M. P. M. (1971a). Social interaction in the first weeks of human life. *Psychiat. Neurol. Neurochir.* 14, 35–42.

Richards, M. P. M. (1971b). A comment on the social context of mother-infant interaction. In Schaffer, H. R. (ed.) *The Origin of Human Social Relations*. London, Academic Press.

Richards, M. P. M. and Bernal, J. F. (1972). An observational study of mother-infant interaction. In Blurton Jones, N. J. (ed.) *Ethological Studies of Child Behaviour*. London, Cambridge Univ. Press.

Sander, L. W., Stechler, G., Burns, P. and Julia, H. (1970). Early mother-infant interaction and 24-hour patterns of activity and sleep. *J. Amer. Acad. Child Psychiat.* 9, 103–23.

Schaffer, H. R. (1971). *The Growth of Sociability*. London, Penguin.

Spitz, R. A. (1965). *The First Year of Life*. New York, Internat. Univ. Press.

Trehub, S. E. and Robinovitch, M. S. (1972). Audiolinguistic sensitivity in early infancy. *Developm. Psychol.* 6, 74–7.

Trevarthen, C. B. (1973). Behavioural embryology. In Carterette, E. C. and Freidman, M. P. (eds.) *The Handbook of Perception*. New York, Academic Press.

Wasz-Höckert, O., Lind, J., Vuorenkoski, J., Partanen, T. and Valarne, E. (1968). *The Infant Cry*. Clinics in Developm. Med. No. 29. London, S.M.I.P. with Heinemann.

Weisberg, P. (1963). Social and non-social conditioning of infant vocalisations. *Child Development*, 34, 377–88.

White, B. L. (1967). An experimental approach to the effects of experience on early human behaviour. In Hall, J. P. (ed.) *Minnesota Symposia on Child Psychology*, Vol. 1. Minneapolis, University of Minnesota Press.

Wolff, P. H. (1963). Observations on the early development of smiling. In Foss, B. M. (ed.) *Determinants of Infant Behaviour*, Vol. 2. London, Methuen.

Wolff, P. H. (1967). The role of biological rhythms in early psychological development. *Bull. Menninger Clin.* **31**, 197–218.

Wolff, P. H. (1969). The natural history of crying and other vocalisations in early infancy. In Foss, B. M. (ed.), *Determinants of Infant Behaviour*, Vol. 4. London, Methuen.

Wortis, R. P. (1972). Child-rearing and women's liberation. In Wandor, M. (ed.) *The Body Politic*. London, Stage 1.

6

Infant–mother attachment and social development: Socialisation as a product of reciprocal responsiveness to signals

Mary D. Salter Ainsworth, Silvia M. Bell, and Donelda J. Stayton

The term 'socialisation' is applied to the process through which a child is *made social*. It refers to what must be done so that a child learns rules, proscriptions, values, and modes of behaviour which fit him to his appropriate role in a social group and which make him acceptable to others. It implies that a child is not social at the beginning, but only gradually becomes social. Learning theory holds that a child learns these responses because they have been reinforced; psychoanalytic tradition implies that he takes over the behaviour of those with whom he identifies. Although dissimilar in many respects these views share the basic assumption that an infant's initial repertoire of responses is ill-suited for living in a social world and that profound alterations must be effected before he is fit for society.

It is our view that infants are genetically biased towards interaction with other people from the beginning. Their sensory equipment is responsive to stimuli most likely to stem from people, and many of their behavioural systems are most readily activated (or terminated) by such stimuli. A child is pre-adapted to a social world, and in this sense is social from the beginning. To be sure, the social role of an infant differs from those of adults, but, as Richards suggests (this volume) an infant is predisposed to become adult. If an infant is reared in a social environment not too dissimilar from that in which the species evolved – an environment in which adults are responsive to the signals implicit in his behaviour – it seems likely to us that he will gradually acquire an acceptable repertoire of more 'mature' social behaviours without heroic efforts on the part of his parents specifically to train him to adopt the rules, proscriptions, and values that they wish him to absorb. Because of these considerations we find the concept of 'socialisation' essentially alien to our approach.

For some years we have been concerned with research into the development of the attachment relationship between an infant and his mother in the first year of life. In the course of this research findings have emerged that seem relevant to issues that are commonly conceived to pertain to 'socialisation'. Two of these issues are considered in some detail in this chapter. Under what conditions does an infant learn to cry less than he did in the beginning and thus become less demanding and less of a nuisance? Under what conditions does an infant come to comply readily with his mother's commands and prohibitions?

Before presenting research findings pertinent to these issues, it is first desirable to discuss the theoretical context of the research itself. This theoretical background has been substantially influenced by ethological principles and findings. It owes much to Bowlby's (1958, 1969) formulations, although it has also been considerably influenced by our own empirical work. The next section gives a condensed account of our attachment theory – a theory that has been presented in more detail elsewhere (e.g. Ainsworth, 1969, 1972, 1973; Ainsworth and Bell, 1970).

I   BACKGROUND OF ATTACHMENT THEORY
    AND RESEARCH

Definitions

An attachment may be defined as an affectional tie that one person or animal forms between himself and another specific one – a tie that binds them together in space and endures over time. The behavioral hallmark of attachment is seeking to gain and to maintain a certain degree of proximity to the object of attachment, which ranges from close physical contact under some circumstances to interaction or communication across some distance under other circumstances. *Attachment behaviors* are behaviors which promote proximity or contact. In the human infant these include active proximity – and contact-seeking behaviors such as approaching, following, and clinging, and signaling behaviors such as smiling, crying, and calling. (Ainsworth and Bell, 1970, p. 50)

Some highlights of attachment theory

Although active proximity- and contact-seeking behaviours are not in evidence until locomotion and reaching have developed, even a newborn human infant has a repertoire of reflex-like behaviours which promote the maintenance of physical contact once it has been achieved – behaviours such as rooting, sucking, grasping, and postural adjustment when held. For increasing proximity or gaining physical contact with his mother, however, a very young infant must rely on his mother's approach in response to signalling behaviours, such as crying and smiling. It is hypothesised that these behaviours are genetically programmed – both those effective at birth or very soon afterwards, and those that

100

develop later but are nevertheless species-characteristic. It is further postulated that adults generally – despite a massive overlay of learned behaviours – are biased to respond to the species-characteristic signals of an infant in ways that are also species-characteristic. To be sure, there are individual differences in maternal responsiveness, presumably much affected by individual experiences and personality development. Thus, for example, some mothers, perhaps because they are depressed or compulsively occupied with other matters, are relatively impervious even to urgent infant signals. Other mothers are so sensitively perceptive of an infant's behaviour that his entire behavioural repertoire has to them a signalling function. Evolutionary theory suggests that a species-characteristic behaviour is adapted to some significant aspect of the environment in which the species evolved, and that social behaviours are adapted to reciprocal behaviours of conspecifics – or of particular classes of conspecifics. Thus, for example, male mating behaviours are adapted to the behaviours of females, and maternal behaviours are adapted to the behaviours of offspring. In this vein, it is reasonable to hypothesise that infant attachment behaviours are adapted to reciprocal maternal behaviours, that a mother responsive to infant signals is a salient feature of the environment of evolutionary adaptedness, and that unresponsive mothers may be viewed as the product of developmental anomalies and likely themselves to foster anomalous development in their infants.

Evolutionary theory suggests further that any species-characteristic behaviour becomes pre-adapted because it fulfils a significant function that forwards survival of individual, population, or species. Although in mammals, one of the common (predictable) outcomes of infant–mother contact is that the infant will be fed, Bowlby (1969) argues that the essential biological function of attachment behaviour and of reciprocal maternal behaviour is protection of the infant, perhaps especially protection from predators. In espousing this view he was influenced both by the phenomenon of imprinting in precocial birds (in which an infant–mother bond is formed rapidly despite the fact that the infant is not dependent on his mother for food), and by Harlow's experimental studies (e.g. 1958, 1961, 1963) in the rearing of rhesus monkeys in which the infant's attachment behaviours – featuring clasping and clinging in this species – lead him to seek proximity and contact more often with an inanimate surrogate mother figure which is soft and claspable than with another which yields milk. Furthermore, Harlow demonstrated that once an attachment has been made to such a figure, the infant is able to use it as a secure base from which he can explore even a strange and otherwise alarming situation, and as a haven of safety when faced with a fear-arousing stimulus.

Whatever role feeding and other aspects of nurturance may play in the development of attachment, it seems to us likely that Bowlby is correct in identifying protection as the essential biological function of attachment behaviour. Although danger from predators seems insignificant in present-day Western environments, Bowlby argues that this was a major danger in the 'environment of evolutionary adaptedness' – presumably the savannah environment in which the human species is believed to have first evolved. In any event, even in present-day Western environments, there are still dangers from which children must be protected, and it is reasonable to view attachment behaviours and reciprocal maternal behaviours as continuing to have a significant protective function. Furthermore, it is clear that conditions of alarm dependably activate attachment behaviour at a high level of intensity.

Development of attachment. Although an infant may be viewed as genetically biased to behave in ways that promote proximity and/or contact with adult figures, it is clear that learning is implicated in the development of attachment. An infant is not attached to anyone at first, but if he is reared in a social environment that approximates the environment of evolutionary adaptedness – an environment in which at least one or more adults are consistently accessible to him – he becomes attached to one or a few specific figures about the middle of the first year of life. There is some evidence that he becomes attached to the figure or figures with whom he has had most interaction.

The learning component of attachment is first conspicuous in an infant's acquisition of discrimination of his mother figure from others. As this discrimination is learnt his attachment behaviour becomes increasingly differential, and specifically directed towards her and/or other attachment figures who have become discriminated concomitantly. Furthermore, as he develops he becomes increasingly effective in seeking proximity and contact to his preferred figures on his own account, for example, through approaching, following, and clinging. He also becomes increasingly able to maintain interaction across a distance through a varied repertoire of signals and communications.

During the second half of the first year of life an infant's attachment behaviour becomes increasingly 'goal-corrected' (Bowlby, 1969). This implies that in any given situation, in accordance with environmental and intraorganismic conditions, a child will have a certain 'set-goal' of proximity to his attachment figure, and his attachment behaviour will be activated if that distance is exceeded. But, by this time, his systems of attachment behaviour, originally distinctively activated and terminated, become somewhat interchangeable and capable of being organised into new patterns of behaviour which are flexibly adjustable and continuously being corrected in order to maintain the set-goal. Or, in Piaget's (1936) terminology, attachment behaviours may be viewed as 'schemata' which have become 'mobile' as a child has become capable of distinguishing between means and ends. Furthermore, as Piaget (1937) demonstrates, an infant at this time begins to be able to search for hidden objects, and thus shows the first substantial beginning of the concept of an object as having permanence despite its absence from his perceptual field. The acquisition of 'object permanence' marks a momentous shift in the nature of infant–mother relations. It is not until a child is cognitively capable of conceiving of an attachment figure as existing while not actually present perceptually that his behaviour can have the time- and space-bridging qualities that distinguish attachments from other transactions with the environment.

Attachment distinguished from attachment behaviour. Elsewhere (e.g. Ainsworth and Bell, 1970; Ainsworth, 1972) we have discussed the implications for the concept of attachment of a child's response to a definitive separation from his attachment figures and his subsequent reunion with them. Although attachment behaviour may be greatly heightened in some phases of a child's response to such a separation and may be entirely absent in other phases, the attachment as a relationship to a specific figure tends to survive undiminished. These and other considerations (some of which will be discussed shortly) have led us to distinguish between an 'attachment', as a stable propensity intermittently to seek proximity or contact with a specific figure, and 'attachment behaviours', through which proximity is promoted or sought.

It has been further suggested (Ainsworth, 1972) that it is useful to view attachment as an inner organisation of behavioural systems which not only controls the 'stable propensity' to seek proximity, but is also responsible for the distinctive quality of the organisation of behaviours through which a given individual promotes proximity with a specific attachment figure. Such a hypothesis implies some kind of stable intra-organismic basis for individual differences in the organisation of behaviour, which must be conceived as interacting with environmental conditions and other 'situational' intraorganismic conditions – neuro-physiological, hormonal, and receptor processes – to activate, terminate, and direct attachment behaviour in any specific situation. The concept of attachment as propensity or inner organisation is of the same order as 'mediating process', 'intervening variable', or 'hypothetical construct'.

Whereas, according to this view, the 'attachment' is stable and enduring, attachment behaviours are variable, intermittent, and situationally determined in regard to both activation and intensity. In particular, it is necessary to view attachment behaviours as interacting with other behavioural systems which may also be activated in a given situation and which may either be compatible or incompatible with them. Of these other systems, exploratory behaviour deserves special notice.

Attachment and exploratory behaviours. In the familiar environment of his own home it is common for a child freely to leave his mother's side to explore and to play, perhaps for extended periods, before returning to her. Under these circumstances attachment behaviour may be described as having a low level of activation, while exploratory and/or play behaviour are more intensely activated. The proximity set-goal may be described as having a wide setting. If mother moves away to another room, the child's attachment behaviour is likely to be activated, however, although perhaps at relatively low intensity, by the fact that set-goal distance is exceeded, and the child will tend to gravitate after his mother, following her into closer proximity before moving off again to play. If, however, she seems about to depart from the house, or if something alarming happens, or indeed if intraorganismic conditions change, the set-goal will shift to one of closer proximity, attachment behaviour will be activated at a high level of intensity, and balance between the attachment and exploratory systems will be tipped away from exploration and towards proximity-seeking.

The dynamic balance between exploratory and attachment behaviour may be seen to have significance from an evolutionary point of view. Whereas attachment behaviours and reciprocal maternal behaviours serve a protective function during the long, helpless infancy of a species such as the human which can adapt to a wide range of environmental variations, exploratory behaviours reflect a genetic bias for an infant to be interested in the novel features of his environment, to approach them, to manipulate them, to explore, to play, and to learn about the nature of his environment and the properties of the objects in it. It is an advantageous arrangement for an infant to be activated to explore without straying too far from an adult who can protect him if he encounters danger, for him to be programmed to maintain a reasonable degree of proximity on his own account without requiring that the adult be always alert to do so, and for him to be activated to seek quickly a closer proximity or contact should he become alarmed.

The advantageous arrangement described above is not unique to the human species. Studies of ground-living non-human primates (e.g. Southwick, Beg and Siddiqi, 1965; DeVore, 1963; van Lawick-Goodall, 1968; Hinde, Rowell and Spencer-Booth, 1964; Hinde and Spencer-Booth, 1967; Harlow and Harlow, 1965) have provided ample evidence that whereas at first mother and infant are in almost continuous contact, soon the infant ventures forth increasingly to investigate his surroundings and to play with other infants, and spends increasingly more time 'off' his mother. His mother, in turn, becomes increasingly less restrictive and retrieves him less frequently. Alarm, or threat of separation, however, tip the balance towards intense activation of attachment behaviour (and maternal retrieving behaviour) and bring mother and infant quickly together again.

Experimental studies of human infants have shown that an infant will explore even an unfamiliar environment freely while his mother is present, although exploration is weak or absent and attachment behaviour conspicuous should she be absent (Arsenian, 1943; Cox and Campbell, 1968; Rheingold, 1969). Nevertheless, an infant will freely leave his mother on his own initiative to enter another unfamiliar room to explore it (Rheingold and Eckerman, 1970). If mild alarm is introduced by the entrance of a stranger, exploration tends sharply to diminish, and if the mother herself departs exploration halts and attachment behaviour is strongly activated (Ainsworth and Wittig, 1969; Ainsworth and Bell, 1970). It appears that whether a strange environment is perceived as novel and elicits exploration or as alarming and elicits attachment behaviour depends in large measure upon the presence of an attachment figure.

Individual differences and previous studies thereof

Our discussion of attachment has thus far described common behavioural trends. There are individual differences even in species-characteristic behaviours, and these common trends must be viewed merely as 'normative' (both in the sense of biologically normal and of statistically average) and by no means as invariable in all members of the species. Our first study of individual differences was directed to the balance between attachment relationship with the mother, showed a smooth balance and vironment during the last quarter of the first year of life and in a strange situation at the end of the first year (Ainsworth, Bell and Stayton, 1971). The most frequent pattern in our sample of twenty-six infants followed the normative trend that might be expected from our theoretical generalisations. These infants, who may be described as having a secure attachment relationship with the mother, showed a smooth balance and integration between attachment and exploratory behaviours. They did indeed use the mother as a secure base from which to explore; they moved freely away from her, active in locomotion and manipulation; they kept track of mother's whereabouts with an occasional glance and moved back to her to make brief contact from time to time; if picked up

105

they responded positively, but they did not want to be held for more than a few moments; when put down they moved happily off to play again. In a strange situation, without exception, their behaviour followed the normative trends described earlier.

Half the sample, however, showed patterns of behaviour reflecting a disturbed balance between attachment and exploratory behaviour, and these same infants similarly showed departures from the norm in the strange situation. A systematic account of these several patterns of disturbance is given elsewhere (Ainsworth, Bell and Stayton, 1971). Here it must suffice to say that they included the following features in various constellations: ambivalence in attachment behaviour, especially in behaviour relating to physical contact; heightened separation anxiety so that very minor everyday separations or threats thereof unduly disrupted exploratory behaviour; passivity, whether intermittent or consistent, that damped down both exploratory behaviour and active attachment behaviour; and proximity-avoiding behaviour that effectively blocked the appropriate activation of attachment behaviour and resulted in a degree of independence that seemed both premature and inappropriate. Findings such as these, together with findings to be reported later in this chapter, strengthened our conviction that there are striking and stable individual differences, even in the first year of life, in the way in which attachment behaviour is organised around and directed towards the mother figure. There seems no doubt that all of these infants had become attached to their mothers. The quality of the attachment relationship differed, however, from one individual to another, and affected both attachment behaviour and exploration even when (as in the strange situation) the environmental conditions remained essentially the same.

Whatever may be the role of constitutional differences between infants in influencing the quality of the infant–mother attachment relationship, there is strong evidence that it is influenced substantially by the kind of interaction with his mother the infant has experienced throughout his first year, and whatever contribution the infant himself may have made to this interaction, his mother's contribution is significant. Later reference will be made to detailed codings of maternal behaviour. Here we shall draw attention to four dimensions of maternal behaviour which were found to be related significantly to quality of infant–mother attachment as reflected in the balance of attachment and exploratory behaviour both in the strange situation and at home (Ainsworth, Bell and Stayton, 1971). These dimensions are labelled as follows: sensitivity–insensitivity, acceptance–rejection, co-operation–interference, and accessibility–ignoring. They were measured by nine-point rating scales, each of which has five anchor points with detailed behavioural specifications.

The first scale[1] dealt with the degree of sensitivity the mother showed in perceiving and responding promptly and appropriately to the infant's signals and communications. It turned out to be a key variable, in the sense that mothers who rated high in sensitivity also, without exception, rated high in acceptance, co-operation and accessibility, whereas mothers who rated low in any one of the other three scales also rated low in sensitivity. Thus, for example, a rejecting mother was insensitive even though she might not also be especially interfering or inaccessible. Without exception, the infants whose mothers rated high in sensitivity displayed the normative behaviour described earlier in the strange situation, and a smooth balance between attachment and exploratory behaviour at home. Without exception, the infants whose mothers rated low in sensitivity displayed one or another of the behaviour patterns (to which reference was made in the preceding paragraph) which reflected a disturbed attachment–exploration balance both at home and in the strange situation. Furthermore, different patterns of infant disturbance were related to specific patterns of maternal behaviour. Thus, for example, the infants showing one pattern tended to have rejecting–interfering mothers, those showing another had rejecting–ignoring mothers, another ignoring but non-rejecting, and non-interfering mothers, and so on.

The mothers whose behaviour facilitated harmonious interaction with their infants and thus attachment relationships of secure quality showed a remarkable lack of emphasis on procedures intended to socialise their babies. Such a mother tended to work with the grain of her baby's social repertoire rather than against it. Although she did not deliberately attempt to train her baby, her transactions with him nevertheless facilitated his acquisition of socially desirable modes of behaviour.

Not all of those mothers whose behaviour was so insensitive as to make for disharmonious interaction and disturbed infant–mother attachments were intent on socialisation, however. Some of them were themselves too disturbed or impervious to act sensitively, but some of them were deliberately insensitive and ignoring, rejecting or interfering in an attempt to train the infant to cry less, to demand less, to adapt to household schedules, to fit into an adult-centred social group, and in general to do what adults wished when they wished it and to learn not to expect to 'get their own way'. Their efforts were largely unsuccessful, and their babies were slower to acquire socially desirable modes of behaviour than were those whose mothers were sensitively responsive.

[1] The sensitivity–insensitivity scale is shown in the Appendix. Copies of the other scales may be obtained from Professor Mary D. S. Ainsworth, Department of Psychology, The Johns Hopkins University, Baltimore, Maryland 21218.

107

In the next two sections we shall deal in more detail with the relationship between maternal practices and two aspects of infant development: first, the changes that take place in one specific attachment behaviour – crying – in the course of the first year of life, and second, the development of infant obedience to maternal commands, a development that emerges as closely related both to infant–mother attachment and to exploration.

II INFANT CRYING

A review of U.S. Children's Bureau *Infant Care* pamphlets between 1920 and 1940 attests to the fact that the fear of 'spoiling' a baby by responding to his cries has been a recurrent theme guiding pronouncements on infant care. A baby should not be picked up in between feedings, mothers are admonished, lest he learn 'that crying will get him what he wants, sufficient to make a spoiled, fussy baby, and a household tyrant whose continual demands make a slave of the mother' (U.S. Children's Bureau, 1926, p. 44).[2] Although more recent advice of the Bureau encourages mothers to follow their natural impulse to respond to crying, the notion that this may result in increased crying persists, perhaps supported by untested and presumably naïve extrapolations from learning theory that assume that to respond to a cry will strengthen crying behaviour.

Crying is classed as an attachment behaviour because it serves to bring mother and baby into proximity with each other. When viewed in the context of attachment theory, both crying and maternal responsiveness to it are seen as behaviours crucial to the survival of the young infant. Crying can be regarded as the earliest communicative signal at the disposal of the child – a signal which is relatively undifferentiated at first, but comes in time to be integrated into a wide range of complex modes of communication. Despite the fact that mothers tend, of necessity, to respond to a large percentage of an infant's cries, crying decreases with age, as more effective modes of communication become operative. The older child, in fact, tends to resort to crying primarily when frustrated and distressed after these other modes have failed. The question before us is to determine which characteristics of maternal care tend to promote this typical outcome.

Bell and Ainsworth (1972) conducted a study of the development of crying in the first year of life. One of the purposes of the study was to explore specifically the relation between maternal responsiveness to crying and changes in the frequency and duration of crying throughout the year.

---

[2] Historical changes in the advice offered by such sources is discussed in detail in chapter 4.

Twenty-six white, middle-class mother–infant pairs were observed in the home for four-hour periods, at three-week intervals throughout the first year of life. Thus, babies were seen, on the average, four times in each quarter of the first year, for a total of sixteen hours per quarter. All instances of crying, fussing, and unhappy vocalisations were recorded, and their duration assessed. In addition, the presence or absence of a maternal response to the cry was noted, as well as the duration of the delay between the onset of the cry and the mother's response.

Two measures of crying were obtained for each baby in each observation period: 'frequency of crying episodes' and 'duration of crying'. The measures of maternal responsiveness obtained were: the number of cries the mother ignored, the length of time that a baby cried without obtaining a response from her – i.e. the duration of maternal unresponsiveness – the types of intervention produced by the mother, and, finally, the conditions which successfully terminated the cry. The information obtained was averaged over the four visits of each quarter, in order to obtain a stable measure of the maternal and infant behaviours characteristic of each three-month period.

Wide individual differences were found both in infant crying and maternal responsiveness. Whereas a mother's tendency to ignore or respond to the cry tended to be stable throughout the year, individual differences in infant crying did not become stable until the second half of the first year of life. The findings indicated that infants achieved a characteristic pattern of frequency and duration of crying as a result of interaction with the mother, and thus that maternal responsiveness was the main factor to account for individual differences in crying.

Table 1 shows the relation between episodes of crying ignored by the

Table 1   *Episodes of crying ignored by the mother and frequency of crying*

		Episodes ignored by the mother			
		First quarter	Second quarter	Third quarter	Fourth quarter
Frequency of crying	First quarter	−0.04	0.34	0.48*	0.21
	Second quarter	0.56†	0.35	0.32	0.29
	Third quarter	0.21	0.39*	0.42*	0.40*
	Fourth quarter	0.20	0.36	0.52†	0.45*

*$p < 0.05$.   †$p < 0.01$.
Note. The figures in italics have been corrected to avoid confounding.

mother and frequency of infant crying. There are three parts of the table upon which to focus. The diagonal, which gives the correlation of maternal and infant behaviours in the same quarter, shows that the relation between episodes ignored and frequency of crying is not significant either within the first nor within the second quarters, but becomes significant in the second half of the year. The lower portion of the matrix shows that maternal ignoring in each quarter correlated significantly with infant crying in the following quarter. Thus, tiny babies do not respond immediately by crying more frequently, but from the third month of life on, they tend to be more insistent in their crying as a result of the past history of mother's ignoring tactics. Finally, the correlations reported in the upper right cells of the table indicate that the effects of infant crying on maternal behaviour are not marked, nor statistically significant, until the fourth quarter. Thus, when inspected longitudinally over the whole first year of life, it seems that maternal ignoring increases the likelihood that a baby will cry frequently from the third month of life on, whereas the frequency of crying has no consistent influence on the number of episodes the mother will be likely to ignore.

Table 2   *Duration of mother's unresponsiveness to crying and duration of crying*

		Mother's unresponsiveness			
		First quarter	Second quarter	Third quarter	Fourth quarter
Duration of crying	First quarter	*0.19*	0.37	0.12	0.41*
	Second quarter	0.45*	*0.67†*	0.51†	0.69†
	Third quarter	0.40*	0.42*	*0.39**	0.52*
	Fourth quarter	0.32	0.65†	0.51†	*0.61†*

*$p < 0.05$.   †$p < 0.01$.
Note. The figures in italic have been corrected to avoid confounding.

Table 2 shows the results of a comparable analysis of the relation between duration of maternal unresponsiveness and duration of crying. The findings are analogous to those obtained in the previous analysis and suggest that crying in each quarter is highly correlated with maternal unresponsiveness in the previous quarter. In addition, this table shows that, by the second half of the first year, an infant's persistence in crying affects the mother, tending to make her more reluctant to respond promptly. This indicates that by the end of the first year a vicious spiral has been established. Babies whose cries have been ignored tend to cry more frequently and persistently, which further discourages prompt responsiveness.

In the first three months of life, approximately three-quarters of the crying episodes were produced when the baby was not in proximity or contact with the mother. Analysis of the types of intervention mothers produced in response to the cry revealed that more than 90 per cent of maternal responses involve mother bridging the distance, if not actively decreasing the distance, between her and the baby. Contact was the most effective response throughout the first year, terminating a cry in almost 90 per cent of the instances in which it was instituted. Even behaviours involving distance interchanges between mother and baby were effective more than 40 per cent of the time in the first quarter, and became increasingly effective towards the end of the first year. Although some maternal responses were more effective than others in terminating a cry, no relationship was obtained between maternal tendency to respond with one or another type of intervention and frequency of crying. Thus, the findings point to the conclusion that the single most important factor associated with a decrease in infant crying, at least in the first year, is the promptness with which the caretaker responds.

Changes in crying were also examined in the context of the general quality of the mother–infant relationship. Four maternal care rating scales were selected for comparison with the infant crying measures. Two of these, mother's 'sensitivity–insensitivity' and 'acceptance–rejection', have been described in an earlier section of this chapter and assess maternal care in the fourth quarter of the first year. Two additional scales, 'appropriateness of mother's social interaction with the baby' and 'amount of physical contact', were used to assess maternal care in the first three months of life. High ratings on these scales suggest that maternal care is appropriate, and that there is a high degree of harmony in the interaction between mother and baby.

The result of the comparison, shown in Table 3, indicates that in the

Table 3   *Rank-order correlations between infant crying and maternal-care ratings*

Crying measures	First quarter		Fourth quarter	
	Appropriateness of interaction	Amount of physical contact	Sensitivity	Acceptance
Frequency of crying	−0.20	−0.32	−0.61*	−0.68*
Duration of crying	−0.51*	−0.64*	−0.72*	−0.71*

*$p < 0.01$.

111

first three months of life the quality of maternal care tends to affect the duration of crying, but is not associated with frequency of crying episodes. By the fourth quarter of the first year, however, both crying measures are highly correlated with maternal sensitivity and acceptance. A more complex statistical analysis,[3] showed that maternal sensitivity was associated with a steady decrease in both crying measures from the first to the fourth quarter of the first year. These findings support the hypothesis that promptness of maternal responsiveness to crying, in the context of a generally accepting and sensitive relationship between mother and baby is associated with a decrease in crying during the first year of life.

Since those babies whose mothers had been responsive cried less frequently in the last quarter, it was of interest to determine whether other modes of communication had developed to replace crying. All the babies were classified into three groups on the basis of the subtlety, clarity, and variety of their communicative signals – a relatively uncommunicative group, a moderately communicative, and a communicative group of babies characterised by the ability to produce a varied range of clear, subtle signals through facial expression, gesture, and vocalisation. The assessment was based on signals observed and described by the observer, whether these were directed towards the mother or another, the assessment did not depend upon how the recipient of the signal responded to it. Table 4 shows that infant communication is negatively

Table 4   *Infant communication in the fourth quarter, crying and maternal responsiveness*

	Fourth Quarter Infant Communication
Duration of crying	−0.71*
Frequency of crying	−0.65*
Mother's unresponsiveness	−0.63*
Episodes ignored by mother	−0.54*

*$p < 0.01$.

correlated to crying, and to mother's unresponsiveness to crying. Thus, babies who, by the end of the first year, had developed the most adequate channels of communication were the same who cried little, and whose cries had been promptly heeded.

These findings suggest that crying is the earliest of a system of signalling behaviours through which proximity and contact with the mother are maintained. Maternal responsiveness tends to terminate an

[3]   By means of a non-parametric analysis-of-variance technique.

episode of crying and to result in the decrease of crying behaviour while it fosters the development of other communicative signals. Although our analysis did not deal directly with maternal responsiveness to these non-crying communications, it seems likely that the more sensitive mothers would tend to be responsive to them as well as to crying signals. Thus, it appears that responsiveness to infant signals of all kinds, including crying, facilitates the development of varied modes of communication while weakening the tendency to signal through crying..

Although a more thorough discussion of the theoretical relevance of these findings is left to the concluding section of the chapter, it is relevant to note here that they support a theory of early social development such as the one described in the earlier sections of this chapter, which ascribes survival function to the child's inherent predispositions to produce signals which elicit a response from certain key members of his surroundings. In order that the mother's protective function be fulfilled, it seems essential (*a*) that a mother should respond to the crying infant and (*b*) that undifferentiated forms of communication, such as crying, become differentiated and used selectively in conjunction with more specific, clearer communicative signals. Our findings indicate that these two essentials are causally linked so that the most appropriate maternal behaviour – i.e. responsiveness – fosters infant development in the most adaptive direction.

The present study, however, was limited to maternal and infant behaviours in the first year of life, as observed in the context of the average middle-class home. It seems plausible that in older children some forms of fussing might be strengthened by over-solicitousness, and it is a fact that under the extremely depriving conditions characteristic of institutions, crying, as well as most forms of infant initiative, can be lessened to a point of near extinction. Within the range of interaction characteristic of mother–infant pairs in the first year, however, maternal responsiveness seems to set the tone for mutual co-operation – the more attentive the mother, the less demanding and impatient the baby learns to be.

III INFANT OBEDIENCE

Although crying, as a particularly changeworthy behaviour, has been a conspicuous target of socialisation practices, the inculcation of obedience is perhaps their major objective. Compliance to commands and prohibitions is generally considered to precede and to be at the core of internalised standards and values that mediate moral behaviour. Until a child – or an adult, for that matter – demonstrates a willingness to comply with the rules, values, and proscriptions of his parents – or society in general

– he is considered to be asocial and a liability to society, if not indeed antisocial and a menace.

Traditional theories of socialisation assume that the social environment modifies a child's asocial tendencies by supplying not only the *standards for behaviour* but also the *motivation* necessary for adopting these standards. A child's motives are generally believed to be hedonistic. Therefore, it is held that he must acquire social behaviour through reward and punishment or through such processes as identification and modelling. In either case, it is generally believed that firm and consistent training and discipline is required if obedience is to develop.

We do not believe that obedience in an infant or very young child should be conceived as the outcome of learning of specific acts and avoidances. Rather, we propose that infant obedience may be best understood as an instance of pre-adaptation, and that it should be viewed within the context of the attachment theory summarised in the introductory section.

Infant obedience, when first observed, consists of compliance to adult signals and communications such as 'No! no!', 'Come here!', 'Don't touch!', and 'Give it to me!'. Later, infants may display a self-imposed compliance to commands previously given but this is relatively rare in the first year of life. A baby shows such 'internalised' control when he arrests himself in the act of approaching a previously prohibited area or reaching for a forbidden object.

To an infant, an adult's commands and prohibitions are probably not at first semantically meaningful; rather he is likely to respond not so much to the verbal content of a command as to the tone of voice with which it is issued, and to accompanying facial expression, gesture, and posture. These, in the context of the baby's activity in progress and the situation as a whole, yield the crudely specific 'meaning' of the command. Often enough, however, compliance is achieved if he stops what he is doing or approaches the adult or both. It is our hypothesis that an infant is biased to respond to some signal properties of commands and prohibitions, and that he is predisposed to comply with these signals under most circumstances.

Obedience in the human infant is usually first observed about the time that his locomotion becomes effective and he is first capable of moving away from his mother or from where she has placed him. As his interest in his physical environment increases and he begins to venture away on his own initiative, his actions in an environment which may be filled with hazards unsuspected by him must, if he is to survive, be modifiable by signals given across some distance by his mother or other protective figure. Obedience to signals may thus be perceived to supplement attachment behaviour in fulfilling the biological function of protection,

114

and may be viewed as particularly useful in the context of infant exploration.

There are both situational and individual differences which affect the likelihood of occurrence of obedient behaviour. Perhaps of first importance is the degree of alarm and threat present in the situation. A mother who signals her infant in a very alarmed and excited (and therefore alarming) manner is more likely to arrest infant exploration and to activate proximity-seeking behaviour than is a placid mother who sends non-alarming signals. Particularly when an infant is preoccupied with exploration, the signal must be intense and urgent if it is to turn his attention back to his attachment figure. This expectation is consistent with the notion that an infant's behavioural systems operate in a dynamic equilibrium and sometimes compete with one another.

The matter of individual differences bears more directly upon attachment theory and the quality of the infant–mother relationship. It is our thesis that a disposition to be obedient, like other social dispositions, is an essential manifestation of the normal infant–mother attachment relationship. As the quality of a mother's care deviates from the degree of responsiveness to which an infant's attachment behaviours are pre-adapted, however, his attachment relationship will deviate from the norm, and anomalies may occur in his social development – including deviations from the norm of obedience.

Stayton, Hogan and Ainsworth (1971) undertook an analysis of the relationship between infant obedience and the quality of maternal care. This analysis was prompted by the impression that infants in our sample who had developed a secure attachment relationship, and who had therefore experienced harmonious relations with their mothers, tended to be compliant to maternal commands and prohibitions without specific training directed towards the learning of obedience. Framed as hypotheses, the expectations were that an infant whose mother is accepting, co-operative, and sensitive to signals will tend to obey her verbal commands and prohibitions more consistently than will an infant whose mother is rejecting, interfering, and insensitive, and that this tendency to comply is independent of the mother's specific socialisation tactics or disciplinary procedures.

The sample for this investigation was the same as that described in the crying study. The observations were also the naturalistic accounts of the home behaviour of the mother–infant pairs, which were made at three-week intervals for four hours throughout the first year of life. For the purposes of the obedience analysis, observations covering the period from age nine to twelve months were used.

The narrative reports were analysed for two infant behaviours:

compliance to commands and internalised controls. *Compliance to commands* was defined by the percentage of instances in which a baby heeded his mother's verbal commands. *Internalised controls* refers to self-inhibiting, self-controlling behaviour. Three groups were distinguished according to whether self-inhibition was clearly demonstrated, ambiguous, or never observed. Infant sex and I.Q. (Griffiths Scale of Mental Development) were also recorded.

Three maternal variables were coded from the narrative accounts to assess the extent to which the mother tried to train, discipline, and/or control the baby's behaviour: the frequency of verbal commands, the frequency of physical intervention, and floor freedom. The *frequency of verbal commands* refers to the mean number of commands and prohibitions issued by the mother per visit. The *frequency of physical intervention* refers to the mean number of discipline-oriented physical interventions by the mother per visit. This included instances of slapping the baby, dragging and jerking him away from things, and the like. *Floor freedom* refers to the degree to which a baby was permitted to be free on the floor or in a walker during his waking hours.

The quality of the mother's care was assessed by three scales: sensitivity–insensitivity, acceptance–rejection, and co-operation–interference. These scales were mentioned earlier in this chapter.[4]

The findings suggest that in the first year of life, an infant is more likely than not to obey his mother's commands. The group mean indicates that the infants in our sample complied 67 per cent of the time to their mother's commands. When mothers were divided into two groups depending on whether they were above or below the median in sensitivity, it was found that the infants of the more sensitive mothers obeyed 86 per cent of the time and infants of the less sensitive mothers obeyed 49 per cent of the time.

The maternal measures and infant variables were intercorrelated (Table 5) and then submitted to a principal components analysis (Table 6). The findings of most relevance here are that neither of the two disciplinary practices, the frequency of the mother's commands nor her physical interventions, were positively related to the measures of infant obedience. The three measures which assess the quality of the mother's care – sensitivity, acceptance, and co-operation – however, were positively related to compliance to commands and internalised controls.

Finally, internalised controls were not found to be significantly correlated with compliance to commands; none the less, internalised control is positively related to the three maternal variables of sensitivity, acceptance, and co-operation as well as to the amount of floor freedom per-

[4] The scale 'accessibility–ignoring' had not been applied at the time the obedience analysis was done.

116

Table 5   *Intercorrelations among maternal and infant variables*

Variables	1	2	3	4	5	6	7	8	9
Maternal variables									
1 Sensitivity–insensitivity									
2 Acceptance–rejection	91†								
3 Co-operation–inter- ference	87†	88†							
4 Verbal commands (frequency)	−14	−05	−35						
5 Physical interventions (frequency)	−44*	−38	−59†	62†					
6 Floor freedom (permission of)	07	00	10	−03	07				
Infant variables									
7 Sex	−28	−19	−11	−14	17	03			
8 I.Q.	46*	45*	44*	06	06	46*	20		
9 Internalised controls	40*	41*	42*	−15	−27	47*	18	52†	
10 Compliance to commands	63†	67†	62†	−08	−22	09	−14	38	35

Note. Decimals omitted.   *$p < 0.05$.   †$p < 0.01$.

Table 6   *Components matrix of maternal and infant variables*

Variables	Factors		
	I	II	III
Maternal variables			
1 Sensitivity–insensitivity	91	−12	−24
2 Acceptance–rejection	90	−09	−29
3 Co-operation–interference	93	−17	03
4 Verbal commands (frequency)	29	40	−77
5 Physical interventions (frequency)	−55	56	−46
6 Floor freedom (permission of)	23	67	25
Infant variables			
7 Sex	−14	42	53
8 I.Q.	58	66	−03
9 Internalised controls	61	47	32
10 Compliance to commands	74	02	−25

Note. Decimals omitted.

mitted the baby and the baby's I.Q. It is our hypothesis that the relationship between compliance to commands and internalised control may have been obscured because self-imposed control was observed in only 20 per cent of our sample and in only those infants most accelerated in cognitive development. This relationship should be explored in children old enough to demonstrate clearly the ability to have such internalised compliance. (The reader is referred to Stayton, Hogan and Ainsworth (1971) for a more detailed analysis of the findings.)

E

The findings suggest that a disposition toward obedience emerges in a responsive, accommodating social environment without extensive training, discipline, or other massive attempts to shape the infant's course of development. These findings cannot be predicted from models of socialization which assume that special intervention is necessary to modify the otherwise asocial tendencies of children. Clearly, these findings require a theory that assumes that an infant is initially inclined to be social and (somewhat later) ready to obey those persons who are most significant in his social environment (Stayton, Hogan and Ainsworth, 1971, pp. 1065–6).

The conclusions drawn from this study gain considerable support from the field studies of other species. Very early compliance to the mother's signals has been described in a wide variety of animals. There is no report of maternal efforts to train obedience; rather naturalistic observations suggest that infants are predisposed to respond to many signals characteristic of their species. McCann (1956), for example, observed wild mountain sheep and reports that when the mother gives a warning snort, the lamb drops immediately to the ground and remains motionless. Altmann (1963) described mother–infant alarm patterns in the moose and elk. When a dam moose freezes with angry bristling, her calf also freezes, ready to follow when she gives intention movements. In the case of the elk, the mother's warning bark causes the calf to drop back and hide.

Primates have more complex communication signals which usually consist of a constellation of vocalisation, gesture, and facial expression. For example, DeVore (1963) noted that a mother baboon may indicate that she is ready to walk away by a swift glance over the shoulder at the infant, by a slight lowering of her hindquarters, by a quick step directly away, or by some combination of these. On several occasions an infant was called down from a tree by his mother who thrust her face towards him, staring intently and lip-smacking loudly. Van Lawick-Goodall (1968) observed that a chimpanzee mother, wishing to move on, may gesture the infant to cling by touching him or gesturing with one or both arms. An alarmed mother may also signal with a 'hoo' whimper. Occasionally, an infant chimpanzee fails to respond when his mother gestures him to cling or to follow, but infants do not refuse to cling when their mothers are in a hurry or alarmed.

Thus, naturalistic studies of subhuman species suggest that the attachment bond between mother and infant disposes the infant to comply with his mother's signals. These studies have not yet focused on individual differences with regard to obedience. It is our thesis, however, that socialisation results from reciprocal mother–infant responsiveness. When the mother is less sensitive and less responsive to her infant than is expected in the social environment of evolutionary adaptedness, the infant more than likely will be less responsive and hence less compliant

118

to the signals of his mother and other social companions. Subhuman infants, as well as human, are affected by the quality of maternal care. However, since deviations in maternal behaviours and reciprocal infant behaviours may endanger a mother–infant pair in the wild, it is not surprising that individual differences are difficult to detect.

Our assumption that obedience is a behavioural predisposition does not exclude the importance of learning. Certainly, learning may facilitate or may even be required for some communications and commands to acquire signal value. Learning is probably a more important factor for humans than other species if only because humans possess such a complex communication system. Our position is that it is the *willingness to be obedient* rather than the understanding of the contents of the communication that is fostered by the attachment bond.

The relationship between obedience in infancy and later obedient acts has not been explored. The typical 'negativism' of the toddler suggests that a child will not always conform to demands of his parents no matter how loving and understanding they may continue to be. Factors such as intellectual competence, peer group, and cultural values begin to play more significant roles. None the less, a willingness to comply with the rules and values of others seems to mediate most social standards of conduct. It is our belief, then, that early attachment relationships must be considered for understanding the development and maintenance of mature moral behaviour.

IV   DISCUSSION

Both our attachment theory and our empirical findings portray an infant as social from the beginning. He does not need to be taught to be social. During his first three months of life he is more likely to cry when he is alone than when he is near his mother, and least likely to cry when he is actually being held by her. When he does cry, the most effective way to soothe him is to give him physical contact. He seems to be programmed to 'want' proximity and contact to judge by the fact that he is well equipped with signalling systems that promote these outcomes. It is in this sense that even the neonate may be described as social; he does not need to learn to signal for someone to come to him. These signalling systems, however, achieve their 'predictable' outcome only because they serve to activate approach and other appropriate behaviours in the adult. To the extent that there is reciprocity between a newborn's attachment behaviours and the behaviour of adult figures who have assumed the responsibility for his care, he may be described as integrated into a social world from the beginning, at least in a prototypical way appropriate to this early stage of development.

119

The success of this early 'integration' seems to depend very largely upon the extent to which his mother figure and/or other figures close to him are programmed (whether through genetic underpinnings or experience or a combination of both) to respond to his repertoire of behavioural signals. To be sure, it must be acknowledged that neonates differ from the beginning in their behavioural repertoire, so that some perhaps signal more effectively than others. But in our sample of normal, healthy infants we found some evidence (as illustrated in our report of infant crying) that differences in infant behaviour seem to be more influenced by maternal responsiveness than does maternal behaviour seem to be influenced by infant characteristics.

Although an implicit assumption of many theoretical explanations of socialisation is that the child is basically asocial, the main thrust of the concept of 'socialisation' is that the natural behavioural dispositions of a child must be altered – whether curbed, redirected, or eradicated – if he is to be integrated eventually as a desirable participant in an adult social world. There is no question that the prototypical integration of the newborn into a loving and protective family must give way gradually to integration into a widening social world at progressively more mature levels. The question is how this 'socialisation' process may best be achieved. According to the most widely held views, it is to be achieved either through consistent efforts by caretakers to train him or to condition him (thus bringing his behaviour under effective environmental control) or through his own efforts to do what is expected of him for fear of losing parental affection. (There are other sophisticated views – such as socialisation through identification – that are not covered by this simple generalisation, but they have had relatively less influence upon childrearing procedures in Western society than have the 'training' and 'loss of love' views.)

A major implication of our findings is contrary to these widely held views, at least in so far as the first year of life is concerned. We have shown that specific efforts to train an infant, or otherwise consciously to push him into the desirable behavioural mould, tend to prolong behaviour deemed to be changeworthy, whereas to accept him as he is, to respect his natural behavioural patterns as valid, to be accessible to him and to respond sensitively to his signals tends to facilitate the development of the kinds of behaviours commonly believed to be desirable in infancy. Specifically, we have reported that maternal responsiveness to infant crying tends significantly to reduce the frequency and duration of crying throughout the first year, and that maternal acceptance, cooperation, and sensitivity to signals are strongly related both to infant compliance with maternal commands and with the beginnings of 'internalisation' of prohibitions.

120

Further evidence is emerging from our study as analysis of data proceeds, although this is as yet unpublished. For example, it has been found that mothers who give relatively much physical contact to their infants in their earliest months, and especially mothers who give relatively long and 'well-rounded' holding during an episode of contact have infants who by the end of the first year not only enjoy active affectional interaction when in contact but also are content to be put down and turn cheerfully to exploratory and play activity (Ainsworth, Bell and Stayton, 1972). To have given the contact that a baby seems programmed to promote does not make him into a clingy and dependent one-year-old; on the contrary, it facilitates the gradual growth of independence. It is infants who have had relatively brief episodes of being held who tend to protest being put down, and who do not turn readily to independent play; indeed they seem highly ambivalent about physical contact – they may seek it, but they do not respond positively to it when they get it, and yet when put down they protest.

Another piece of evidence comes from an analysis of infant responses to mothers' everyday departures from the room in the familiar home environment (Stayton and Ainsworth, 1973; Stayton, Ainsworth and Main, 1973). Babies who have experienced sensitively responsive mothering do not, in the second half of the first year, protest consistently when their mothers leave the room; they are more likely to follow her than they are to cry; they can tolerate her brief and accustomed absences in a familiar environment as though they had confidence that they knew where to find her if they wished and trusted that she would soon return in any case. (In a strange environment, however, they tended to protest mother's departure, and to have attachment behaviour strongly activated both during her absence and upon her return (Ainsworth, Bell and Stayton, 1971).) Babies who had experienced relatively insensitive mothering tended to be more intolerant of everyday separations in the home environment; they were the ones who did not want to let mother out of sight and who were more frequently distressed by her departures.

Both the normative trends and the individual differences in our sample are congruent with the evolutionary implications of our attachment-theory model. An essential focus of this model is the protective function of attachment behaviours and reciprocal maternal behaviours, and equally essential corollaries are the advantage of an interlocking balance between these behaviours and infant exploratory behaviour and the close relationship between them and fear behaviours. It is of survival advantage for an infant to emit signals that draw adults to him and activate their protective and other caretaking behaviours. It is advantageous also that he rapidly develop various active modes of seeking proximity and contact on his own account, to supplement his repertoire of signals. It is not only of immediate survival advantage but also in the interests of his integration into a wider social group that he expand his repertoire beyond simple signals such as crying and smiling to include other modes of communication, such as varied facial expressions, gestures, and non-crying vocalisations, also including intentional communications eventually embracing language. It is a finding of very considerable interest that maternal responsiveness to the more primitive signals including crying promotes the development of a wider repertoire of communication.

The survival advantage for an infant of both crying and other later forms of communication[5] is illuminated by an attempt to picture an

---

[5] Here we are considering other modes of communication only as they may be viewed as substituting for crying and as serving the same function, namely, protection through bringing the mother into closer proximity. The relationship between communication and attachment is a complex one. Since attachment behaviours promote proximity between an infant and his mother, they also promote interaction between them and thus the gradual development of more complex communication. As an infant's attachment behaviour becomes organised on a goal-corrected basis, not only do its separate components become more or less interchangeable, but also the primitive set-goal of contact or close proximity may change to permit communication across some distance to substitute for other behaviours. Thus, for example, conversation or exchanges of facial or bodily gestures may take the place of crying or smiling and meet the requirements of a new set-goal operating occasionally and in non-alarming situations, that specifies communication rather than increased proximity. Communication, although it may serve attachment, and although its development may have been facilitated by an attachment relationship, is by no means specific to attachment. Just as locomotion may be implicated in exploration, in attack, in flight, and in food seeking, as well as in approach to an attachment figure, communication may serve many purposes.

The substantial proportion of time an infant or young child spends in close proximity to his mother provides him with much opportunity for learning not only communication but also other social and cognitive skills. Since such skills are obviously very useful in fitting him to play a more mature role in the society in which he lives, some have suggested that the biological function of attachment behaviour is the provision of opportunity to learn rather than protection. Bowlby (1969, pp. 223–8) acknowledged that both protection and opportunity for learning contribute to survival, but cited evidence that makes it seem likely that protection is that consequence of infant–mother proximity which, in the course of evolution, led attachment behaviour to be incorporated into the biological equipment of a species. His argument will not be repeated here. In addition to the points he raises, however, we would add that attachment theory holds that attachment behaviour becomes organised toward one or a few specific figures, and this makes sense when its function is viewed as protection.

It is an open question whether opportunity to learn is of necessity greater when a child is with an attachment figure rather than with other adults or with peers as playmates. On one hand, it seems likely that the behaviour of an attachment figure is more often contingent upon his own behaviour than that of a peer-playmate or unfamiliar adult and thus facilitates learning, and that an attachment figure is a more potent model for observation learning or imitation. Furthermore, a child is likely to learn most from interaction with that figure with whom he spends the most time, and in infancy his attachment behaviour and reciprocal maternal behaviour may lead him to spend most time near his mother. On the other hand a child can ob-

infant in the original environment in which man is believed to have evolved, in which relatively much time may be presumed to have been spent away from shelters and relatively much on the open ground where predators and other dangers were not unlikely. In such an environment it would be advantageous for an infant to emit clear signals – and soon more varied communications – whenever alone, alarmed, or in general distressed, and for a mother to respond to these by coming to him promptly. It would be advantageous for an infant to redouble his crying should his mother ignore him at first. On the other hand, a crying infant might attract the attention of predators, so it would be even more advantageous for his mother quickly to come to quiet him. Finally, it seems adaptive for an infant to come to reserve crying for the more alarming of the situations he encounters, and to use less urgent modes of communication otherwise – as elucidated in the folktale of the boy who cried 'Wolf!' too often.

As an infant develops locomotion and can actively approach novel features of his environment to examine them more closely and to manipulate them, signals across a distance become perhaps even more important than before. But at this point of development it becomes clearly more urgent than previously for an infant to respond to his mother's signals. If he did not so respond, his mother could not fulfil a protective role if she allowed him out of arm's reach. Of course, should the child become alarmed by some novel or otherwise frightening or painful feature of his environment his attachment behaviour would be elicited, and he would seek proximity to his mother. But natural clues to danger (cf. Bowlby, 1973) do not cover all dangerous contingencies, and an adult's experience may be a safer guide than a baby's predispositions to respond to certain clues such as loud noises, looming objects, and the like. Under these circumstances it is of obvious survival

---

viously learn through observation of or interaction with figures to whom he is not attached. Furthermore, the behaviour patterns resulting from learning – communication *qua* communication, and other social and cognitive skills – are to a large extent non-specific as to figure. Therefore, it is not clear that the tie-in of opportunity to learn with infant–mother attachment is more than coincidental. Infant–mother attachment may ensure proximity that is a necessary condition for much useful learning, but a child, once his behaviour has become organised on a goal-corrected basis, does not seek out an attachment figure as providing an opportunity to learn with the same specificity or with the same urgency with which he seeks proximity to such a figure when alarmed.

Attachment theory cannot pretend to encompass all that is coincident with or contingent upon attachment. On the other hand, there is no essential incompatibility between the attachment model and other models that seek to throw light on the development of cognitive processes and the learning of the many culture-specific skills that are of undoubted significance in facilitating a child's becoming eventually a competent adult, well equipped to participate in the specific society into which he happens to be born.

advantage if the adult can control an infant's behaviour across a distance, inducing him either to stop his activity or to come quickly back or both in sequence. It is probably not mere coincidence that in the human infant locomotion, attachment, and compliance to parental signals develop at about the same time in the second half of the first year of life. As pointed out earlier, it is likely that the infant responds to commands that convey an alarming urgency, and that comprehension of verbal content comes later. Despite the tendency for infants whose mothers had been relatively responsive and sensitive to heed such commands more readily than those whose mothers had been relatively insensitive, the incidence in our sample of compliance – irrespective of maternal efforts to enforce obedience – was so great as to support the hypothesis that it is a natural outcome of attachment that an infant tends to comply with the signals received from an attachment figure. This implies that there is an initial 'willingness' to comply upon which 'socialisation' can build. A child does not have to learn a desire to be obedient, at least not initially, even though he may have later to learn much of the specific content of what is expected of him. How he learns this after the end of the first year of life we cannot say from our observations; this is a significant area for further research.

Let us turn now to the implications of our unpublished findings relevant to physical contact and response to separation. These too are congruent with our model. Despite the programming we infer that an infant has to achieve proximity and contact with a conspecific, it would be disadvantageous for his development if he continued to seek to be close to his mother figure and failed to explore and to learn about his environment. In this light, it is altogether reasonable to find that infants who have enjoyed relatively much physical contact early in the first year – and, according to our findings, physical contact that is tender, affectionate, and unhurried, rather than abrupt, inadequate, and brief – are most likely by nine months of age to demand relatively little contact under ordinary circumstances and to accept cheerfully being put down where they can turn to independent exploration and play. It seems a misconception to believe that 'independence' must be deliberately fostered; it seems clear, not only from our studies but also from field studies of non-human primates that an infant is biased to leave his mother to explore the world as soon as he is able. It is true that in the rhesus macaque and in the baboon (Hinde, 1969; DeVore, 1963) maternal rejection is conspicuous in pushing offspring towards independence and away from clinging in later infancy. But such rejection has not been observed in apes (e.g. van Lawick-Goodall, 1968) and it was not observed in our sample in most of the infants who were content to be put down.

Perhaps our findings in regard to separation anxiety may have seemed incongruent with our model at first glance. It is well established that the departure of the mother, especially if it be sudden or in a strange environment, tends dependably to activate behaviour that brings an infant into close proximity with his mother as soon as can be. If we consider only attachment behaviour and its biological function, it seems obvious that it is indeed adaptive for attachment behaviour to be activated by separation. On the other hand, if we consider the desirable dynamic balance between attachment and exploratory behaviour, our findings emerge as not at all paradoxical. If an infant is to be freed for exploration and learning, it would be disadvantageous if he were so constantly concerned about his mother's whereabouts that he dared not let her leave his side under any circumstances. In a familiar environment, in which presumably danger is minimised, it would be advantageous for an infant to widen the range of his set-goal for proximity (Bowlby, 1969), and to pursue his own autonomous activities without undue disturbance as long as his mother moves about through a known and expected range. On the other hand, it is certainly advantageous for his immediate survival, if he mobilises rapidly his proximity-seeking behaviour if his mother should move off in a strange environment, under unaccustomed circumstances, or beyond her usual range. Similarly, it may be viewed as advantageous for an infant whose mother seems to him to move unpredictably and inconsistently (and whom he has not been able to learn to trust) to monitor her movements with exceptional alertness and to evince disturbance whenever she moves off quickly or out of sight.

It has been impossible to avoid acknowledgement of individual differences, even while emphasising the course that an infant's development seems 'programmed' to take. Individual differences were substantial even in our normal white middle-class sample of babies – and also in Ainsworth's (1967) Ganda sample. Their prominence serves as a reminder that species-characteristic behaviours are adapted to certain features of the environment, and draws attention to the general principle that to the extent that the present environment differs from the environment of evolutionary adaptedness the behaviours in question may fail to fulfil the function for which they have been evolved. Even though some degree of environmental lability may be inherent in certain of these behaviours – and of course here we have attachment behaviours in mind – too great a discrepancy between the present environment and the environment to which the behaviours were originally adapted may occasion developmental anomalies. In regard to attachment, it is clear that the kind of interaction an infant has with his attachment figure(s) shapes the course of development of his attachment behaviours and, in time, the way these are organised together into his attachment relationship(s). It may be

125

considered an anomaly of development should an infant explore too intrepidly without due concern for the whereabouts of an attachment figure, should he be so anxious about the whereabouts and intentions of an attachment figure that he dare not leave 'home base' to explore his environment, or, indeed, should he not develop an attachment relationship with any figure. Even short of these potentially dangerous or grossly inhibiting anomalies, certain kinds of behaviour linked to insecure attachment relationships (e.g. ambivalence) may hamper a child in becoming integrated into his social world – in becoming 'socialised'.

We have found that an infant becomes well-socialised if he has enjoyed a harmonious attachment relationship with his mother figure. The picture is one of mutual co-operation – or reciprocal responsiveness to signals. The mother has accepted the baby and responsibility for his care, despite the fact that he interferes with her other activities. She respects his autonomy as a separate individual and indeed enjoys noticing his individuality and the ways in which he asserts his wishes. She remains consistently accessible to him – or is careful to provide adequate substitute care when she feels she cannot be there. She is sensitively aware of his signals, and responds to them promptly. Infants naturally respond to such mothers co-operatively, and become increasingly responsive to the signal qualities of maternal behaviour. Rather than becoming 'spoiled' or overdependent, these infants can best be characterised as secure. They tend to cry little, to be affectionate and unambivalent towards the mother, to explore and play eagerly on their own, and to obey her commands. In short, they come to exhibit a desirable balance between independent competence and harmonious interaction with others.

Clearly, the fear of 'spoiling' a child by responding to his signals is not borne out by our data. An infant who might be labelled 'spoiled' is fussy, demanding, unco-operative, and generally difficult to handle. This label is more appropriate for infants in our sample whose mothers have been insensitive to signals, unduly interfering with infant activity, rejecting, punitive, and/or inaccessible. Closely connected with the fear of spoiling is a fear of fostering overdependence in a child, and also a fear that a child whose signals are heeded may gain tyrannical control over his mother. Associated with this fear also is the apprehension that babies who have been responded to may become children who are unable to understand and to respect the point of view of others.

Since our investigations have focused on the first year of life, we cannot with assurance state that secure attachment relationships in the first year guarantee a continuance of co-operative and 'socialised' interaction – but we hypothesise that they are likely to do so provided that maternal co-operation does not undergo an abrupt change. Certainly in the first year independence seems fostered rather than hampered by a secure and harmonious attachment relationship, whereas 'overdependence' seems a product of insensitive mothering. Also in the first year sensitive mothering seems to make an infant progressively less demanding rather than more so. Finally, much of the basis of the security of a one-year-old seems to be that he can trust his mother – that he can anticipate her actions, her absences and her returns, and her response to his communications – whereas much of the insecurity of the fussy, ambivalent and demanding one-year-old seems due to the fact that his mother is unpredictable. It seems reasonable to suppose that trust in the predictability of an attachment figure is the first step towards understanding the motivations and set-goals of that figure – a clear step away from 'egocentricity' and towards empathy and understanding and respecting of another's point of view. On the other hand, a figure who is unpredictable is impossible to understand.

Perhaps the long-standing uncertainty about the causes of spoiling and continuation of egocentricity has been based upon a widespread failure to perceive the biological function of infant behaviours that constitute an inconvenience to the adult caretaker. Crying, demands for contact, intolerance of separation, and other such phenomena have been widely viewed as changeworthy behaviours. Although it has been asknowledged that a young infant is helpless and defenceless, he has also been viewed as infinitely malleable. To be sure, one great asset of the human species is the environmental lability of his behaviours, but this lability is not unlimited. It is when we set aside our admiration of human flexibility, and our concern with moulding and changing behaviour, and begin to study a child's development in his naturalistic setting, that we come to appreciate both the fact that changeworthy behaviours have a significant function and that development proceeds optimally when an infant's caretakers provide an environment for his development which does not depart in important respects from the environment to which the behavioural equipment of the infant of the species is adapted. Of course, only research can identify the limits of variation in the infant-care environment that hamper social development or, in the extreme, produce developmental anomalies that are difficult to reverse.

APPENDIX. SENSITIVITY VERSUS INSENSITIVITY TO THE BABY'S COMMUNICATIONS

This variable deals with the mother's ability to perceive and to interpret accurately the signals and communications implicit in her infant's behaviour, and given this understanding, to respond to them appropriately and promptly. Thus the mother's sensitivity has four essential components: (*a*) her awareness of the signals; (*b*) an accurate interpretation of them; (*c*) an appropriate response to them; and (*d*) a prompt response to them. Let us consider each of these in turn.

The mother's awareness of her baby's signals and communications has two aspects. The first is the same as the issue covered in the scale 'accessibility versus ignoring and neglecting'. In other words, the mother must be reasonably accessible to the baby's communications before she can be sensitive to them. Accessibility is a necessary condition for sensitive awareness. It is not a sufficient condition, however, for a mother can maintain the 'baby' in her field of awareness without fulfilling the other condition for sensitive awareness. The second aspect of awareness may be described in terms of 'thresholds'. The most sensitive mother – the one with the lowest threshold – is alert to the baby's most subtle, minimal, understated cues. Mothers with higher thresholds seem to perceive only the most blatant and obvious communications. Mothers with the highest thresholds seem often oblivious, and are, in effect, highly inaccessible. This second aspect is very closely related to the question of interpretation of the baby's signals, for usually the mother who is alert to minimal cues also interprets them correctly. This is not invariably the case, however. For example, some mothers are alert to the slightest mouth movements, and sometimes incorrectly interpret them as hunger – or they notice minimal tensions or restlessness and incorrectly interpret them as fatigue.

The mother's ability to interpret accurately her baby's communications has three main components: (*a*) her awareness, as previously discussed; (*b*) her freedom from distortion; and (*c*) her empathy. An inattentive, 'ignoring' mother is, of course, often unable to interpret correctly the baby's signals when they break through her obliviousness, for she has been unaware of the prodromal signs and of the temporal context of the behaviour. But even a mother who is highly aware and accessible may misinterpret signals because her perception is distorted by projection, denial, or other marked defensive operations. Mothers who have distorted perceptions tend to bias their 'reading' of their babies according to their own wishes, moods, and fantasies. For example, a mother not wishing to attend to her baby might interpret his fussy bids for attention as fatigue and, therefore, put him to bed; she being in a hurry, might perceive any slowing down in the rate of feeding as a sign of satiation; or a mother who is somewhat rejecting of her infant might perceive him as rejecting and aggressive towards herself. Mothers who least distort their perceptions of their babies have some insight as to their own wishes and moods, and thus can more realistically judge the baby's behaviour. Furthermore, they are usually aware of how their own behaviour and moods affect their infant's behaviour.

128

The mother must be able to empathise with her baby's feelings and wishes before she can respond with sensitivity. That is, a mother might be quite aware of and understand accurately the baby's behaviour and the circumstances leading to her baby's distress or demands, but because she is unable to empathise with him – unable to see things from the baby's point of view – she may try to tease him back into good humour, mock him, laugh at him, or just ignore him. The mother's egocentricity and lack of empathy may also lead to detached, intellectual responses to the baby rather than to warm sensitive interactions with him.

A high threshold of awareness and inaccurate perceptions certainly lead to insensitive responses. Nevertheless, the mother may be highly aware and accurate in her interpretation and still be insensitive. Therefore, in the last analysis, the appropriateness and promptness of the mother's response to communications are the hallmarks of sensitivity.

The quality of the mother's interaction with her infant is probably the most important index of her sensitivity. It is essential that the mother's responses be *appropriate* to the situation and to the baby's communications. Often enough, at least in the first year of life, the sensitive mother gives the baby what his communications suggest he wants. She responds socially to his attempts to initiate social interaction, playfully to his attempts to initiate play. She picks him up when he seems to wish it, and put him down when he wants to explore. When he is distressed, she knows what kind and degree of soothing he requires to comfort him – and she knows that sometimes a few words or a distraction will be all that is needed. When he is hungry she sees that he soon gets something to eat, perhaps giving him a snack if she does not want to give him his regular meal right away. On the other hand, the mother who responds inappropriately tries to socialise with the baby when he is hungry, play with him when he is tired, or feed him when he is trying to initiate social interaction.

In play and social stimulation, the mother who responds appropriately to her child does not overstimulate him by interacting in too intense, too vigorous, too prolonged, or too exciting a manner. She can perceive and accurately interpret the signs of over-excitement, undue tension, or incipient distress and shifts the tempo or intensity before things have gone too far. Similarly, she is unlikely to underestimate the child, because she picks up and responds to the signals he gives when he is bored or when he wants more interaction than has heretofore been forthcoming.

In the second year of life, and sometimes also towards the end of the first year, it is maximally appropriate for the mother to respond to the baby's signals not so much in accordance with what he ostensibly wants as in terms of a compromise between this and what will make him feel most secure, competent, comfortable, etc., in the long run. This is a tricky judgement to make, for so much that is done 'for the baby's own good' is done both contrary to his wishes and according to the mother's convenience, whim, or preconceived standards. Nevertheless there are situations in which limit-setting, even in the first year, clears the air even though it is initially contrary to the baby's wishes. Similarly there are situations in which the baby's signals might lead the mother to increase the tempo of interaction to the point of discomfort for him, and in which it is appropriate gradually to diminish intensity. Furthermore, there is a fine point of balance at which the mother can begin to show that baby that she is not an instrument of his will, but a co-operative partner whose participation must be elicited appropriately. In such instances the mother will slightly frustrate the baby's imperious demands but warmly encourage (and reward) behaviours which are inviting or requesting rather than demanding. Nevertheless in such interactions the sensitive mother acknowledges the baby's wishes even though she does not unconditionally accede to them. The chief point is that a sensitive, appropriate response does not invariably imply complete compliance to the baby's wish – although very frequently compliance may be the most appropriate response.

The final feature of appropriate interaction is that it is well-resolved, or well-rounded and completed. For example, when the baby seeks contact the sensitive mother holds him long enough to satisfy him, so that when he is put down he does not immediately seek to be picked up again. When he needs soothing, she soothes him thoroughly, so he is quite recovered and cheerful. When he seeks social interaction she enters into a more or less prolonged exchange with him, after which, often enough, he is content to entertain himself. In contrast, some mothers with low sensitivity seem to be fragmented and incomplete; these mothers may try a series of interventions as though searching for the best method or solution. Highly sensitive mothers have completed, easily and well-resolved interactions.

Finally, there is the issue of the *promptness* of the mother's response to the baby's communication. A response, however appropriate, which is so delayed that it cannot be perceived by the baby as contingent upon his communication cannot be linked by him to his own signal. On the assumption that it is a good thing for a baby to gain some feeling of efficacy – and eventually to feel cumulatively a 'sense of competence' in controlling his social environment – it seems a part of sensitivity to acknowledge the baby's signals in some effective way and to indicate that one is at least preparing to accede to them. During the first quarter of the first year, a mother's sensitivity is most easily judged by her latency in response to the baby's distress signals such as hunger. However, during the last quarter, the mother's prompt response to the baby's social communication and signals is probably a more critical measure. A mother is inevitably insensitive when she fails to respond to the baby's outstretched arms, to his excited greeting, or simply to his smile or gentle touch.

An issue which cuts across the various components of sensitivity concerns the timing of routine activities and play. In general, arbitrary or very rigid timing of major interactions cannot but be insensitive to the infant's signals, moods, and rhythms. The mother who arranges and organises day-by-day activities with her infant in order to most convenience herself, or the mother who thinks by the clock, has little or no consideration of the infant's tempo and current state.

In summary, highly sensitive mothers are usually accessible to their infants and are aware of even their more subtle communications, signals, wishes, and moods; in addition, these mothers accurately interpret their perceptions and show empathy with their infants. The sensitive mother, armed with this understanding and empathy, can time her interactions well and deal with her baby so that her interactions seem appropriate – appropriate in kind as well as in quality – and prompt. In contrast, mothers with low sensitivity are not aware of much of their infant's behaviour either because they ignore the baby or they fail to perceive in his activity the more subtle and hard-to-detect communications. Furthermore, insensitive mothers often do not understand those aspects of their infant's behaviour of which they are aware or else they distort it. A mother may have somewhat accurate perceptions of her infant's activity and moods but may be unable to empathise with him. Through either lack of understanding or empathy, mothers with low sensitivity improperly time their responses, either in terms of scheduling or in terms of promptness to the baby's communications. Further, mothers with low sensitivity often have inappropriate responses in kind as well as in quantity, i.e. interactions which are fragmented and poorly resolved.

9 *Highly sensitive.* This mother is exquisitely attuned to B's signals, and responds to them promptly and appropriately. She is able to see things from B's point of view; her perceptions of his signals and communications are not distorted by her own needs and defences. She 'reads' B's signals and communications skilfully, and knows what the meaning is of even his subtle, minimal, and understated cues. She nearly always gives B what he indicates what he wants, although perhaps not invariably so. When she feels that it is best not to comply with his demands – for example, when he is too excited, over-imperious, or wants something he should not have – she is tactful in acknowledging his communication and in offering an acceptable alternative. She has

'well-rounded' interactions with B, so that the transaction is smoothly completed and both she and B feel satisfied. Finally, she makes her responses temporally contingent upon B's signals and communications.

7 *Sensitive*. This mother also interprets B's communications accurately, and responds to them promptly and appropriately – but with less sensitivity than mothers with higher ratings. She may be less attuned to B's more subtle behaviours than the highly sensitive mother. Or, perhaps because she is less skilful in dividing her attention between B and competing demands, she may sometimes 'miss her cues'. B's clear and definite signals are, however, neither missed nor misinterpreted. This mother empathises with B and sees things from his point of view; her perceptions of his behaviour are not distorted. Perhaps because her perception is less sensitive than that of mothers with higher ratings, her responses are not as consistently prompt or as finely appropriate – but although there may be occasional little 'mismatches', M's interventions and interactions are never seriously out of tune with B's tempo, state and communications.

5 *Inconsistently sensitive*. Although this mother can be quite sensitive on occasion, there are some periods in which she is insensitive to B's communications. M's inconsistent sensitivity may occur for any one of several reasons, but the outcome is that she seems to have lacunae in regard to her sensitive dealings with B – being sensitive at some times or in respect to some aspects of his experience, but not in others. Her awareness of B may be intermittent – often fairly keen, but sometimes impervious. Or her perception of B's behaviour may be distorted in regard to one or two aspects although it is accurate in other important aspects. She may be prompt and appropriate in response to his communications at some times and in most respects, but either inappropriate or slow at other times and in other respects. On the whole, however, she is more frequently sensitive than insensitive. What is striking is that a mother who can be as sensitive as she is on so many occasions can be so insensitive on other occasions.

3 *Insensitive*. This mother frequently fails to respond to B's communications appropriately and/or promptly, although she may on some occasions show capacity for sensitivity in her responses to and interactions with B. Her insensitivity seems linked to inability to see things from B's point of view. She may be too frequently preoccupied with other things and therefore inaccessible to his signals and communications, or she may misperceive his signals and interpret them inaccurately because of her own wishes or defences, or she may know well enough

132

what B is communicating but be disinclined to give him what he wants – because it is inconvenient or she is not in the mood for it, or because she is determined not to 'spoil' him. She may delay an otherwise appropriate response to such an extent that it is no longer contingent upon his signal, and indeed perhaps is no longer appropriate to his state, mood, or activity. Or she may respond with seeming appropriateness to B's communications but break off the transactions before B is satisfied, so that their interactions seem fragmented and incomplete or her responses perfunctory, half-hearted, or impatient. Despite such clear evidence of insensitivity, however, this mother is not as consistently or pervasively insensitive as mothers with even lower ratings. Therefore, when the baby's own wishes, moods, and activity are not too deviant from the mother's wishes, moods, and household responsibilities or when the baby is truly distressed or otherwise very forceful and compelling in his communication, this mother can modify her own behaviour and goals, at this time, can show some sensitivity in her handling of the child.

1 *Highly insensitive.* The extremely insensitive mother seems geared almost exclusively to her own wishes, moods, and activity. That is, M's interventions and initiations of interaction are prompted or shaped largely by signals within herself; if they mesh with B's signals, this is often no more than coincidence. This is not to say that M never responds to B's signals; for sometimes she does if the signals are intense enough, prolonged enough or often enough repeated. The delay in response is in itself insensitive. Furthermore, since there is usually a disparity between M's own wishes and activity and B's signals, M, who is geared largely to her own signals, routinely ignores or distorts the meaning of B's behaviour. Thus, when M responds to B's signals, her response is characteristically inappropriate in kind, or fragmented and incomplete.

REFERENCES

Ainsworth, M. D. S. (1967). *Infancy in Uganda: Infant Care and the Growth of Love.* Baltimore, Johns Hopkins Univ. Press.

Ainsworth, M. D. S. (1969). Object relations, dependency and attachment: a theoretical review of the infant–mother relationship. *Child Development*, **40**, 969–1025.

Ainsworth, M. D. S. (1972). Attachment and dependency: a comparison. In Gewitz, J. L. (ed.). *Attachment and Dependency.* Washington, D.C., V. H. Winston and Son (Distributed by Wiley, New York.)

Ainsworth, M. D. S. (1973). The development of infant–mother attachment. In Caldwell, B. M. and Ricciuti, H. N. (eds.). *Review of Child Development Research*, Vol. 3. Chicago, Univ. Chicago Press.

Ainsworth, M. D. S. and Bell, S. M. (1970). Attachment, exploration and separation: illustrated by the behaviour of one-year-olds in a strange situation. *Child Development,* **41**, 49–67.

Ainsworth, M. D. S. and Witting, B. A. (1969). Attachment and exploratory behavior of one-year-olds in a strange situation. In Foss, B. M. (ed.). *Determinants of Infant Behaviour*, Vol. 4. London, Methuen.

Ainsworth, M. D. S., Bell, S. M. and Stayton, D. J. (1971). Individual differences in strange situation behavior of one-year-olds. In Schaffer, H. R. (ed.). *The Origins of Human Social Relations.* London, Academic Press.

Ainsworth, M. D. S., Bell, S. M. and Stayton, D. J. (1972). Individual differences in the development of some attachment behaviors. *Merrill-Palmer Quart.* **18**, 123–43.

Altmann, M. (1963). Naturalistic studies of maternal care in moose and elk. In Rheingold, H. L. (ed.). *Maternal Behavior in Mammals.* New York, Wiley.

Arsenian, J. M. (1943). Young children in an insecure situation. *J. abnorm. soc. Psychol.* **38**, 225–49.

Bell, S. M. and Ainsworth, M. D. S. (1972). Infant crying and maternal responsiveness. *Child Development,* **43**, 1171–90.

Bowlby, J. (1958). The nature of the child's tie to his mother. *Int. J. Psychoanal.* **39**, 350–73.

Bowlby, J. (1969). *Attachment and Loss*, Vol. 1, *Attachment.* London, Hogarth Press.

Bowlby, J. (1973). *Attachment and Loss*, Vol. 2, *Separation.* London, Hogarth Press.

Cox, F. N. and Campbell, D. (1968). Young children in a new situation with and without their mothers. *Child Development* **39**, 123–31.

DeVore, I. (1963). Mother–infant relations in free-ranging baboons. In Rheingold, H. L. (ed.). *Maternal Behavior in Mammals.* New York, Wiley.

Harlow, H. F. (1958). The nature of love. *Amer. Psychol.* **13**, 673–83.

Harlow, H. F. (1961). The development of affectional patterns in infant monkeys. In Foss, B. M. (ed.). *Determinants of Infant Behaviour*, Vol. 1. London, Methuen.

Harlow, H. F. (1963). The maternal affectional system. In Foss, B. M. (ed.). *Determinants of Infant Behaviur*, Vol. 2. London, Methuen.

Harlow, H. F. and Harlow, M. K. (1965). The affectional systems. In Schrier, A. M., Harlow, H. F. and Stollnitz, F. (eds.). *Behavior of Nonhuman Primates*, Vol. 2. New York, Academic Press.

Hinde, R. A. (1969). Analyzing the roles of the partners in a behavioral interaction – mother–infant relations in rhesus macaques. *Ann. N. Y. Acad. Sci.* **159**, 651–67.

Hinde, R. A. and Spencer-Booth, Y. (1967). The behaviour of socially-living rhesus monkeys in their first two and a half years. *Anim. Behav.* **15**, 169–96.

Hinde, R. A., Rowell, T. E. and Spencer-Booth, Y. (1964). Behavior of socially-living rhesus monkeys in their first six months. *Proc. Zool. Soc. Lond.* **143**, 609–49.

Lawick-Goodall, J. van (1968). The behaviour of free-living chimpanzees in the Gombe Stream Reserve. *Anim. Behav. Monog.* **1**, part 3.

McCann, L. J. (1956). Ecology of the mountain sheep. *Am. Midl. Nat.* **56**, 297–324.

Piaget, J. (1936). *The Origins of Intelligence in Children* (2nd ed. 1952). New York, Internat. Univ. Press.

Piaget, J. (1937). *The Construction of Reality in the Child* (2nd ed. 1954). New York, Basic Books.

Rheingold, H. L. (1969). The effect of a strange environment on the behavior of infants. In Foss, B. M. (ed.). *Determinants of Infant Behaviour*, Vol. 4. London, Methuen.

Rheingold, H. L. and Eckerman, C. O. (1970). The infant separates himself from his mother. *Science*, **168**, 78–83.

Southwick, C. H., Beg, M. A. and Siddiqi, M. R. (1965). Rhesus monkeys in North India. In DeVore, I. (ed.). *Primate Behavior: Field Studies of Monkeys and Apes*. New York, Holt, Rinehart and Winston.

Stayton, D. J. and Ainsworth, M. D. S. (1973). Individual differences in infant responses to brief, everyday separations as related to other infant and maternal behaviors. *Developmental Psychology*, **9**, 226–35

Stayton, D. J., Ainsworth, M. D. S. and Main, M. B. (1973). Development of separation behavior in the first year of life: Protest, following, and greeting. *Developmental Psychology*, **9**, 213–25

Stayton, D. J., Hogan, R. T. and Ainsworth, M. D. S. (1971). Infant obedience and maternal behavior: the origins of socialization reconsidered. *Child Development*, **42**, 1057–69.

U.S. Children's Bureau Publications (1926). *Infant Care*, Washington, D.C., U.S. Government Publications.

7

The institution as an environment for development

Jack and Barbara Tizard

In industrial societies the proportion of children who are brought up in residential institutions during the whole, or for substantial parts, of their childhood is considerable. King (1970) has estimated that out of a population of 11.5 million children under the age of sixteen years in England and Wales in 1963, there were 146 500 who were 'deprived of a normal home life'. Of these approximately 78 000 were 'deprived' children in the care of local authorities or voluntary agencies and a further 15 000 were 'protected' children in foster homes for reward or adoption. Delinquent children in approved schools or remand homes numbered over 10 000, and handicapped children in special boarding schools nearly 24 000. A further 19 000 handicapped children were in hospitals or mental subnormality units. In all, they amounted to 1.3 per cent of the child population.

Though very substantial numbers of children are admitted to temporary care by local authorities and voluntary agencies because of mother's confinement or some family crisis, the very great majority of children actually in care at any one time are long-stay cases who have been away from home for more than six months. On 31 March 1963 long-stay cases made up 93 per cent of the total in residence (Packman, 1968).

Nearly half of all children admitted to the care of local authorities and voluntary organisations are boarded out in private families, but the remainder live in residential institutions, as do the great majority of handicapped and delinquent children classified by King (1970) as deprived of a normal home life. In 1963, and indeed today, the total number of such children in long-stay institutional care must have been 80 000–90 000, many of whom would spend the whole of their childhood in establishments staffed by paid professional staff and organised in a manner very different from that of an ordinary home or foster home (King, Raynes and Tizard, 1971; Tizard and Tizard, 1971).

The numbers of children in such institutions has remained much the same during the last few years. Thus in March 1970 there were 78 274 children in the care of local authorities or voluntary organisations, as

137

compared with 78 025 in 1963. Of these children, 5500 were under two, and 10 700 were aged two to four years.

Residential care of this sort has a long history; it serves a necessary social function in providing for the needs of children who are destitute, in physical or moral danger, or otherwise deprived of normal family care. From a social viewpoint therefore residential establishments serving the needs of children are important institutions.

Because patterns of upbringing in residential institutions are inevitably different from those found in a normal family, or in a foster home, residential institutions also offer opportunities to the investigator to explore the effects of different environmental circumstances upon the development of children. Furthermore, because such places contain numbers of children under one roof, and because they are more open to public scrutiny than are private households, they are convenient as well as important places to study. Little systematic study has however been made of them.

The present paper is concerned primarily with factors affecting the development of young children in long-stay residential care, but reference is made to other types of residential institution in order to put the topic in context. Short-stay care is not discussed.

INSTITUTIONS HAVE A BAD NAME

Residential children's homes, unlike prisons, concentration camps, barracks and some other types of residential establishment, are benevolent rather than punitive or coercive in intention. In spite of this they have a bad name, and there is virtually no type of children's institution except the kibbutz which has not at some time been the subject of recurring public scandal. Thus, in London during the eighteenth century, 80 per cent of children under three admitted to the care of certain workhouses died within a year (Pinchbeck and Hewitt, 1969). Things were admittedly no different elsewhere for pauper children: in 1763 the parish of St James, Westminster, resorted to paying a bonus of a guinea to foster mothers whose foster children survived the first year of life. Conditions in workhouses during the nineteenth century remained 'Dickensian'; and even as late as the end of the Second World War the plight of children in workhouses and barrack type children's homes shocked the Curtis Committee (1946) which investigated the care of children deprived of normal home life. During the last decade in England, public inquiries have been held to examine and report on the ill-treatment of children in approved schools, mental subnormality hospitals, and some boarding schools. The bleakness of life in children's hospitals has also been a subject of unfavourable report (Platt, 1959; Oswin, 1971).

England is not alone in this respect. Bowlby (1951) summarised much of the comparative literature from other countries. More recently Wolfensberger (1969), Blatt (1967, 1969), and others in the United States have presented graphic accounts of institutional neglect of the mentally handicapped in that country. The situation affecting infants and children in residential institutions in Italy is currently a major public scandal, and it would not be difficult to find examples of ill-treatment or neglect in most, if not all, countries.

It is not only, or indeed not especially, children's institutions which have earned themselves a bad name. Residential institutions for adults have an even more dubious status, portrayed and analysed by Goffman (1961) in his memorable essay on total institutions. Today, perhaps even more than in the past, public attitudes are strongly opposed to institutional care for the handicapped, the weak or the dependent – so much so that the question is often asked as to whether all forms of institutional life, for adults as well as for children, are not inevitably harmful. Many social workers, psychiatrists and staff in Local Authority welfare departments, appear to think they are. However as Titmuss (1961) has pointed out, when we criticise institutions it is always the bad ones we point to – the Poor Law institution, the old-fashioned asylum, not the public school or the Oxford College.

CHANGES IN POLICY

Attempts to reduce the numbers of children admitted to residential care have led to a major review, during the last fifteen years, of alternatives open to those concerned with public policy for deprived and handicapped children. It has been shown that better 'preventive' social case work with families, coupled with much more adequate personal social services for people living in their own homes, can sometimes prevent family breakdown and, more often, make it possible for families to cope with children at home in times of crisis (Heywood, 1965; Fitzherbert, 1967; Schaffer and Schaffer, 1968). Even severely handicapped children who would otherwise require hospital or institutional care can usually be looked after at home if adequate services are made available (Tizard, 1964). However, the development of domiciliary services has been slow, and the number of deprived children in care per 1000 of the population under eighteen has remained almost constant since 1966.

Attempts to increase the number of foster home placements have been scarcely more successful; the proportion of children in care who are boarded out has remained at about 48 per cent for some years. Hence residential institutions remain with us. During the last twenty years however they have changed remarkably. One of the major reforms here has been the almost total replacement of large children's communities, frequently housed in barrack-type institutions, by smaller, scattered homes. Today, in southern England, it is difficult to find residential children's establishments (except hospitals and schools) which contain more than thirty children. Public policy favours siting the small children's homes in residential areas rather than in disused manor houses or abandoned farmhouses deep in the country. Where conditions permit it, homes which contain more than six to eight children are subdivided into smaller family groups, each of which has its own staff of houseparents. Children normally attend ordinary schools, and efforts are made to keep children in close contact with relatives, to encourage visiting, and visits home. Child care officers with a social work training are responsible for case work with parents and children.

Equally great changes have taken place in establishments for the care of infants and preschool children. Residential nurseries have been thoroughly reorganised. They are better staffed and much better equipped. Efforts are made to retain links with parents and to foster outside contacts which provide breadth of experience for the children. Normally, children under the age of about nine months are cared for in a special baby nursery, but as soon as possible they are moved into small mixed age units of about six children, each with its own staff of trained nursery nurses and helpers. Increasingly, children are being kept in residential nurseries until they are six to eight years of age, in order to avoid a sudden break at the time of starting school. Some authorities are able to dispense with residential nurseries altogether, by putting even the youngest children in all age homes so that a subsequent move becomes unnecessary, and from their earliest years they will have opportunities to mix with older children.

By no means all children's institutions achieve what are regarded as good standards of child care. The organisation of mental subnormality hospitals and of some long-stay units for other types of handicapped children in general compares very unfavourably with that of children's homes for 'ordinary' children deprived of normal home life. Institutions dealing with delinquent children also differ in other ways from ordinary children's homes. But here too changes have occurred and new developments (e.g. in the provision of small boarding homes for mentally retarded children, and 'community homes' for difficult and delinquent children) are occurring.

The enormous changes in child care policy which have occurred during the last twenty years are unfortunately less well known to those not professionally concerned with it than are the defects of old-fashioned institutions and the scandals that still make the headlines about those that remain repressive or inadequate. Rather than discuss these further, it is more useful to turn to questions of current concern; how suitable *can* a children's home be as a place for children to grow up in? More generally, what differences in development are likely to be found in children growing up in a modern child-oriented institution, as compared with similar children growing up in their own homes?

THE COMPLEXITY OF THE PROBLEM

The care of children presents problems which are different from, and more complex than, those of adults. Children are more vulnerable than adults both to physical and mental trauma, the effects of which are likely to be longer lasting or even irreversible. They are more defenceless than adults, poor witnesses in a Court of Law and totally dependent upon adults for help and protection. They are also *developing* creatures whose needs change rapidly with age and vary according to their genetic and environmental history. A discussion of the effects of institutional up-bringing on children has therefore to take account of the age, handicaps and length of stay of the children in residence, the type and quality of the care provided in the institution, the alternatives actually or in principle available for children not able to be brought up in their own homes, and, above all, the consequences for the child and for the family of leaving the child at home. Most of the classical studies of institutional care have not done this: they have been insufficiently specific and analytical. Nearly all of them were carried out in institutions which were overcrowded, meanly provided for and understaffed; and conditions in these have been compared with those that obtain in ordinary families, close knit, stable, reasonably well housed and economically secure. The indictment of institutional neglect is entirely justified, but it is misleading to generalise about institutional upbringing on the basis of findings obtained only in establishments which are poor and bleak.

A COMPARATIVE STUDY OF INSTITUTIONS

Our own approach has been concerned with attempts to analyse, measure, and account for differences between institutions, and to show how these differences affect the development of children growing up in them. We start from the observation that residential institutions caring for the same type of inmate differ widely one from another, and that in particular establishments characteristic patterns of function tend to remain relatively constant over long periods of time, despite changes in

141

staff and inmate population. Our viewpoint is that an institution tends to function in one way rather than another not simply because of personal factors associated with particular individuals, or idiosyncratic circumstances, but because of the characteristics of its organisation. Thus individual units belonging to a particular class of institutions (e.g., small residential hostels) tend to resemble each other more than they resemble members of another class (e.g., large hospitals) irrespective of whether the inmate population is normal or retarded and irrespective of the personality of the various staff members.

If it is true that the characteristics of institutions remain more or less constant over substantial periods of time, practices which differentiate one establishment from another and which impinge on the children who are resident should result in differences in the way in which children in long-term care develop. This is especially true because the residential institutions are encompassing institutions, in that the child's environment is almost entirely circumscribed by the institution in which he lives. Hence the child's world is very largely shaped by the adults who care for him.

The object of our studies has been to explore the implications of this argument, using objective and reliable indicators which would permit the testing of specific hypotheses and admit of replication. Taking a particular inmate population, e.g., severely retarded children, we have selected for study a number of institutions which differ markedly in their mode of organisation. A systematic study was then made of the quality and frequency of interactions between staff and children in the different establishments.

The next step was to attempt to relate differences in staff–child interactions to the characteristics of the organisation in which the staff worked, using scales to measure those organisational aspects which were considered relevant.

Thirdly, systematic studies were made of individual children to see whether any effects of differing patterns of upbringing could be discovered. Relations were thus sought between three kinds of data: observations of staff–child interactions, measures of organisation, and assessments of the children's development.

A full description of the mental subnormality studies has been published (King, Raynes and Tizard, 1971). They comprised field studies of a large number of different mental subnormality and child care units, and a detailed observational survey of mental subnormality hospitals and small hostels all caring for severely or profoundly retarded children. Large and characteristic differences, measured by an objective Child Management Scale, were found in child care practices, as between small hostels in which child care practices were strongly *child oriented* on the one hand, and mental subnormality hospitals where child care practices were *institution oriented*. The evidence suggested that differences in child care practices were not due to differences in the handicaps of the children.

Child care practices varied with the size of the institution, and the size of the child care units in which the children lived, but differences in unit size did not seem able to account for differences in child management patterns. Nor could differing child care practices be ascribed to differences in assigned staff ratios, though in child-oriented units more staff were available in peak periods (i.e. at such times as getting up and breakfast time, and at the end of the day) whereas in institution-oriented units staffing was neither increased during peak units nor decreased during those periods of the day in which there was less for them to do.

The organisational structure of child-oriented and institution-oriented units was very different and it was this which appeared to be the principal determinant of differences in patterns of child care. In child-oriented units the person in charge had very much greater responsibility to make decisions about matters which affected all aspects of the unit's functioning. Perhaps because they were accorded greater autonomy, senior staff in those establishments tended to share their responsibilities with their junior colleagues; role differentiation was reduced (e.g. senior staff were more often engaged in child care than were their counterparts in institution-oriented units who spent far more time on administration and even domestic work, and far less time in child care.) Staff stability was also much greater in child-oriented units, partly because staff were not moved from one unit to another to meet crises in units which were short staffed, partly because students in training were not moved about in order to 'gain experience'. Role performance also differed. In child-oriented units staff were more likely to involve the children in their activities. They spoke to them more often, and were more 'accepting' of them, and less often 'rejecting'. Junior staff tended to behave in ways similar to those in which the head of the unit acted.

Though the social organisation of the institution appeared to be largely responsible for the differences in staff behaviour which we observed, the nature of staff training also seemed important. Trained nurses were in general less child-oriented than were staff with child care training. They were more authoritarian, and when the person in charge was a nurse the unit tended to be characterised by sharp role differentiation.

Mentally handicapped children in units which were child care oriented were significantly more advanced in feeding and dressing skills, and in speech, than were those in institution-oriented units. Though no very

143

adequate study was made of other personality characteristics of the children, fewer of those in child-oriented institutions appeared to be psychiatrically disturbed.

UPBRINGING IN RESIDENTIAL NURSERIES

Our mental subnormality studies left many questions unanswered. Furthermore, mental subnormality institutions have some special characteristics which mark them off from institutions responsible for the care of normal children. In a later series of investigations, which are still continuing, more detailed studies have therefore been made of the manner in which young normal children living in group care are being brought up in modern child-oriented nurseries. Differences in child care practices in different institutions are being examined and attempts made to assess their consequences for the children.

The nurseries we have studied do not present gross organisational differences of the kind found amongst institutions for the retarded. None the less pilot studies indicated that there were important differences in the way in which they were organised, and suggested that these would be likely to affect the quality of staff talk and behaviour, and hence the level of language development of the children. It was therefore decided to examine, as in the mental subnormality studies, relationships between three sets of data. The first set, obtained from records and by interview, was concerned with organisational structure in the nurseries; the second, obtained through direct observation using time-sampling techniques, measured the 'verbal environment' of the children; the third, obtained through formal psychological testing, comprised measures of both verbal and non-verbal development. An earlier inquiry (described below) had shown two-year-olds in residential nurseries to be somewhat backward in language, and we wished to ascertain whether or not language retardation increased as the children got older. Language development may be regarded as one indicator of general social development, and all the healthy two- to five-year-old children in the thirteen nursery groups which were intensively studied were tested with the Reynell Developmental Language Scales, and the non-verbal scale of the Minnesota Preschool Scale.

RESULTS

The results indicated the fruitfulness of the approach and threw some light on general problems of institutional upbringing in nurseries which maintained high standards of physical and social care (Tizard *et al.*, 1972).

144

Though all nurseries were divided into mixed age groups of six children, differences in organisational structure were apparent. The autonomy of the nursery group appeared to be of especial importance: in some nurseries the nurse in charge had almost as much freedom as a foster-mother to run her unit as she wished. In these groups also the children were allowed a great deal of freedom. At the other extreme, there were some nurseries in which the nursery matron exercised a dominating role over all the nursery groups. In these, the nurse in charge of a group had little authority, and her tasks were so well defined that someone else could easily take her place. Most decisions not made on an entirely routine basis were referred to the matron, and the freedom of both nurse and child was very limited. Thus the children were not allowed to leave the group room unattended and the nurse would have to ask permission to take the children for a walk or to turn on the television set.

In the more autonomous groups considerable efforts were made to broaden the children's experiences. Special excursions, e.g. to the cinema, zoo, or sea-side, occurred at least as often as in a contrast group of London working-class families, and ordinary social experiences, e.g. shopping, visits to cafés, bus and train trips, were nearly as frequent. The lower the autonomy of the group, the more restricted were the child's experiences. Differences between groups in various characteristics of organisational structure were assessed on quantitative scales. Differences in scale scores were strongly associated with differences in patterns of staff–child interaction. In the least centrally organised groups the staff spent more time talking, reading and playing to the children, and doing things with them in which the children were rated as 'active' rather than 'passive'. The quality (but *not* the amount, which was high in all nurseries) of staff talk to the children also differed. Staff in nursery groups which had most autonomy offered more informative talk, spoke in longer sentences, gave fewer negative commands, and were more likely to explain themselves when they told the child to do something, than were those in the institutionally oriented groups. Thus the linguistic, as well as the general, social environment differed subtly but substantially among the nurseries.

The differences were related to specific differences in the children's attainments. In non-verbal intelligence the mean scores of children in nurseries with differing autonomy did not differ: the mean was 104.9. In verbal attainments however there were marked differences. The mean verbal comprehension score of the three nursery groups which had the highest autonomy was 114.9, 1.5 standard deviations higher than those in the three most institutionally oriented groups – a difference in mean scores equivalent to that found between the verbal comprehension

145

scores of ordinary children of professional families growing up in their own homes, and children of manual workers. The mean language expression score in the same three nurseries was 100.0, 0.5 standard deviations higher than those in the most institutionally oriented.

In all nursery groups the analysis of staff talk indicated that older children tended to be spoken to more frequently than the younger ones. There were no significant differences between the institutions in this respect. It was noteworthy therefore that the older children scored significantly *higher* rather than lower in the verbal comprehension test: thus the hypothesis that institutional children become progressively more retarded in language as they get older was not confirmed. Inasmuch as linguistic attainments are indicators of the social and intellectual adequacy of the environment, this set of nurseries could be said to have attained good standards of care; the best of them were very good indeed. The language studies supported our general belief that the nurseries provided a less adequate environment for some of the younger children, but from the age of $2\frac{1}{2}$ the children scored well above the population means. Since most of the children came from lower working-class parentage it is likely that their cognitive development was more advanced than it would have been had they remained in their own family.

INSTITUTIONS AND THE DEVELOPMENT OF PERSONALITY

Bowlby's (1951) highly influential monograph presented an extensive body of data in support of his thesis that institutional upbringing almost always led to dire consequences. It was plain, he said, that when deprived of maternal care 'the child's development is almost always retarded – physically, intellectually, and socially – and that symptoms of physical and mental illness may appear . . . retrospective and follow-up studies make it clear that some children are gravely damaged for life. This is a sombre conclusion which must be regarded as established' (p. 15).

Later studies, including our own, have shown that these conclusions were too sweeping. We have been able to show that the level of language development depends very much on the characteristics of the institution: in the best residential nurseries the children we studied were not only healthy but intellectually normal, linguistically advanced, and exposed to a near-normal range of general experiences. No study was made of personality development, and we have no evidence of the ways in which differences in institutional environment affect this variable. However, in an ongoing study we are comparing the all-round development of a group of young children who have spent virtually the whole of

146

their lives in good nursery care with others from a similar nursery environment who between the ages of two and four years were adopted or restored to their parents. A contrast group of London working-class children living at home forms part of the study.

In the first stage of the study thirty children admitted to residential nurseries before the age of four months were examined at the time of their second birthday (Tizard and Joseph, 1970; Tizard and Tizard, 1971). Compared to the contrast group of London children living at home, the institution children were found to be slightly backward in speech and verbal intelligence, and to be somewhat more fearful of a stranger and of separation from a familiar adult. Fewer had achieved bowel and bladder control. Thumb and finger sucking were more common among them, sleep disturbances less so. There was evidence of a relationship between the extent of the children's timidity and the paucity of their previous experience with strangers. Gross disturbances were rare: withdrawn, apathetic or depressed children were not encountered.

A major area of difference between the nursery and home children lay in their relationships with their caretakers. Most of the home two-year-olds showed a marked preference for their mother; they tended to follow her about the house, and to be upset if she left the house without them. However, few of them were disturbed if she left the room. Such relationships result from a close family structure where the mother is the principal if not the sole caretaker and is almost always accessible to the child. By contrast, in the residential nurseries which we studied large numbers of different staff cared for each child, and because of scheduled off-duty hours and study leave particular staff members were by no means always accessible to the child. Moreover, following an adult round the house was not allowed in most nurseries. The attachments of the children were not surprisingly diffuse – although all showed preferences between adults – most children were described as showing attachment to anyone they knew well, that is they tended to cry when any staff they knew well left the room, and to run to be picked up when any familiar staff entered the room. Their behaviour was thus not only more indiscriminate but more immature than that of the home children.

The question arises as to whether deviance in attachment behaviour at twenty-four months is reversible, and if not whether it presages subsequent deviance in personality development. Bowlby (1969) in his recent monumental study of affective development maintains that harmonious social and emotional development is dependent upon the early development of attachment behaviour to a specific adult. He describes in convincing detail the ontogeny of attachment behaviour in human infants, and draws extensively upon animal studies to argue that attachment behaviour serves a biological, protective function, and that primates deprived of the usual mothering experience develop abnormally. So impressed was Bowlby by the bias of a child to attach himself especially to one person, and also of the far-reaching implications of this attachment, that he coined a special term, monotropy, to describe it.

With respect to reversibility, it seems probable that in this as in many other respects human behaviour is more modifiable by experience than animal behaviour. In our study of four-and-a-half-year-old children who had been adopted or restored to their parents from an institution after the age of two we found that in most cases close attachments *had* developed. On the other hand, many of the children who remained in the institution showed markedly deviant attachment behaviour by the age of four and a half; their nurses tended to complain either that they 'didn't care about anyone' or that they would 'follow anyone who took an interest in them'. A number of these children also showed behaviour disturbances, as did some of the children living at home. The analysis of the data is not yet complete, but the evidence suggests that rather different behaviour patterns characterise institutional, adopted, and restored children. Continued institutional care appears to be associated with a particular kind of deviant behaviour.

Two further relevant questions are whether the development of normal attachment behaviour is possible within an institutional setting, and whether some deviant forms of attachment behaviour are compatible with healthy personality development. It is by no means certain how far Bowlby is generalising about human development from a study of the nuclear Western family. In other societies extended families have existed, and these may develop here in the future; in these the care of children is shared among a number of loving adults. In such circumstances it is possible that healthy development may occur in the absence of specific attachments. However present-day children's institutions differ from such extended families in a number of respects, most of which are related to the professionalism of the staff. Unlike members of a family, staff work limited hours, and have personal and professional needs which in modern society result in fairly frequent job changes. Multiple caretaking is combined with instability of care. The staff are therefore likely to protect themselves and the children by keeping emotional relationships cool, reasoning that difficulties would be created for themselves and the children if the children demanded the care of a particular nurse. Indeed very often the institution will be organised to prevent the development of specific attachments – each child will be cared for by any of the staff on duty, rather than assigning the care of specific children to specific staff. In this way, because care is impersonal, less attempt is made to reduce the number of caretakers or their constant turnover.

Changes in staff are an inevitable feature of modern institutions: however it is possible to organise institutions in such a way that the number of caretakers per child is drastically reduced by assigning the care of specific children to specific staff members, with one or two regular deputies for off duty hours. In these circumstances much closer attachments are likely to develop, but at the risk of a series of almost inevitable bereavements. We found a number of examples in our study of prolonged and marked grief reactions in young children following the departure of their nurses. Thus whilst attempts to mimic a nuclear family within an institutional setting are feasible, they are likely to result in a different pattern of disturbance for the child. Multiple caretaking, changes of caretaker, and impersonal care are features of most but not all institutions, and would seem likely to produce deviant personality development. Unfortunately, the alternative solutions for many deprived children may be unfavourable in other respects – e.g. foster home care may be both impersonal and unstable, whilst the child's own family may be hostile, unstable or neglectful.

DISCUSSION

It should by now be apparent that the title of this chapter needs restating; institutions are many and diverse, and their effects on development may be benign or malignant. In the studies outlined above, and reported in detail elsewhere, an attempt has been made to show that important aspects of the institutional environment can usefully be measured, and that the factors responsible for these aspects can be assessed, as can their effects on children's development. It thus becomes possible in principle to specify the kinds of institutional environment likely to promote different kinds of development, and the kinds of organisational structure in which staff are most likely to produce such environments.

This has already been done to some extent in regard to physical and cognitive (including linguistic) development. Evidence about the effects of different child care patterns upon personality development is less satisfactory – partly because few useful measures of social and emotional development exist, partly because no *systematic* comparative studies of residential institutions for young children have been carried out to examine the complex interactions which presumably influence the personality development of children brought up in differing environments. Neither our own studies, nor those of other research workers, have systematically explored these problems. There is a wealth of data to show that poor institutional child care practices have adverse effects upon children; and a number of long-term follow-up studies indicate that

children exposed to such conditions in early childhood are more likely
to be disturbed or delinquent in adolescence and adult life. However the
interpretation of long-term follow up data poses formidable problems,
in that information about the quality of the early environment is usually
sketchy, and because a high proportion of the children who are neglected
or ill-treated at one point in their lives are likely to continue to live in
highly unsatisfactory circumstances.

A further, practical point weakens the use that can be made of
longitudinal data by those concerned with child care policy: institutions
themselves are liable to have changed so much before their long-term
consequences for children become manifest that inferences drawn for
current practice from primary data which relate to conditions existing
fifteen to thirty years ago must be treated with circumspection.

However it would not seem impossible to carry out studies designed
explicitly to measure the 'emotional climate' of institutions serving the
needs of young children, to explore the organisational arrangements
which facilitate different types of staff–child interaction, and to assess
the effects of these upon the children's emotional well-being. Only when
this is done will it be possible to assess the effects of different strategies
at present advocated as being likely to overcome or mitigate the consequences of discontinuities of institutional upbringing. In our own mental
subnormality studies for example we found it possible to rate the quality
of observed staff–child interactions very reliably, using a simple threefold classification (accepting, tolerating and rejecting). In the nursery
studies it was found that staff in different nursery groups differed greatly
in the *quality* of their verbal exchanges with the children, as well as in
the continuity, and the nature, of their relations with them. These differences were related to differences in patterns of nursery organisation, and
were likely to have affected the children's behaviour. The study of two-
year-old children showed that there were significant differences in
attachment behaviour and in responses to strangers between those in
nurseries and a contrast group living at home, and the longitudinal
studies in progress throw light on short-term consequences of particular
patterns of care, and particular changes in patterns of care.

However indicators such as we have used require further development. The most difficult problems are likely to be encountered not in
developing further measures of organisational structure, or of the
emotional 'tone' of staff–child interactions, but in quantifying differences
in child behaviour. To date, most psychological research concerned with
non-cognitive aspects of behaviour during the preschool years has dealt
with behavioural pathology. But gross pathology is uncommon in good
modern nurseries; and the most rewarding studies in the future are likely
to be those which explore differing rates of social and emotional develop-

ment in children of different age groups, and those which relate differences in children's behaviour in different nursery settings to particular qualities of the nursery environments. Our own studies lead us to believe that behavioural ratings by staff are likely to be too unreliable to be useful for this type of comparative study. Instead, one must rely on direct observation, and clinical and experimental examination of individual children.

The conceptual and technical problems of devising such procedures are of central importance to developmental psychology. And inasmuch as our concern is with environmental determinants of behaviour, comparative research carried out in institutions offers unique opportunities in which to study the development of children in settings in which environmental and hereditary influences are not hopelessly confounded.

REFERENCES

Blatt, B. (1967). *Christmas in Purgatory : a photographic essay in mental retardation*. Boston, Allyn and Bacon.
Blatt, B. (1969). Purgatory. In Kugel, R. B. and Wolfensberger, W. (eds.). *Changing Patterns in Residential Services for the Mentally Retarded*. Washington, D.C., President's Panel on Mental Retardation.
Bowlby, J. (1951). *Maternal Care and Mental Health*. Geneva, W.H.O.
Bowlby, J. (1969). *Attachment and Loss*, Vol. 1, *Attachment*. London, Hogarth Press.
Curtis, M. (1946). *Report of the Care of Children Committee*. London, H.M.S.O. Cmd 6922.
Fitzherbert, K. (1967). *West Indian Children in London*. Occas. Papers on Soc. Admin. No. 19. London, G. Bell.
Goffman, E. (1961). *Asylums: Essays on the Social Situation of Mental Patients and Other Inmates*. New York, Doubleday.
Heywood, J. S. (1965). *Children in Care : the Development of the Service for the Deprived Child*. London, Routledge and Kegan Paul.
King, R. D. (1970). A Comparative Study of Residential Care for Handicapped Children. Unpublished Ph.D. thesis, Univ. of London.
King, R. D., Raynes, N. V. and Tizard, J. (1971). *Patterns of Residential Care : Sociological Studies in Institutions for Handicapped Children*. London, Routledge and Kegan Paul.
Oswin, M. (1971). *The Empty Hours: a Study of the Weekend Life of Handicapped Children in Institutions*. London, Allen and Lane.
Packman, J. (1968). *Child Care: Needs and Numbers*. London, George Allen and Unwin.
Platt, H. (1959). *Report of the Committee: The Welfare of Children in Hospital*. Ministry of Health Central Health Services Council, London, H.M.S.O.
Pinchbeck, I. and Hewitt, M. (1969). *Children in English Society*, Vol. 1, *From Tudor Times to the Eighteenth Century*. London, Routledge and Kegan Paul.
Schaffer, H. R. and Schaffer, E. B. (1968). *Child Care and the Family*. Occas. Papers on Soc. Admin. No. 25. London, G. Bell.

151

Titmuss, R. (1961). Cited by J. K. Wing (1962) in Institutionaiism in mental hospitals. *Brit. J. soc. clin. Psychol.* **1**, 38–51.

Tizard, J. (1964). *Community Services for the Mentally Handicapped*, London, Oxford Univ. Press.

Tizard, B. and Joseph, A. (1970). The cognitive development of young children in residential care. *J. Child Psychol. Psychiat.* **11**, 177–86.

Tizard, J. and Tizard, B. (1971). The social development of two-year-old children in residential nurseries. In Schaffer, H. R. (ed.) *The Origins of Human Social Relations*. London, Academic Press.

Tizard, B., Cooperman, O., Joseph, A. and Tizard, J. (1972). Environmental effects on language development: a study of young children in long-stay residential nurseries. *Child Development*, **43**, 337–58.

Wolfensberger, W. (1969). The origin and nature of our institutional models. In Kugel, R. B. and Wolfensberger, W. (eds.). *Changing Patterns in Residential Services for the Mentally Retarded*. Washington, D.C., President's Panel on Mental Retardation.

8

Attachment: some problems and possibilities

Judith Bernal

Much of the impetus to examine the early relationship between mother and child has come from the work of John Bowlby (1969). His discussion of attachment encompasses both the function of the bond between mother and child in an evolutionary context, and its importance for the development of the individual. Bowlby's emphasis on the biological function of the bond as one of protection for the child during the long period of immaturity has led to a concentration of attention on the proximity-seeking and proximity-maintaining aspects of the relationship. While the gains of an approach that highlights and defines key features of the relationship in a specifically testable fashion are clearly reflected in the studies that have grown from it, there are also some problems in understanding the growth of the mother–child relationship in these terms. In this chapter two of these questions will be discussed, first the difficulty of defining and measuring the affectional bonds between the child and those to whom he becomes attached, and secondly the question of how the child's relationship with his mother, or chief attachment figure, differs from his relationship with others, and what significance this difference has for later social development.

CRITERIA OF ATTACHMENT

One criterion that has been used to test for the formation of the attachment bond is the response of the child to separation from the mother, either in everyday occurrences or in standardised laboratory situations. While this separation response may be useful as a test for assessing the age of onset of specific attachments, it cannot be taken as a sole criterion of the attachment bond, as a study by Ainsworth and Wittig (1969) showed. Among those children in this study who protested intensely when separated from the mother were 'some whose protests reflected strong attachment and others whose attachment was full of ambivalence or anxiety. Among those who responded with minimal distress were babies who seemed to have relatively weak attachments, but also at least one child whose attachment was strong and secure . . .' (p. 135).

The child's response to separation from the mother can then be

153

difficult to interpret, and would be of limited use in understanding individual differences in attachment patterns if it were the sole criterion applied.

The stress on proximity-seeking and maintenance as an index of the attachment bond has grown out of the discussion of the biological function of attachment as primarily one of protection for the child. While the selective advantage of the protection ensured by the attachment bond during the long period of dependence and immaturity of the human baby is obvious, the question of the function of the bond can also be asked in terms of the specifically human characteristics of the relationship. What are the possible developmental consequences of the attachment that may be relevant and important for the human child – for language acquisition, for cognitive and social development?

To answer these questions it seems important not to limit the aspects of the interaction between mother and baby that are to be examined. Bowlby (1969, p. 332) has suggested that a difficulty in using what first-hand accounts of attachment we have is that data concerning a child's attachment behaviour is not always kept distinct from the amount and kind of interaction he has with his mother. But are we in a position to make a distinction between attachment behaviour and interaction? The evidence from studies looking at the interrelations of various measures of attachment behaviour suggests that this sort of dichotomy is too simple. In Lewis and Ban's (1971) study of individual differences in attachment and the stability of these differences between the ages of one and two years, four attachment measures were used: time spent touching mother, looking at mother, vocalising to her, and being in proximity to her. It was found that the four measures did not vary together, touching and proximity tending to be negatively related across age, and looking and vocalising positively. The individual differences in the patterns of attachment behaviour and the way these changed with age were marked; sex differences were also large.

Defining and assessing the relationship between mother and infant in terms of the proximity maintained between them does present some specific problems in dealing with the child's exploratory behaviour and growing independence. The balance for the child between exploring the world and contact with the caretaker is obviously of central importance, and work such as that of Appell and David (1965) suggests that there is a richness and subtlety in the variations of balance achieved by different mother-and-child pairs, styles of interaction and communication that may vary over a wide range of intensities and media. Physical proximity is too crude a measure for this range of communication and understanding. By limiting the aspects of the interaction studied to those related to the distance between the two we may be missing important facets of the relationship, and further, the proximity maintained between mother and child may mean very different things in different relationships: Escalona's study (Escalona and Corman, 1971) of two mother–child pairs from birth to twelve months showed that while the presence of the mother had a marked effect both on how children behaved, the direction of the effect was opposite in the two children. One child became more active and responsive in all areas of behaviour, the other decreased in general alertness, responsiveness and animation.

Ainsworth (1969) resolves the problem of exploration versus attachment by distinguishing attachment behaviour from the underlying attachment bond. She uses a dimension of security of attachment by which the securely attached child is seen as the child who explores with confidence and who, she suggests, 'uses mother as a base from which to explore' as a criterion for being attached. While the notion of security of attachment is clearly very important, the behavioural indices by which it can be assessed are not yet described, and we are left with the difficulties of distinguishing, for example, the physical separation indicating non-attachment from that shown by a securely-attached, exploring child. The security of the attachment bond remains a concept which has to be distinguished from behavioural measures, and needs further specification before it can be useful in explanation: the Appell and David study referred to indicates that detailed observational work will be needed before the ways in which the balance between exploration and contact is achieved are understood.

With the difficulty of reconciling security of attachment as measured in proximity terms and exploratory behaviour, the cognitive developmental approach of setting social development in the context of the stages of cognitive growth provides a helpful model. Schaffer's studies (Schaffer, 1971) draw attention to the distinction between recognition of the mother – evident early in the first six months (Yarrow, 1967) – and the ability to recall the memory of the mother in her absence. This, he points out, is a relatively complex cognitive process, one that is required before the infant can for example perceive a stranger not only as unknown but as different from the mother. Once the infant has a clearly formed and retrievable representation of the mother, the internalised mother 'provides him with the security which formerly only her physical presence provided. The more soundly the internal representation is established and the more easily the child can evoke it the greater the gaps of time for which she can be away' (Schaffer, 1971, pp. 151–2).

This approach avoids the difficulty of using exploration and proximity as measurements of the same bond; the question of how the early interaction with the mother affects the establishment of the internal representation remains open.

It is argued then that rather than attempting to measure the strength of an attachment bond, attention could usefully be paid to qualitative differences in patterns of interaction between children and their attachment figures. The importance of understanding the origins and implications of individual differences in attachment patterns has been underlined by Hinde's studies of separation experiences in infant rhesus monkeys (Hinde and Spencer-Booth, 1970; Hinde and Davies, 1972). These show that the effects of the separation-experience on the rhesus infant are very much influenced by the relationship with the rhesus mother *before* the separation, and that the pattern of the relationship was influenced by both maternal and infant variables. Rutter (1972) comments on the value of these studies in discussing the differences in children's vulnerability to 'maternal deprivation'; this again underlines the importance of understanding how individual differences in mother–child relationship arise. Two key conditions in the formation of the attachment bond are emphasised in various studies (Bowlby 1969, Schaffer and Emerson, 1964, Ainsworth and Wittig, 1969) in accounting for differences in the intensity of the attachment, the sensitivity of the mother figure, and the amount and nature of interaction between mother and infant. It is perhaps worth a close look at some of the problems involved in using the notion of sensitivity, as it is directly related to the 'quality' of the interchange.

MATERNAL SENSITIVITY

If the idea of sensitive mothering is to be used, a distinction must be made between maternal responsiveness that in an immediate sense terminates the baby's demands, and the long-term connotations of the appropriateness of the maternal response, which seems to assume knowledge of the implications for development of the possible maternal responses or strategies. The study by Sander and his colleagues (1970) of babies reared in three different early environments does provide evidence that to equate the caretaker's responsiveness to the infant cry with a blanket idea of sensitivity can be extremely misleading. In one part of Sander's study each baby was cared for by nurse X or nurse Y alone in a rooming-in situation, after being in a nursery for the first ten days. He showed that the two nurses had dramatically different effects on the amount of crying the babies did, those looked after by nurse Y crying much less. But examination of the automatically monitored record of the caretaking interventions showed that in fact nurse X was responding more quickly to the baby's cry, and that the frequency of her response to the cry was higher. Nurse Y's caretaking interventions were, however, longer. If this result is interpreted as showing that the differences in crying seem to be related to what happens in the interaction rather than to the speed of response, it emphasises that 'sensitivity' is not simply a matter of latency of response. It could however be seen as showing that babies looked after by X learnt that crying produced a quick response, whereas with Y it did not work so well. If the notion of sensitivity of response to crying is to be used, it should be borne in mind that even in the neonatal period there may be considerable differences between babies in what causes or terminates crying. Is 'sensitivity', then, learning the characteristics of the individual baby?

The difficulties with using the idea of appropriateness of maternal behaviour are illustrated with another point from Sander's study. The babies in nurse X's care, though they had much higher crying scores, slept much longer. As Sander *et al.* (1970, p. 116) point out 'There are requirements over the longer course of development which draw upon different facets of maternal character and preclude premature judgment of long-term effectiveness.'

One immediate problem of rating or assessing mothers along the continuum of sensitivity or responsiveness is that of separating the parts played by the two partners in interaction. If a mother is rated as behaving appropriately when her baby's demands cease, this could be telling us as much about the ease with which the baby's requests are satisfied as about the relevance of the maternal response. In most studies of mothers and infants it is impossible to separate the effects of the two partners on each other. (An outstanding exception is the Moss study (1967) referred to below, whereas in animal studies the same problems are approached with more methodological sophistication (Hinde and Spencer-Booth, 1968; Rosenblatt, 1970).) There is now some acknowledgement of the mistake of minimising the child's part in the development of the relationship. Bell (1968), for example, has offered reinterpretations of several studies in terms of child effects on parents, and he discusses the historical reasons for the attitudes that lie behind the minimising of the child's importance. The problems of separating the mother and baby effects can be illustrated by some data from a study of breast-fed and bottle-fed babies (Richards and Bernal, to be published). During the first ten days there were marked differences in the patterning and the amount of sleeping and crying behaviour of the two groups. The breast-fed babies showed a more extreme twenty-four-hour pattern of restlessness and higher crying scores. It is impossible from these data to make any statement about how far these differences are due to differences between the babies, and how much can be attributed to differences in their mothers' care and interaction. But we do have some assessment of the babies which is outside the interaction situation – neurological and sucking tests done on the eighth day after birth. In the sucking test the breast-fed babies react more quickly and with more crying to the removal of the teat; they are as a group different by the eighth day. This means that already a spiral of differences is set up; when comparing the mothers who breast-feed with those who bottle-feed, we must be aware that their babies are different. The breast-feeding data suggest that when looking for continuities in baby behaviour it is not enough to assume that by taking the baby in the first month or so the contamination of 'socialisation' effects will be avoided. Waldrop and Bell's (1966) original study using the sucking test showed that the density with which the births were spaced affected what the babies were like in the first week. That the effects of the baby on the mother can be shown in the first weeks was demonstrated by Moss (1967); the boys in his sample were more irritable in the third week than the girls, and their mothers spent more time responding to them. By the twelfth week, however, the mothers of the irritable boys were responding less, finding them difficult to pacify. It would be interesting to know more of the stability or lability of the mother's response to the child, and how this varies with developmental changes in the child's behaviour.

Another illustration of the importance of considering the child's contribution to the interaction is Schaffer and Emerson's (1968) study of non-cuddly babies. Babies who do not seem to enjoy contact comfort have been commented on in several studies. While it is sometimes assumed that this must be due to inappropriate handling on the mother's part, in Schaffer and Emerson's study it is concluded that 'the non-cuddlers' avoidance of close physical contact is concerned with a phenomenon that is not peculiar to the relationship with the mother or indeed to social relationships in general'. The babies' resistance to physical contact, which the authors tentatively conclude is a function of inherent characteristics of these restless and hyperactive children, does mean that the nature of the interaction with the mother is greatly affected.

The complexities of separating influences, and assessing maternal responsiveness in interaction with a newborn, underline the problems of looking at interaction with a one-year-old, whose large range of communication skills is now used in a subtle, goal-directed manner and whose parents respond in the context of understanding this.

SECURITY, ATTACHMENT AND OTHER SOCIAL RELATIONSHIPS

The second question raised in this chapter centres round the nature of the child's bond with the mother figure: whether and how this differs from his relationships with others. The essence of the relationship with the attachment figure is that she provides a source of security, and the work of Bowlby and Ainsworth has drawn attention to the importance of understanding the way proximity to the mother contributes to the child's security and ability to explore. Bowlby refers to the experiments of Harlow (1961) who reared rhesus monkeys with wire surrogate mothers, in stressing the role of physical contact in the development of security; the later development of coping and mastery behaviour is suggested to be linked with the security provided by the mother as a base from which to explore. What is not yet clear is how the security aspects of the relationship are related to later social behaviour, or to the child's relationship with other people. In Rutter's view (1972) the main bond with the attachment figure does not differ in kind from the child's relationships with others. He argues that most children develop bonds with several people and that it is likely these bonds are basically similar: the presence of a sib or the father can, for instance, reduce the insecurity of an anxious child in hospital. The chief bond is seen as particularly important because of its greater strength.

Kohlberg (1969), on the other hand, sees the security aspects of the relationship, the importance of proximity and physical contact, as irrelevant to the development of social behaviour. Drawing on the work of Piaget and Mead, he develops a concept of human social attachment that stresses features of sharing and identification between self and others, a position that he summarises: 'A social attachment or bond is conceived of as a relationship of sharing, communication or co-operation (or reciprocity) between selves recognising each other as selves. In contrast, all popular child psychology theories have denied that experience of, or desire for, sharing and communication between selves are the primary components of a human social bond.' While commenting that the prerequisites for human attachment are present in infant behaviour in that positive social attachment develops out of intrinsic motivation to engage in social interaction, he dismisses those aspects of contact-security that Bowlby stresses. He cites Harlow's experiments (Harlow and Harlow, 1965) as evidence that the cloth mother, while providing security, does not generate social behaviour, whereas playing with peer-group monkeys does provide a formative base from which complementary reciprocal sharing behaviour develops. He argues that 'the physical need for the presence and services of the other does not itself generate social bonds because it does not involve a motive to share between self and other, or to be guided by the response of the other'.

Kohlberg stresses that the changes with age of the attachment relationship are generated by cognitive structural change, citing as evidence for the infant stage Decarie's work, showing:

(*a*) close age parallels between Piagetian progressions in physical object concepts and social object relations, and

159

(*b*) correlations between the two such that infants advanced in one are advanced in the other.

He questions whether there are steps in the formation of a mother attachment which indicate something more than the child's cognitive growth in response to external objects, whether physical or social; he suggests too that it is doubtful whether the relationship with the mother is more important for the development of social bonds than, for example, the relationship with siblings.

Kohlberg's view of the relationship with the mother in the first years involves two issues which will be considered separately; first, the relationship of physical contact and security behaviour to later social behaviour, and second, the dismissal of mother–infant interaction in the first year as unimportant for later social relationships.[1]

Taking the issue of physical contact first, if the evidence from Harlow's studies is to be used to emphasise that physical contact as provided by the cloth mother, while enabling the infant monkey to explore a potentially frightening novel object, was not enough to ensure the development of a socially adequate adult, it should be pointed out that Harlow himself (Harlow and Harlow, 1965, p. 292) believes that 'Intimate physical contact is the variable of primary importance in enabling the infant to pass from the stage of comfort and attachment to the state of security, specific security to a specific mother figure.'

It is not yet at all clear empirically what developmental continuity there is between physical contact behaviour in the first year and later social behaviour, or between physical contact behaviour and other forms of attention-seeking at any one age. The Lewis and Ban study (1971) referred to earlier showed negative correlations between 'proximal' behaviour at one and two years, particularly touching. The pattern of 'transformation' of touching behaviour varied very much with individuals. There is plenty of research on 'dependent' behaviour in slightly older children, but much of it is confusing and inconsistent, especially if attempts are made to interpret it in terms of a unified trait of behaviour. For example, Sears, Rau and Alpert (1965) in a study of nursery-school children, found positive correlations for girls between measures of seeking physical proximity, comfort and reassurance and attention-seeking; these were related to demands of attention from the mother. For boys, however, proximity and physical comfort-seeking seemed related to each other but not to seeking attention from the mother. In a study by Radke-Yarrow, Campbell and Burton (1968), while teachers' ratings of the children's seeking closeness and attention correlated, there was no relation to the child's reaction to separation from the mother. If the diffi-

[1] This problem is also discussed by Harré in chapter 12.

160

culties in making sense of these differences lie in attempting to interpret them as part of a unitary system of dependent behaviours, the same difficulties may apply to trying to relate 'emotional dependency' to attachment behaviour in the first year, as Ferguson (1970) has suggested, in that there may well be continuities between particular aspects of the early relationship with the mother and later behaviour but these may vary not only with sex but with individuals.

A common feature of many of the various preschool studies is to distinguish two main groups of attachment behaviour, proximity-seeking or contact-behaviour, and attention-seeking; these are differentiated, for instance, in the age-changes in shifts of target, attention-seeking generalising from being directed to adults to children, but proximity-seeking remaining directed at adults. Maccoby and Masters (1970) suggest that a unitary primary affectional system of attachment in infancy becomes differentiated by three or four years into proximity-seeking and attention-seeking clusters. They point out that the differentiation of target for the two types of behaviour may be related to the response of the target – adults being more likely to respond to a need for physical comfort in a satisfactory way, while peers may be as *interesting* as adults to interact with. What must be emphasised is how little is known of the relation between the responses of mother or peers to infant behaviour.

In considering Kohlberg's dismissal of mother–infant interaction as unrelated to later social development, the question of the potential importance of the early reciprocal behaviour of mother and infant must be examined.

The suggestion is frequently made about Harlow's rearing experiments that the inadequacy of the relationship with the cloth mother lies in the lack of reciprocal interaction, the lack of salient responses to the infant. (It is interesting however that young monkeys reared so that they can *see* other members of the same species are much more socially adequate, though they have no opportunity for physical interaction (Rowland, 1964).) Ferguson (1971) suggests there is a continuity between the earliest 'reciprocal' behaviour such as mutual gaze, vocalisation, and smiling with the mother, and the later reciprocal interactions which are seen as the way in which the child begins to distinguish self and other. There would of course be difficulties in showing what sort of continuity there is between early matching behaviour and later exchanges. If a positive relationship was demonstrated between early matching behaviour and later, this might also be explained by continuity of the mother's behaviour – each group of the child's matching behaviours related independently to different sets of maternal behaviour. If it was shown that particular sorts of reciprocal exchange are essential in the early years and that later aspects of social behaviour do not appear without them, we are still profoundly ignorant of the relationship between the two, and should perhaps be wary of giving the same label to both interchanges: a common description as 'communication' implies a continuity that may be inappropriate.

The question of the relation of the interchange between mother and child to the acquisition of both social and cognitive skills remains wide open. Ryan (this volume) has drawn attention to the importance in acts of communication of recognising intentions in order to 'secure uptake'; the importance for early language development of an adult 'tuned-in' to a continuity of exchange with the infant may have more general implications for cognitive development. Bruner (this volume) draws attention to the important part social relationships play in the development of skills, and in Piaget's view the chief importance of the mother is as the most central source of reciprocal exchange because she is most available and most responsive.

In discussing the effects of institutionalisation on children he says (Piaget and Inhelder, 1969, p. 27): 'It is not necessarily the maternal element as affectively specified (in the Freudian sense) that plays the principal role, but the lack of stimulating interactions, but these may be associated with the mother in so far as she creates a private mode of exchange between a given adult with her character and a given child with his.'

Perhaps the reciprocal exchange that is possible with a sensitive, receptive and constantly present adult provides possibilities that exchange with a less involved adult will lack.

Studies of children in residential care, such as those of the Tizards (this volume) may provide valuable evidence here. In one study (Tizard *et al.*, 1972) they demonstrated a relationship between the development of language in children in long-stay nurseries and the way the nursery was organised. A variable of particular importance was 'the quality of staff talk', and this variable they suggest was crucially related to the social relationship between staff and children, and among staff. In another study (Tizard and Tizard, 1971) they have described the difference in patterns of attachment that develop with prolonged stay in institutions. There is no significant correlation between language development and attachment behaviour as measured by separation protest (Tizard, personal communication), but as the authors point out the institution children who protested very much at separation were able to spend very little time with their favourite person, and so these data cannot be used to answer the question of how far other dimensions of the attachment relationship, such as time spent in close interaction with the attachment figure, may be important in language development.

The question of *how* the interaction with the mother figure relates to advances the baby makes in developing skills is another problem that observational work will help to solve. There are suggestions in Escalona's earlier studies (1969) that while new cognitive capacities are first demonstrated (passively as a response) in social situations with the mother, the active applications of the capacities as mastery behaviour is developed with inanimate objects, and only later appears in interchanges with people. On the other hand her observations also suggest that in many cases the baby's behaviour during interchange with the mother was either more complex or more complex and sustained. With the mother continually varying her behaviour in response to the baby, providing 'affective critical support' (see Bruner in this volume), it would be easy to understand this as the context for advances in behaviour.

The idea of the pleasure involved in the exchange introduces a third point arising from considering Kohlberg's challenge to the attachment concept, the issue of the distinction between cognitive and non-cognitive (affective?) aspects of the interaction. It is interesting that Kohlberg (1969), while suggesting that there is no reason to assume 'that early experience should have a basic effect on capacities for later social attachment unless early deprivation or trauma were so extreme as to retard responsiveness to external stimuli and cognitive development in general' comments in general on the damaging effects of institutionalisation on social development: 'It seems to be due to the absence of stable and pleasurable social interaction, rather than a lack of maternal caretaking which produces weakened ties.'

It is not clear why Kohlberg should make a distinction between lack of stable interaction that leads to 'weakened social ties', and the mother–child interaction in the first years that he suggests is unrelated to later social development. The elements that make the interaction 'stable and pleasurable' may be closely related to the aspects of the mother's behaviour in the first year that make her a source of security, but while these elements remain so unspecified, the relation between the reciprocal interchange and the security aspects of the relationship, and between the security aspects and later social development must remain an empirical question.

While the difficulties of using ideas of sensitivity and security of attachment have been underlined, it is not disputed that they may be of central importance; rather it is suggested that before they can be used in an explanatory way a first stage of careful description of the development of physical contact behaviour, attention-seeking and other aspects of the interaction is required, in terms that make it possible to examine both their separate development and their interrelations, and the course of change with age of the channels used. It is investigation of the qualitative differences in patterns of relationships between parent and child,

163

rather than attempts to measure the strengths of a bond, and a more careful separation of the parts played by the partners in interaction that is needed before we can understand both the source of individual differences in attachment and the wider significance of the bond between mother and child during the first year.

ACKNOWLEDGEMENT

The Richards and Bernal work cited is supported by grants from The Nuffield Foundation.

REFERENCES

Ainsworth, M. D. S. (1969). Object relations, dependency and attachment: a theoretical review of the infant-mother relationship. *Child Development*, **40**, 969–1025.

Ainsworth, M. D. S. and Wittig, B. A. (1969). Attachment and exploratory behaviour of one-year-olds in a strange situation. In Foss, B. M. (ed.). *Determinants of Infant Behaviour*, Vol. 4. London, Methuen.

Appell, G. and David, M. (1965). A study of mother–child interaction at 13 months. In Foss, B. M. (ed.). *Determinants of Infant Behaviour*, Vol. 3. London, Methuen.

Bell, R. Q. (1968). A reinterpretation of the direction of effects in studies of socialisation. *Psychol. Rev.* **75**, 81–95.

Bowlby, J. (1969). *Attachment and Loss*, Vol. 1, *Attachment*. London, Hogarth Press.

Escalona, S. K. (1969). *The Roots of Individuality*, London, Tavistock.

Escalona, S. K. and Corman, H. H. (1971). The impact of mothers' presence upon behaviour: the first year. *Human Developm.* **14**, 2–15.

Ferguson, L. R. (1970). Dependency motivation in socialisation. In Hoppe, R. A., Milton, G. A. and Simmel, E. C. (eds.). *Early Experiences and the Processes of Socialisation*. New York, Academic Press.

Ferguson, L. R. (1971). Origins of social development in infancy. *Merrill-Palmer Quart.* **17**, 119–37.

Harlow, H. F. (1961). The development of affectional patterns in infant monkeys. In Foss, B. M. (ed.). *Determinants of Infant Behaviour*, Vol. 1. London, Methuen.

Harlow, H. F. and Harlow, M. K. (1965). The affectional systems. In Schrier, A. M., Harlow, H. F. and Stollnitz, F. (eds.). *Behavior of Non-human Primates*, Vol. 2. New York, Academic Press.

Hinde, R. A. and Davies, L. M. (1972). Changes in mother–infant relationship after separation in rhesus monkeys. *Nature*, **239**, 41–2.

Hinde, R. A. and Spencer-Booth, Y. (1968). The study of mother–infant interactions in captive group-living rhesus monkeys. *Proc. Roy. Soc. B.* **169**, 177–201.

Hinde, R. A. and Spencer-Booth, Y. (1970). Individual differences in the responses of rhesus monkeys to a period of separation from their mothers. *J. Child Psychol. Psychiat.* **11**, 159–76.

Kohlberg, L. (1969). Stage and sequence: the cognitive–developmental approach to socialisation. In Goslin, D. A. (ed.), *Handbook of Socialization: Theory and Research*. Chicago, Rand-McNally.

Lewis, M. and Ban, P. (1971). Stability of attachment behaviour: a transformational analysis. Paper presented at Society for Research in Child Development Meetings, symposium on *Attachment: Studies in Stability and Change*. Minneapolis, April 1971.

Maccoby, E. and Masters, J. C. (1970). *Attachment and Dependency*. In Mussen, P. H. (ed.). *Carmichael's Manual of Child Psychology*, Vol. 2 (3rd ed.). New York, Wiley.

Moss, H. A. (1967). Sex, age and state as determinants of mother–infant interaction. *Merrill-Palmer Quart.* **13**, 19–36.

Piaget, J. and Inhelder, B. (1969). *The Psychology of the Child* (trans. Weaver, H.). London, Routledge and Kegan Paul.

Radke-Yarrow, M., Campbell, J. D. and Burton, R. V. (1968). *Child-rearing – an enquiry into research methods*. San Francisco, Jossey-Bass.

Rosenblatt, J. S. (1970). Onset and maintenance of maternal behavior in the rat. In Aronson, L. R., Tobach, E., Lehrman, D. S. and Rosenblatt, J. S. (eds.). *Development and Evolution of Behavior*. San Francisco, Freeman.

Rowland, G. L. (1964). The effects of total social isolation upon learning and social behavior in rhesus monkeys. Unpublished doct. dissert, Univ. Wisconsin.

Rutter, M. (1972). *Maternal Deprivation Reassessed*. London, Penguin.

Sander, L. W., Stechler, G., Burns, P. and Julia, H. (1970). Early mother–infant interaction and 24-hour patterns of activity and sleep. *J. Amer. Acad. Child Psychiat.* **9**, 103–23.

Schaffer, H. R. (1971). *The Growth of Sociability*. London, Penguin.

Schaffer, H. R. and Emerson, P. E. (1964). The development of social attachments in infancy. *Monogr. Soc. Res. Child. Devel.* **29**, No. 94.

Schaffer, H. R. and Emerson, P. E. (1968). Patterns of response to physical contact in early human development. *J. Child Psychol. Psychiat.* **5**, 1–13.

Sears, R. R., Rau, L. and Alpert, R. (1965). *Identification and Child Rearing*. Stanford, Stanford Univ. Press.

Tizard, J. and Tizard, B. (1971). The social development of two-year-old children in residential nurseries. In Schaffer, H. R. (ed.). *The Origins of Human Social Relations*. London. Academic Press.

Tizard, B., Cooperman, O., Joseph, A. and Tizard, J. (1972). Environmental effects on language development: a study of young children in long-stay residential nurseries. *Child Development*, **43**, 337–58.

Waldrop, M. F. and Bell, R. Q. (1966). Effects of family size and density on newborn characteristics. *Amer. J. Orthopsychiat.* **36**, 544–50.

Yarrow, L. J. (1967). The development of focussed relationships during infancy. In Hellmuth, J. (ed.). *The Exceptional Infant*, Vol. 1. New York, Brunner–Mazel.

9

The organisation of early skilled action

Jerome S. Bruner

Competence, of course, is a term that covers a wide range of skills and their appropriate deployment. The attainment of varied forms of competence in infancy and early childhood and the significance of such attainment for growth has been the topic of a 1972 C.I.B.A. Conference, and a volume of papers presented there is in process of being edited (Connolly and Bruner, 1974). For convenience, the forms of early competence can be divided into those which regulate interaction with other members of the species, and those involved in mastery over objects, tools, spatially and temporally ordered sequences of events. Obviously, the two cannot be fully separated, as witness the importance of imitation and modelling in the mastery of 'thing skills'. In the pages that follow, we shall be concerned principally with the early acquisition of skills relating to the manipulation of things – though perforce the role of certain social skills will be treated in the interest of explicating that topic. We do well to bear in mind that the growth of manipulatory skill – the use of the hands for solving problems – is not only a classic topic in developmental psychology (e.g. Gesell, 1926; Halverson, 1931; Mc-Graw, 1935), but also a key issue in the study of the evolution of the hominids and emergence of man (e.g. Napier, 1962; Washburn and Howell, 1960; LeGros Clark, 1963). For the human hand–eye–brain system makes possible not only high manual adaptability and dexterity, but also the emergence of the tool.

In the growth of such competence in infants, three themes are central – intention, feedback, and the patterns of action that mediate between them. These are the themes that are central to the present article; feedback needs brief discussion first, for it is often oversimplified. Feedback is now known to have at least three aspects: *internal* feedback that signals an intended action within the nervous system (sometimes called feed-forward for it occurs *prior* to overt action); *feedback proper* from the effector system *during* action; and *knowledge of results* that may occur only *after* action has been completed. Viewed in terms of these three functions, it can readily be seen as something more than the negative feedback of a control system.

We shall concentrate principally upon infants during the first year of life. The competences achieved during the first year can be roughly divided into five broad enterprises: feeding, perceiving or attending, manipulating the world, locomoting, and interacting with members of the species. There is another that is somewhat more subtle: it has to do with control of internal state, and this may be a sphere different from the others. In each of the five enterprises the infant comes early to solve problems of high complexity and does so on the basis of encounters with the environment that are too few in number, too unrepresentative, or too erratic in consequence, to be accounted for either on the basis of concept attainment or by the shaping effects of reinforcement. Initial 'learning' has a large element of preadaptation that reflects species-typical genetic instructions. But it is highly flexible preadaptation as we shall see. The initial patterns of action that emerge through exercise then become the constituents for new patterns of action directed at more remote or complex objectives. Here, too, the role of learning in the conventional sense is not clear. Indeed, what is striking about the opening year of life is how specialised and circumscribed the role of learning turns out to be. In the interest of clarity, the progress of a skill during the first year will first be described in programmatic terms and then later instanced with some specific examples of behavioural development.

We begin with the initial arousal of an intention in the infant by an appropriate object. Intention as used here involves an internal discharge in the nervous system whereby an act about to occur is not only produced in the effectors by the usual motor volley, but is also signalled to related sensory and co-ordination systems by a corollary discharge (Sperry, 1950) or efference copy (von Holst and Mittelstaedt, 1950) – or as Evarts (1971) now proposes to call it, by internal feedback preceding action. Even at the simplest level of postural adjustment or effector movement, it is impossible to conceive of directed action without the compensation made possible by such prior signalling of intention. Oscarsson (1970) has in the last years gone so far as to show the internal feedback loops that connect cortex to cerebellum and back to cortex, whereby 'voluntary' motor discharges from precentral gyrus downward are signalled to the cerebellum to regulate balance and, in turn, are modulated by the most recent input from balance organs better to generate an appropriate motor command. Intention viewed abstractly may be at issue philosophically. But it is a necessity for the biology of complex behaviour, by whatever label we wish to call it.

It is possible to argue at length about the 'origin' of intention in early infancy, and such arguments may indeed be fruitful in stimulating research. Intention, viewed behaviourally, has several measurable features: anticipation of the outcome of an act, selection among appropriate means for achievement of an end state, sustained direction of

168

behaviour during deployment of means, a stop order defined by an end state, and finally some form of substitution rule whereby alternative means can be deployed for correction of deviation or to fit idiosyncratic conditions. It can be argued from evidence that the *capacity* for all of these is present from birth (e.g. Bruner and Koslowski, 1972; Kalnins and Bruner, 1974) and that the patterned behaviour that initially occurs 'reflexly' or 'instinctually' is, by virtue of these capacities, converted into intentional action when the infant has had an opportunity to observe the results of his own acts.

The characteristic initial accompaniment of aroused intention in the infant is prolonged orienting accompanied by triggering of anticipatory consummatory activity. It is the nature of objects or states that arouse such intentionality that they operate like triggers or releasers, more like threshold phenomena than like reflexes in which stimulus magnitude determines response magnitude.

Initial arousal is often followed by a loosely ordered sequence of constituent acts that will later occur in an appropriate serial order to achieve the end state towards which the intention appears to be steering. Meanwhile, during this clumsy athetoid phase, the consummatory response will continue, and even the wrongly orchestrated constituent acts can be shown to have an appropriate adjustment with respect to the goal. The development of visually guided reaching is typical of this pattern. An appropriate free-standing object, of appropriate size and texture and at an appropriate distance (and these can be quite specifically described), first produces prolonged looking and, very shortly after, there is action of the mouth and tongue and jaws – the area to which a captured object will be transported once effective, visually guided reaching develops. If the intent persists, one can then observe anti-gravitational activity of arms and shoulders, clenching of fists in a 'grab' pattern, movement of arms, ballistic flinging of clenched fist, etc. (Bruner, May and Koslowski, 1972).

These constituent acts or subroutines are aroused, but they do not yet occur in the correct order for successful object capture. Yet it can be shown that in a diffuse way, each of the components is adapted to the goal though there has been no feedback from the effectors during the consummatory act (which has not occurred) nor can there be said to be 'knowledge of results' (for the same reason). Alt (1968) has shown, for example, that the ballistic flinging of the arm is well aimed, even when a blinder is placed at the side of the infant's eye, preventing a view of his active hand. And Koslowski and Bruner (1972) have indicated that the hand and arm movements are, though unsuccessful in capturing an object, roughly appropriate to the size of the object evoking activity towards it.

169

In time, and probably by virtue of sheer practice of the act in the presence of the releasing stimulus, which permits the co-ordination of internal and peripheral feedback, the act is successfully executed. An object is captured and brought to the mouth. Doubtless some of this progress depends on morphological maturation of relevant tracts in the nervous system, particularly tracts in the corpus callosum for much of the activity involves bilateral hand use, and the maturation of relevant callosum tracts is known to be slow (Conel, 1939–63). But we also know from the work of White, Castle and Held (1964) and of Held (1965) that practice is crucial in the perfection of such reaching. It is this practice that makes possible the form of co-ordination noted above – allowing the development of appropriate synchrony between feed-forward corollary discharges and feedback from the effectors, finding out how to put them into an orchestrated form much as the kittens in the Held and Hein (1963) experiments required active practice to put prismatically displaced visual input into synchrony with efferent discharges to the muscles and to the sense organs regulating the muscles – representing the intended as well as the completed action in the sensory system.

It is often difficult, to be sure, to distinguish between constituents and the larger-scale acts into which they are combined in carrying out a skilled act. For it is often the case that a highly practised complex skill becomes the constituent for a still more comprehensive skilled performance: walking, which is a complex serial structuring of component acts, very soon becomes so automatic as to fit easily into a variety of higher order acts. Paul Schiller (1952) puts it well in a highly important but overlooked paper entitled, 'Innate constituents of complex responses in primates':

Just which response is complex and which simple is not easily decided in the light of embryological behavior studies. Elements of complex responses are admitted to be ready prior to specific learning, but the question is whether the organism is not producing the compounds we observe without any training, just as its effectors mature. Experiments on maturational factors *versus* experience have led to contrasting results with various species and various tasks. In a long forgotten study Spaulding (1875) has shown that flying in birds was unimpeded after he prevented early practice. Essentially the same was found by Carmichael (1926) in the swimming of tadpoles, by Gesell (1926) in the climbing behavior of human twins. On the other hand, Shepard and Breed (1913) recorded that chicks have to learn how to peck seed in a few days of practice, whether freshly hatched or fed artificially for a considerable period allowing for maturation. Similarly Stone (1926) and later Beach (1942) have found severe impairment of copulating behavior in rats isolated from early contact with mates.

The contradiction in these results can be resolved by a dichotomy. The *constituents* of the motor pattern themselves mature. Due to internal, prefunctional factors, they appear at a certain stage of development (many of them traced in embryos) ready formed. Their application to external stimulus con-

170

figurations is something that must be learned. Such a dichotomy was reported by Mosely (1925) who found that pecking, striking and swallowing were unlearned responses whereas seizing of the grain was formed by practice.

Here we come to a puzzle. Once the act is successfully executed and repeated with success, i.e. constituents are put stably into proper serial order, there often appears a sharp alteration in the structure of the act used for achieving an intended outcome. For example, shortly after the first successful taking of an object, the fist rather than being closed prematurely which often happens before successful capture, now remains open at maximum extension until the object being sought is touched. There appears to be a reorganisation of components, with a substitution of hyper-extension ended by contact with the object for the previous routine of closure that begins with the extension of the arm. A constituent is drastically altered to fit the task requirements, in this case the alteration being in direct contrast to the act replaced.

At this point in the progress the effects of reinforcement seem to take over. Completion of the act with wide-open hand is now frequent enough to be effective. But reinforcement produces a *modification* of the action pattern-in-being rather than, as sometimes suggested, *selecting* elements from a trial-and-error pattern. Its effects are threefold, the first two quite unexceptional, the last puzzling. The first effect is to increase the anticipatory patterning of the act: e.g., the hand now begins to close gradually to the shape of the object as it approaches, rather than after it gets there. (By the way, we know from the work of Twitchell (1965) that the tactile-dominated 'instinctive groping reaction' shows months earlier a comparably patterned pronation and supination to fit the shape of objects touched, but not looked at.) The second effect is what we have come to call modularisation – the act gradually becomes less variable in latency and in execution time and more economical in expenditure of energy. The third and puzzling effect is that the now increasingly successful act is soon supplanted by a new pattern of action which may in fact include the previously mastered act as a component part. Thus, in place of the by-now well-modularised bilateral pounce reach (Bruner, 1968), the infant now six or seven months old, reaches in two steps: the first extends the hands out to the plane of the object, and the second closes in with the familiar anticipatory hand-closure pattern, a pause of some hundreds of milliseconds separating the two. The old programme does not 'disappear'; under stress, with overload, in unfamiliar surroundings it appears intact – as also when the more complex act fails of attainment (Bruner and May, 1972).

Again, reinforcement operates to modularise this newest pattern. But, there is still a question of what brought the new act into being. It is a question that is constantly forced upon us in many of the studies we conduct on reaching under visual guidance, on search patterns involving looking, on social interaction, and, indeed, in our research on nutritive behaviour as well. A new act is mastered, only to be supplanted by a 'higher-order action' that usually encompasses it as a subroutine. It is very much like the pattern found in the classical studies of Bryan and Harter (1899) on telegraphy code learning: once a lower-order pattern begins to work effectively, there is a shift to a higher-order pattern – individual letters, then words, then phrases, etc.

What leads to the emergence of particular higher-order action programmes is a puzzle many of us share. They plainly are not selected by a process of reinforcement from a 'lexicon' of random or near-random response elements. The new pattern emerges with an adaptive, serially ordered structure that reflects some internal principle of organisation that is triggered by the environment. The puzzle has an analogue in linguistic development where the child goes from one level of syntactic complexity to a higher one with no 'in-between' at all. Practice is necessary, to be sure, but not in a specific sense of successful practice with reinforcement selecting constituents or rules (cf. Brown, Cazden and Bellugi, 1969). When, in our studies, for example (Bruner, Lyons and Kaye, 1973) the child has routinised the task of holding two objects, one in each hand, there then occurs a first 'storage' activity for dealing with a third object placed before him – placing blocks in the crook of the arm or in the lap, and then recovering them. It is no more nor less mysterious than the presumably unprovoked first occurrence of imbedding in speech, which it formally resembles.

My speculation about what makes possible these quantum jumps in performance is very much in line with information-processing theories of development as noted above. Modularisation frees available information-processing capacity for further use in task analysis, just by virtue of constituent sub-routines requiring less attention. The reduction in attention is accomplished when co-ordination is achieved between internal feedback, peripheral feedback, and knowledge of results involving not only the co-ordination between different sense modalities as Birch and Lefford (1967) have proposed, but also synchrony within modalities as Evarts (1971) and Hess (1964) among many have pointed out. Similarly, 'preoccupation with means' abates with practice (Koslowski and Bruner, 1972) so that means–end scanning can be instituted anew. The mechanism that makes possible the achievement of serial order in behaviour is the ubiquitous 'feed-forward' loop mentioned earlier. But most important, given modularisation and the reduction in attention necessary to regulate an act, that act can then be incorporated into a higher-order, longer-sequence act without requiring so much attention as to disrupt regulation of the higher-order act.

172

What about the further 'task analysis' that is made possible by more available information-processing capacity? Welford (1968) in his analysis of skill proposes that there is a task translation process by which an operator converts a set of givens into requirements for carrying out an intended action. Feature extraction is guided by the instrumental requirements of achieving a given objective. This is the typical attention of somebody doing something. The more skilful we become in doing a task, the better and more relevant is this kind of task-relevant feature analysis. As the child develops, his *general* skill in task analysis improves markedly, as attested to by the increasing appropriateness of his *initial* efforts at dealing with new tasks. We shall return later to this crucial point. We know very little about such activity, though monographs on problem-solving behaviour like Duncker's (1945) and Maier's (1937) and studies like Saugstad's (1952) provide interesting leads concerning the combinatory nature of hypothesis in problem-solving – whether involving external objects used in a task or internal thought elements.

Goal-directed, skilled action, then, may be conceived of as the *construction* of serially ordered constituent acts, whose performance is modified towards less variability, more anticipation, and greater economy by benefit of feed-forward, feedback, and knowledge of results. The 'stock' of constituents from which such performances are constructed is in no sense (save perhaps initially) to be thought of as made up of fixed action patterns in the ethological sense. Nor is it something in the form of a fixed lexicon from which elements are drawn for use by a sentence generator. For one thing, there is too much variability in the component acts that go into skilled performance to be at all like a lexicon. In so far as they have a kinship with language, it is much more at the level of phonology, resembling the production of speech sounds. Like speech gestures, gestural components of a skilled motor act are generated intentionally to meet a specification. And like articulatory acts in speech, they are within anatomical limits capable of continuous variation in various attributes (e.g., open to closed hand is analogous to front to back vocalising). But in both instances, the continuous domain is rendered discontinuous. Not all positions are used for vowel production and not all positions of the hand are used in manipulating. In the case of speech articulation, the bases for discontinuity are not, contrary to earlier belief, arbitrary, but result from acoustic properties produced naturally by the articulatory mechanism and detected easily in speech perception – a simple reason why the distinctive features of speech sounds differ so little from language to language. The criteria by which component motor acts develop are more extrinsic: they fit the requirement of holding objects for precision uses or power uses, for cupping fluid or granular substances, for exploring with sensitive fingertips, etc. In the evolution

173

of the hand (Napier, 1962), it is plain that morphology has been selected to improve the efficiency of these effective hand gestures – as indeed, it may one day be shown that the evolutionary transformation of speech articulation served to increase the match between speech perception analysers and speech sound-generating mechanisms. But in both cases, articulation and skilled manual action, there is also enormous variation in execution, either to take into account the starting position of the articulatory mechanism or other 'local conditions', or to take account of the requirements imposed by the task at hand in manipulation.

K. N. Stevens (1971) puts the matter succinctly for the articulatory case in summarising the work on distinctive features of speech over the past decade.

(1) Examination of the relationships between articulatory configurations and the properties of the resulting acoustic signal suggests that there are, so to speak, preferred ranges of articulatory gestures. This range of articulation gives rise to acoustic outputs with attributes or properties that are distinctively different from the outputs for other articulatory gestures . . .

(2) Experiments on the perception of speech and speech-like sounds indicate that the auditory mechanism responds selectively to acoustic stimuli that possess specific attributes. When a stimulus is perturbed in a way that moves it outside the region encompassed by a given attribute, there is a sharp change in the perception of the stimulus. These experimental findings suggest that the human auditory mechanism is endowed with a set of 'property directors'.

(3) An attribute that is matched to the property generating capabilities of the articulatory mechanism and to the property detecting capabilities of the auditory mechanism is, in some sense, optimal as a building block which forms an element of the language code. Such a building block is often called a distinctive feature of language.

(4) During natural speech, in which a given distinctive feature may occur in various contexts, its ideal acoustic attributes may be modified . . .

In the case of component gestures of the manipulatory system, again there are preferred positions and, as noted above, criteria not of perceptibility but of utility with respect to object handling. These are what make the initial stock of 'building blocks' from which acts of manipulation are constructed. And like the distinctive features of speech, to paraphrase Stevens' four points, they vary from their ideal form to fit the requirements of an ongoing task.

We can better understand, in the light of the above, the significance of certain preadapted patterns of manipulatory activity that are evoked by sight of an object, though there may have been no prior experience in manipulating them – as in patterns of groping at a virtual object in the study by Bower, Broughton, and Moore (1970) or with size-appropriate gesturing towards objects before the child can effect a visually guided reach, as reported by Bruner and Koslowski (1972). These are probably highly overdetermined responses with a long evolutionary history that constitute a 'launching stock' from which initial skilled action is constructed. In this sense, they are like the first speech sounds acquired by the child in the stage of babbling that immediately precedes speech (Miller and McNeill, 1968).

Obviously, speech is more idealised or standardised than skilled action. It is not that the intention to transmit a given message is any more precisely defined than the intention to produce a given effect by one's motor action. Both may be equally precise. The difference comes, rather, from the requirement of communication, of sharing with another human being, using a common code. Take two examples, both from the gestural level: waving good-bye and scratching an itch.[1] We can scratch our heads with any or all fingers, by rubbing a palm or the back of the hand on the itchy spot, by rubbing an arm on it, etc. With respect to 'waving bye-bye' the range of variation is sharply constricted. Turning the hand towards ourselves is meaningless, relaxing the wrist beyond a certain limpness signals something quite different, half-closing the hand gives the appearance that one is clawing the air in desperation. It is only when an activity (i.e., defined by an intended outcome and an appropriate means) must be *demonstrated to another* that it becomes standardised or idealised (cf. Bruner and Olson, 1973 for a further discussion of demonstration, the 'symbolisation' of action). The point is mentioned here in this much detail better to illustrate the similarity and the difference between the activity of speech and skilled manipulatory activity. Both are governed by rules of productive combination of means for the achievement of intended outcomes – i.e., both involve the *construction of behaviour* rather than the *acquisition of responses*. But one is constrained by the nature of a shared code that is idealised in order to reduce ambiguity.

The picture of development drawn thus far is much too task-directed, too playless to be characteristic of the first year of life. For it is not until we consider early play that we understand more fully how the child achieves his growing competence. There is, of course, much problem-solving in the first year, episodes where an intention is held invariant while the means used to attain its objective are varied. But there is also much behaviour that seems to be without clear-cut means–end structure, where the activity seems more playful, where ends are changed to fit available means, and means and ends become admixed.

[1] I am grateful to George Miller for the example.

Vygotsky (1967), speaking of somewhat older children, remarks that 'a child's play must always be interpreted as the imaginary, illusory realization of unrealizable desires'. Play at this higher level is wish fulfilment of a displaced or diffuse kind, often helped by what Vygotsky calls a pivot – some prop that carries externally a feature of the wished-for state – e.g., a stick serves as a horse to ride on. While I agree with Vygotsky, I think that the achievement of this kind of symbolic play in late infancy and early childhood is preceded by an earlier type of play, the exercise of which is crucial for development during the first year or year and a half.

It might best be called mastery play, and its form is playful means–end matching. Rather than taking the form of 'illusory realization of unrealizable desires' it consists precisely in extending to new limits already achieved skills. Several examples drawn from our own studies at Harvard will illustrate what appear to be pleasure-giving variations of newly acquired routines. The six-month-old infant, having learned to hold on to an object and get it easily to his mouth, then begins a programme of variation. When he takes the object after mastery has been achieved, he holds it to look at, he shakes it, he bangs it on his high chair, he drops it over the edge, and before long he manages to *fit the object into every activity* into which it can be put. Inversely, when the young infant masters a new step in sensory-motor development, as in simultaneous use of power and precision grips so that he can hold an object steady in one hand while exploring it with the fingers of the other, he very soon uses this new act *on any object* that has a 'loose end' or 'pick-at-able' property. In the first case, a new object is fitted into as many routines as available; in the second, a newly mastered act is addressed to as many different objects as available. Both are absorbing work (or play) for the child. It has been surprising to us how long the infant will stay with such variation of activity – a six- to eight-month-old up to half an hour.

This type of mastery play is particularly characteristic of higher primates. Many examples can be found in Köhler's *Mentality of Apes* (1927). A particularly striking example of placing an object into as many possible contexts as available is provided by the following observation of a chimpanzee at the London Zoo made by Caroline Loizos (1967) over a forty-five-minute period.

I bounce a tennis ball in front of the cage several times so that she hears as well as sees it and place it inside on the floor. She backs away, watching ball fixedly – approaches with pouted lips, pats it – it rolls. She backs hurriedly to the wall. Hair erection . . . J. pokes at it from a distance, arm maximally extended, watching intently; looks at me; pokes ball and immediately sniffs finger . . . She dabs at ball and misses, sniffs finger; she backs away and circles ball from a distance of several feet, watching it intently. Sits and watches ball . . . (pause of several minutes) . . . walks around ball. J. walks past the ball again even closer but quite hurriedly. She left some of the woodwool in the cage to peer at the ball from a new angle, approaches ball by sliding forward on stomach with arms and legs tucked underneath her, so that protruded lips are very close to ball without actually touching it. Withdraws. Pokes a finger towards it and sniffs finger . . . Returns to ball, again slides forward on stomach with protruded lips without actually connecting. Pokes with extended forefinger, connects and it moves; she scurries backwards; more dabs at it with forefinger and it moves again (but not far because of the woodwool in that area of the cage). J. dabs, ball rolls and she follows, but jumps back in a hurry as it hits the far wall. She rolls the ball on the spot with her forefinger resting on it, then rolls it forward, watching intently the whole time. She dabs again – arm movement now more exaggerated, flung upwards at end of movement. Tries to pick ball up between thumb and fore-finger very gingerly . . . fails. Rolls it *towards* her, sniffs with lowered head. Picks it up and places it in front of her – *just* touches it with lips – pushes it into straw with right forefinger – touches it with lower lip pushed out – pokes, flicking up hand at end of movement, but backs away as it rolls towards her. Bites at own thumb. Dabs at it with lips, pulls it towards her and backs away. Examines own lip, squinting down, where it touched ball. Picks at it with fore-finger and covers ball as it rolls (walking on all fours, with head down to watch ball as it rolls along at a point approximately under her belly). Pushes with outside knuckles. Stamps on it, dabbing at it with foot. Sits on it, rolls it with foot; carries it gingerly in hand and puts it on the shelf, climbing up to sit beside it. It drops down – she holds it in one hand and pats it increasingly hard with the other. Holds it in right hand, picks at stripe on ball with her left. Rolls it between two hands. Rolls it between hand and shelf. Holds and pats; bangs it on shelf. Holds and *bites*, examining ball after each bite. Ball drops from shelf and she pats at it on ground with right hand. Lies on her back, balances ball on her feet, holding it there with hands; sits up, holds ball under chin and rolls it two or three times round back of neck and under chin. It rolls away and she chases it immediately and brings it back to shelf. Lies on backs and holds it on feet. Presses it against teeth with her feet and bites – all fear appears to be gone – lies and bites at ball held in feet, hands. Rolls it in feet, hands. Climbs to ceiling, ball drops and she chases it at once, J. makes playface, rolls and tumbles with ball, around, over, under ball, bangs it; bites it, rolls it over her own body.

Morris (1967) has argued that one can roughly divide species into those whose adaptation is highly specialised (e.g., tree squirrel) and those that are more despecialised or 'opportunist', with the latter group requiring more curiosity and more play, what he calls 'neophilia'. But one instance of a fairly specialised bird might give us pause. Cullen (1971) reports that the fledgeling common tern is early capable of running along hard sand and taking wing in low flight – provided the flying is carried out with no seeming objective and in isolation from a broader programme of goal-directed behaviour. If now, one moves a dummy predator overhead at a speed that requires flying to escape, the young birds resorts to the earlier developed form of running. The young tern is also flightless if one tempts it with food moved along at a speed such that it could be caught by flying pursuit but not by running. The initial flying of the bird appears to be 'flying in play'.

Play, then, has the effect of maturing some modular routines for later incorporation in more encompassing programmes of action. It also seems to 'trial run' a range of possible routines for employing already established sub-routines. Not *all* forms of activity need such exercise – as we know from such pioneering studies as those by McGraw (1935) on Johnny and Jimmy, particularly where such tightly knit synergies as walking are involved. But certainly manipulation does require it, and certainly complex oculomotor scanning of visual displays (e.g., Mundy-Castle and Anglin, 1969; Mackworth and Bruner, 1970; Vurpillot, 1968; and Gardner, 1971), and certainly social interaction (e.g., Harlow, 1959; Ainsworth and Bell, 1969; Bowlby, 1969). And as Schiller remarks, whenever action involves the serial application of constituents to external stimuli with the objective of altering a state of the world, then exercise is particularly needed. For exercise to be highly flexible, play must precede it.

I shall speculate that the more productive the programme of action of the adult of the species, the greater the likelihood of mastery play earlier on in development in that species, with higher primates and man being at the top of the scale. But here one would also do well to bear in mind Morris' point (1967) on the types of 'opportunist' adaptations that might require of a species more opportunity for play.

Much has been left out of this account of the development of early competence, but one omission is unpardonable. The human infant is above all else helpless and reliant upon caretaking by a mother or somebody standing in that role. There is an enormous reliance upon adequate social relationships if the child is to get on with the kind of skill development we have been considering. This is the sort of diffuse, affective yet critical support the child needs in order to thrive. Without it, sustained intention-directed behaviour flags and we have an infant 'failing to thrive'. The range of competences involved in such behaviour, recently brought together in a masterful review by Bowlby (1969) could equally well be the subject of a paper entitled, 'The competence of infants'. Bowlby's work, indeed, provides a justification for the special direction pursued in this paper. But I would like to concentrate briefly upon an aspect of competence that is peculiarly social; it is 'modelling'.

Modelling is a powerful means for transmitting highly patterned behaviour. The mechanisms whereby one organism patterns his behaviour on another's is, to be sure, poorly understood (e.g., Flanders, 1968). This is not the place to explore these mechanisms; rather let me comment, as Hamburg (1968) has most recently, on the widespread occurrence of 'adult-watching' among young primates from the pongid apes through man, a pattern in which the observation of adult behaviour is followed by the incorporation of observed patterns into play among the young. Careful studies of the young in simple hunter-gatherer human societies (Marshall and Marshall, 1963; Lee, 1965; Fortes, 1938) all highlight this same pattern. I should like to comment in passing that in order to do such observational 'learning' the child must be able to construct complex behaviour to match the sample. A major accomplishment of the kind of initial skill-learning we have been discussing is precisely that it provides the means for the young to enter such observation–play activity. Studies by Wood and Ross (1972) at the Center for Cognitive Studies indicate that the child's *skill* at a complex construction task *per se* determine to what extent he is capable of taking advantage of skilled behaviour being modelled by the experimenter. The task involves putting together flats of four blocks by a moderately difficult peg system, then arranging these flats into a pyramid. The child skilled only in putting together pairs will often take apart the experimenter's proffered four-block constructions to follow her way of putting together pairs. So we do well to recognise that preliminary skill mastery provides the basis for utilising modelling and for carrying out imitation. Note as well in the young that the 'imitation' of adult patterns takes place not directly, but through incorporation in play.

Two closely related points, one practical, the other theoretical, will serve to conclude the discussion. There is inherent in the description given of the growth of infant skill an emphasis on self-initiated, intentional behaviour. Surely, the chief practical recommendation one would have to make on the basis of what has been said thus far is that the infant should be encouraged to venture (or at least not discouraged), rewarded for venturing his own acts, and sustained against distraction or premature interferences in carrying them out. It is a point of view very alien from such ideas as preventing 'deprivation' or providing 'enrichment', both of which are highly passive conceptions. From a practical and theoretical point of view, the controlling motif of skill acquisition as presented here is 'opportunity to initiate and sustain action' in play and in carrying out intentions with a further opportunity this provides for co-ordinating feed-forward, feedback, and knowledge of results. It goes without saying that there are many affective and social factors that directly affect this kind of development – the nurturing conditions discussed by Bowlby (1969), by Ainsworth and Bell (1969), and by Harlow (1959).

Elsewhere I have argued (Bruner, 1970) that 'cultures of failure' resulting from persistent poverty often have the effect of signalling very early to the young and to the caretakers of the young a discouragement with or a frustration-saving reduction in the setting of goals, the mobilising of means, the cultivation of delay in gratification. The effects are very widespread in terms of development, and there is reason to believe that they begin early, though they may not show up until later testing. Poverty does not necessarily produce the signals of powerlessness and defeat that get through to the young, though the important work of Philip and Maxine Schoggen (1971) suggests that in the economically depressed home there are fewer challenging 'environmental force units (EFU)' tempting the child into activity on his own.

Children in middle-income homes as compared to children in low-income homes had EFU characterized by a higher percent of units in which they were (1) *given or asked for information*, (2) *engaged in more extended interaction*, (3) *given an obligation to perform* some specific action, (4) *in harmony* with the goal of the agent, and (5) receiving and giving messages through a *verbal medium*. By contrast, the children in low-income homes, as compared to children in middle-income homes had higher percents of EFU in which they were (1) asked to do *or to stop doing* something, (2) given *negative feedback* and prohibiting obligation, (3) utilizing signals or *physical contacts* in communication, and (4) *in conflict with* and receiving negative affect from the EFU agents.

We would do well, now, to examine by experimental means not only the factors that affect the kind of skill acquisition that has concerned us, but also the social ecology that sustains or impedes it. For it may well be that we have, in our dismay over the effects of stunting environments, failed fully to appreciate the nature and importance of environments that are both supportive and challenging. The theoretical conclusion to which we must come on the basis of the present discussion is that a great deal of the orderliness in early skilled behaviour comes from internal biological sources and is, so to speak, shaped but not constructed by the environment. The first orderly, skilled behaviour is virtually 'released' by appropriate objects in the environment, presented under appropriate conditions of arousal. A close examination of skill acquisition following this initial, pre-adapted stage suggests that a capacity for the appropriate *construction* of skilled action, designed to achieve intended ends, is operative. Skilled acts, to put it in simplest terms, are constructed by the serial deployment of constituent subroutines. The role of learning in the classical sense is to shape and correct these constructions to meet the idiosyncratic nature of particular instances of tasks encountered. Much of the task of 'learning' to put constituent acts together for the appropriate attainment of intended objectives occurs in play, as we have argued. Learning, under the circumstances, deserves to be put into quotation marks, since under conditions of play, there is no reinforcement for the sorts of sequences that will later appear in skilled behaviour. If one chooses to call play 'latent learning' (e.g., Tolman, 1932) or think of it as providing an opportunity for S-S and R-S learning, one can have no quarrel. To speak of early skill as being *constructed* or selected by contingencies of reinforcement is, on the basis of the evidence, both contrary to fact and obscurantist in effect.

The ubiquitousness of transfer in skill-learning, moreover, cannot by the same token be accounted for by a principle of generalisation – be it of response or stimulus. Rather, skilled acts are constructed to fit the requirements of a task. A task can be conceived of as an hypothesis about how to fulfil a given intention under given conditions. And just as one may conceive of a language-generating device as capable of instancing an intended meaning by a variety of paraphrases, so too one can posit that an intended result will be achieved by a variety of actions, each one generated by a device that is capable of constructing paraphrases of the intention, each designed to meet different local conditions.

The study of skill acquisition, as Lashley (1951) long ago urged, must take into account the serial structure of acts and the extent to which they achieve intended results in the light of local conditions, and how they are modified when they do not. It is this process that underlies the growth of competence in the infant as well as in the adult, with the principal difference being that the latter has many more and particularly many more higher-order constituent routines for combining, a much more sophisticated capacity for task analysis, and a better mastery of 'time-binding'. What this means methodologically is that one cannot proceed in the study of skill and its growth by choosing arbitrary responses followed by arbitrary contingencies. There are, as the ethologists have insisted, natural 'chunks' of behaviour, natural orderings of constituents, etc. The ordinary operant conditioning paradigm – choose any operant and bring it under the control of an S and a reinforcer – is no more revealing of the growth of skill than the rate of learning of paired associates is relevant to the learning of language.

REFERENCES

Ainsworth, M. D. S. and Bell, S. M. (1969). Some contemporary patterns of mother–infant interaction in the feeding situation. In Ambrose, A. (ed.). *Stimulation in Early Infancy*. New York, Academic Press.

Alt, J. (1968). The Use of Vision in Early Reaching. Unpublished honours thesis, Department of Psychology, Harvard Univ.

Beach, F. A. (1942). Comparison of copulatory behaviour of male rats raised in isolation, cohabitation, and segregation. *J. Genet. Psychol.* **60**, 121–36.

Birch, H. G. and Lefford, A. (1967). Visual differentiation, intersensory integration, and voluntary motor control. *Monog. Soc. Res. Child Development*, **32**, 1–87.

Bower, T. G. R., Broughton, J. M. and Moore, M. K. (1970). The co-ordination of visual and tactual input in infants. *Percept. Psychophysics*, **8**, 51–3.

Bowlby, J. (1969) *Attachment and Loss*, Vol. 1, *Attachment*. London, Hogarth Press.

Brown, R., Cazden, C. B. and Bellugi, U. (1969). The child's grammar from I to III. In Hill, J. P. (ed.). *Minnesota Symposium on Child Psychology*. Minneapolis, Univ. Minn. Press.

Bruner, J. S. (1968). *Processes of Cognitive Growth: Infancy*. Heinz Werner Lecture Series. Barre, Mass., Clark Univ. Press.

Bruner, J. S. (1970). *Poverty and Childhood*. Occasional paper, Merrill-Palmer Institute, Detroit, Mich.

Bruner, J. S. (1974). The uses of immaturity. In Connolly, K. and Bruner, J. S. (eds.). *The Early Growth of Competence* (C.I.B.A. Foundation). New York, Academic Press.

Bruner, J. S. and Koslowski, B. (1972). Visually preadapted constituents of manipulatory action. *Perception*, **1**, 3–14.

Bruner, J. S. and May, A. (1972). *Cup to Lip* (film). New York, Wiley.

Bruner, J. S. and Olson, D. R. (1973). Learning through experience and learning through media. *National Society for the Study of Education Yearbook, 1973*.

Bruner, J. S., Lyons, K. and Kaye, K. (1973). On handling multiple objects. In Bruner, J. S. (ed.). *The Growth of Skill*. New York, W. W. Norton.

Bruner, J. S., May, A. and Koslowski, B. (1972). *The Intention to Take* (film). New York, Wiley.

Bryan, W. L. and Harter, N. (1899). Learning a hierarchy of habits. *Psychol. Rev.* **6**, 349–59.

Carmichael, L. (1926). The development of behaviour in vertebrates experimentally removed from the influence of external stimulation. *Psychol. Rev.* **33**, 51–8.

Conel, J. L. (1939–63). *The Postnatal Development of the Human Cerebral Cortex*, Vols. 1–6, Cambridge, Mass., Harvard Univ. Press.

Connolly, K. and Bruner, J. S. (1974). (eds.). *The Early Growth of Competence* (C.I.B.A. Foundation). New York, Academic Press.

Cullen, M. (1971). Personal communication.

Duncker, K. (1945). On problem-solving (trans. Lees, L. S.). *Psychology Monographs* **58**, No. 248.

Evarts, E. V. (1971). Feedback and corollary discharge: a merging of the concepts. *Neurosc. Res. Prog. Bull.* **9**, 86–112.

Flanders, J. P. (1968). A review of research on imitative behaviour. *Psychol. Bull.* **69**, 316–37.

Fortes, M. (1938). Social and psychological aspects of education in Taleland. Suppl. to *Africa*, **11**, No. 4.

Gardner, J. (1971). The Development of Object Identity in The First Six Months of Human Infancy. Unpublished Ph.D. dissertation, Harvard Univ.

Gesell, A. (1926). Maturation and infant behaviour pattern. *Psychol. Rev.* **36**, 307–19.

Halverson, H. M. (1931). An experimental study of prehension in infants by means of systematic cinema records. *Genet. Psychol. Monog.* **10**, 107–284.

Hamburg, D. (1968). Evolution of emotional responses: evidence from recent research on non-human primates. *Sci. Psychoanal.* **12**, 39–54.

Harlow, H. F. (1959). Love in infant monkeys. *Scientific American*, **200**, 68–74.

Held, R. (1965). Plasticity in sensory-motor systems. *Scientific American,* **213,** 84–94.

Held, R. and Hein, A. (1963). Movement-produced stimulation in the development of visually guided behaviour. *J. Comp. Physiol. Psychol.* **56,** 872–6.

Hess, W. R. (1964). *The Biology of Mind* (trans. von Bonin, G.). Chicago and London, Chicago Univ. Press.

Holst, E. von, and Mittelstaedt, H. (1950). Das Reafferenzprinzip. *Naturwissenschaften,* **37,** 464–76.

Kalnins, I. and Bruner, J. S. Control of visual focus by sucking. *J. Child Psychol.* in press.

Köhler, W. (1927). *The Mentality of Apes* (trans. Winter, E.). New York, Harcourt Brace.

Koslowski, B. and Bruner, J. S. (1972). Learning to use a lever. *Child Development* **43,** 790–9.

Lashley, K. S. (1951). The problem of serial order in behaviour. In Jeffress, L. A. (ed.). *Cerebral mechanisms in Behavior: the Hixon Symposium.* New York, Wiley.

Lee, R. (1965). Subsistence Ecology of !Kung Bushmen. Unpublished Ph.D. dissertation, Berkeley Univ. Calif.

LeGros Clark, W. E. (1963). *The Antecedents of Man.* New York, Harper.

Loizos, C. (1967). Play behaviour in higher primates: a review. In Morris, D. (ed.). *Primate Ethology.* London, Weidenfeld and Nicolson.

Mackworth, N. H. and Bruner, J. S. (1970). How adults and children search and recognise pictures. *Human Development* **13,** 149–77.

Maier, N. R. F. (1937). Reasoning in rats and human beings. *Psychol. Rev.* **44,** 365–78.

Marshall, L. and Marshall, L. (1963). The bushmen of Kalahari. *National Geographic,* **23,** 866–88.

McGraw, M. (1935). *A Study of Johnny and Jimmy.* New York, Appleton-Century-Crofts.

Miller, G. A. and McNeill, G. D. (1968). Psycholinguistics. In Lindzey, G. and Aronson, E. (eds.). *Handbook of Social Psychology.* Reading, Mass., Addison-Wesley.

Morris, D. (1967). (ed.). *Primate Ethology.* London, Weidenfeld and Nicolson.

Moseley, D. (1925). The accuracy of the pecking responses in chicks. *J. Comp. Physiol. Psychol.* **5,** 75–97.

Mundy-Castle, A. C. and Anglin, J. (1969). The development of looking in infancy. Presented at Biennial Conference of the Society for Research in Child Development, Santa Monica, California.

Napier, J. (1962). The evolution of the hand. *Scientific American,* **140,** 1070–6.

Oscarsson, O. (1970). Functional organization of spinocerebellar paths. In Iggo, A. (ed.). *Handbook of Sensory Physiology,* Vol. 2, *Somatosensory System,* Berlin, Springer-Verlag.

Saugstad, P. (1952). Incidental memory and problem-solving. *Psychol. Rev.* **59,** 221–6.

Schiller, P. H. (1952). Innate constituents of complex responses in primates. *Psychol. Rev.* **59,** 177–91.

Schoggen, M. and Schoggen, P. (1971). Environmental forces in the home lives of three-year-old children in three population subgroups. D.A.R.C.E.E. Papers and Reports, Vol. 5, No. 2. (John F. Kennedy Center for Research on Education and Human Development, George Peabody College, Nashville, Tenn.)

Shepard, J. F. and Breed, F. S. (1913). Maturation and use in the development of an instinct. *J. Anim. Behav.* **3**, 274–85.

Spalding, D. (1875). Instinct and acquisition. *Nature*, **12**, 507–8.

Sperry, R. W. (1950). Neural basis of the spontaneous optokinetic response produced by visual inversion. *J. Comp. Physiol. Psychol.* **43**, 482–9.

Stevens, K. N. (1971). Perception of phonetic segments: evidence from phonology, acoustics, and psychoacoustics. In Horton, D. L. and Jenkins, J. (eds.). *The Perception of Language.* Columbus, O., Charles Merrill Publishing Co.

Stone, C. P. (1926). The initial copulatory response of female rats reared in isolation from the age of twenty days to the age of puberty. *J. Comp. Physiol. Psychol.* **6**, 73–83.

Tolman, E. C. (1932). *Purposive Behavior in Animals and Man.* New York, Appleton-Century-Crofts.

Twitchell, T. E. (1965). The automatic grasping response of infants. *Neuropsychol.* **3**, 247–59.

Vurpillot, E. (1968). The development of scanning strategies and their relation to visual differentiation. *J. Exper. Child Psychol.* **6**, 632–50.

Vygotsky, L. S. (1967). Play and its role in the mental development of the child. *Soviet Psychology*, **5**, 6–18. (From *Voprosy psikhologii* 1966, **12**, 62–76).

Washburn, S. L. and Howell, F. C. (1960). Human evolution and culture. In Tax, S. (ed.). *The Evolution of Man*, Vol. 2. Chicago, Univ. Chicago Press.

Welford, A. T. (1968). *Fundamentals of Skill.* London, Methuen.

White, B. L., Castle, P. and Held, R. (1964). Observations on the development of visually directed reaching. *Child Development*, **35**, 349–64.

Wood, D. and Ross, G. (1972). Planning in three- to five-year-olds: a developmental study. Centre for Cognitive Studies, Harvard Univ.

10

Early language development: towards a communicational analysis

Joanna Ryan

I INTRODUCTION

It is a sociological commonplace that language is an important instrument of socialisation. As such, various features of language have been extolled, particularly its 'detachability from the here and now' (Berger and Luckman, 1967). This, expressed in different forms by other writers, is seen as allowing the efficient transmission of cultural norms, of presenting absent realities, of allowing quick and abstract thought, and of facilitating the definition and communication of subjective experience. Relatively little attention has been given within sociological writings to what makes these crucial instrumental roles of language possible. The process of acquiring language in itself constitutes a form of socialisation. This is particularly true of the very earliest stages of development when the child first comes to participate in dialogues with others, and when she first uses signs whose meaning is socially rather than individually determined.

Within psychology, recent psycholinguistic work has neglected the earliest, presyntactic, stages of language development, concentrating exclusively on the details of the child's subsequent mastery of grammar. This approach can be characterised as exclusively cognitive, in the sense that it regards language as something to be studied as the *object* of the child's knowledge, and ignores all the other skills that determine actual language use. This neglect of what has come to be known as 'communicative competence' is not only serious in itself, but has also led to a distorted view of the child's grammatical abilities. This distortion is seen most clearly in McNeill's (1966) exaggerated claims as regards the child's 'achievements' in acquiring syntax with such alleged speed. If the acquisition of syntax were seen in a broader developmental perspective, as based on the child's pre-existing social, communicative and verbal skills, it would not seem quite the 'mystery' that McNeill (1970) supposes it to be. This recent neglect of presyntactic language development is in marked contrast to the importance attached to it in the writings of earlier psychologists and linguists.

The aim of this chapter is to provide a framework for the analysis and description of the communicative skills that a child acquires in the first

185

two years of life. As will become apparent, many of the problems that face an investigator in this field are at present primarily descriptive and conceptual ones – how to talk about communication. We currently lack any means of analysing human communication at anything more than a physical and mechanistic level (e.g. Goldman-Eisler, 1968). Recent work in the philosophy of language (e.g. Grice, 1957) and in social psychopathology (e.g. Watslavick, Beavin and Jackson, 1968) do however suggest some guidelines for constructing such a framework. This lack of any framework is particularly serious when early language development is considered. It is one contention of this chapter that before the appearance of marked syntactic forms in a child's speech, the child is developing skills that are at least as essential to speaking and understanding language as the mastery of grammar is supposed to be. The so-called 'one-word stage' cannot be regarded as simply the mere accumulation of a vocabulary, in preparation for its incorporation in later sentences. Rather, during this time, a child is learning a lot about how to talk, how to do many different things with words. Not only are the conventional meanings of words learnt, but so also are various nonlinguistic conventions about the appropriate utterance of such words, particularly as regards participation in mutual dialogues with others. Further the use and understanding of standard words develops at a time when the ability to communicate non-verbally is well established, in the sense of being able to influence the behaviour of others, and of indulging in reciprocal interchanges of various kinds.

'Communicative competence' is an extremely complex notion, and one that is in danger of being used in an oversimplified way, as a panacea for all psycholinguistic ills. Hymes (1971) presents a sociocultural analysis, emphasising the diversity of communicative means. Campbell and Wales (1970) define communicative competence as the ability to produce or understand utterances which are 'appropriate to the context in which they are made' (p. 247), a definition very similar to that of Marshall's (1971). Campbell and Wales in their criticisms of Chomskian notions of linguistic competence advocate greater attention to 'situational' factors involved in the production of utterances, as well as to the nature of adult–child interaction, in attempting to explain language acquisition. Marshall argues that any adequate model of language use has to characterise the shared knowledge, 'the semantic congruence between the contents of two minds' (p. 46), that makes the successful performance of acts of communication possible. In both these accounts the task for the psychologist is to analyse how the ability to produce 'appropriate' responses is grafted on to other linguistic abilities, that is, to explain how linguistic abilities are *applied* in various limiting social conditions.

186

Habermas (1970) criticises Chomskian notions of linguistic competence, not on the grounds that Campbell and Wales do, of insufficient attention to social context, but instead on more radical grounds. His arguments also apply to Campbell and Wales' attempts to analyse communicative competence. His main criticism is of the 'monologic' model of communication that is implied, such that successful communication is attributable to the fact that both speaker and hearer are previously equipped with the same pre-established code.

Habermas argues that verbal communication cannot be understood only as an application of linguistic competence, limited by prevailing empirical conditions, but instead that the 'structure of intersubjectivity' that makes such application possible has to be explained. Intersubjectivity between any speakers capable of mutual understanding is made possible by what he calls 'dialogue constitutive universals', and communicative competence is defined as mastery of these. Such universals allow for the interlacing of perspectives between speakers, for the relating of speakers to the referents of conversation, and for other pragmatic aspects of the speech situation. Habermas maintains that these 'dialogue constitutive universals' are expressed in discourse by linguistic elements, such as personal and demonstrative pronouns, expressions of space and time, and forms of address. Whilst one might query the explicitly linguistic nature of Habermas' dialogue universals, his emphasis on the structure of intersubjectivity presupposed by successful speech is extremely important. This is particularly so when considering what contribution non-verbal forms of reciprocal interaction between adults and children make to subsequent language development. It is also important when considering the active role of adults in interpreting children's early utterances. Various forms of interaction between adults and children that contribute to the establishment of intersubjectivity of meaning will be discussed in section III of this chapter. The next section is a critique of previous work.

II CRITIQUE OF PREVIOUS WORK

Presyntactic language development has been studied from many different points of view. The various interests have very little connection with each other as yet, although there are some common themes. There are no detailed theories, only some rather broad views, with a scattering of facts.

(1) One line of investigation – one which provides at least apparent facts – is developmental in the following sense. Using various criteria as indicators of beginning to speak, reliable group differences are found.

Thus girls in general speak earlier than boys (e.g. Illingworth, 1966), first-borns slightly earlier than second-borns (e.g. Morley, 1957), twins later than singletons (e.g. Day, 1932), children in institutions later than those reared at home, children with middle-class parents earlier than those with working-class ones (e.g. Templin, 1957), children with subsequent average I.Q.'s earlier than those with very low I.Q.'s. These generalisations are of course crude, in that there is both great overlap between the groups, and great individual variation within groups. However all these early group differences persist in later language development, and in some cases, for example those related to social class, grow larger.

Much effort has been put into the collection of this kind of material, into obtaining age norms for various measures, into devising more reliable and detailed tests of language development, and providing remedial or intervention programmes for those who fall behind. Such work, whilst it certainly provides facts and correlations that any complete theory of language development has to explain, does not in itself throw any light on the origin of group or individual differences. The measures used are often too superficial and global to do justice to the complexity of processes involved. This is particularly true at the earliest stages. One common criterion used in developmental tests to assess the onset of speech is 'first uses words *with meaning*' (e.g. Illingworth, 1966, my italics). Developmental tests are uniformly unhelpful as to how the tester or mother is to decide when a child uses words with meaning, or without, or indeed what is to count as a word at all. Other tests shelve the problem of meaning and specify only that the child must use one (or more) word, clearly, consistently and appropriately (e.g. Griffiths, 1954). Such a criterion raises an equally difficult problem about 'appropriateness' and again evades the question of what is to count as a word. The unsatisfactory nature of such criteria may well contribute to the very large variation in age reported for the beginning of speech. Morley (1957) for example finds a range of 8–30 months for the 'first word'. It is not clear at present whether this very large age range is a real phenomenon or an artefact of the measure used.

In much of this work there is a preoccupation with *rate* of development as the most important dependent variable. This preoccupation obscures important differences between individuals – differences which potentially can throw more light on the processes involved than can overall measures of speed of development. Assessment procedures designed to measure relative advancement in language development necessarily rely on norms of development. They thus tend to emphasise the generality and distinctiveness of 'stages', and to view development as a series of universal quantative accretions. How misleading this can be is shown by some of Cazden's (1968) work. The three children in the Harvard longitudinal study were compared on the basis of a somewhat global measure, mean length of utterance (M.L.U.). The child who on this measure was furthest behind for her chronological age was, for any M.L.U., furthest ahead in respect of the acquisition of various noun and verb inflections. Thus the course of this child's language development was not simply the same but slower than that of the apparently fastest-developing child, but differed in ways that are important for understanding the possible processes involved. At younger ages, similarly misleading impressions are obtained if a vocabulary count is taken as an index of rate of development, as is commonly done. Such vocabulary counts assume that progress in development will be reflected in the number of different words produced by the child. Detailed diary studies (see below) have shown that there is a substantial mortality in children's use of words, especially at the youngest ages. Words are used for a short time and then drop out; new words appear. What in terms of vocabulary counts looks like a 'plateau' in the child's development (and has been described as such), thus hides a particular form of new learning.

Attempts to explain these group differences in language development often make some reference to the supposed nature of the effective environment, particularly to the amount and quality of maternal speech. However there is very little direct evidence on, for example, the speech of working-class as opposed to middle-class mothers towards their infants, or of mothers in general towards boys as against girls. Attempts to explain the differences between groups in such terms are complicated by the fact that many other aspects of development apart from language also show similar correlations with the variables in question.

(2) Diary studies of individual children provide the most detailed and valuable information about the earliest stages of language development. They are of very uneven quality, varying from the anecdotal to Leopold's (1939) painstaking and monumental account. Other extensive studies include those of Stern and Stern (1907) and Lewis (1936).[1] For the last two or three decades such individual studies have been unfashionable; this is due partly to the lack of interest in the very beginnings of language, and partly to the obvious shortcomings of the methods involved. Recently, however, Bloom (1971) has provided a detailed and in many ways new diary study.

These diary studies do not have much in common apart from the methods used. Some of the ideas and findings that have emerged from thm will be discussed below (p. 196). In some of the studies (e.g.,

[1] See Leopold (1939) for a critical and comprehensive bibliography of early studies.

Stern and Lewis) attempts are made to trace the origins of early speech in previous vocalisations of the infant. In all the early studies there is considerable emphasis on the form (phonological characteristics) of early speech and the changes in form with age. Much attention is also paid to the function of early utterances, and to the related question of categorising the infant's utterances. However, the underlying problem concerning the criteria for deciding the meaning of utterances is never really explored, except in Bloom's study. Whilst these studies provide a wealth of information about the form and possible functions of early speech, they neglect the process of interaction between child and adults. The only exception to this is Lewis, who does advance some rather general considerations about the role of adults in maintaining some patterns of speech. In none of these studies is there any systematic consideration of the speech heard by the child.

Leopold provides an exceptionally detailed account of the growth of his child's vocabulary, and the changes in the apparent meanings of words.

(3) Piaget (1946) is the only psychologist so far to have shown a sustained interest in the non-verbal prerequisites for the beginnings of language, although Vygotsky (1934) and Bruner (1968) have some interesting speculations on the topic. Bloom's (1971) study also raises questions about the relationship between linguistic and cognitive development. Piaget's work on the origins of language development has received virtually no attention since it was published; considerable space is therefore given to it here and elsewhere (Ryan, 1973). Despite the difficulties inherent in much of Piaget's theorising, he does at least try to do what no one else has done in any detail so far, namely, to view language development as part of the general development of intelligence.

Piaget describes language development within the general framework of the transition from sensory-motor to representational modes of thought. His interest is not primarily in the form or structure of early speech, nor in the details of interaction with adults who speak to the child. Piaget does not regard language as *sui generis*, something that requires special equipment to explain its appearance, independently of other cognitive development. Nor does Piaget regard language as something to be studied as the object of the child's knowledge, in the way that current phycholinguistic theory does. Rather, apart from the very early stages, he sees it as a means of knowing and thinking. He has neglected all subsequent linguistic development as a topic in its own right, although recently Sinclair and Bronckart (1971) have worked on this within the Piagetian tradition. Further, whilst Piaget has some fairly general remarks to make about the importance of symbolic modes of thought in the efficiency with which logical operations can be carried out, he shows little interest in the gradually increasing control that verbal processes have over children's behaviour. Psycholinguistics emphasises the unique nature of language and the complexities facing the developing child; Piaget sees language as simply one facet of cognitive development, providing an economical means of representing reality. From a Piagetian perspective, psycholinguistics has exaggerated the 'achievements' of a child in acquiring language.

There are two important features of Piaget's account, the first of which is related to similar issues in the work of other writers, to be discussed below. This is Piaget's notion of the representative or symbolic function, and the associated distinction he draws between the 'true' and objective use of words, and their earlier changing and subjective use. Piaget distinguishes two senses of 'representation'. In the narrow sense, representation involves the ability to differentiate what Piaget calls 'signifiers' from what they signify, and thus the ability to 'evoke' absent realities by means of a verbal sign or other mental symbol such as an image.[2] In the broader sense 'representation' is identical with thought, i.e. all intelligence which is based on a system of concepts or mental schemes and not merely on perceptions and actions (Piaget, 1946, p. 67). Further, representation 'goes beyond the present, extending the field of adaptation both in space and time' (*ibid.* p. 273). Representative thought in this broader sense develops concurrently in different areas, in the child's conception of objects, space, time and causality. Language, in its early development, is seen as somehow part of this non-verbal development, but it is not really clear what kind of connections are supposed to exist. Piaget sees the two as mutually interdependent, thus: 'the collective institution of language is the main factor in both the formation and socialisation of representations, *but* the child's ability to use verbal signs is dependent on the progress of his own thought' (*ibid.* p. 273, my italics). This simultaneous and mutually dependent development in several different areas is characteristic of Piaget's notion of 'stage'. The plausibility of viewing language development as part of the wider development of representational thought must depend on a closer analysis of the notion of 'stage', and particularly of what relations are posited between different areas of development. The relations Piaget supposes exist between language and other development are similarity (in that representative thought is found in all areas), concurrence in time (of the appearance of representation in all areas), and as quoted

---

[2] Piaget draws an idiosyncratic distinction between symbols and signs. 'Symbols' are 'motivated' signifiers, in virtue of their resemblance to the signified; 'signs' have no natural or individual connection with what they signify, but only a conventionally determined and thus, to the child, 'arbitrary' relation (Piaget, 1946, p. 68).

above, mutual dependence. Concurrence in time has never been empirically checked, though in principle it could be. Mutual dependence is quite unanalysed as regards the causal relations involved.

The other important feature of Piaget's account is his tracing of the origins of both language development and representative thought in general in previous non-verbal development. The non-verbal roots of representation are to be found in imitation and play. Piaget gives a fairly detailed description, based on observations of his three children, of the changes in imitation and play during the sensory-motor period. Very little subsequent work has been done on these topics, so it is not all clear whether Piaget's account is empirically correct or not, as regards the succession of different substages.

According to Piaget, imitation develops so that by the final stage of the sensory-motor period the child is able to reproduce, without prior practice, unfamiliar models and actions in their absence. Such ability must involve some system of internal representation on which the deferred imitation is based, and Piaget suggests mental images for this role. Thus, 'imitation is no longer dependent on the actual action, and the child becomes capable of imitating internally a series of models in the form of images or suggestions of actions' (*ibid*. p. 62). The mental image is 'the symbol', or 'interior copy or reproduction of the object', and 'the product of the interiorisation of imitation' (*ibid*. p. 70). Piaget maintains that such images and memories are essentially individual and idiosyncratic, 'a translation of personal experiences' (*ibid*. p. 71). Imitation is also an instance of pure accommodation in that reality is copied and not distorted.

The function of such deferred imitation in the development of language and representation generally, is that it 'provides' differentiation and co-ordination between 'signifiers' (in this case mental images) and what is 'signified' (the absent model). It is not clear what the nature of this provision is. Piaget draws a distinction between the representative relationships involved in deferred imitation and in language. He contrasts the individual nature of mental images with the externally and socially determined nature of words, as regards the form of representation. Otherwise, as regards their representative functions there are important similarities between the two, with imitation providing the earlier and less social form. This would seem to imply that the development of deferred imitation in other areas is necessary before language can appear, and one might look for empirical relationships on this account. However this inference is rendered invalid by Piaget's further claim that the first words are not 'true signs', but are intermediate in their nature between such signs and the idiosyncratic images (symbols) of imitation. This intermediate status is seen in the changing and subjective meaning that

192

the first words have (a topic to be elaborated below), and also in their allegedly imitative nature. They are held to be either onomatopaeic, and thus direct imitations of the sounds, or else to be isolated imitations of words used by adults. It is thus not clear from Piaget's writings whether the development of deferred imitation is necessary before this earliest use of words can appear, or only before the subsequent development of 'true' verbal signs. If the latter is the case, then it is not clear what other relationship is being posited between the representative abilities involved in deferred imitation and those in the first use of words, than that of parallel and simultaneous development. How does the ability developed in one sphere transfer to another? Piaget at one point (*ibid*. p. 3) says they 'interact' but he never elaborates on this.

Whilst imitation is supposed to supply the child with the ability to copy absent models, play is supposed to supply what Piaget calls the 'meanings of symbols' (*ibid*. p. 3). By the end of the sensory-motor period pretence or make-believe play develops. In this the child chooses objects to stand for other objects, in their absence, and out of the context in which they occur normally. The object or activity which is chosen as a play substitute may have little or no natural connection with what they represent; rather the connection is what Piaget calls 'motivated', being the product of individual imagination and needs. Pretence play resembles imitation in its 'representational element whose existence is proved by the deferred character of the reaction' (*ibid*. p. 98). They differ from each other in that in play there is no accommodation to objective reality, but instead there is 'subjective assimilation' and a distortion of reality. In imitation, by contrast, the child's activity is predominantly determined by the external reality she is copying. While in extreme cases Piaget's distinction between imitation and play, between copies and distortions of reality, is clear, there are many intermediate cases where there appears to be an element of both. However 'distorted' the symbolisation involved in play is, there is always some element of copying of an earlier or absent model.

Piaget maintains that ludic assimilation and imitative accommodation eventually become closely co-ordinated, having been differentiated during the sensory-motor period. This progressive integration appears to take the form of the same objects being involved in simultaneous accommodation and assimilation of this kind (*ibid*. p. 213). Again Piaget only makes passing and scanty reference to what this process of integration and co-ordination consists in, maintaining however that the 'constitution of the symbolic function is only possible as a result of this union' (*ibid*. p. 3).

His account of the non-verbal origins of language, and of the simultaneous development of the 'representative function' in many aspects of

193

behaviour solves several internal problems, as far as Piaget's general theory of development is concerned. His account of the origins of language in the non-verbal sensory-motor developments of play and imitation allows him to preserve his overall thesis of functional continuity but structural discontinuity that he sees in all development. How useful is this account to the analysis of early language development? As the foregoing critique has emphasised Piaget's theory seems to be least testable at the most crucial points – i.e. at the *links* between the various allegedly related areas of development. In many places, his account is so overdetermined, in the sense of everything being different from but essentially similar to or related to everything else, that it is difficult to see what empirical substance it has. However, theory apart, there seem to be at least two valuable aspects that can be extracted. These are his observations and descriptions concerning imitation, and those concerning the child's earliest use of words, and the concomitant development of word meaning. Imitation, verbal and otherwise, is clearly important in allowing the child to establish correspondence of a particular kind between her behaviour and that of others. Correspondence and reciprocity are essential ingredients of any form of communication; and as such they have been much neglected in the study of language. Piaget does not directly address himself to the topic of communication, nor does he view language in the perspective of dialogue between mother and infant, but his observations provide some illustrations of how exchanges of various kinds are built up between the child and others.

(4) The final approach to be considered can be broadly characterised as behaviourist. This approach has never got off the ground, consisting of statements of the general Skinnerian position, of speculation and of armchair anecdotes; no empirical data has been generated within this framework, and there is surprising ignorance of the existing data of other writers. A variety of analyses have been offered, the most detailed being those of Mowrer (1960), Jenkins (1969) and Quine (1960).

The following assumptions are common to all such approaches: the randomness of the child's vocalisations prior to the first intelligible words, the association of such words with particular objects or events, and with reinforcement, and the importance of the child's imitation of adult words. The instructional role of adults is also emphasised. The assumption of randomness in babbling, and the differential sensitivity of adults to particular sounds has serious empirical objections to it (see p. 200). It further neglects any possible function that a child's preverbal vocalisations may have in interaction with others, and the importance of such interaction for subsequent verbal development. This is just one instance of the failure of this approach to consider language acquisition

194

in any developmental framework, or in any broader context than that of contiguous association. The assumption of the ubiquity of reinforcement is open to all the familiar objections. However the most fundamental objection is the oversimple conception of what it is to talk and understand. For Jenkins, the use of language consists in objects or other stimuli eliciting the correct words; understanding consists in the association of words with objects, and words with 'appropriate' responses. (Quine, it should be noted, is not open to this criticism, since he is mainly concerned with how children come to learn the reference of words, and with what kind of reference they learn, and not with actual use.) The main function of utterances is thus reduced to labelling or naming. This ignores all other functions and of course runs into difficulties with function as opposed to content words.

Despite these criticisms the behaviourist approach does have the advantage that it focuses attention on the exact, albeit hypothetical, situations and ways in which children might come to associate particular sounds with particular objects or events. Such association is one necessary component of acquiring language; it is clearly particularly important in the earliest stages when there is no pre-existing linguistic system into which new words can be fitted. The mistake of the behaviourists is to elevate such association into the one necessary and sufficient component of language acquisition. There is very little description in the literature about the fine structure of events concerning such association: Leopold (1939) provides the only detailed account. He emphasises how the earliest apparent comprehension develops slowly as a result of repeated instruction on the part of the mother; how a few months later the child learns both to comprehend and produce words spontaneously, without such teaching; how words are first understood and produced with application to objects in one specific situation, and how this restriction loosens, so that words are increasingly applied to the same objects in other situations, and to whole classes of objects. Bullowa, Jones and Duckert (1964) also attempt to trace the acquisition of a word over several months, but with less detail than Leopold. They too emphasise how the restriction of the word on the part of the child to the presence of the object, and to the occurrence of the word in the mother's speech, is gradually loosened.

One further point that emerges from Leopold's (1939) and Bloom's (1971) accounts is that the occurrence of overt imitation of words is not a necessary feature of language development as supposed by behaviourist accounts. Leopold and Bloom both state that their children did not imitate adult speech at all. However, there are many examples of children who imitate adult speech frequently. Such differences may reflect important individual variations in how language is learned. In general, the role of imitation, for those children who do imitate, is unclear, and probably much more complex than that suggested by the behaviourist account, as argued in Ryan (1973).

Running through much of this work, especially that in sections 2 and 3 are several common theories concerning developmental sequences and changes in the child's use of language. One general claim seems to be that before developing something that is variously regarded (by different authors) as the 'true' use of language, other verbal but less complete and more primitive functions develop. Two themes, variously expressed, recur particularly often, although not always separated from each other, as here:

(i) The change from predominantly expressive or emotional use of words to their factual or descriptive use.

(ii) The change from presymbolic use, when words are regarded as properties or attributes of objects or situations, to their fully symbolic use, when words stand in some more abstract but unspecified relation to objects, events, etc.

The first theme is found most clearly in Lewis' (1936) attempts to trace the origins of speech in earlier cries of discomfort and pleasure. These cries are mainly associated with hunger and its expression by use of mouth movements connected with feeding. For example, the child's 'earliest words . . . are fundamentally the child's own expressive utterance, which has begun almost with his earliest cry'. Lewis sees the alleged origin of speech as leading to a similarity, between children, in both the form and meaning of the earliest words. These early words are 'stabilised' by various processes of interpretation, by adult expectations, and by imitation on the part of the child, so that 'the meanings of (his) first words are therefore fundamentally expressive, as well as socially determined'. Leopold (1939) classified what he calls 'the syntactical purposes' of one-word utterances into the following categories: emotional interjections, wishes, questions and statements of fact. Whilst he admits that fine distinctions between what he calls the emotional and intellectual nature of speech cannot be drawn, he does claim that questions of predominance can be settled, and that a child's earliest utterances are predominantly emotional rather than intellectual. Unlike Lewis, he does not offer any explanation of this alleged sequence.

The second theme is found most prominently in Vygotsky's (1934) writings. Thus Vygotsky distinguishes a stage at which words are 'properties' but not 'symbols' of objects. Vygotsky elaborates this by maintaining that 'the child grasps the external structure word-object earlier than the inner symbolic structure' (1934, p. 50). This symbolic structure is the 'internal relation sign-referent' (*ibid*. p. 28), or 'word meaning' (*ibid*. p. 5). The external relation is one in which words 'substitute, as in conditioning, for objects, persons, actions, states or desires' (*ibid*. p. 43). It is not at all clear what the empirical criteria for making such a distinction could be, and Vygotsky is silent on this point. One simple criterion might be the use of words in the presence as against the absence of their referents, but there are difficulties about this. How would the symbolic as against the non-symbolic use of a word be distinguished when the referent is present? Further, some uses of words in the absence of their referents, as in requests, develop early on, and are in one sense very intimately tied to the immediate situation for the child (e.g. requesting food when hungry).

Vygotsky does however, tie the development of the 'symbolic function' of words to the 'intellectual phase' of speech. The earlier stages of speech he sees as having nothing to do with thinking, but rather as being 'affective-conative' in function. However this does not throw much light on what the 'symbolic function' is supposed to mean. Vygotsky also claims that even at much later ages, in the learning of new words, children initially conceive of the word as a property of an object, before discovering its function as a sign.

In his description of 'preintellectual' speech as 'a predominantly emotional form of behaviour' (*ibid*. p. 42) Vygotsky's distinction between words as properties of objects and words as symbols seems to have become conflated with the other theme mentioned above – namely, the evolution of the descriptive use of words from their earlier emotional or expressive use. There does not seem to be any necessary connection or identity between words as properties of objects (assuming some meaning can be given to this) and their allegedly emotional function. Vygotsky again does not elaborate on this point, and confuses the question further by comparing early infant speech with animal communication, in its emotional release function.

The two themes are also found conflated in Marshall's (1971) account. Marshall adopts Bühler's distinction between (i) indicative or expressive, (ii) stimulative or releasing, and (iii) representational or descriptive functions of speech, and supposes the first two to be more primitive and to develop earlier than the third. He argues that the first two functions can be given a Skinnerian account, whereas the third cannot. Marshall regards the 'essence' of languages that they can function semantically as systems of representation. He criticises Stern's criterion for the onset of 'true' language – the child's discovery that everything has a name, and the generalising ability Stern thinks this implies – on the grounds that the tendency to ask for names does not in itself imply any 'general symbolic activity' but only a tendency to produce the same eliciting words ('What's that?') on all occasions when he does not know any specific words. Marshall argues that the representational or symbolic use of language has to be given an analysis in terms of the ability to distinguish between true or false statements.

This claim, that the truth-functional use of language is somehow basic, and that the ability to make true or false statements is what separates human language from animal systems of communication, is, as Marshall notes, an old and familiar one. Psychologists and neurologists have almost always taken a strictly positivist attitude to language. However, as recent work in the philosophy of language has emphasised, we do many different things with words, and making statements is only one of many possible speech acts. Further, truth or falsity is only one of many possible criteria that we apply to utterances; many of the other criteria, such as appropriateness as regards the circumstances of utterance, nullity or otherwise of presuppositions, sincerity of the speaker, consistency of implication, are ones with which we evaluate non-truth-functional utterances.[3] To suppose that the assertion of potentially true or false propositions is somehow the fundamental function of language is to distort and oversimplify the richness and complexity of human speech. This perspective suggests that psychologists should abandon essentialist attempts to find single defining criteria of human language, and with it the parallel attempt to decide when children develop 'true' language. Instead, attention should be focused on what children do with the words they use. This would involve establishing empirical criteria as regards the behaviour of the speaker and listener, and as regards the effective context, for describing and categorising children's utterances into different types of speech acts.

Piaget (1946) also conflates these two themes, the primarily expressive function of early speech, and its presymbolic nature, although in a very different way from Marshall. For Piaget words are used at first with an individual and changeable meaning, in the sense that their application is determined by the child's own interests and perceptions, and not by external and objective usage. Further the earliest words 'represent schemas of actions, not objects'. This change in the range of application of words is discussed below (p. 205).

In the work so far reviewed, the idea of developmental changes in the child's use of words occurs frequently, in various forms. It has been argued that one of the changes described, that of the presymbolic to symbolic use of words, does not make sense in that there are no possible empirical criteria on which such a distinction could be based. The other main theme – that of the initial predominantly emotional or expressive

[3] See section IV for further exposition of this.

use of words – is potentially more susceptible to empirical evaluation. Such evaluation would depend on setting up criteria for distinguishing between the various kinds of utterances that it is supposed children make, such as requests, protests, comments, identifications, questions, etc. (see below, p. 202 for a further discussion of this).

III   INTERACTION AND INTERPRETATION

The accounts of language development discussed above entirely neglect the effective environment in which the child develops. No descriptions are given of the interaction between the child and others, and there are no characterisations of the speech of others to the child; instead the child's speech has been treated as an isolated phenomenon. Recently, however, some observations have been made of maternal speech (Brown and Bellugi, 1964; Bingham, forthcoming; Phillips, (1973); E. Lieven, pers. comm.); these allow some suggestions to be made about the forms of interaction and communication between adult and child.

In this section, I wish to approach the problem of providing a framework for the description of language development from two rather obvious starting points. The first is that much of what a child utters in the early stages is difficult to understand, if not unintelligible. The second is that much of a child's speech and other vocalisations take place within a context of interaction with adults who are motivated to understand the child's utterances. There is no systematic information at present about the extent to which infants vocalise or speak in the presence of adults, as opposed to their absence, (but it is known that the amount of vocalisation can be increased by contingent responding on the part of adults.) Nor is there any quantitative evidence about the extent to which a child's utterances can be said to be directed at others, as part of an attempted dialogue or other kind of interaction, as opposed to an autistic monologue. Despite the absence of such information it is clear from tape-recordings and observations made of mother–infant interaction by Lieven (pers. comm.) and by Richards and Bernal (pers. comm.) that many young children experience extensive verbal interchanges with their mothers. During these the mother actively picks up, interprets, comments on, extends, repeats and sometimes misinterprets what the child has said. This can happen even if the child has not obviously directed his utterance to her or to anyone else. Brown and Bellugi (1964) in their study of older children, also observed that mothers frequently responded to their child's utterance by 'expanding' it – that is, by reproducing it and also adding something to it, or otherwise changing it. Such expansion was primarily interpretive of the child's utterance, delimiting its meaning more precisely, rather than corrective. Explicit corrections were extremely rare, a finding since replicated by Lieven with younger children.

Adults also modify their speech towards children in the direction of greater distinctiveness, slowness, and simplicity. Brown and Bellugi noticed that adults mostly used short and grammatically correct sentences when speaking to children. In a more detailed investigation, Phillips (1973) compared mothers' speech to children of different ages with that to an adult interviewer. She found that the adult-directed speech contained longer utterances, more verbs and more verb forms, more modifiers, more function words, fewer 'concrete nouns', and that it was less repetitious. Speech to 28-month children was more complex than that to 18-month ones, on most of the measures that distinguished adult-directed speech from that to children generally. Similar results were found by Bingham (forthcoming). Such findings concerning greater simplicity and distinctiveness are hardly surprising, but they emphasise how mothers provide a more helpful linguistic input for the child than has been assumed in much recent work.

Early language development thus appears to take place in a context that provides a child with frequent interpretations of his utterances. It is on this active interpretive process that I wish to concentrate, since it illustrates several important features of what a child has to learn in order to speak and understand, and how this is mediated by interaction with adults.

There are several distinct forms of difficulty that adults can experience when trying to understand infant utterances:

(1) The child may be making unrecognisable noises with no familiar intonation or gestures, and with no apparent relation to the context or the preceding speech of others. In such a case no interpretation is possible. Much of what is described as 'random babbling' would be included in this category. However this assumption of randomness is mistaken. There is evidence that from very early on children's babbling reflects some features of the language spoken around them. Thus Weir (1966) cites a study in which the babbling of 4–6-month infants of Chinese and American parents could be distinguished by linguists. Lieberman (1967) found that the fundamental frequency of several children's vocalisations reflected the frequency of those voices (male and female) that they had most recently heard. There is thus evidence of systematic selectivity in the production of sounds before recognisable speech appears. Conditioning studies on 3-month-old infants suggest that the discriminatory capacity for distinguishing various speech sounds is present from a very early age (Eimas *et al.*, 1971). It therefore appears that long before parents think they can recognise familiar sounds

in the vocalisations of children, the sounds made do in fact bear some resemblance to the native language.

(2) The child may be making noises that are unrecognisable because they are not part of the standard adult vocabularly, but she may be making them in such a way that adults think she is trying to say something. Whether or not it is true that the child is 'trying to say something', and whether or not this is something that is in principle ascertainable, it is an important fact about adults that they do behave towards children in this way – that is, as though the child was trying to say something. In an effort to understand what are regarded as attempts at speech, mothers often repeat or extend the child's utterance, or alter some aspect of the non-linguistic context. There are several different features of the child's behaviour that both leads adults to credit her with 'trying to say something' and also are used in the interpretation of the utterance. These features can be described as follows, using a categorisation of Austin's (1962), developed for a different purpose:

(*a*) *Aspects of the utterance*, such as intonation patterns, which are variously interpreted as insistence, protest, pleasure, request, etc. The basis for such interpretation is what adults do, and what adults express by particular stress and emphasis patterns. The assumption is that children are using intonation in the same way and to the same ends as adults would. Bloom (1971), however, has queried this assumption, in that she and others do not find any consistent or distinctive use of intonation until after syntax develops. However, even if Bloom is correct, it can be argued that what is important is that adults interpret children's use of intonation in a systematic way, thus allowing children to learn what is conventional usage.

(*b*) *Accompaniments of the utterance*, on the part of the child, such as pointing, searching, playing with specific objects, refusing; the physical state of the child.

(*c*) *Circumstances of the utterances*, such as the presence or absence of particular objects or people, the relation of these to the child, any immediately preceding events or speech, the relevant past experience of the child.

One interesting phenomenon, which is likely to be related to this process of interpretation, is that non-standard sounds are often identified as the 'child's word' for something. Thus both Leopold (1939) and Bloom (1971) report the existence of non-standard 'words' in their child's vocabulary. In many such cases mothers seem confident that they know what the child's word means, as does Leopold in the cases he discusses. In other cases, and in Bloom's example, no adult interpretation seems possible, in that no consistent usage can be worked out, even though the 'word' occurs with considerable frequency. In such cases the grounds for giving an uninterpretable but persistent sound the status of a 'word' for the child appear to lie in other features of the utterance, such as those listed above, (*a*)–(*c*).

It is of course possible that non-standard 'words' may arise as deviant imitations of adult forms. Leopold considers this possibility for his child, and concludes that this is unlikely in more than a few cases, given the sounds and apparent meanings involved. The existence of non-standard 'words' which cannot be explained as deviant imitations, implies that the child has learnt something general about speech, independent of specific forms learnt from adult speech. She appears to have learnt something general about the notion of a word, as regards its circumstance and manner of usage, that is not tied to any particular actual instance. Such overgeneralisation is also seen later on in development, when children produce non-standard forms of nouns and verbs that it is most improbable they have heard (e.g. using regular verb endings for irregular verbs). Such overgeneralisation is taken to show the 'creative' and rule-governed nature of children's speech (McNeill, 1966). Similar 'creativity' seems to be shown in presyntactic development.

(3) A further kind of difficulty can arise when a child utters a recognisable word but it is unclear what she means by uttering it or why she has said it – that is, what sort of an utterance it is. In such cases, the same kinds of clues to interpretation as listed above can be used. It should be noted that these clues are similar to those we use in trying to understand adult speech, in cases of ambiguity, lack of proficiency in the language, distortion, etc.

One consequence of this kind of interpretive process is that the child is described as using the same word with a variety of meanings on different occasions. This description occurs in the various early accounts of child speech (e.g. Stern, 1924; Leopold, 1939). It would probably be more accurate to say that the child is using the same word to make several different utterances, on different occasions. There is nothing strange about this in that adults use similar or identical sentences to make different kinds of utterances – the differences depending on the ways in which speakers intend their utterances to be taken, and on various features of the utterance and the context. It is a mistake to suppose that children are special in the variety of interpretations that can be given to their utterances of the same single words, as is implied in the literature. However there clearly is much more scope for ambiguity and misinterpretation than with adults. There would appear to be at least two sources of this. One is the obvious one that the form of one-word utterances conveys much less information than does the form of more complex utterances. The second is that we do not know much about what kind of utterances children are capable of making, nor what concepts they are capable of expressing, nor the ways in which their utterances are related by them to other linguistic or non-linguistic aspects of the total situation. It is generally true, as Bloom (1970) points out, that in order to understand the speech of young children we usually have also to know what they are doing. In this sense, and also in the sense that children's speech is often about features of the immediate context, their speech is much more closely tied to aspects of the immediate situation, than is that of adults. Bloom's (1971) account of what her child talked about is much more detailed than Leopold's classification of utterances into emotional interjections, wishes, questions, and statements of fact. For example, Bloom interprets her child as using the names of familiar adults and of herself in the following ways: initially as pointing out or naming one person to another, as a greeting and to call for someone; subsequently she used the same names to indicate objects that belonged to the person so named, and also to name the agent of an action she was either performing or wanting performed by someone else; she very rarely named people who were objects of actions or events. Noun forms that were not names of people were used with increasing frequency, mostly, according to Bloom, to point out or name the object in question. Bloom also describes her child's use of certain function and relational words, such as 'more', 'no', 'up', 'away', etc. 'More' was used initially to request the recurrence of objects that had ceased to exist or been consumed, then later as a comment on the occurrence of another instance of a class of objects or events; it was never (at this age) used in a comparative sense. There was also evidence in the child's use of 'no', 'away', 'all-gone' and 'stop' that she was commenting on the non-existence, disappearance and cessation of objects, etc., that were expected to exist in certain contexts, or whose existence ceased.

Bloom's kind of analysis needs carrying out more systematically and with much more detail concerning the various features of the context that are used in interpreting the child's utterance. There are several instances where alternative interpretations are possible, and where the evidence is ambiguous. There are further problems, which she does not raise, about what metalinguistic terms to use in describing the child's speech. How, for instance, do we decide whether or not a child is using words to name, to comment on, to describe, to assert the existence of something, to request, to refuse, to point out related features for which the appropriate words are not known, to greet – plus all the other plausible functions that a child's utterances can be interpreted as having?

It is crucial for any full account of language development that we should know what kind of acts young children can perform with words, and particularly what developmental changes occur in this respect.

The view outlined in section II, that speech begins by being used in a predominantly 'emotional' or 'expressive' way before being used to state or describe, receives limited support from some of Bloom's (1971) analyses. For example she finds that some words are used as requests or refusals before being used to comment on the situation or object in question.

A common claim in the literature on early speech is that one-word utterances are really sentences. Thus Stern (1924) maintains that 'children's utterances are really whole sentences, because one and the same unit is used with a multitude of meanings'; Leopold (1939) that 'one-word sentences constitute for the child a complete expression of thought and feeling'; McNeill (1970) that 'single-word utterances express complex ideas and are thus equivalent to the full sentences of adults'. Taking a narrowly grammatical definition of a sentence, as something having internal structure and constituent parts, these claims are clearly false. The truth of what is being claimed seems to lie in the way children's utterances are interpreted by adults, namely as having at least some of the same potential functions that utterances expressed with complex sentences have.

Is there an alternative to this view, that the child is somehow expressing more than the simple form of his utterance would suggest? McNeill (1970) takes an alternative view to be one which describes the child as simply naming or labelling the referent of the word uttered. This alternative he attributes to Quine (1960) and to the general Skinnerian viewpoint. As Marshall (1971) points out, a strictly consistent behaviourist account would not permit the use of terms such as 'naming' to describe the child's behaviour. This aside, it seems wrong to suppose that the only function of one-word utterances is naming or labelling. Simply naming objects or events is a rather specialised function of speech. It is something adults do when explicitly teaching new words to children. It has a certain plausibility with children in that they have to learn many new words, and also in that they may imitate the often exaggerated behaviour of adults in pointing things out to them. Children can sometimes be observed naming a succession of objects, but this tends to happen relatively late on in the one-word 'stage', often when they have begun to ask the names of objects. Many other uses of words are established before this happens. Further many of a child's earliest words do not refer to anything visualisable, and hence the naming relationship has much less plausibility with such words. Thus, although children may sometimes be described as naming objects, etc., with their one-word

204

utterances, this cannot be the only and invariable function of these utterances.

These views of the nature of early speech are essentially interpretative ones, and should be more accurately described as views about how adults understand (or fail to understand) child speech than as views of the speech itself. This is because they have tended to conflate the means (listed above) by which an adult interprets a child's utterance with the devises it is assumed a child uses to express herself, given her limitation to the one-word form. That is, they assume a child uses the same devices to convey her meaning as an adult uses in interpreting the utterance. The question arises of whether we can in principle tell if such an assumption is correct or not. In some cases we can tell with some confidence if we are wrong in our interpretations (for example, if we do something we think is appropriate and the child screams); however very often we cannot. Clearly there is scope here for much empirical observation, and for decisions about what metalinguistic terms it is appropriate to use with respect to children's utterances. However it is possible that what is most important for the child is not whether she is correctly interpreted by adults, but that she is interpreted at all. The context of rich interpretation provided by many mothers, combined with the considerable ambiguity of many one-word utterances, provides an extremely informative situation for the child as regards what she is taken to be meaning. We cannot assume when a child starts to produce one-word utterances, that the possible meanings of her utterances are as clearly delimited for her as they are for the adults who interpret them.

(4) A final source of difficulty on the part of adults can arise because a child uses standard and recognisable words with unconventional reference. Such unconventional reference takes two forms; extension to objects, etc., not usually covered by the words in question, and restrictions to a subclass of the objects, etc., usually referred to. Extension seems to be an extremely common phenomenon, as it is noted by most writers; restriction seems to be much less common, but this may be because it causes much less confusion. Associated with this overextension is also variability in reference; children's words change in their reference as adult usage is approximated.

The question arises of what the basis of this extended reference is; how does the child classify objects, etc., not usually classified together? In most cases of extended reference it is unlikely that the child is confusing or failing to distinguish between the referents, in that her nonverbal behaviour shows discrimination. Extensions often appear to have a functional basis, or one that is related to the child's needs and perspectives. However, it is difficult to tell from the literature whether this is always the case, because words that are extended to objects, etc., that have no obvious relationship to the conventional referents are much less likely to be interpreted at all, and thus will not be noticed as an extension. Piaget maintains that this extension in reference is determined by the assimilation of objects, etc., seen by the child to its own point of view, and he gives as one example of this the use of one word to refer to many different objects seen from the child's balcony (Piaget, 1946, p. 216), from which she had seen the object first named by the word. Leopold (1939) has many examples of extension based on the perceptual characteristics of the objects in question, e.g. soft material, round shapes.

Piaget describes this extended use of words as 'subjective' and as characteristic of the earliest stage of language development, before words are used more objectively. However Leopold's work suggests that extension in general persists long beyond the earliest words, although as the child's vocabulary enlarges the reference of particular words becomes more restricted. Leopold's examples also indicate that the basis of the extended reference may be much more objective or externally orientated than Piaget claims.

Extension is interesting, not only as an indication of ways in which children perceive and classify, but also because it is further evidence of how a child's utterances are not, even at the earliest stages, derived in any simple way from those of adults. The extended use of words is not something a child could have imitated from adults; it suggests generalisation, in a systematic if individual way, of something that may initially have been learnt as an imitation. Extension can also be seen as a partial consequence of the child's lack of particular words, combined with a desire to talk about increasingly many things.

Four kinds of difficulty that adults experience when trying to understand young children have been described. To summarise, these were (1) difficulty due to the fact that the child makes noises with no speech-like characteristics at all, such that adults would not readily say she was even trying to speak, (2) difficulty due to the fact that the child's noises are not recognisably part of the adult vocabulary, but that she makes (utters) them in such a way that she would be described as trying to speak, (3) difficulty due to the fact that a child utters a recognisable standard word but what she means by uttering it is unclear, (4) difficulty due to the unconventional reference with which a child uses a standard word. This categorisation cuts across the more traditional descriptions of what a child has to learn prior to syntax, namely the sounds (phonology) and meanings (semantics) of words. What it adds are various features pertaining to the intentionality of the act in question: whether the utterance of a particular noise is to count as an instance of communication at all, and what kind of an utterance it is to be understood as; (2) suggests that a child can be counted as speaking in the sense of meaning something even though the noises she makes do not have any conventional meaning, (3) that even when words with conventional meaning are used, there can still be a question as to what the child meant by uttering those words. In the next section an attempt will be made to give a fuller analysis of these suggestions.

IV INTENTION AND COMMUNICATION

Recent work in the philosophy of language provides some helpful concepts and distinctions for the analysis of discourse and acts of speaking. Grice's (1957, 1968) account is an attempt to analyse sentence and word meaning in terms of certain intentions on the part of the speaker and the recognition of these intentions by the hearer. Grice draws a distinction between (i) notions of meaning involved in saying that a given sentence, word or phrase means 'x', and (ii) an allegedly more basic notion of meaning involved in specifying what the speaker means by uttering 'x'. He tries to give an account of (i) in terms of (ii). Although this attempt, as a theory of meaning, has certain objections to it, the distinction drawn between (i) and (ii), and the analysis of (ii) are useful in a variety of ways.

In Grice's earliest account, someone, S, means something by an utterance, x, if S intends to produce a certain effect, or response, r, in his audience, A, by means of A's recognition of S's intention. Subsequently Grice qualifies this by supposing that the effect that the speaker intends in his audience is not necessarily that the audience should believe any proposition or do any action, but rather that the audience thinks that the speaker believes something, or that the audience should intend to do something (rather than actually do it). This is thus a tripartite analysis involving:

(i) S's intention to produce a certain response, r, in A;
(ii) S's intention that A shall recognise S's intention (i) to do this;
(iii) S's intention that this recognition of S's intention (ii) is the reason, or part of it, for A's response, r.

Strawson (1964) adds as a further qualification,

(iv) S's further intention that A should recognise S's intention (ii).

Grice's account of what it is for someone to mean something by an utterance is not necessarily restricted to linguistic cases; his analysis is applicable to other instances of an agent's meaning something by the performance of particular actions.

Grice's attempt to give an account of meaning in terms only of utterer's meaning has been criticised on several grounds. The most general ground is that sentence-, word-, or phrase-meanings are not totally dependent on communication taking place, or even on the possibility of communication. Ziff (1967) provides several counter-examples, where communication and meaning are clearly separable. His counter-examples include the following:

(*a*) Someone can be uttering nonsense or gibberish, but still fulfill all Grice's conditions, as regards his intentions. His utterance does not mean anything, although the speaker means something by uttering it. Ziff's example is one in which S intends to annoy A by producing x (gibberish). Here A will not be annoyed by S uttering x, unless he recognises that S intends to annoy him and is trying to do so by the production of x.

(b) *Soliloquy*, where there is no question of the recognition of the speaker's intentions by an audience, does not thereby render utterances meaningless.

(*c*) Someone can utter something unaware that there is an audience or that he is saying anything, for example, when delirious. Here it is not the case that the speaker meant anything by uttering x, but x still means something.

Thus, as an account of meaning, Grice's analysis is both too wide and too narrow; it allows in nonsense utterances, and excludes meaningful sentences where there is no intention to communicate. However incomplete it is as a total account of meaning, Grice's analysis does suggest some important features of human communication – linguistic or otherwise – that are helpful in describing what infants have to learn to do. This is particularly true of his analysis of the non-linguistic conditions necessary for communication in discourse of various kinds. Here work of Austin's (1962) and Strawson's (1964) is also relevant.

Austin initially drew a distinction between utterances which are sayings (such as statements, descriptions) and utterances which are doings (such as warnings, orders, promises, bets). Only the former are in principle capable of being true or false. In the latter (the performatives) the speaker is *giving* a warning, or *making* a promise, and this is not something which criteria of truth and falsity are applicable, although other criteria for the evaluation of such utterances are relevant. All the different kinds of speech acts were named illocutionary acts. They were distinguished from other sorts of effects (often unintended) that speakers may have on hearers, such as boring them or amusing them; these were named perlocutionary acts.

Subsequently Austin argued that making statements or giving descriptions were as much performing acts as were promising, ordering, etc. He tried to show that statements or descriptions, in addition to being liable to be true or false, were also subject to the same criteria as explicit performatives. These criteria concern the appropriateness of the utterance to the circumstances in question; they include the nullity or otherwise of presuppositions, the sincerity of the speaker, consistency with what is entailed and implied, whether or not the speaker is in a position to state what is being stated. Austin described many of the various things that people may do in saying something, and tried to show the vast detail and complexity that exists with respect to how we evaluate their utterances. He drew a distinction between the 'meaning' of an utterance and its 'illocutionary force'. The meaning of a serious utterance always limits its possible illocutionary force, and is determined by linguistic conventions. Sometimes, as with explicit performatives the meaning totally exhausts its force. Where it does not exhaust it, and where the meaning of an utterance is known, there remains the question of how the speaker meant what he said, how he intended the utterance to be taken by the audience.

Essential to the notion of performing an illocutionary act is that of 'securing uptake' – bringing about the understanding of the meaning and force of the utterance. Strawson's (1964) account of this is preferable, namely that the *aim*, if not the achievement, of securing uptake is at least a standard, if not an invariable, element, in the performance of illocutionary acts. He extends Grice's analysis of what it is for someone to mean something by an utterance, to what it is to understand, and thus for uptake to be secured. Strawson suggests that for A to understand something by S's utterance x, there must be some intention of the kind described in (ii) above, that A takes S to have (namely, S's intention that A shall recognise S's intention to produce a certain response, r, in A). In order for A to understand S's utterance *correctly*, it is necessary for A to think that S has the intention (ii) that S does in fact have. Thus (iv) and (ii) must be fulfilled for correct understanding.

This analysis of adult discourse has been presented extremely briefly, in a way that does not do justice to the subtlety of the arguments for it, nor to the objections to it. However, even in such bare outline, it does provide some means of systematising the previous considerations about child speech. Firstly, the distinction between linguistic conventions, what words and sentences mean, and what people mean by uttering words, etc., is important. Traditionally, accounts of language development have concentrated only on the first aspect, although the distinction has not been clearly recognised. This neglect of utterer's meaning has of course contributed to the acommunicational view of language development implicit in all previous accounts (see section II). The analysis presented in section III, of the various kinds of difficulty adults can experience in trying to understand children's speech, shows how important the distinction is for any full account of language development. Secondly, Grice's analysis of acts of communication as crucially dependent on the recognition of various complex intentions, makes it intelligible how in various limiting cases the standard meaning of words, etc., is a dispensable element. This is clearly relevant to much of what passes for pre-verbal, or just verbal, communication in children. The major problem then arises of identifying and describing the kind of intentions involved, and how the necessary mutual recognition develops. It seems likely that the various non-verbal but vocal 'dialogues' often observed between mothers and infants are important in this respect. Mothers often imitate the sounds of their very young infants, and this appears to happen before the infants start to imitate their sounds. Other non-vocal sequences involving the interleaving, correspondence and matching of various activities also occur. However much more detail is needed on the precise kinds of sequences involved before this analysis can be extended. Thirdly, the analysis of illocutionary force is applicable to the kind of difficulty of interpretation described in III (3) above – that of intelligible one-word utterances whose meaning is ambiguous. What is needed, as argued above, is detailed description of the kinds of utterances children make, and are taken by adults to make.

A very different analysis of communication is presented by Watslavick, Beavin and Jackson (1968). 'Communication' is for them synonymous with 'behaviour'. All behaviour is seen as part of some interaction or relationship, and therefore as always influencing others: because of this all behaviour has 'message value'. Just as one cannot not behave, one cannot not communicate in all that one does. 'Communication' thus includes all interaction, and is analysed in terms of consequences and effects. The term is not restricted to those cases of intentional and successful interchange, where there is mutual understanding, but includes unsuccessful and distorted communication.

This all-inclusive definition has certain advantages in the analysis of paradoxical or pathological situations. Watslavick *et al.* produce many entertaining examples where there is disagreement between two people as to what passes between them, when there is little or no communication in the sense of mutuality or reciprocity, but where there is clearly influence and interaction. However, their definition confuses information with communication, as can be seen by an example. Suppose X sneezes. This will *inform* Y that X has a cold. It may also *influence* her behaviour; she may pass X a tissue, or move away. However, X has not communicated anything to Y by sneezing. For this to be the case, there would have to be an understanding between X and Y about what X's sneezing meant. For example X and Y may previously have agreed that when X sneezed, Y would leave the room. Here X's intention in sneezing is to produce in Y a certain response, leaving the room, by means of Y's recognition of this intention. In such a case, X's sneezing is an instance of communication.

Watslavick *et al.*, following Bateson, draw a distinction between the 'report' and 'command' aspects of any communication. The report aspect refers to the content of a message, to the information conveyed. The command aspect refers to what sort of a message it is to be taken as, and thus to the relationship between the sender and receiver. The same content may occur with very different command features. Watslavick *et al.* claim this relationship aspect of communication is essentially a metacommunication – a communication about the message. It may take a verbal form as in 'I am only joking', or a non-verbal form as evidenced in the tone of voice of the speaker. It may be implicit in the circumstances of the utterance, or the identities of the speaker and hearer. Watslavick *et al.* maintain that the command features of any communication classify the report aspect, and that the ability to metacommunicate is a *sine qua non* of successful communication. Their main argument for this is the ambiguity of contextless or insufficiently located messages. Under the 'command' aspects of communication would be included virtually all the non-linguistic features of an utterance as well as some linguistic ones. No distinctions however are made between the various conditions, circumstances and features involved. It should be noted that much of what falls under the 'command' aspects of communication are included in Austin's (1962) detailed analyses of various speech acts.

The importance of Watslavick *et al.*'s analysis lies in the emphasis given to the pragmatic, as opposed to the syntactic or semantic, basis of communication. Both this analysis, and the previous philosophical considerations, show how inadequate it is to regard 'communicative competence' as the appropriate application of linguistic skills to the prevailing social context. Any analysis of human communication must include a description of the structure of intersubjectivity between participants in a dialogue. This chapter has suggested that this intersubjectivity consists, at least in part, of the mutual recognition of certain kinds of intention. Certain modes of interaction between child and adult, that might help establish such intersubjectivity, have been described. In this respect the interpretive role of adults has been especially emphasised. What is needed next is an analysis of the development of different forms of intentional behaviour in the child, combined with detailed descriptions of the preverbal dialogues and other reciprocal interchanges that adults and children participate in.

Joanna Ryan

ACKNOWLEDGEMENTS

I should like to thank Elena Lieven for many helpful discussions. The work is supported by a grant from the Nuffield Foundation.

REFERENCES

Austin, J. L. (1962). *How to do Things with Words*. London, Oxford Univ. Press.

Berger, P. L. and Luckmann, T. (1967) *The Social Construction of Reality*. London, Allen Lane.

Bingham, N. E. (forthcoming). Maternal speech to prelinguistic infants.

Bloom, L. (1970). *Language Development*. Cambridge, Mass., M.I.T. Press.

Bloom, L. (1971). One word at a time. Paper presented to the Conference on Developmental Linguistics, 1971, Summer Institute, Linguistic Society of America, Buffalo Univ.

Brown, R. and Bellugi, V. (1964). Three processes in the child's acquisition of syntax. In Lenneberg, E. (ed.). *New Directions in the Study of Language*. Cambridge, Mass., M.I.T. Press.

Bruner, J. S. (1968). *Processes of Cognitive Growth: Infancy*. Barne, Mass., Clark Univ. Press.

Bullowa, M., Jones, L. G. and Duckert, A. R. (1964). The acquisition of a word. *Lang. and Speech*, **7**, 107–11.

Campbell, R. and Wales, R. (1970). The study of language acquisition. In Lyons, J. (ed.). *New Horizons in Linguistics*. London, Allen Lane.

Cazden, C. B. (1968). The acquisition of noun and verb inflections. *Child Development*, **39**, 433–48.

Day, E. J. (1932). The development of language in twins: 1. A comparison of twins and single children. *Child Development*, **3**, 179–99.

Eimas, P. D. Siqueland, E. R., Jusczyk, P. and Vigorito, J. (1971). Speech perception in infants. *Science*, **171**, 303–6.

Goldman-Eisler, F. (1968). *Psycholinguistics*. London, Academic Press.

Grice, H. P. (1957). Meaning. *Phil. Rev.* **68**, 377–88.

Grice, H. P. (1968). Utterer's meaning, sentence-meaning, and word-meaning. *Found. of Lang.* **4**, 1–18.

Griffiths, R. (1954). *The Abilities of Babies*. London, Univ. London Press.

Habermas, J. (1970). Introductory remarks to a theory of communicative competence. Reprinted in Dreitzel, H. P. (ed.). *Recent Sociology*, No. 2. London, Macmillan.

Hymes, D. (1971). Competence and performance in linguistic theory. In Huxley, R. and Ingram, E. (eds.). *Language Acquisition: Models and Methods*. London, Academic Press.

Illingworth, R. (1966). *The Normal Child*. Edinburgh, Livingstone.

Jenkins, J. (1969). The acquisition of language. In Goslin, D. A. (ed.). *Handbook of Socialization Theory and Research*. Chicago, Rand-McNally.

Leopold, W. F. (1939). *Speech Development of a Bilingual Child*. Evanston, Ill., Northwestern Univ.

Lewis, M. M. (1936). *Infant Speech*. London, Routledge and Kegan Paul.

Lieberman, P. (1967). *Intonation, Perception and Language*. Cambridge, Mass., M.I.T. Press.

212

McNeill, D. (1966). Developmental psycholinguistics. In Smith, F. and Miller, G. A. (ed.). *The Genesis of Language*. Cambridge, Mass., M.I.T. Press.

McNeill, D. (1970). *The Acquisition of Language*, New York, Harper and Row.

Marshall, J. C. (1971). Can humans talk? In Morton, J. (ed.). *Biological and Sociological Factors in Psycholinguistics*, London, Logos Press.

Morley, M. E. (1957). *The Development and Disorders of Speech in Childhood*. Edinburgh, Livingstone.

Mowrer, O. H. (1960). *Learning Theory and the Symbolic Process*. New York, Wiley.

Piaget, J. (1946). *Play, Dreams and Imitation in Childhood* (English trans. 1951). London, Routledge and Kegan Paul.

Phillips, J. R. (1973). Syntax and vocabulary of mothers' speech to young children: age and sex comparisons. *Child Development*, 44, 182–85.

Quine, W. V. (1960). *Word and Object*. Cambridge, Mass., M.I.T. Press.

Ryan, J. F. (1973). Interpretation and imitation in early language development. In Hinde, R. and Hinde, J. S. (eds.). *Constraints on Learning: Limitations and Predispositions*. London, Academic Press.

Sinclair, H. and Bronckart, J. P. (1971). La structure d'ordre S.V.O. Un universal linguistique. Unpublished paper.

Stern, C. and Stern, W. (1907). *Die Kindersprache*. Leipzig.

Stern, W. (1924). *Psychology of Early Childhood*. London, Allen and Unwin.

Strawson, P. F. (1964). Intention and convention in speech acts. *Phil. Rev.* 4, 4–60.

Templin, M. (1957). *Certain Language Skills in Children*. Minneapolis, University of Minnesota Institute of Child Welfare.

Vygotsky, L. S. (1934). *Thought and Language* (English trans. 1962). Cambridge, Mass., M.I.T. Press.

Watslavick, P., Beavin, J. H. and Jackson, D. D. (1968.) *The Pragmatics of Human Communication*. London, Faber.

Weir, R. (1966). Some questions on the child's learning of phonology. In Smith, F. and Miller, G. A. (eds.). *The Genesis of Language*. Cambridge, Mass., M.I.T. Press.

Ziff, P. (1967). On H. P. Grice's account of meaning. *Analysis*, **28**, 1–8.

Since this chapter was completed an important new study of language acquisition has appeared:

Nelson, K. (1973). Structure and strategy in learning to talk. *Monog. Soc. Res. Child Development*, **37**, No. 4.

11

The development of personal powers

John Shotter

Strange to say, babies born to us need not grow up to be what we think of as human; their humanity seems to be transmitted to them after birth in an as yet ill-understood negotiation or transaction between the babies and chiefly among others their mothers – and its seed may never blossom as Itard's (1801) *The Wild Boy of Aveyron*[1] attests. As far as we can tell, the primeval state of man was hardly different from that of today's apes. But, from being totally surrounded by nature, man is now all but surrounded by his own artefacts; from being hardly more skilful than the beasts, he is now the possessor of countless bodily and mental skills. And this transformation has been brought about, it seems, by factors operating solely within men themselves – they have created and are still creating the characteristics of their own humanity.

Man inherits his humanity then, not like blue eyes, but like the houses and cities, the tools, and the other more material artefacts and his predecessors. They pass on the forms they have fashioned, and besides teaching him a skill at using them, teach him a skill at fashioning more. Being socialised, becoming a person, then, is not a natural process, it is, some would say, a praxis (see Ingleby, this volume); people are made by other people, and they attempt to make them in their own image – the praxis involved is not, however, as straightforward as all that, beliefs and interests between and within mothers and their children often conflict, and the process is one of continuous negotiation and renegotiation. If a child's development is thought of as a natural process (determined by natural laws which the scientific psychologist must discover), it is difficult to see how such factors as these can enter into and exert their influence on the process. It is the purpose of this essay to construct a framework of thought within which the praxis of child development can be understood and projects worth further empirical investigation formulated.

---

[1] In 1799 a boy of about eleven or twelve years was found in the woods of Aveyron and brought to Paris for exhibition. Itard took him up, but in spite of devoted attention the boy never became a full human being – chief amongst his deficits was his lack of speech.

John Shotter

PSYCHOLOGY AS A MORAL NOT A NATURAL SCIENCE

The first part of this essay will be spent in making a number of general comments about the nature of (human)[2] action – the activity in which human agents, selves, or individual personalities formulate and pursue intentions or projects, i.e., praxis. These comments are necessary because at the moment psychological theory is deeply divided between at least three major schools of thought, and two of these 'reify' (see Ingleby, this volume) praxis as process, conceive of actions as sequences of events, treat psychology as a natural rather than a moral science.

One school believes that man's behaviour can be accounted for within a mechanistic conception or its equivalent (e.g. Sutherland, 1970; Broadbent, 1971; Skinner, 1953, 1972). For them, man consists of a number of objective parts, which, because they are thought to retain their character unchanged irrespective of their context of existence, can be investigated in isolation from the totality in which they play their part. The task of these workers is to discover the natural laws thought to be governing the behaviour of the parts, and from this knowledge plus a knowledge of the relations between the parts, infer man's total functioning. The second school, however, believes a more wholistic, organismic (v. Bertalanffy, 1952, 1968) or a more biological approach (Piaget, 1971, 1972) is required. They feel that as man is an entity which grows itself, so to speak, it cannot consist of distinct parts like a machine at all. At any one moment in time, man's parts owe not just their character but their very existence, not only to one another, but to his parts at some earlier point in time – they have grown from them, and a temporal as well as a spatial, a historical as well as a logical aspect characterises their interdependence. It is the task of this school, given the logical structure of the ends towards which organisms develop, to account for the developmental processes involved in attaining them.

This is a far richer approach than the first. Bertalanffy's organismic system or Piaget's constructive structural approach does what Sutherland's and Broadbent's simple mechanistic approach cannot: it makes the *construction* of 'mechanisms' within the organism a possibility, for mechanisms as such cannot be made to construct themselves. Organisms may be thought of as constructing 'mechanisms' within themselves during the course of growth – *viz.*, Bertalanffy's doctrine of

---

[2] If what follows below is correct, then the word 'human' is redundant, for only human beings will be capable of *action* as such. While animals may be able to behave intelligently, they cannot behave *intentionally* and thus be said to act. It will be *intentionality* which will mark off the realm of the personal from the realm of the beasts.

216

'progressive mechanisation' or Piaget's 'formal operations' stage, where contingent relations finally make way for necessary ones. However, while these approaches may make the construction of mechanisms intelligible, neither can give an adequate account of *meaning*, an account of when, where, how and why a particular 'mechanism' is *used* in the co-ordination of one organism's behaviour with another's. Neither this school nor the mechanistic one treats the *social sphere* realistically: (1) They make no mention of how the *source* of an action is ascertained and how the attribution of responsibility for it influences subsequent action; they make no distinction between what a person *does* and what merely happens to or within him. Yet, I shall argue, this is of fundamental importance in human affairs: it is just because a mother can (or not, as she so chooses) treat her child's actions as if 'he' were responsible for them that she can influence his development in the way that she does (see Ryan this volume). (2) Furthermore in ignoring the attribution of responsibility, neither school distinguishes the subjective from the objective aspects of a person; they make no distinction between a person and what he *uses* in the formulation and the attainment of his goals. They condemn the idea of an active subject realising itself in the objective world as vitalism, as the introduction of 'occult entities' of the worst kind. Both treat an organism's response to a situation as the immediate resultant of some total system of interacting elements materially present in the world at the moment of response. These charges of vitalism can, I believe, be overcome, and I shall turn to them in a later section.

Because of the above and other deficiencies in the social sphere an even richer approach than the structuralist one seems called for. A third school, to which I assign myself, feel that nothing less than a *personal* approach to human affairs is adequate (e.g. MacMurray, 1957, 1961; Hampshire, 1959; Taylor, 1966; Bannister and Fransella, 1971; Harré and Secord, 1972; Harré, this volume). However, in taking this approach, psychology is removed from the realm of the natural sciences and is placed among the moral sciences. This alters its character entirely. Most importantly it becomes concerned with *negotiations*, with negotiations between people rather than with interactions between things. Values, opinions, beliefs, feelings, intentions, etc., once again assume a crucial role in human affairs. While classical science demands that everything be studied ultimately as if it were matter in motion according to an absent God's pre-established laws, *persons* seem able on occasions to act from a belief, a mere *conception* of a law, thus, apparently, exempting themselves from this demand. And in attempting to live thus, according to the conception of a law, people may fail; they may act inappropriately, rightly or wrongly, legitimately or illegitimately, etc., for conceptions decree only what *should* or *might be* the case, not what is. Attempting to live according to laws inevitably involves the judgement of other people.

This, then, I shall take as a basic fact of life: that *people* living in relation to one another co-ordinate their affairs in terms of concepts. And what it is for people to conduct their affairs in a rational and responsible manner is for them to direct their behaviour towards the attainment of socially constructed and established goals, sensing and correcting deviations from this task in the course of their behaviour – constructing its own goals in this way is something no other species of animals can do. Man's social life is essentially a moral affair. And it's no use hoping, as many psychologists do, to replace the essentially moral practices regulating human affairs with 'natural' principles; for science, the process of discovering 'natural laws' is itself a moral enterprise: it is only because I can act in accord with a (shared) conception of a *possible* natural law and sense what accords and what departs from it that I can plan and conduct an experiment in the attempt to verify it. No more fundamental basis for deciding the truth of empirical matters can be found – in the organisational complexity of matter, say (Sutherland, 1970) – for how would it be established as a true base? In the end, even the formulation and choice of 'natural laws' via which to control our circumstances seems to involve negotiations between people; 'an "objective fact" is simply one that can be shared by different individuals' (Hyman, 1964, p. 103).

The concern of this essay, then, is with how it is possible for people to behave responsibly and with how the ability is developed. Its growth seems to involve different kinds of interactions and negotiations between mothers and their children over a considerable period of time. And it is the central aim of this essay to construct a framework of thought within which the significance of observations on these activities might be interpreted. It suggests that a baby's development is not wholly a natural process but is partly an intentional one, and as such is a product of human thought and deliberation, belief and ideology. In other words, as other writers in this volume suggest, it is a process into which the interests and ideas of a culture as well as the ideologies of a class can enter.

RESPONSIBLE ACTION FROM A PRACTICAL
STANDPOINT

To be counted an autonomous individual in social life, we must be solely responsible for our own actions. If when so acting we want to be said to be acting reasonably, in a way intelligible to our fellows, we must attempt to make our actions intelligible to ourselves in *their* terms; that is, we must attempt to assess the value of our performances in relation to interests other than our own immediate and idiosyncratic ones. George Mead (1934, p. 73) put this point thus:

Such is the difference between intelligent conduct on the part of animals and what we call a reflective individual. We say the animal does not think. He does not put himself in a position for which he is responsible; he does not put himself in the place of the other person and say in effect, 'He will act in such a way and I will act in this way.'

Mead later imagines the situation to be as if when relating our actions to one another, we did it within the context of a game or set of games, and moved in relation to one another according to rules – an analogy also proposed by Wittgenstein (1953) and now gaining much favour. For the game-analogy is more comprehensive than the models of sign-using and rule-following previously used. Our task is, however, to be more comprehensive still, for we have to understand not only how we can conduct ourselves within the context of a game, but how in the first place we set them up.

As a first step in this attempt, I am going to adopt the position that it is practical activity not thought which is primary in human life . . . in the beginning was the deed not the word, and the deed was social. Now perhaps it may be felt by some that as the Piagetian slogan, 'thought is internalised action', is now so well known and accepted that such a view hardly needs examination here. But let me point out that the mainstream of modern thought, indeed Western thought since the Greeks has concentrated upon man-as-a-thinker, upon man as an isolated subject set over against the world as an object, and not upon man-as-a-doer, upon man as an agent who makes something happen, and certainly not upon man as a social self (Mead, 1934), acting responsibly. It is the 'cognitive' image of man which has structured *and still does structure* all our more reflective activities. And perhaps the most important consequence of this is that they all issue, not in improved powers of responsible action, but in plans for more effective action – means towards ends in a material world.

The inadequacies in the 'cognitive' image are perhaps nowhere more apparent than in the 'psycholinguistic' attempts to understand the child's development of language. As Ryan (this volume) points out, studying language not as praxis but as an 'object of the child's knowledge' ignores all the other skills entering into its actual *use*. If this essay were to be a critique of Piagetian psychology (and other structuralist approaches, even constructivist ones) it would centre just upon the way in which the social implications of such standpoints have not been realistically treated. In being concerned only with the attainment of logico-mathematical knowledge Piaget has ignored all those human activities not directed towards the attainment of definite ends, all the creative activities to do with bringing ends into existence, actions directed towards what does not yet exist. And as Harré (this volume) remarks, one sphere in which this creative activity seems to be manifested early on is in the creation and use of ritual and ceremonial acts which establish and maintain a social order. Concerned only with cognition, Piaget has failed to take into account both our actions upon one another and our non-cognitive springs of action. Also he makes no distinction between deliberate and spontaneous activity, intentions and their formulation play no part in his thought. In this essay the concept of intentionality[3] (Brentano, 1924) will play a central part.

In our everyday practical affairs we do, and must, distinguish between what we as individual personalities do and know ourselves to be doing, and what we just find happening. For, if we are to be accepted as rational beings, we are expected to appreciate the consequence of our actions, and to be responsible for what we do; we must know no matter how dimly the goal towards which we are directing our actions, i.e., we must in some sense appreciate our own intentions and act in relation to their regulative force. *This is fundamental.* No more fundamental distinction can be found to replace my sense of responsibility for my own actions – as I have pointed out, the conduct of science itself rests upon it. I shall therefore take the distinction between *acts* and *events*, *doings* and *happenings* as absolutely basic and interpret its significance from a practical rather than a cognitive standpoint. Straightaway some startling implications emerge – and in the rest of this section I follow Macmurray (1957, 1961).

Briefly, in acting we do something; using something else we make something take on a form other than the form it would have had if we had not acted; we determine the world. For this to be possible, the world must be capable of being given a structure that it does not already possess; that is, the world must be essentially *indeterminate*. Contrary to the classical deterministic view of natural science, the billiard ball universe, the possibility of action seems to require the possibility of alternative futures, as William James (1917, p. 151) pointed out some time ago. Indeterminism, he said:

admits that possibilities may be in excess of actualities and that things not yet revealed to our knowledge may really be ambiguous. Of two alternative futures which we conceive, both may now really be possible; and the one becomes im-

---

3   It was Franz Brentano who was responsible for introducing the concept of intentionality into modern philosophy. In attempting to clarify the distinction between mental and physical phenomena he suggested that every mental phenomenon is characterised by what the Schoolmen of the Middle Ages called the 'intentional inexistence' of the object. In other words, mental activity is directed upon an object, or has a content, or is regulated in relation to an end. And it is this, its intention, which distinguishes one act from another, not the temporal order of behavioural *events*.

220

possible only at the very moment when the other excludes it by becoming real itself. Indeterminism thus denies the world to be one unbending unit of fact. It says that there is a certain ultimate pluralism in it; and so saying it corroborates our ordinary unsophisticated view of things.

Usually we do seem able to intervene in ongoing processes and make something happen in one way rather than another, as if both possibilities had been intrinsically available in the process. And indeterminism thus implies that action necessarily involves *choice*. As James points out, when one among a set of possibilities is realised the rest become impossible. To do anything is to do this *and not that*.[4] This does not mean that action is *preceded* by choice; that some mysterious mental act of choosing occurs before we actually act. While reflective activity may precede action, it is only a theoretical choosing, a possible choice as is shown by the fact that the action so 'chosen' need not be performed. Actual choosing is the doing of an action, whether preceded by reflection or not. This suggests a further important characteristic: distinctions such as intelligible and unintelligible, legitimate and illegitimate, right and wrong, etc., are *intrinsic* in action (but not necessarily in thought). This is illustrated in the fact that we can and usually do speak grammatically without it first being necessary for us to think about how to do it. Reflection upon grammatical possibilities is only necessary when we run into difficulties.

Now one crucial aspect of action which must be mentioned here is that it is, as we have already said, *intentional*. While an *event* is to be explained by discovering its *cause*, an *act* is to be explained by giving its *reason*, by saying what the person was trying to do in performing it. Now, by suggesting that human behaviour is to be explained by reference to an end, it may seem that we are suggesting human behaviour can be explained teleologically. And as this is the form of explanation applied to animal behaviour, it may be thought that human behaviour can be explained in the same way as animal behaviour. This would be mistaken. Whereas, in understanding animal behaviour teleologically, our point of reference is the end which actually occurs as the final stage of a behavioural process, it is the end *proposed or intended* by the person, not any *actual* end he may attain, which is crucial in explaining his behaviour. His behaviour may be understood, then, as a more or less successful attempt to fulfil his intention.

Not all human behaviour, however, has this characteristic: besides the execution of intentions there are also activities to do with their

---

4   In Shotter (1970) I discuss some aspects of Kelly's (1955) personal construct theory. His *construct systems* are sets of interrelated bipolar distinctions. In these systems too, things are known both for what they are *and* what they are not; categories necessarily imply their own contrastives. Such personal construct systems involve intentional distinctions rather than existential ones.

formulation. In Shotter (1970, pp. 238–42), drawing upon Dreyfus (1967), I discuss the situation of a wild-boy divorced from any human community. He developed his knowledge both of the nature of his needs and of the structure of his environment in terms of *what he had to do* in order to alleviate vague and indeterminate states of discomfort and restlessness. It was argued there that he could make his vague knowledge of himself and his environment determinate via the elementary principle of doing, when he was again in a restless state, what he did last time but this time not as the result of a prolonged trial-and-error process but directly as an attempt to alleviate his restlessness, evaluating his attempt in the process by an 'inner sense of gratification' (Dreyfus, 1967). This principle, however, provides only one 'construal' of his situation, one which ties his actions to his own immediate needs. If he is ever to put different construals on to situations in order to assess their significance in relation to other than his own idiosyncratic needs and interests, then negotiations with others are necessary. And helping the child to formulated ends worth pursuing in the social world is the major part of the task a mother faces in her efforts to 'bring her child up'. She must help him to construct something like a 'target', or a system of 'targets', or even a system for generating and relating 'targets' at which to aim while conducting his own behaviour in relation to others, systems of rules via which he can regulate his own behaviour responsibly.

The doctrine of intentionality has, thus, an ideal, a creative, or a prospective aspect to it. Not all human social behaviour need be directed towards explicitly determinate ends or systems of ends (although it often is); some may be involved in the determination, in the making or construction of such ends. Intentionality has both a rule-using and a rule-making aspect. Thus to say that people's behaviour is intentional and not teleological is not to say that they possess some mysterious *élan vital* denied to animals, but simply to say that they direct their conduct in relation not to their own immediate interests and needs but to actual or potential socially constructed ones. Now it is in this sense that intentionality is central to this essay. For I want to suggest that to the extent that a mother interacts with her baby with the intention of bringing him up to be a responsible adult his development is not natural but intentional. Such an intention is perhaps one of the most general and indeterminate that there is, but no less real for all that. In one form or another, to make a person of him, is the reason mothers would give for much of what they do in interaction with their child. And it is in their attempts to make their intentions determinate to themselves in deciding upon some definite practical activity regarding their child that the child care literature (such as that mentioned by Newson and Newson, this volume) and other sources of social influence can take their effect.

The development of personal powers

Human babies are not born into any direct relation with nature, but into a home, not into a natural habitat but into a humanly created setting, an institution designed in advance through artifice and foresight to provide for human needs, both biological and personal. And sometimes this foresight and artifice may be defective in one way or another (see Tizard and Tizard, and Hubert, this volume). However, to represent the process of human development even at its earliest stages as an organic process, a process of development towards a pre-determined final structure, would be to exclude all reference to these and to other exclusively human aspects of the process. As he cannot think or act for himself his survival depends upon the thought and actions of others. It is only within this process of development, a process in which the intentions of others are of crucial significance, that he achieves a relative independence and autonomy by acquiring his own powers of responsible action. From all this it follows that a baby is not a machine although he may be said to possess mechanisms; nor an animal although in some respects he may be said to function organically; if he is to develop as an individual personality he must be treated as a full term in a personal relationship, as a being amenable to rationality. If nobody intends his survival and acts with the intention to secure it, he does not survive. Thus a mother's reasons for her actions (which usually follow from her beliefs about the nature of people and things), no matter how inarticulate and vague, play an important part in the upbringing of her child.

And this highlights an important methodological point, an error in much psychological and social research. Personal relationships and other human groupings do not exist and function as matters of fact, but are maintained by the intention of their members to maintain them; without such intentions they collapse. Thus they cannot simply be observed and described from the standpoint of an external observer, for, as was made clear above, it is their projected or prospective ends which structure people's actions not their attained ends. Personal relationships need to be described in a way exclusively human; in terms of what the people involved in them are trying to do. Lock (in press) has described a form of participatory experimentation on the development of communication with very young children which incorporates this approach, and I will say more about this later.

POWERS

Implicitly, I have been introducing above an entirely new image of physical reality to replace the old classical billiard-ball universe; and it includes a radically different principle of causality. Central to this new image is the idea that things or substances have *powers*. This is related to the old Aristotelian nation of *efficient causes*, and has recently been reintroduced into science and philosophy by such writers as Taylor (1966), Ayers (1968), Harré (1970), and Harré and Secord (1972). An efficient cause used to be thought of, not simply as a state or event which preceded another state or event in a principled manner, but as a definite thing or substance which had an *intrinsic* power to make something happen. Now I have discussed this idea at length elsewhere (Shotter, 1973), and so will only mention aspects of it relevant to my purpose here.

The concept of powers is related to that of a field of possibilities, to indeterminism. If we say that a person's past does not determine just one possibly real future of him but a number, then we must say that at a certain moment in time he possesses an intrinsic power or potentiality to express himself in a whole range of different ways, the way he chooses depending upon his circumstances at the time. Now classically, a vexing problem with this formulation has been that of saying in what a thing's or substance's potentialities consist before they are actualised; for, if they do not exist before they are realised (a contradiction in terms), how is prediction ever to be possible? – to mention but one difficulty. While in an indeterministic world it may be impossible to predict a man's future in detail, it certainly must be possible to predict its general form – and this is the whole point of introducing the concept of powers – for his future emerges from a *particular present state* within a *definite field of possibilities* (possibilities, we can say, structured according to rules, for that, at least, is how personal powers are expressed). And indeed, if we are ever to find one another's actions intelligible as a matter of course (as in talking, for instance), such prediction must be possible – we may go so far as to surmise that such prediction is made possible by the construction of a system, a generative and transformational system of formal targets at which to aim while speaking, and that this is the nature of man's achievement in his invention of language. His *knowledge of language*, as an abstract object, functions to regulate the *form* of his speech. So, although in an indeterministic world people are under no necessity to act in an orderly manner, if they want to live with one another, they must. And if we describe the general structure of their intentions in doing so (the rules they use in the regulation of their actions), then, even though individual personalities might seem to have a character of their own, the powers they all share can be made public. The classical problem of saying in what potentialities consist before they are actualised cannot be solved, nor need it be. We can keep it in abeyance by ascribing to the thing concerned a *power*. And to quote Harré

(1970, p. 85), 'to ascribe a power to a thing asserts only that it can do what it does in virtue of its nature, whatever that is. It leaves open the question of the exact specification of the nature or constitution in virtue of which it has the power. Perhaps that can be discovered by empirical investigation later.' But fully describing the powers of things is to give, Harré says, at least a *schematic* explanation of its intrinsic nature, an explanation which, with the growth of knowledge, would not need to be changed in outline, merely filled in with detail.

So far, I have discussed the application of the concept of powers in general; I now want to go on to discuss its special application here. Above, I introduced the fundamental distinction which we can make in our experience of our own behaviour: between what I as an individual personality can make happen and what simply happens, a distinction between acts and events, reasons and causes. Now clearly, much of what goes on between and within people merely happens; they do not as people make it happen – it happens *naturally* I shall say. For when I decide to do anything, the nervous and muscular co-ordinations required to express the intention happen automatically without me as such intending them, and are included in the doing of what I intend. As an individual personality *I* merely seem to *modulate* an ongoing natural process. I shall, thus, distinguish two aspects of man: man as a child of Culture, that aspect of himself which he makes, and man as a child of Nature, the aspect for which, we shall say, Nature is responsible. In line with this we can view men both as *individual personalities* with *personal powers* and as *natural agents* with *natural powers*; as the former we can view them as living in a culture, responsible for their actions, and assessing the value of their actions in relation to shared aims and interests, as the latter we can view them as living with one another like animals, not responsible for their actions, and acting only in relation to their own immediate interests and needs.[5]

In our investigations, while we may intend these distinctions in practice, they are not actually distinctions in the nature of man's existence; they are *teleological distinctions* rather than *distinctions of existence* (Dewey, 1896) or *matters of intention* rather than *matters of fact* (Macmurray, 1957). And having distinguished them we must now seek their relation to one another. Below I shall suggest that a child derives his personal powers from his natural powers in the course of his upbringing; that deriving them is not something he can do (at first, if ever) on his own; that the help of someone who already possesses them is required,

---

[5] These two different views define two different spheres of study: the natural and the man made. And it would be surprising if the same frameworks of thought and techniques of investigation were appropriate to both, a point Vico first made in 1744.

and usually that help is supplied by a mother – not necessarily the biological mother, but someone who is in what I shall call a *love* relation to him. (But see Harré, this volume, who suggests that children have worlds of their own; that there is more in the child's world than ever appears in the adult world; and that in a sense it is complete in itself. This is, of course, with children of three years and older who seem able to act, as Harré puts it, not according to rules but in relation to 'images'. I shall discuss this in a later section.)

Specifically then, I want to discuss what goes on between and within a mother and her child during that part of his early development which results in him being transformed from an almost wholly natural agent into an individual personality, his acquisition of personal powers.

THE INITIAL STAGES OF 'PSYCHOLOGICAL SYMBIOSIS'

The most obvious fact about the human baby is his total helplessness. As Macmurray (1961) puts it, he seems to be 'adapted', to speak paradoxically, to being unadapted; he is adapted to a complete dependence upon an adult human being. He is born into a love relationship which is inherently personal; he must be treated as if he were a person who could intend purposes; he cannot think for himself, yet he cannot live without thought, so some way must be found of having his thinking done for him. Until he has constructed his own thought mechanisms, I shall propose that he *uses* his mother as a 'mechanism' to do the thinking required in the realisation of his intentions.

Very young babies *do* very little; while most of the essential physiological rhythms are established, and *perhaps* a few automatic reflexes, they have no power of behaviour. Around the end of the first week of life they do, however, begin to respond to some cues. One such cue is said to be a change of *equilibrium*. If, after the eighth day, a breast fed baby is lifted from the crib and held in a nursing position, he turns his head towards the breast. In contrast, if he is held in a vertical position he does not (Spitz, 1965). In general, however, for the first two months of life the child could not be said to 'perceive' his surroundings at all. After that time an approaching adult begins to acquire a unique place in the child's environment. At this stage, a hungry, crying child begins to perceive, in his sense of the term, an approaching adult visually: he will become quiet, open his mouth or make sucking movements. But this is said (Spitz, 1965) to take place only when the child is hungry; the response is to a totality of both internal and external factors. Two or three weeks later there is further progress: when the infant 'perceives' a human face, he follows it with concentrated attention. Later, at three months, he will smile, and this smile is, Spitz maintains, the first manifestation of active, directed (and, he says, intentional)[6] behaviour on the child's part. This is the end of what Spitz calls the 'objectless stage' (the stage of no active relationship with the mother) and the beginning of what he calls 'psychological symbiosis'. This is a very interesting and important stage, a true love relationship for total attention to one another is required. Now during this period of 'psychological symbiosis' the formative processes which terminate in the child seem to have their source in the mother and their influence is transmitted to him in the course of affective exchanges. That is, they are transmitted to him in the course of exchanges in which one individual responds in an immediate and unconsidered manner as a result of the way he apprehends the immediate and unconsidered reaction of the other individual to him. Richards (1974) mentions a number of these kinds of exchange; it is often the mother's timing of what she does that is all important. For instance, while breastfeeding her infant she times her talking and smiling to him to occur in the pauses between sucking. As Mead (1934) points out, such interlaced activities are a form of *communication*, but they are not of the form in which a stimulus affects the individual who makes it in the same way as the one who receives it. It is thus not a language proper; it is the communication of natural agents (he would say, biologic individuals). The sort of perception involved in these exchanges the expression of feeling or affect, is very primitive, and all writers on the child's early development (Schaffer, 1971; Spitz, 1965; Koffka, 1921) note that distinctive reactions to different forms of human expression appear a few months before differential reactions to 'things' or 'thing-qualities'. As such affective or unreflective exchanges between human beings as natural agents are central to my whole thesis, I must break off here for a brief discussion of this form of perception.

THE PERCEPTION OF EXPRESSION AND THE PERCEPTION OF THINGS

A classical problem of perception is at issue here: Do we perceive people's psychological states is some direct way, or do we perceive them indirectly, via, say, a process of 'unconscious inference' (Helmholtz) from the objective characteristics of their expression? As the child reacts differentially to human expressions of joy and anger, friendliness and hostility *before* he reacts differentially to colours and other thing-characteristics (Koffka, 1921) it would seem to be the former. But this suggests that ostensively more complex judgements are made at an earlier

---

[6] We will not say intentional as at this stage, although the smile may be directed, it could not be said to be a *self*-directed activity.

age than apparently more simple ones – simpler, that is, if one holds the classical image of man in which cognition is primary. The resolution of this issue involves matters of (1) *access* to the relevant data, (2) the *determination of its significance*, and (3) the *determination of its source*, so I will discuss each of these in turn.

(1) Take joy, for instance: anyone can, in principle, report on whether a person is behaving joyfully or not, but only the person himself can say whether he is aware of being joyful. Thus it seems that two distinct kinds of criteria are involved here, one private and the other public. And in the past, both philosophers and psychologists have supposed that, as the seemingly private criteria are not open to scrutiny, only the public ones can be used as a basis for ascribing psychological predicates to people. But this, Harré and Secord (1972, p. 121) point out, is mistaken; both criteria are necessary and *are* available for scrutiny. 'There are always some situations for any state-of-mind predicate where others have some degree of access to that state of mind, even in another person', they say. Our feelings, moods, beliefs, intentions, etc., are *shown* in our actions, and although they may not involve reference to objective criteria, they do involve readily observable criteria which can be made 'logically adequate' (Harré and Secord, 1972, pp. 14–123) as required, i.e., they are negotiable. What has misled philosophers and psychologists, Harré and Secord argue, is their failure to distinguish between *access* and *authority*: although a person is often (but not always) the best authority on what he is doing – he is, after all, his own closest observer – *he is not the only one to have access to the relevant data*. One way or another that is made available in his behaviour for all to grasp, and indeed, when it comes to assessing the nature of his own behaviour, i.e., satisfying Mead's criterion, he is in no better position than anyone else. Only as his intentions issue in performance is he able to tell whether he is successfully executing them or not – a point we shall take up again when later we discuss talking. While he usually (but not always) knows what he intends, he must judge the adequacy of his own performances as others do, as they occur in both time and space – it being the temporal sequencing of the spatial possibilities which reveals the person's choice and thus manifests his intention.

(2) Now, if the criteria involved in the assessment of psychological states are not private, and people do show their psychological states in the temporal organisation of their behaviour, how do we determine these states? Consider for a moment a related situation. We distinguish a joyful person *outside* us from the feelings (of joy or otherwise) which he

occasions *within* us. If, however, we accept that all our experiences are derived from outside us,[7] this distinction can only be a function of the way in which we *determine* these categories. One aspect of our experience is determined as *outer* and ascribed to an object (in space), the other is determined as *inner* and ascribed as feeling to ourselves (in time) – space and time being, respectively, the forms of outer and inner perception (Kant). Returning now to our problem I want to suggest that when confronted by a person it is open to us, to determine the aspects of his behaviour similarly. Now when attempting to determine the nature of a real object it does not, so to speak, answer back; it neither acts nor reacts. Thus, in this case, the categories of outer perception can be made as determinate as an investigator pleases (and his categories of inner perception are idiosyncratic and irrelevant to all except himself). However, a non-object, a source of expression cannot be determined as one pleases, for it does answer back. So there is an essential indeterminacy associated with the categories of perception in this case which can only be resolved *via negotiation and agreement with the source being investigated* – to approach a point about negotiation made by Harré and Secord (1972, p. 161) from another direction.

So the essential difference between the processes involved in the perception of expression and the perception of things seems more to do with *the way in which these categories are made determinate* than anything to do with the perceptual process itself. The criteria of inner perception involve negotiation and agreement with the source (or are otherwise left indeterminate, and people do not know exactly their feelings), while those of outer perception, at least in their objective paradigm form, do not involve such negotiation.

(3) Now if the process of inner perception works on 'expressions' and determines them *irrespective of whose expressions they are,* the classical theories of our experience of other minds are quite redundant. It is unnecessary, usually, to even unconsciously infer people's beliefs, intentions, etc., from sequences of behavioural events objectively perceived in outer perception. We can perceive or apprehend mental activity directly in what I have called our inner sense.[8] But, if this is the case, as in our interactions with other people there must be a continuous flux of activity within us, *undifferentiated as to theirs or ours,* the problem becomes one, not of appreciating the nature of mental activity in others, but of distinguishing that which has its *source* in us from that which has

[7]   Strictly, we should say that all our experiences are derived from outside *us* as individual personalities responsible for our own actions etc.; from outside *ourselves* that is. For often we want to talk about our experience of the motions of our own bodies as well as our experience of the motions of other people's.

[8]   A distinction not of existence but in intention.

its source in them. And this, I think, is the young infant's problem in his period of 'psychological symbiosis'. He has to discover for which, of all things happening, he is or can be responsible.

CONTINUATION OF THE 'PSYCHOLOGICAL SYMBIOSIS' PERIOD

As Spitz said, the smile is the first directed expression of affect on the child's part. At first (at three months) the individuals to whom the infant responds with a smile are freely interchangeable. This is because the three-month-old does not perceive the human face as such at all, as Spitz has established experimentally, he perceives only a 'sign Gestalt': a specific configuration within the face as a totality, consisting of just the forehead–eyes–nose sector, triggers the infant's smile response after the manner of an 'innate releaser mechanism' (an I.R.M. – Tinbergen, 1951). But as Spitz (p. 95) remarks:

this sounds quite mechanical: sign Gestalten, releaser mechanisms triggering innate responses. The reader may well ask: couldn't a mechanical doll, fitted with the sign Gestalt rear our children just as well? No, it could not . . . Only a reciprocal relation can provide the experiential factor in the infant's development, consisting as it does of an ongoing circular exchange, in which affects play the major role. When the infant experiences a need, it will provoke in him an affect that will lead to behavioural changes, which in their turn provoke an affective response and its concomitant attitude in the mother; she behaves 'as if she understood' what particular need of the infant causes his affective manifestation.

Although the relationship between a mother and her child is clearly an unequal one, they do have the power in some sense to complete or fulfil one another's intentions. And the situation cannot be simply as Ainsworth (this volume) states it, that the baby 'becomes attached to the figure or figures with whom he has had most interaction'. It is the quality not the quantity of interaction which must be significant. To the extent that a mother can interpret her baby's behaviour as having a mental content or intentional structure – and the extent to which she can do that is up to her – she can attempt to complete its intention and 'negotiate' with him a satisfaction of his needs, i.e., alleviate his state of discomfort or restlessness. But the mother pursues intentions within the interactive scheme also, she wants her baby to suck, to stop crying, to acknowledge her by looking into her eyes, to grasp her finger, etc. And she discovers strategies and tactics via which she can elicit these responses from her child. Thus, both gain a great deal of idiosyncratic knowledge about one another as individuals, knowledge which at this stage is very important, and which makes the mother irreplaceable.

Now within the totality of the child and his mother, she constitutes a 'mechanism' or 'set of mechanisms' via which he can execute actions in the world. (That even very young children (four to eighteen weeks) will execute 'actions' if given access to the appropriate mechanisms has been strikingly demonstrated by Bruner (1969).) It is only via her instrumentality that he comes to differentiate the forehead–eyes–nose sign Gestalt as a meaningful entity. She appreciates in his movements, in his manifestations of feeling or affect, the nature of his mental state and responds to them in such a way that she presents him with the characteristic Gestalt just at the time she is gratifying his needs. It thus only appears and functions within the ongoing circular affective exchange which has its source and its terminus in the child, but which is mediated via the 'mechanisms' the mother provides. The child could not have distinguished the sign Gestalt entirely by his own devices. Currently, he can only act because his mother acts 'as if she understood' him, and it is in this sense that the child of three months is in 'psychological symbiosis' with his mother. He can only differentiate himself from her by constituting within himself some of the 'mechanisms' the mother now provides.

THE CONSTITUTION OF 'MENTAL' TOTALITIES

Now we can only surmise about the processes going on within the child responsible for constituting the forehead–eyes–nose sign Gestalt. But there is no doubt at all that we must postulate the existence of something like, to use Chomsky's (1972) term, intrinsic processes of mental organisation. For clearly, there are natural processes within us which take sensory data and organise them in such a way that subsequent data are not regarded *de novo* but are treated in a characteristic way preconditioned by past data.

What this characteristic way is has been elucidated recently by some experiments of Garner (1966). He gave people experience of (incomplete) families of visual (and auditory) patterns, presented singly and constructed according to a family style. But as he remarks 'a single stimulus can have no real meaning without reference to a set of stimuli, because the attributes which define it cannot be specified without knowing what the alternatives are'. And he found, in fact, that people seemed to 'infer', as he put it, even from their limited experience what the appropriate family of alternatives might be. But they did not do this consciously, they did not do this as individual personalities who knew what they were doing; it must have been, we shall say, as natural agents that they did it, using their natural powers of mental organisation or determination in such a way that the principles of

231

determination, used to match the already encountered situation, could also be used to determine as yet unencountered situations in the same style. In other words, it is a natural power that a person augments such a task.

The determination of such totalities seems to be an active process at every level, and Bohm (1965) has elucidated other aspects of it. He points out that nothing is seen without movements and variations on the retina of the eye, and the characteristics of these variations must play some part in determining the structure of what is seen. The relevant data must be extracted from the *relations* between the outgoing movements and their incoming consequences. So we do not at any level perceive just what is in front of our eyes, what we perceive contains 'structural features which are not even on the retina of the eye at a given moment, but which are detected with the aid of relationships observed over some period of time' (Bohm, 1965, p. 203). In fact, Bohm goes on to argue, the attempt to base our idea of perceptual processes upon some physical time-order of events can only lead to confusion for 'the order of signals is not essentially related to the order of time' (p. 210) – as, for instance, in the constitution of images in a television picture. It is the way a person *relates* his actions and their consequents that matters, and to some extent, that is up to him, i.e., it is an intentional process. Perceiving is a skill: 'a person must actively meet his environment in such a way that he co-ordinates his outgoing nervous impulses with those that are coming in. As a result the structure of his environment is, as it were, gradually incorporated into his outgoing impulses, so that he learns how to meet his environment with the right kind of response' (Bohm, 1965, p. 211). As Garner says, the perceiver actively participates in the process of perceptual organisation, but if Bohm is right, in realms way beyond those Garner has so far investigated experimentally.

Garner's work suggests why the forehead–eyes–nose sign Gestalt only functions within the totality of the human face: stimulus configurations only have their significance in relation to some mentally constituted totality of possible configurations. Bohm's arguments suggest that the sign Gestalt (and later the mother herself, personally) is singled out because the mother co-ordinates her activities closely with her child's. She is the only one who can be incorporated in the circuit of activities which has its source and terminus in the child. It is via his own actions *and* her instrumentality in them that he singles out the sign Gestalt (and will later single out her); and it is via his own activities that he will eventually differentiate himself from her, and end the period of 'psychological symbiosis'.

THE END OF THE PERIOD OF 'PSYCHOLOGICAL SYMBIOSIS'

The child thus begins to do things on his own, and as a natural agent he may manifest powers in an apparently directed and regulated way. But it is not behaviour in which he *knows what he is doing*. It is not, as Harré and Secord would say, *monitored* behaviour; it is not yet *self-directed* activity. There is some way to go before that.

The notional end[9] of the period of psychological symbiosis is indicated by the development of the child's ability (around fifteen months) to actively deny his mother the option of influencing him, in other words, by him learning effectively to say 'No'; he is now beginning to move around. Until this time it was simply the mother's task to gratify or not the needs and wishes of her infant, now she has to curb and prevent some of his initiatives. And apparently, when acting as an agent in his own right, as a self, he will not easily tolerate being forced back into a purely reactive role; he attempts to sever the links via which she exerts her control over him. The period of social games can now begin. For, if one is to play one's part in a game properly, that is, be solely responsible for what happens, one must cut oneself off from the influence of others while doing it; however, only if one is open to the influence of others does one know *when* to play it. Thus the child if he is to be able to play social games must first develop a clear distinction between people and things (animate and inanimate), and learn as his first social skill how to open and close the social link at will. And part of being able to do that is being able to acknowledge (as Harré, this volume, points out) the humanity, the autonomy and cognitive status of the other by some form of greeting – even if only a smile.

THE EXERCISE OF NATURAL POWERS IN PLAY AND THEIR REGULATION ACCORDING TO RULES IN SOCIAL EXCHANGES

The three-year-old still reacts to adults affectively, but in contrast to early childhood these affective reactions are directed and regulated in a generalised manner, e.g., the child acts as if he senses an adult's authority, etc. His behaviour manifests the influences of his past exchanges with adults and the physical world and is, presumably, regulated by some internally constituted structures.

Now, in Vygotsky's (1966) view, the child's play at this stage is

---

9 Rejections and refusals are apparent, of course, all the way through the infant's early development. I am indebted to John Collinson for this point.

essentially a generalised expression of affect: an expression of his basic needs and desires, structured as a result of his earlier action exchanges with adults and the world. Thus the child when he plays does not understand *what* he plays, he simply plays in accord with some internal structure, what Vygotsky calls an 'imaginary situation'. It would be wrong then, to say that he plays 'according to rules', he does not. He simply seems to be attempting to play out the possibilities inherent in his internally constituted mental totalities. The establishment of rules or rule-systems, is, as we shall see, a final consequence of this process, *not an essential part of it*. So, although the child's play may seem to be regulated by rules, and someone may extract rules from it and use them to re-enact his play, to extract the rules is not to reconstitute their original basis in an 'imaginary situation'. The rules would only characterise the possibilities realised in that situation, not necessarily the whole field of both realisable *and unrealisable*[10] tendencies in it. Any rules there might be in the child's play are not formulated in advance, but issue in the course of playing with others in a co-ordinated way, i.e., they issue in the invention of a game. It is at this point that I think the capacity for ceremonial emerges, which Harré (this volume) so rightly emphasises as of crucial significance in the child's life. Of particular interest here are the rituals and comfort habits of the young child (Newson and Newson, 1968) and his linguistic incantations (Weir, 1962); these phenomena both occur on the child going to bed, at a time free of external demands. One could go on at this point to investigate the relation between ritual, myth, and ceremonial in child and primitive thought as indeed Cassirer (1957) has done partially, but it would be out of place in this essay.

Now, most importantly, playing in accord with an 'imaginary situation' involves *meanings*. Usually, the 'things' in a young child's environment dictate what he must do, but in play in an 'imaginary situation' they do not. Here, he is regulating his own behaviour not by reference to the 'things' actually present in his own environment at all. In that sense, he is detached from it, and is acting in a cognitive or mental realm. The 'things' in his environment may be incorporated into his play, not for what they are in themselves, but for their meanings. That is, they may be incorporated to the extent that they fall in with or offer no resistance to those aspects of his play regulated by his 'ideas'. His behaviour has ceased to be wholly *context-dependent* and begun to be *structure-dependent*, in Chomsky's (1972) sense of the term; that is, its elements come to have their significance in terms of the part they play in relation

---

[10] Rules specify possibilities, and not all the possibilities they specify are necessarily realisable. That is why, of course, we have to test theories, and why also mistakes are often intelligible.

to the field of possibilities inherent in his image. And the most unlikely things may enter into his play in all sorts of guises. All that matters is that whatever 'thing' is used it must allow for the execution of at least some of the same actions as the imaginary thing in an imaginary situation. (And in this sense, of course, a child's mother can be the best 'play-thing' he has.) Now we are not at the stage of symbolism involving *rules* yet, such play still essentially operates in affective terms, but now the affective meanings he assigns to 'things' dominates and determines his behaviour towards them. But as long as they are used as *enactive* representations (Bruner, 1966), as long as 'things' can mean almost anything in play, how can meanings and 'things' ever become linked in any determinate fashion? The role of other people in this process seems to be crucial.

Vygotsky (1966, p. 9) discusses a situation in which two sisters (five and seven years) play at being 'sisters'. The vital difference between simply being sisters and playing at it is that, in play, they intend to be sisters and are conscious of one another's aim. They thus distinguish and discuss what it is to be a sister; they enact whatever emphasises their relationship as sisters *vis-à-vis* other people: they are dressed alike, they walk about holding hands, the elder keeps telling the younger about other people – 'That is theirs not ours'. Everything associated with the children's intuitions of what it is to be a sister is expressed in one way or another and emphasised, and presumably on occasions, discussed amongst themselves and accepted, modified or rejected accordingly. Thus, to quote Vygotsky, 'What passes unnoted by the child in real life becomes a rule of behaviour in play.' Now this situation is most interesting for the sisters are, in fact, playing at reality. They are interacting with one another not in terms of what they are to one another in any immediate sense, but in terms of how they imagine one another to be; they are interacting in terms of what they *mean* to one another in their *roles* as sisters. Each is playing their proper part in a social game. Clear criteria have been adduced, some in action others in discussion, and, what it is to be a sister has, for the moment at least, been decided between them. They have laid down the rules for their 'sisters-game'; they thus know what criteria they must meet in order to be sisters; they can thus now be self-directing in sisterly activities.

But the function one sister performs for the other here is the function a child's mother continually performs for him: in her play with him she gets him to co-ordinate his activity with her's in relation to definite criteria which are important to her in some way. She cannot in this situation instigate his activities for him, but she can none the less exert a powerful controlling influence. She can do this because she is still the means of his gratification, and because she and her child know one another personally from their earlier inarticulate and affective relationship. She makes use of this relationship time and again to draw him into involvements which, if left to his own devices, he would never otherwise undertake. And in so doing, surely has something to do with the *modularisation* and *differentiation* observable in the child's development of skilled performances (see Bruner, this volume).

It is thus, in the course of these informal involvements, that 'language games' (Wittgenstein, 1953) are established. Now there is nothing absolute about the rules or criteria functioning as the reference points in such exchanges. As Wittgenstein (1958, p. 25) remarks

remember that in general we don't use language according to strict rules — it hasn't been taught us by means of strict rules, either. We are unable to clearly circumscribe the concepts we use; not because we don't know their real definition, but because there is no real 'definition' to them. To suppose that there *must* be would be like supposing that whenever children play with a ball they play a game according to strict rules.

Clearly, they do not. What they do is to negotiate the rules as required. And clearly, this is the one most important skill the child acquires in the course of his 'games' with his mother, the skill the sisters manifest in their 'sisters game', the skill to make the meanings of their actions determinate as required by co-ordinating their behaviour with others, and by making implicit or explicit agreements with them one way or another.

This then is the nature of people's activity in social exchanges: it is as if one were making moves in a great political game such as 'Diplomacy', for one is. But the relationships that people have to one another, besides having an aspect of mutual use, also provide a reciprocated access to being — people help one another to be themselves. Now it is a common assumption that the social world is the product of emotional bonds. But, to quote Harré (this volume), 'a much more accurate response is to stand back in astonishment in the face of the maintenance in existence of forms of social cohesion in actual situations of emotional flux'.

NATURAL AGENTS DETERMINE FORMS: INDIVIDUAL PERSONALITIES MONITOR THEM FOR THEIR MEANINGS

We have arrived now at the stage when social games are possible, and we can begin to touch upon the nature of personal powers, the powers whose exercise is monitored by the individual exercising them. These, I have suggested, are derived from a person's natural powers. Now Mead (1934, p. 347) in distinguishing between the 'biologic individual' and the 'socially self-conscious individual' brings out the contrast (and the relation) between these two forms of powers:

The distinction answers roughly to that drawn between the conduct which does not involve conscious reasoning and that which does, between the conduct of the more intelligent of the lower animals and that of man. While these types of conduct can be clearly distinguished from each other in human behavior, they are not on separate planes, but play back and forth into each other, and constitute, under most conditions an experience which appears to be cut by no lines of cleavage. The skill with which one plays a fast game of tennis, (etc.) . . . seems to belong to the organic equipment of the same individual, living in the same world and subject to the same rational control.

Such skills reflect, Mead continues, 'our biologic inheritance from lower life', but they are transformed in the sphere of social exchange.

Now, within the limits prescribed by rules people can act as they please; but animals act as they must, *in their own interests*. Thus they cannot be said to act in accordance with rules, for rules, by definition, involve negotiated agreements between individuals.[11] But when playing games such as tennis, men's activities although unreflective *are* none the less regulated according to rules; men's 'organic equipment' does come to reflect their social life. The personal powers they derive from their natural powers in social exchanges, in reality, 'play back and forth into each other' and are marked by 'no lines of cleavage'. The distinction is a matter of intention, not a matter of fact – for them just as much as for us as their investigators. However, although the spontaneous, unreflective exercise of certain skills comes to be directed according to rules, they are not activities which can be said to be *self*-directed; it is only in their deliberate activities that people as individual personalities know what they are doing and why, and can be said to be exercising their personal powers.

Now in discussing the development of personal powers it will be convenient to concentrate our attention upon the activity of speaking. Clearly, no explicit agreements making meanings determinate are possible until the child has learnt the skill of making agreements verbally, and he must first learn 'language games', and the agreements they involve, implicitly, by participating in 'forms of life' (Wittgenstein, 1953). It is via action exchanges that he co-ordinates his activities, including their *vocal* aspect, with the activities of others. The processes discussed above suggest how this might be done; thus there is no necessity and indeed no warrant to assume that, at first, he vocalises according to rules: he vocalises, presumably, according to internally constituted

---

[11] While animal behaviour may indeed be *directed* or *regulated* it need not be *rule-regulated*. *Regulation* is a characteristic of all processes in 'open systems' maintained in a 'steady state' according to 'system parameters' (v. Bertalanffy, 1968), rules involve agreements.

mental structures in both an immediate and unconsidered fashion. His vocalisations are not, of course, always intelligible; the constitution of his natural powers of vocalisation allow for the expression of a whole field of possibilities appropriate in some tenuous way to the current situation. His vocalisations are thus regulated but not yet rule-regulated; he still has to discover which of all the possibilities are the actual ones used in his speech community and to acquire skills at using them. (Some of these issues are discussed by Ryan, this volume.) It is via *instruction* that these skills are acquired (Vygotsky, 1962). It is via the intervention of others that *spontaneous* actions can become transformed into *deliberate* ones, that personal powers can be derived from natural ones. 'In order to subject a function to intellectual and volitional control, we must first possess it,' says Vygotsky (p. 90). And he goes on to discuss (pp. 100–1), as an example, a situation in which although a child cannot say 'sk' deliberately, out of any sort of context, he can say 'Moscow', when asked, with ease. It is only later thanks to instruction in grammar and writing that he becomes aware of what he is doing in such speech performances and learns to use his skills consciously, and realises that 'sk' is a part of 'Moscow'. But in being instructed in grammar someone other than the child himself – who monitors his own speech for its *meanings* – must observe his speech *forms* and draw his attention to them. It is attending to the form of a performance while at the same time monitoring it for its meaning that even the most highly practised performers find difficult. Reflecting back to one the form of one's actions – treating them as a sequence of *events* rather than *actions* – is a service that another person can provide; a service that is essential if one's performance is to be structured into components which can then be arranged and re-arranged as one pleases. Here again, then, in the structuring, or *modularisation* (see Bruner, this volume) of skills, the role of others is crucial.

Now considering his speech at a much later stage, when he has begun to construct lengthy utterances: while it may be correct to assume that he is aiming at definite articulatory 'targets' in his *determination* of word-forms, and definite syntactic criteria in his *determination* of sentence-forms, it is still not necessary to assume that he is *using* words and sentences according to any definite criteria at all. To suppose that there must be strict rules for using words and sentences 'would be like supposing that whenever children play with a ball they play a game according to strict rules'. A sentence is something one *uses* to express one's meaning, and it is not an expression of a meaning itself; its meaning is a logical construction to be completed both by oneself and one's listener out of the influences exerted by one's utterance. And one may find, just as one's listener does, that the sentence just uttered was

238

inadequate to the purpose intended; one may find even in the course of uttering it that it is inadequate, hesitate, and begin again.

The construction of a sentence (as an instrument) is thus to be distinguished from the uses to which it can be put. And, although sentences are clearly constructed for precise and special functions, it would still be a mistake to think that its use was completely specified by its construction. Rather than specifying a single actual use, its construction seems to specify a field of possible uses. And as I said earlier, only if necessary, for particular practical purposes, are the criteria making its use determinate established and agreed upon, and there are all sorts of strategies for doing that, some drawing on agreements made before the use of the sentence, some made during, and some after its use.

What then is the relation between personal powers and rules? Do we speak in accordance with rules? While speaking we obviously remain sensitive to our listener's nods of comprehension and grimaces of bafflement, and modify our talk accordingly. It is just not the case, empirically, that we turn our eyes inward, shut ourselves off from our environment, and refer to some pre-established inner plan to determine what we say. We can in some cases, but usually we do not. Face-to-face conversations are not mediated solely by linguistic 'rules'. In any case, such rules are couched in terms of *idealisations*; the assignment of utterances and their constituents to linguistic categories depends upon a prior grasp of their meaning, and idealised linguistic categories need play no part in the understanding of spontaneous speech. Rather, what seems to be the case is that we continually monitor the construction of our expressions in relation to our intended purpose. And we do this by constructing as we utter them their meanings, in just the same way as our listener must construct them. We can say that our natural powers present us with possible forms of expression and regulate their forms, while our personal powers allow us to select among them the expressions whose meanings are appropriate to our purposes.

So, while the determination of linguistic forms need not be *self-directed*, but simply, directed, the use of linguistic forms in a purposeful manner is. And besides being self-directed, potentially at least, their use is also rule-regulated – but I say *potentially* for it may very well be that the agreements which will actually make the meanings of one's utterances determinate may only be reached *after* one's utterance, in the course of subsequent exchanges. So what people seem to be aware of while they talk are not the regulations determining the possible *forms* of their talk, but the possible criteria (and thus the possible operations) necessary in determining what is *meant* by their talk. And these are in no way fundamental. They reflect just as much aspects of one's experience as 'the general character of one's capacity to acquire knowledge' (Chomsky, 1965, p. 59).

CHILD DEVELOPMENT AS A CONCEPTUAL PROBLEM

Now the theme of this essay has been that the human child does not develop psychologically according to 'laws of nature', but his development is intended; that is, the concepts in terms of which we interact with him play an important part in determining the form of his psychological development. It is the idea of *intentionality* which has been central; the idea that action is the realisation of possibility; and the idea that action is essentially social exchange. Now the end of an act, being a conceptual matter, a matter of intention rather than fact, is indeterminate; it is determined or not as the case may be by the agent in action. Action is thus not teleological but intentional. Although some classes of act, i.e. skills, are properly described and understood by reference to an end (or system of possible ends as described by a grammar), this is by no means true of all acts – truth seeking being perhaps the most obvious and childrearing being perhaps one of the least obvious examples. Grammars can only be produced for activities where the end, or system of ends is determinate before the sequence of acts begins and remains unmodified throughout their performance. This seems likely to be the case in the production of linguistic forms – most likely at the phonological level and less likely at the syntactic level. The determination and maintenance of grammars, being a matter of intention rather than natural law, are aspects of Culture for which man is responsible; it is in the sense of discovering how to make his meanings determinate by referring to an open, but, determinable, system of ends while speaking that we can say, man, out of his ingenuity, out of his natural powers 'invented' language.

Now if action is the realisation of possibility, we must suppose that alternative futures really are possible; the concept of intrinsic powers thus is a necessary theoretical adjunct to the concept of action – it is a device via which we can use our knowledge to date in order to predict the range of future possibilities open to an individual. And, as I said earlier, which one is actually realised depends upon the individual's future circumstances, which we cannot predict.

Above, I have suggested that we can, as a matter of intention, view people both as natural agents and as individual personalities, and that they derive their personal powers from their natural powers in the course of their psychological development, their personal powers being used sometimes to augment in turn their natural powers. To possess personal powers is to manifest not just directed, but *self*-directed activity; one has to do more than just direct one's activities in an ordered manner, one has

240

to express *meanings* in one's actions. That is, one has to make one's activities intelligible to oneself in other's terms, and in doing so make our actions relevant to other than our own immediate needs or interests. We must put ourselves in a position for which we are responsible, Mead would say. It seems that in order to do this we must, in a manner of speaking, possess within ourselves at any moment in time some internally constituted totalities, structures, or images, and be able, not only to interpret and operate on one's objective world in their terms, but co-ordinate one's actions with other people's in the terms of such images also. Only in relation to such an internal standard could one direct one's own activities in such a way that they could be said to be self-directed and rule-regulated, thus meeting the fundamental requirements to be an individual personality.

If the important aspects of a child's psychological development are conceptual, that is, if they depend upon the intentions we pursue in interaction with him, how can empirical investigations be conducted in this sphere? Well first, let us be clear as to what the aim of such investigations might be. Surely, it can only be understanding how to increase people's powers of responsible action, making moral progress. With this aim in mind, empirical investigations take the form of experimental attempts at *instruction*, with personal knowledge of one's pupil playing a crucial part in such attempts. Lock (in press) has taken a first step in this direction; he reports some observations and interactions involving a young infant, R, between 239 and 289 days of age. It was, to quote him, 'because I was able to construe R's actions as being equivalent to meaning "Do that again" I was able to make his actions effective'. Up to 258 days R waved his arms, not with the intention of communicating his wants, but only in the presence of an agent, with the intention of making something happen again. 'He will produce the scheme (arm waving) for preserving and repeating events that I make happen, but not for fortuitous events where there is no agent to appeal to to recreate the event.' But at 289 days, R plays with a football and it rolls out of his reach, he looks at Lock, waves his arms, and then looks at his ball. Lock retrieves it for him and R continues playing quietly. While on earlier occasions R waved his arms with only the apparent intention of making something happen again, Lock treated his actions *as if* he were communicating and the arm-moving pattern became a sign established between them meaning 'I want it again'. It was not yet, however, in Mead's sense, a significant symbol, for the child was not able to stimulate himself with it in the same way as he stimulated Lock.

Lock's work is one example, but it needs supplementing. While he knew what his intentions were, he knew little about his own performance of them. Video-tape studies of mothers instructing their children score

on this point; but unless a definite task is involved, as only their performances are recorded, their intentions may remain quite opaque –
especially when in a sense the mother is also 'experimenting' with her
child and perhaps even with herself, knowing neither his nor her own
intentions in any determinate fashion. In such a case it can only be via
a rather trial-and-error sort of 'negotiation' that the mother can reach a
satisfactory settlement. Such studies can none the less reveal a great deal,
not least, to other mothers attempting the same tasks. Treble (1972) is
an example of such a study. In neither is an attempt made to attribute
what occurs to determination by natural laws.

In this essay, then, I have tried to construct a conceptual framework
within which we can conduct and make sense of empirical findings in
this area of research. It has been concerned with the concept of personal
powers and their development; i.e., with what empirically is involved in
developing into an individual personality. I have done this in the hope
that by properly understanding how our children develop into fully
autonomous and responsible people, we will be able all the better to help
them realise their potential. In it I have attempted to give the general
form of some of the criteria involved in distinguishing persons from
things, actions from movements, etc., in the hope of establishing a way
of recognising human action when we see it. But I have not been able to
detail the actual criteria in all practical situations, for to satisfy the
criteria to be a person in one situation is not to satisfy them in general,
and in any case the criteria are not general but negotiable – we have to
intend personhood continually and discover empirically in each practical
situation how to fulfil it. And this is not a natural scientific but a moral
task. As Pico della Mirandola described man: 'As the maker and
moulder of thyself in whatever shape thou shalt prefer, thou shalt have
the power to degenerate into lower forms of life, which are brutish. Thou
shalt have the power, out of thy soul and judgement to be reborn into
the higher forms which are divine.' And that choice is for ever present
to us.

ACKNOWLEDGEMENT

I would like to thank the members of the Unit for Research on the
Medical Applications of Psychology, University of Cambridge, especially
amongst them Bob Phillips, who let me try out on them an earlier draft
of this essay. Their patient and considered responses to it made me see
the issues it raises as at least some others see them, and thus forced me to
what I hope is a much clearer expression of them than I would otherwise
have been able to achieve.

REFERENCES

Ayers, M. R. (1968). *The Refutation of Determinism*. London, Methuen.

Bannister, D. and Fransella, F. (1971). *Inquiring Man*. London, Penguin.

Bertalanffy, L. v. (1952). *Problems of Life*, New York, Harper and Row.

Bertalanffy, L. v. (1968). *General System Theory*, New York, George Braziller.

Bohm, D. (1965). Relativity and Perception. Appendix to *Relativity*. New York, Benjamin.

Brentano, F. (1924). *Psychologie vom empirischen Standpunkt*. Leipzig, Meier.

Broadbent, D. E. (1971). Cognitive psychology: introduction. *Brit. Med. Bull.* **27**, 191–4.

Bruner, J. S. (1966). *Toward a Theory of Instruction*, New York, W. W. Norton.

Bruner, J. S. (1969). On voluntary action and its hierarchical structure. In Koestler, A. and Symthies, J. R. (eds.). *Beyond Reductionism*. London, Hutchinson.

Cassirer, E. (ed.) (1957). *The Philosophy of Symbolic Forms*, Vol. 3. New Haven, Yale Univ. Press.

Chomsky, N. (1965). *Aspects of the Theory of Syntax*. Cambridge, Mass., M.I.T. Press.

Chomsky, N. (1972). *Problems of Freedom and Knowledge*. London, Fontana.

Dewey, J. (1896). The reflex arc concept in psychology. *Psychol. Rev.* **3**, 13–32. Reprinted in Dennis, W. (ed.) *Readings in the History of Psychology*. New York, Appleton-Century-Crofts.

Dreyfus, H. L. (1967). Why computers must have bodies in order to be intelligent. *Review of Metaphysics*, **21**, 13–32.

Garner, R. (1966). To perceive is to know. *Amer. Psychol.* **21**, 11–19.

Hampshire, S. (1959). *Thought and Action*. London, Chatto and Windus.

Harré, R. (1970). Powers. *Brit. J. Philos. Sci.* **21**, 81–101.

Harré, R. and Secord, P. (1972). *The Explanation of Social Behaviour*. Oxford, Blackwell.

Hyman, R. (1964). *The Nature of Psychological Inquiry*. New York, Prentice-Hall.

Itard, J-M-G. (1801). *The Wild Boy of Aveyron*. New York, Appleton-Century-Crofts, 1962.

James, W. (1917). The dilemma of determinism. In *The Will to Believe and other Essays in Popular Philosophy*. New York, Dover, 1956.

Kelly, G. A. (1955). *The Psychology of Personal Constructs* (2 vols.). New York, W. W. Norton.

Koffka, K. (1921). Die Grundlagen der Psychischen Entwicklung Osterwieck am Harz, quoted in Cassirer, E. (1957), *The Philosophy of Symbolic Forms*, Vol. 3, pp. 64–5. New Haven, Yale Univ. Press.

Lock, A. (in press). From out of nowhere. To appear in *Proceedings of the International Symposium on First-Language Acquisition* held at Florence, September 1972.

Macmurray, J. (1957). *The Self as Agent*. London, Faber and Faber.

Macmurray, J. (1961). *Persons in Relation*. London, Faber and Faber.

Mead, G. H. (1934). *Mind, Self and Society*. Chicago, Univ. Chicago Press.

Newson, J. and Newson, E. (1968). *Four Years Old in an Urban Community*. London, Allen and Unwin.

Piaget, J. (1971). *Biology and Knowledge*. Edinburgh, Edinburgh Univ. Press.

Piaget, J. (1972). *Principles of Genetic Epistemology*. London, Routledge and Kegan Paul.

Richards, M. P. M. (1974). The development of communication in the first year of life. In Connolly, K. and Bruner, J. S. (eds.) *The Early Growth of Competence*. London, Academic Press.

Schaffer, H. R. (1971). *The Growth of Sociability*. London, Penguin.

Skinner, B. F. (1953). *Science and Human Behaviour*. New York, Macmillan.

Skinner, B. F. (1972). *Beyond Freedom and Dignity*. London, Cape.

Shotter, J. (1970). Men, the man-makers: George Kelly and the psychology of personal constructs. In Bannister, D. (ed.). *Perspectives in Personal Construct Theory*. London, Academic Press.

Shotter, J. (1973). Prolegomena to an understanding of play. *J. for the Theory of Social Behaviour*, **3**, 47–89.

Spitz, R. (1965). *The First Year of Life*. New York, International Univ. Press.

Sutherland, N. S. (1970). Is the brain a physical system? In Borger, R. and Cioffi, F. (eds.). *Explanation in the Behavioural Sciences*. London, Cambridge Univ. Press.

Taylor, R. (1966). *Action and Purpose*, New York, Prentice-Hall.

Tinbergen, N. (1951). *The Study of Instinct*. London, Oxford Univ. Press.

Treble, S. (1972). The development of shape perception in young children. Unpublished Ph.D. Thesis, Univ. of Nottingham.

Vygotsky, L. S. (1962). *Thought and Language*. Cambridge, Mass., M.I.T. Press.

Vygotsky, L. S. (1966). Play and its role in the mental development of the child. *Soviet Psychology*, **12**, 6–18.

Weir, R. H. (1962). *Language in the Crib*. New York, Humanities.

Winch, P. (1958). *The Idea of a Social Science*. London, Routledge and Kegan Paul.

Wittgenstein, L. (1953). *Philosophical Investigations*. Oxford, Blackwell.

Wittgenstein, L. (1968). *Blue and Brown Books*. Oxford, Blackwell.

12

The conditions for a social psychology of childhood

Rom Harr

Rom Harr

INTRODUCTION

The study of the social psychology of childhood is dependent upon, but not wholly dependent upon an adequate psychology of the adult world. The profound changes that have taken place in the latter in the last two or three years must have some reflection in whatever programme of research is undertaken in the former.

The obvious point that students of the development of social skills by children will know what to look for only if they have a clear and correct idea of the skills deployed by adults and the problems their exercise allows to be solved, must be qualified in two ways. It may be that some adult skills have no precursors in childhood, though there is little evidence of this. But a much more likely qualification derives from the fact that there may be autonomous social worlds in childhood, at some age/development levels, which are not precursors of the adult social world at all, or perhaps only in a strictly limited way. I shall be taking the radical step of suggesting that the attachment theory (Bowlby, 1969) is very likely to describe one such world.

With these important qualifications in mind I shall first of all set out the current ethogenic conception of the adult social world, and the skills and conceptual resources which it seems to demand from those capable of mastering it. The point made by David Ingleby in this volume is an integral part of the ethogenic point of view, which aims at the disentangling of the systematic properties of the social worlds which lie behind any ideology, a feature which leads to the making of common cause with phenomenology.

If one takes the ethogenic point of view, there are several important consequences for the study of the social psychology of childhood. Rather than Piagetian 'stages', which seem to me to carry with them always the vectorial quality of being 'stages towards adult mastery', I will suggest that there are at least two social worlds in childhood, one of which, the school child's world, is a precursor of the adult social world, while the other, a much earlier creation is not. Each may be mounted upon a scaffold of stages, some common to both, some directed only to one. I am afraid I shall be sketching a very complicated situation, but that in itself suggests the beginnings of verisimilitude where human life is concerned. I shall develop the argument on the assumption that there are only two social worlds in childhood, one the 'autonomous world' and the other the 'precursor world'. But I want to insist on the provisional and revisable character of that assumption, in that in the end we may come to see that there are more autonomous worlds than the one I shall refer to in this paper.

It will be useful at this point to anticipate one strand in the general line of argument in order to make it quite clear that the radical proposals of this paper suggest *complementary* and additional lines of study to those already proceeding, rather than any root and branch revision. The ethogenic point of view in adult social psychology envisages the social world of adults as a construction, the product of two processes. One is the exercise of certain imaginative capacities of a generally dramaturgical cast, *social* make believe in preparation for social action. I shall be claiming that this capacity is common both to the autonomous and the precursor world. I should like to hear more from developmental psychologists about the origins of this capacity, the incredible sophistication of which amongst even quite young children is illustrated by Vigotsky's beautiful example of the sisters who played at being sisters. The second process, which is perhaps the trademark of ethogenics, is the creation and maintenance of social order by *ceremonial* means. This involves the manipulation and recognition of meaning. I believe that the fact that the human solution to the problem of the creation and maintenance of the social order is ceremonial (as opposed say to pheromonic) is related to the human capacity for dramaturgical performance, in that in both, a kind of conceptual distance from the actual manifest behaviour, the vehicle for the action, is taken. Both are manifestations of a fundamental structural feature of the human organism conceived of as an information processing system.

In Schaffer's otherwise admirable review of the state of developmental social psychology (Schaffer, 1971) the problems for developmental psychologists created by the pervasive ceremonial character of adult social life are untouched. Schaffer (1971, p. 30) offers three progressive problem fields for investigation. First there is the problem of identifying the basis of the general attraction of infants to people (and following Richards of people to infants). Then there is the problem of the basis of the infant's specific capacity to distinguish his mother. Finally for Schaffer there is the problem of the origin and development of the capacity to form lasting emotional bonds.

To leave the matter there, as Schaffer does, suggests very strongly that he (and indeed most psychologists influenced by the attachment theory) suppose that the adult social world is a product of such bonds. Nothing could be further from the truth. The astonishing thing about the adult social world, as revealed by ethogenic analysis, is that it forms and transforms itself with little reference to emotional bonds; lasting or ephemeral. Social glue is of an altogether different stuff. Indeed one detects an excessively sentimental view of the adult social world in the background of Schaffer's analytical remarks, and coupled with it, a naïve view of the genesis of the social order. It is, I think, a common assumption to suppose that emotional bonds cause social cohesion. A much more accurate response is to stand back in astonishment in the face of the maintenance in existence of forms of social cohesion in the actual situation of emotional flux.

If we take the ethogenic point of view we shall see that there emerges a fourth level of problem, the investigation of which seems to me to offer scope for some fascinating research. How and when, and in what cognitive company, does the capacity to manage ceremonial acts appear, and what are its component skills? One must dispute then at least the letter of Schaffer's claim that social behaviour does not constitute a class apart from all other forms of behaviour. Sophisticated social behaviour is indeed a class of ways of acting which are wholly apart from anything found in the problem fields delineated by Schaffer's three questions. But of course the skills and capacities that go into the construction and maintenance of a social world by ceremonial means are connected with forms of symbolic action, and so are part of that range of capacities which are deployed in linguistic and paralinguistic interaction. As I understand it the present orthodoxy tends to assume that the power of symbolic thinking and acting arises at a fairly late stage in the developmental sequence. Perhaps if we seek its early manifestations in ritual and ceremonial acts we may find ourselves obliged to upset the Piagetian stages in yet another aspect. This would not be too surprising since in Gallic fashion he seems to assume that the performance of logical operations is the highest flight of which an intellect is capable.

In order to grasp the kind of social capabilities we are deploying in managing adult social life one must begin with an *a priori* analysis of the social world in search of an adequate specification of its problematic character which our social abilities allow us to master. To the ethogenist (and particularly to the ethnomethodological wing of that movement) the problematic character of the social world goes pretty deep. At no level of social interaction among humans can we assume that a wholly automatic meshing of interactive stimulus and response occurs. There is then no ground level of simple ties out of which social interaction can be built. How far this is true of all other animals is uncertain. But it is certainly true of a great many more species than had once been suppposed (Hinde, 1972).

Once it is clearly seen that certain specific forms of cognitive processes intervene at every stage of the process of social construction, then a radical change must be made in the conceptual system used for the analysis of social action. In particular, as I shall emphasise later, we are required to look at social actions as acquiring their social character only as they are meaningful, and as they are so understood by actor and interactor. With that transformation of view there is a complete change of scene. The productive 'forces' which generate social action, are such that they find their most natural expression in ritual and ceremonial. The adult social world is not, I believe, generated by the constraints which derive from our emotional lives, such as anxiety for love, and the like. This would be an overly general application of the socially formative forces at the 'attachment' level of infant social functioning. Recent studies of the adult social world (Goffman, 1972) and of the social world of school children (Opie and Opie, 1959) provide very little evidence that there are such 'forces' *active* in the generation of forms of social order. It may well be that in the 'attachment' stage, so much illuminated by Bowlby, we have a genuinely autonomous social world, whose skills are useless in the later social world and whose expectations are a source of great social danger.

I do not propose, in this paper, to say much about the nature or the general form of social order. I intend to illustrate the points I want to make by some rather small-scale examples of that order, its maintenance and the way that threats to it are coped with. I shall be relying heavily on recent work in social psychology, particularly that of Goffman (1971). I particularly do not want to be thought to imply by my use of the phrase 'social order' that that order is defined by an existing system of social relations.

A SKETCH OF THE ETHOGENIC STANDPOINT

The existence of any form of order, and consequentially reliable forms of civility, involves an almost continuous stream of solutions to certain kinds of problems that beset the microsocial order. They fall into two interlocking classes. There are the problems created by the sudden appearance of other and strange human beings, and the need to quickly run up some sort of viable relationship with them. Then there are the problems created by threats and challenges to an existing fragment of order. To the former we manage socially *constructive* solutions, to the latter socially *maintaining*.

The general form of one important class of miscrosocial problems for which socially constructive solutions have to be found, can be illustrated by the simple case of the meeting of a stranger on a narrow mountain path. There are two environmental contingencies involved. There is first the presence (accidental, from each actor's point of view) of the other and previously unknown human being. Then there is the structure of the permanent physical environment which makes the accidental presence of the other problematic. In a sufficiently wide or busy street, social confrontation with another can be avoided. This simple point allows us to see something of what it is to be in social confrontation. It involves the obligation to acknowledge the social identity of the other. Contrast the relation between the furnace attendant and the corpse in a crematorium, or the surgeon and his victim on the operating table. Neither is required to acknowledge the social identity of the other as a human being.

The problem having been created by the recognition that the situation *is* problematic, what is involved in its solution? Let us first exclude patently non-social solutions to the problem created by the second person on the path. To bash or shoot the other and throw him over the edge, i.e. to exercise raw physical causality upon him as an object, seems to be a solution that clearly lies outside any social order. I shall return later in the paper to brood upon the delicate line of demarcation that separates meaningful violence from raw physical causality. But a hint may be in place here. Should the aggressor cry 'Die, violator of my solitude!' we should no doubt condemn his action, but we would be obliged to admire his grasp of ethogenic principles, in that by giving his push meaning he has made it part of the social world.

But the archetype of a social solution to the problem created by the appearance of the stranger might run something like this: each catches the eye of the other, a slight smile and, pace Eibl-Eibesfeldt (Hinde, 1972, p. 299) an eyebrow flash are exchanged; each person, now acknowledged as social actor, makes incipient ushering movements, and one of them completes these fulsomely; the other passes while the usherer squeezes himself back against the wall, and each makes a little acknowledging head movement. At no point have they gone so far as to discover whether they belong to the same linguistic community. This interchange might clearly be said to have a strongly ceremonial character.

Let us analyse the creation and maintenance of this ephemeral microsocial world, from an ethogenic point of view. The first distinction to be made is, following Burke (1969) and Goffman (1969a) that between the 'scene' and the 'action'. The scene contains not only the physical scenery and props against which the action is played out, but the crucial conceptual element which has been called the 'situation', to the definition of which some part of the initial action is directed. In our scenario the situation is defined in the short sequence of gestures, expressions, etc., of which the eye-catching and the slight smile are components. This is the minimal form of *greeting,* and is acknowledgement of the humanity of the other. In a similar way one may *greet* a strange dog with a 'Here, boy' hoping to bind him thereby into a primarily *social* encounter. Now this situation is not just a social scene, that it is not just an encounter that is thus defined, but in the defining of the scene in a certain way each actor is committed to a line, to use Künkel's useful notion (Künkel, 1941), the toeing of which requires the presentation of a certain style of self. There are refinements. Each actor must grasp the exact meaning of the smile, for should it be a trifle too narrow, it betokens the recognition of the appearance of an opportunity for mischief, exhibited to the innocent other as part of the exquisite preparation for a sadistic shove, unsatisfying unless the victim knows he's for it. And of course overdoing the style of the self being presented is one of the minor pleasures of the briefer forms of social interaction. In the action that ensues a flamboyant gesture to pass can be permitted to oneself, *and permitted with some degree of awareness.* And even with the awareness that the other is not unaware of that awareness. The enormously socially important activity of the presentation of selves is undertaken through a stylistic gloss on the basic form of the action. But to present a self as the basic action itself is universally condemned in human society, so far as I can ascertain.

The action itself consists in the resolution by ceremonial means of the problem created by the original contingencies, i.e. who has priority of passage, and, since this is a social analysis, who come out best socially from the negotiation of that priority? Clearly the one who concedes passage may by the manner of his concession, exhibit a lofty condescension that does him great credit. The basic moves in this negotiation and its metagame, as Szasz (1961) calls it, can be seen at any counter window, swing door, or lift gate, any day of the week.

The enormous importance of metagames in our analysis of the social world can hardly be overemphasised. I illustrate this with another microsocial example. To lash out when someone bumps into one is not a social solution to the problems of getting through a crowded public place, and the reason is clear. To lash out is *already to have lost the metagame.* To accept the 'I say, I'm sorry' with a forgiving 'That's *quite* all right' is both to create and sustain a microsocial world of great civility and thereby to present oneself in the best possible light. And, as we noticed with the case of the dog, it is to push the other into a show of equal civility and into the presentation of a civil self in action of an equally polished style. Altercasting, as this beautiful mutuality has been barbarously called, can be practised in any Woolworth's by smiling at those notoriously gloomy assistants, and thus earning for oneself some service and a brief though satisfying social reputation. But exercises like that are recommended only for the most experienced machiavellians.

In summary then, the microsocial worlds that we create apparently casually are defined by some form of greeting, in which the humanity, that is the *autonomy* and *cognitive status* of the other is acknowledged. The subsequent action is double-tiered, involving the ceremonial solution of some practical problem (who goes first), and in the style of the action, a competitive metagame to present the most acceptable self. Civil society is characterised by the choice of semantic devices (and I believe syntactic forms) in preference to raw physical causality, for the achievement of the lowest order task, in that in the use of mere physical causality no self is presented at all. One must not make the mistake of supposing that the violence of the villainous is raw physical causality. Great attention is paid to style, and the manifestation of a self pleasing to those whose social arbitration the actor recognises. And I would be strongly inclined to defend my analysis, even to the details of the opening moves as a kind of greeting, in application to the interaction of a random victim and those who practise violence upon him. Eyes must be met, challenges given (and even acceptances manufactured) before the action can begin. A savage beating up of the innocent can be, analytically, a proper part of civil society. Indeed it must be, if it is to serve as a move in the metagames by which selves are built and sustained.

How is a social order maintained? The best way to understand this is again to look at some microsocial episodes, and to identify their characteristics. Broadly speaking two items can be threatened in a challenge to social order. There can be a threat to one's territory (literal and metaphorical), or there can be a threat to the image of self that one has been promoting. The most percipient study of such threats and the manner of their treatment is to be found in Erving Goffman's recent study *Relations in Public* (Goffman, 1971). Broadly speaking violations and threats of violation are dealt with by a variety of ameliorative rituals, or ceremonies. Goffman offers a model drawn in part from the ideas of Radcliffe-Brown and Durkheim, in that he looks upon the general form of the interaction as shaped by the 'sanctity' of the self and its preserves, and the ritual surrounding these as having the general form of that which preserves and punishes the violation of the sacred.

For the purpose of this paper I shall lump together the self and its territories, and consider only one broad distinction in modes of dealing with violations, because it is a distinction that leads backward to some important conclusions about the processes by which the ability to manage oneself in the social world might be acquired. One way of dealing with any action perceived as a violation is to admit that it is a violation, means what it seems to mean, and then employing some ritual, say an

251

apology and its receipt, to ameliorate the offence. Goffman has offered a detailed analysis of the modes and forms of such interaction rituals. But another way of dealing with violations, only touched on in his book, is the method of redefinition. That is the action is admitted to have occurred, but the act performed in the action, its social meaning, is reconstrued so that it no longer constitutes an offence.

There are two main ways in which the reconstrual of meaning can occur. There is what I shall call 'situational discounting' in which an action, which would in most scenes be a violation of the self and its pre-serves, is set in a scene which automatically discounts it. For instance it is an offence against the self to sit with one's hip pressing hard against that of another person, *unless it is on the crowded seat of a rush hour bus*. This illustrates the reciprocal character of the relation between scene and act, that is between the situation conceived socially and the meaning of the actions performed within it. Now one method of dealing with a violation is for either the offender or the offended to rapidly sketch in a new scene around the action, within which its import is harmless. The fact that sometimes the offended can take this way out illustrates a point emphasised by Goffman, that by and large people co-operate in reducing the threat of violation (Goffman, 1969b). There is something socially incompetent about someone who so stands upon his dignity that every violation and indeed potential violation must be ritually ameli-orated by he who is the initiator of the action.

Machiavellians can make use of this feature of social life to commit a good many violations against the persons of others, and get away with it. Once detected they may rapidly run up a metascene rather than have to take the mean part in a ritual of amelioration, though as I pointed out earlier one can use stylistic glosses on rituals of amelioration to win a metagame, or higher order character contest. In looking for the origins of these skills in the young and the very young we must ask what cognitive resources are necessary for these skills to be exercised. It is plain that *in addition to knowledge of the rituals of the culture we must know its standard scenes*, since I believe that situational discounting will turn out to be at least as common and important a means of maintaining social order, that is maintaining inviolate the selves and their territories.

An important animating idea of ethogenic approaches is that society is not found, it is constructed, and that on a day-to-day, moment-to-moment basis (Lyman and Scott, 1970). Ephemeral microsocial struc-tures are coming into being and dissolving, transforming one into another, as people move from scene to scene in their daily lives. Ethogenists, I think, tend to hold that the larger society, on the description and explanation of which much traditional sociology has been bent, is an epiphenomenon of a certain feature of the myriad of microsocial interactions that make up daily life. This feature is the presence in our cognitive resources of an image of a larger order, with the help of which we create and explain certain actions, and give meaning to certain acts, and indeed in the more refined form of social life find acts for the presentation of certain meanings. Provided that there are certain minimal homologies between the images of a sufficient number of us, in certain crucial fields, a larger society can be said to exist. But its being is no more than a likeness and meshing of conduct animated by the rough homologies between people's images.

When a conceptual scheme is applied to an empirical field that field loses its former uniformity, and a texture becomes manifest in it. The day-to-day social world gains a new texture from applying the scene–action, problem–ritual solution conceptual scheme I have just outlined. Thanks to the ethogenic movement, we can at least see what is happening in the microsocial world and it becomes clear that there are two classes of solutions available to the usual run of problems a social actor encounters. Again a grasp of the distinction I shall now elaborate is of enormous importance to making a proper study of the origin and development of childhood social skills. I propose to distinguish *standard* solutions to social problems from *non-standard* solutions. In a standard solution there is a ceremonial form proper to carrying out the ritual task, the use of this form is widespread, and there is some tendency to enforce a certain particular form as having exclusive claim to propriety. For instance the proper ceremonial form for acknowledging the human status of another to whom one has been introduced (at least in Britain), is for both to mutter 'How do you do' (no query) and (at least outside Oxford and Cambridge) to shake hands. This is not the proper form of address when one has been introduced to an animal. I have noticed that when introduced to a cat the proper form in Anglo-American circles is to exclaim upon the beauty of the animal, and then to call it and to stroke it. People and their cats are likely to show some measure of offence if this ritual is not complied with.

In general then we have a problematic situation, say the presence of a stranger amongst us. His mere existence there poses at least four problems, to which solutions must be found before we can safely interact with him. These problems are part empirical: (i) What is his name? (ii) Is he friendly? (iii) What is his relative status? and partly non-empirical (ii *a*) Can he be alter-cast into a friend? (iii*a*) Can he be bested in a status run-in? (iv) Can he be bound to the home side? And even for solving the apparently empirical problems, social care must be exercised. Some people feel that they are too well known for it to be polite to ask their name. So unless one gets it on the first round one must make do without it. And of course, as Shakespeare noted in the encounter between Hotspur and the Prince, a name may of itself carry a move in the status game. The ordinary process of introducing a stranger can be seen to achieve, amongst other acts, *standard* solutions to these, amongst other problems. The ritual or ceremonial form into which introduction is cast has then a twofold function, in the process of social creation. It serves to ensure that all the most useful questions are answered; and that no problematic, dangerous material is introduced that might violate the sanctity of the selves of the interactants. And of course as with every other social performance this twofold action is capable of performance glosses in which selves are promoted, flourished, deflated and so on, sometimes not wholly in accordance with the official lines taken in the basic action.

At this point it might be useful to state in a preliminary way the structural characteristics of a ritual, such as the greeting and introducing ceremonial. It is a sequence of actions, the structure of which is standard, each component action of which has a certain meaning. By saying that the structure is standard I mean that the order of kinds of action elements is fixed, and that violation of that order is recognised as an impropriety. For example I have found in some crosscultural studies of introduction ceremonies that the name of the person of higher ostensible status must be given first, in a ceremonial exchange of names. Failure to observe this rule is considered improper both in Britain and Belgium. Here I am sure we are on the borderline of syntax. I would like to suggest that at least for ceremonial forms, we apply the semantics–syntax distinction in a fairly direct way. I am inclined to think from the crosscultural studies that I have mentioned that the application of transformational rules to the analysis of the processes of genesis of specific forms of ceremonial can be very illuminating. And behind that looms the enticing prospect of some syntactical universals.

There is a hint in Bruner's paper in this volume, that seems to be well worth pursuing. He points out that there is evidence of the innateness of certain routines, which later become sub-routines in more sophisticated trains of actions. It is characteristic of such sub-routines to have always been performed completely. Perhaps there are, as it were, unit ceremonial forms of a similar character, and of a similar provenance.

Non-standard solutions to problematic situations have precisely the aim of standard solutions, i.e. the creation and maintenance of the appropriate measure of order, i.e. of reliable expectations of a structured future. For a non-standard solution to work it must use already existing elements which do have a meaning, or it must involve however curtailed, moments at which meanings are given. A non-standard solution, once embarked upon, may become suddenly problematic through a challenge to the meanings of the elements employed. And most important of all, a non-standard solution may involve agonistic or game-like actions. The agonistic character can tend to seep upwards, leading to agonistic inter-actions as to the definition of the meanings of the actions, at any level.

It is a moot point just how far cross-cultural solutions to a socially problematic situation are non-standard. It will depend upon whether there are or whether there are not social universals. There certainly seem to be some crude semantic universals (Eibl-Eibesfeldt, 1972), though their significance is not great since a great deal seems to turn, in any microsocial encounter, on the more refined semantics of the cultural locality (Leach, 1972).

The non-standard solution seems to arise in those problem situations where for one reason or another experience as to the standard solutions is not readily available. Until recently each couple must have devised their own etiquette for sexual intercourse, using an idiosyncratic variety of semantic elements and syntactic forms for managing the social aspect of the action. So that for a couple newly entering into this form of action the social problems encountered would require and acquire non-standard solutions. Just as Levi-Strauss has noticed about the ritualisa-tion of competitive games, so in this case I am tolerably certain research would reveal that the social forms of the action, each originally a one-off non-standard solution to an immediate problem, become fixed as cere-monials, unique to each couple. The advent of manuals which not only deal with the mechanics of sex but with its social and ceremonial aspects, is bound to lead to the spread of standard forms of ceremonial by which the social order is preserved even in so private a form of public action.

Where, in the action of one human being upon another, do we pass outside the realm of the social? I have already proposed a criterion which echoes Kant's delineation of the moral world (Kant, 1785). The social has to do with the recognition of the humanity of the other, and the minimal mark of that recognition is the endowment of the action with meaning. It is not only an intentional action as seen by the actor, but is a meaningful social act as seen by the one upon whom the action impinges. That it must not only be a push delivered deliberately, i.e. intended as a meaningful social act, but, in order to be part of the social world, that push must be read as an insult (playful shove) etc. Grimaces, and uttered sounds generally speaking effect very little, unless endowed with meaning, but exercising mechanical causality upon another does have a very considerable and noticeable effect. This is why physical violence is such an instructive example for analysis. I take two very different samples to illustrate the way in the adult world the borderline between the social and the non-social is defined by the endowment of action with meaning.

Violent actions which descend upon their victims at random, attacks upon individuals for which no reason can be found, are the antithesis of the social. They destroy the social order, and with it normal expectations. It is just because they create a non-social world that they are the most common means of 'social' control used by totalitarian regimes. In a similar spirit T. Szasz (Szasz, 1961) objects to much of the treatment of the 'mad' encouraged by adherence to the medical model, in that what is done to these unfortunate people is meaningless from their point of view, and thus carries them outside the social order. Goffman (1961) has also noticed the bracketing of 'treatment' by little clumps of proper civilities at its very beginning and very end. In between the individual is right outside the social order. I would like to put this in the form of a principle:

People seek, above all, to endow their social experiences with meaning.

We must return for a moment to the form of the solutions, standard and non-standard, to the problems posed in the creation and maintenance of a microsocial world. In order for any group of people to apply a standard solution to a problematic situation and so resolve it, they must be able to recognise what that situation is, and if it is as yet not clearly differentiated, so act as to define it as of a certain kind. Furthermore in the carrying out of a ritual the various rites in the ceremony must be undertaken by various people, not *in propria persona*, as this or that named individual, but as they represent or take upon themselves the lineaments of types. I differ at this point from Schutz (1972) and the phenomenologists, who mistakenly treat the face-to-face microsocial interaction of one with another as a true 'we' reaction, with each acknowledging the individuality of the other and that, only as 'contemporaries' in mediate interaction, do we interact as types. I believe that ethogenic research will show that in the social world our microinteractions are still as types. Some recent work of Argyle and Little (1972) underlines this point firmly.

Non-standard solutions too involve the definition of situations and interaction as social types or personas, but in this case both situations and identities are negotiated in the course of arriving at a solution. So that in either case we have to decide or determine what situation we are in, and what sort of people we are being when in it. Two items of resource are obvious. We must have some knowledge of what situations are recognised in our culture, and of what personas are authentic in those situations. Of course skilled machiavellians may, for some flamboyant effect, aim a higher order synthesis of order by rolling out an apparently unsuitable persona and then bending the initial situation round it.

By this means we are at least given the chance of recognising the scene and picking the right characters for the play. But what of the scenario? How do we control the action? Ethogenists hold that our knowledge of what is proper action in a given scene and with given characters can most usefully be described and its application explained by using the model of rule-following. Now it is obvious, and we don't need telling, that much of human social action is not generated by the conscious and explicit rule-following that characterises some of it. But the ethogenist conceives of rule-following as a source of concepts for the analysis of 'enigmatic' action. The methodology for the discovery of 'rules' and rules has been set out in detail elsewhere (Harré and Secord, 1972).

But adherence to the rules does not wholly determine propriety. For one thing the manner of the performance, in which so much that is social resides, is not easily or plausibly thought of as governed by rule, even when this concept is used metaphorically. Rather style has a unity around some kind of image that is being presented. This aspect of the control of action seems as a matter of fact, to be taken by an element we would call the 'arbiter'. In planning a piece of social action, say an excuse ritual, we are inclined to think that many people make recourse to a small number of images of actual people, whose imagined reactions to their imagined performances, they consider. That is the actor decides the manner of his performance rather than the matter (which will be pretty stereotyped anyway) by reference to the imagined reactions of his arbiter.

An adult human being then, at his social best, is capable of contemplating a model of himself in a model social environment, and imagining a run through of a variety of forms of some episode in which he is about to engage, as well as rueful re-runs of those affairs he has botched, with splendidly successful alternative forms offered. There surely is play social action, conforming to Bruner's analysis of play motor action (cf. this volume). And within it we need to look for *ceremonial* sub-routines, corresponding to Bruner's manipulative sub-routines. I would venture a hypothesis of the autonomy of these routines and differ again from Schaffer, who argues for the *derivation* of social responsiveness; 'the infant's sensitivity to certain kinds of sensory input, and . . . the fact that other people . . . are structured in such a way . . . to provide those inputs' (Schaffer, 1971, p. 38). I would go so far as to suggest the 'innateness' of ceremonial sub-routines, which become fixed in their role experientially, just as Bruner has shown manipulative ones do.

The resources upon which this skilled performance depends can be expressed in a matrix. Each row represents an integrated systematic resource for coping with a certain type of situation S, requiring an appropriate persona P, for which each person has an arbiter J, and for which there are rules (R) for the proper development of the action.

The columns represent the total variety of each item available to an individual:

$$s_1 - p_1 - j_1 - (r_1)$$
$$- - - - - - -$$
$$- - - - - - -$$
$$s_n - p_n - j_n - (r_n)$$

The matrix as it appears in the diagram is somewhat misleadingly simplified, in that each element is itself complex. A situation is a very complex entity, and a persona even more so. It has been suggested to me that the methods of Kelley (Bannister and Mair, 1968) might be suitably resorted to for an elucidation of the details of the structure.

For the student of human social development much follows, since each fully socially competent person must have an adequate matrix of conceptual resources. At least one form of defective preparation for action in the social world seems to be due to inadequate development of these essential resources. It has been suggested to me that some forms of violent delinquent behaviour in juveniles seem to stem directly from a mismatch between columns 1 and 2 of the matrix, in that they are capable of recognising a wider range of situations than they have personas prepared for (De Waele, 1972). When in the situation and the persona is called for, their recognition of their inability to produce it and be recognised as appearing in appropriate guise may lead to a resolution of the situation by violence; an extreme form of the uneasiness felt by the underdressed on a formal occasion, which is both the occasion and the excuse for social aggression.

THE SOCIAL WORLDS OF CHILDHOOD

There are two possible relations that might hold between the adult social world and the social worlds constructed by and for children. It might be that the social worlds of children are created and sustained by processes essentially similar to those by which adults sustain and create their worlds. As we have seen these means involve the use of ceremony and ritual for the creation and maintenance of social order, the presentation of selves by the stylistic qualification of lower order performances, and the imaginative rehearsal of social action as a test of propriety. The social world of the child would differ then only in content. This is the kind of childhood social world I called a 'precursor'.

But it may be that there is a social world of childhood which is created and sustained by methods and processes other than those resorted to by adults. This is the kind of world I called 'autonomous'.

Thanks to the work of Opie and Opie (1959) we can be fairly sure that the schoolchild's child-child world differs only in content from a normal mature adult's adult–adult world, and that its method of management is essentially similar. This gives us some conceptual leverage on that world. We can give it texture by approaching it with the hypothesis that there are ceremonies to be discovered and that there are personal styles to be identified, and that this group of humans, too, prepare in their imagination for social action. Looked at from this standpoint the social world of school-age children may show a quite different appearance from the way it looks from the standard Piagetian perspective, in which what is visible tends to be that which fluoresces in the light of the content of later performances. For though it may be a precursor world, in the sense that the very same capabilities are exercised in its management as are required for the adult world, from the point of view of content, it may be complete in itself. The child–child social world of schoolchildren, though not autonomous, is, I believe, best looked at as an independent society.

As Opie and Opie put it:

The schoolchild, in his primitive community, conducts his business with his fellows by ritual declaration. His affidavits, promissory notes, claims, deeds of conveyance, receipts and notices of resignation are verbal, and are sealed by the utterance of ancient words which are recognized and considered binding by the whole community ... Of barbarian simplicity, the schoolchild code enjoins that prior assertion of ownership in the prescribed form shall take the place of litigation; and that not even the deliberately swindled has redress if the bargain has been concluded by a bond word. Further it will be noticed that the gestures with which the significance of the language is stressed, for example, spitting, crossing fingers, and touching cold iron, are gestures which have been an accepted part of ritual since times long before our own. (Opie and Opie, 1959, p. 121)

I would like to take issue with this description only on the matter of the unsuitability of the evaluative phrases 'primitive community' and 'barbarian simplicity'. The schoolchild's world is neither primitive, barbarian nor simple. It is a precursor, but it is independent. It is a precursor in that, amongst other things, it depends upon the power of the *word*, alone. Important formulae such as 'Bags I' are effective by themselves, and have no need for supplementary threats of supernatural retribution for their violation. They are truly ritual.

But the ritual is creative and confirmatory of an independent array of social acts. The 'Please and Thank you' problem illustrates this. It is notorious how difficult it is to teach even very intelligent schoolchildren to say 'Please' and 'Thank you' even in the simplest situations as a matter of course. Rational persuasion based upon even so banal a principle as rational self-interest fails, and so does operant conditioning. Why? What is so difficult about it? Currently no one knows. But there are two complementary hypotheses in the field. The one is that this verbal ceremony is much more complex conceptually than it looks. And that it cannot be inculcated reliably unless the conceptual development, involving such matters as the realisation of the autonomy of the other person, is complete. In short the difficulty may have a kind of quasi-Piagetian explanation. There may also be a further maturational element involved, in that there may be similarities with the case of the 'tag-question' problem studied by Brown, in which total inability to get the 'logic' of 'Isn't it?', 'Weren't they?', etc., is suddenly transformed into a complete mastery.

But there is another and additional hypothesis. And this is that in the child–child social world this ceremony just has no place. A social relationship of gift and receipt has no place in the child's catalogue of authentic relationships. His world is ordered otherwise. As the Opies point out it is a world of bagging, swopping, bribing, and placating with sacrifices. And so the ceremonial expression of gratitude has no role. A relationship that is patently authentic for us, and for most adult cultures, may not exist at all in child–child culture. Children cannot learn the Please and Thank you routine since they are quite unable to see what it means.

It has often been pointed out that at some relatively early stage in a child's conceptual development the notions of the animate and the inanimate separate out. A consequence of this step in conceptual mastery is that a child learns not to treat physical things as say intending things for or against him. At the same time he is likely to be taught that mere words are not likely to achieve much in the manipulation of inanimate nature. But it has not so often been emphasised that a child must hang on, at all costs, to the idea that those things which are animate do harbour intentions towards him and plans for him, and that in the social world words and other symbolic forms are about the only things that do have power. Even to make his acts of violence social he must learn to give them a symbolic gloss. Social maturation into the precursor world and hence into the adult world does not consist in confirming the ability to treat one's experiences objectively but in being able to read them for the meaning they do or even more important, could contain. The magical stance which endows every contingency with meaning and every word and gesture with power is the very stance that must be adopted in order to be socially competent. Perhaps the poverty of the social accomplishments of the members of our culture is a reflection of the sophistication of our view of physical nature.

What of the social world I called 'autonomous'? It seems to me that Bowlby (1969) has made out an extraordinarily strong case for his 'attachment' analysis of the child–mother social world, that develops its form during the first year of life, flourishes as an autonomous culture until the end of the third year, and declines in importance thereafter (Bowlby, 1969, pp. 204–5). The contributions of Richards (this volume) to the close analysis of the form of the mother–child relationship serve to reinforce my impression of the autonomy of this culture. I take issue with Bowlby only in his extrapolation of the concept into the adult social world. 'Attachment behaviour (among adults), he says 'is a straightforward continuation of attachment behaviour in childhood' (Bowlby, 1969, pp. 206–7). He instances the strong mother–adult-daughter bonds as examples of this. But it seems that it is at least as likely that those 'bonds' can be given an ethogenic explanation, as epiphenomena of rituals of social maintenance. They may of course be decked out in the language of emotion but this is more likely I believe to turn out on investigation to be a formal expression, or perhaps part of a stylistic gloss, rather than a description of feeling. Bowlby has noted the abrupt change in attachment behaviour that occurs at the beginning of the fourth year, which is the point at which an ethogenist would be inclined to look for the first examples of effective ritual behaviour.

I want to make the radical proposal that the mode of world ordering ('attachment'), which characterises the autonomous world, must perish before adulthood is possible. The intermediate world of the schoolchild comes into being as the proper precursor of adulthood. The social skills of the attachment world, emphasised by those who have pointed out the social power that very young children have over their mothers, must be abrogated, and a wholly different set of skills develop. It is not too difficult to see an adaptive basis for this complexity, nor to view the attachment world as the social equivalent of milk teeth.

In summary then, adopting the ethogenic viewpoint would suggest a further extension of the current cognitive-developmental approach, rather than any revolutionary new line. But this extension would involve students of infant and junior forms of social life operating with a vastly extended conceptual system, in the light of which that life might take on a revolutionary texture. In this way ethogeny suggests a step beyond Bowlby and the theory of attachment, not replacing it by something else, but complementing and transcending it with an investigation of the origin and development of the capacity for ceremonial, and of the cognitive resources by which the effective performance of ceremonial is controlled.

ACKNOWLEDGEMENTS

I am very grateful to Miss Julie Rutowska for some penetrating criticisms of an earlier draft of this paper.

REFERENCES

Argyle, M. and Little, B. R. (1972). Do personality traits apply to social behaviour? *J. Theory Soc. Behaviour*, 2, 1–35.

Bannister, D. and Mair, J. M. M. (1968). *The Evaluation of Personal Constructs*. London and New York, Academic Press.

Bowlby, J. (1969). *Attachment and Loss*, Vol. 1, *Attachment*. London, Hogarth Press.

Burke, K. (1969). *A Grammar of Motives*. Berkeley, California Univ. Press.

De Waele, J-P. (1972). Personal communication.

Eibl-Eibesfeldt, I. (1972). Similarities and differences between cultures in expressive movements. In Hinde, R. A. (ed.). *Non-Verbal Communication*. London, Cambridge Univ. Press.

Goffman, E. (1961). *Asylums*. New York, Doubleday.

Goffman, E. (1969*a*). *The Presentation of Self in Everyday Life*. London, Allen Lane.

Goffman, E. (1969*b*). *Where the Action Is*. London, Allen Lane.

Goffman, E. (1971). *Relations in Public*. London, Allen Lane.

Goffman, E. (1972). *Interaction Ritual*. London, Allen Lane.

Harré, R. and Secord, P. F. (1972). *The Explanation of Social Behaviour*. Oxford, Blackwell.

Hinde, R. A. (1972) (ed.). *Non-Verbal Communication*. London, Cambridge Univ. Press.

Kant, I. (1785). *Groundwork of the Metaphysic of Morals* (trans. Abbott, T. K., 1959). London, Longmans.

Künkel, F. (1941). *God Helps Those* . . . New York, Washburn.

Leach, E. (1972). The influence of cultural context on non-verbal communication in man. In Hinde, R. A. (ed.). *Non-Verbal Communication*. London, Cambridge Univ. Press.

Lyman, S. L. and Scott, M. B. (1970). *A Sociology of the Absurd*. New York, Appleton-Century-Crofts.

Opie, I. and Opie, P. (1959). *The Lore and Language of School-Children*. Oxford, Clarendon Press.

Schaffer, H. R. (1971). *The Growth of Sociability*. London, Penguin.

Schutz, A. (1972). *The Phenomenology of the Social World*. London, Heinemann.

Szasz, T. (1961) *The Myth of Mental Illness*. London, Secker and Warburg.

13

Ethology and early socialisation

N. G. Blurton Jones

INTRODUCTION

Comparative ethology, the school of animal behaviour research originated by Konrad Lorenz (1970) and developed by Niko Tinbergen (1963), has been brought to the attention of people interested in human behaviour by a number of popular books. These elicited a just mixture of scorn and interest. But there are aspects of ethological work on social behaviour which may be of more lasting use. One aspect is the direct application of ethological methods of studying interactions between individuals, advocated by Hutt (1970) and Hutt and Hutt (1970*b*) and represented by most of the contributions to Blurton Jones (1972*a*). In this aspect ethology has total overlap of subject matter with psychology.

The other aspect, more exciting to the zoologist but more controversial for the social scientist, is the approach to the human social sciences which draws on ethology's origin in zoology and in the study of evolution. This approach attempts to give an all-round biological framework to studies of social behaviour. This includes comparative studies, so long as they are carried out with more concern for academic standards of evidence and comparability than is seen in some popular accounts. This aspect is represented by the work of Bowlby (1969) on the child's attachment to its mother, Crook and his colleagues (1970*a*, *b*), and Gartlan (1968) on the relationships between social organisation and ecology in non-human primates, and Freedman (in press), and others. In anthropology it has a direct counterpart in the work largely instigated by Washburn (e.g. 1964); a contemporary example being DeVore and Konner (in press) where features of behaviour of contemporary hunter-gatherers are considered in relation to their survival value. It is best to point out immediately that this approach has nothing to do with the 'social Darwinism' of the early 1900s. There is no dedication to the 'organism' analogy of society (this is not to say that society cannot be regarded as a 'system' in the (cybernetic) engineering sense, which it undoubtedly could be, with great benefit to research in this area) nor any interest in ranking societies on a scale of 'evolution'. For that matter there is a marked lack of dedication among contemporary zoologists for ranking animals on such a ladder from lowest to highest. Comparative

263

psychologists too have recently found that such a ranking procedure has its limitations (Hodos, 1970), totally ignoring as it does the importance of adaptive radiation.

APPLICATION OF ETHOLOGICAL METHODS IN STUDIES OF HUMAN BEHAVIOUR

Most of the few ethologists who have looked at behaviour in childhood have worked either on newborns or in nursery schools. In some cases this has been because in nursery school it is easy to see large numbers of children in a setting relatively uncontrolled by the observer but it is also because children in that age group behave as much as, or more than, they talk about behaving. Studies done so far have been very exploratory, testing the applicability to human behaviour of techniques of observation and analysis of social behaviour that have developed in studies of animals.

Most of these workers have perhaps too much ignored earlier work and the established theories, but they have done so out of a profound dissatisfaction with certain features of traditional methods. For example as a source of information about behaviour, asking people what they or their children do is very unsatisfactory. It tells you about what people say, not what they do; it gives plenty of interesting, if difficult, material but it is not data on what people do. One may for instance consider which would be the most interesting things to get out of a conversation with a chimpanzee! When the chimpanzee baby Washoe (Gardner and Gardner, 1971) says 'you tickle me' it is surely more interesting to see that she uses personal pronouns than to see the apparent confirmation that tickling was reinforcing, which had been shown by direct experiment some years previously by Mason (1965). It is of course also interesting that a chimp will use language-like communication to mediate a quite normal piece of chimp interaction. However, now that several field studies of chimps exist it seems that the interesting things conversations with Washoe give (apart from their insight into the nature of language) are things to do with what it is like to be a chimp and not about what chimps do. Confusing data on behaviour with data on attitudes for example makes it impossible to investigate the relationships between attitudes and behaviour.

A second traditional method, rating people on predetermined scales, is fitting an artificial, untestable, and culturally biased pattern on to their behaviour. Even counting ill-defined or interpretative categories (like 'aggressive acts', 'bids for attention', etc.), especially when they are defined only by examples, leaves other researchers wondering just what was observed.

The most lucid, balanced and authoritative account of the methods and viewpoint of ethology that is available is probably that by Tinbergen (1963). A number of good textbooks of animal behaviour which cover most of the points he raises are now available, e.g. Manning (1967), Hinde (1966) and Marler and Hamilton (1967). There have been several papers describing possible contributions of ethology to psychiatry (e.g. Zegans, 1967; Hutt and Hutt, 1970*a*), anthropology (Tiger and Fox, 1966; Freeman, 1966) and studies of human behaviour in general (Freedman, 1967; Ambrose, 1968). Bowlby's (1969) discussion of attachment includes a useful summary of many features of ethological thought. Most of these concentrate either on contributions from the findings on animal behaviour or on the evolutionary viewpoint (sometimes also with reference to the highly canalised developmental systems often thought to be required by natural selection). Attempts to describe features of ethological methods which may be important to the human behavioural sciences were made by Grant (1965), Hutt (1970), Hutt and Hutt (1970*b*) and Blurton Jones (1972*b*).

Although no practical definition of who is or is not an ethologist is possible or even worth while, there seem to be two fundamental features of an ethological approach. One is the conscious attempt to treat behaviour in the same way as a zoologist treats any other feature of an animal such as an organ or other structure. The other (brought about originally by the futility of trying to empathise with animals) is the intention to deal with observable behaviour, and in this respect (and perhaps only in this respect) ethologists are frequently at one with behaviourists. A number of more or less distinct features of ethology spring from these two fundamentals. These are dealt with only briefly here as they are more fully described by Hutt (1970) and in the papers in Blurton Jones (1972*a*).

1. *Description of observed behaviour*

Ethologists argue that any science must begin by describing the phenomena that it wishes to explain. In behaviour there are two outcomes of this: (*a*) the natural history phase of a study in which the phenomena are described, which process may incidentally generate hypotheses to explain the observations; (*b*) behaviour is described in terms of what one sees happening, in almost anatomical terms so that any observer from whatever culture may tell from the description what the observed behaviour looked like. The meaning of the behaviour is something to be discovered not something to be assumed. The anatomical descriptions can also be used to describe behaviour in many different cultures (e.g. Eibl-Eibesfeldt, 1972). One advantage of this may be the more precise description of differences between behaviour of people in different cultures.

2. *Explanations based on the discrimination in zoology of four kinds of questions about behaviour (the four whys)*

When it comes to explaining their observations ethologists have been saved a certain amount of preliminary disorder by referring back to general zoology. Tinbergen (1951) has pointed out that there are four different kinds of question that may be meant when one asks 'why did he do that?' They are the same as the questions asked about any biological event: (1) What caused it to happen now? (i.e. the short-term causes and physiology of the event), what is the mechanism? Mechanisms can be described at either the behavioural (e.g. cybernetic descriptions) or the physiological (neuro-physiological and endocrine) levels. (2) How did the individual develop to be an individual that reacts that way? (i.e. long-term causes of the mechanism, the embryology and ontogeny of the event). (3) Why does this kind of animal develop such responses? What are the effects of the behaviour and its advantages under natural selection? (i.e. what is its survival value?). (4) Why does this kind of animal solve those problems of survival in this way? (What is the evolutionary history of the behaviour? How has the interaction of its phylogeny with multiple selection pressures proceeded? Its ancestry may have committed the animal to certain kinds of solution to problems of survival.)

Thus, if we take smiling in infancy as an example, the causal question (1) would be answered by the data on the visual stimuli that elicit smiling, the behavioural contexts in which it occurs in the neonate (Emde and Konig, 1969), by factors influencing responsiveness to these stimuli such as 'state', by the behaviour and situations associated with it (Grant, 1969) and by theories such as those of Kagan (1971) on the cognitive background to smiling. The developmental question (2) is illuminated by the studies such as those of Ahrens (1953), Ambrose (1966) and Fantz (1967) on the changes in the optimal visual stimuli for smiling, studies of the operant conditioning of smiling, e.g. Brackbill (1958) and on development of this pattern in twins (Freedman, 1967) and in blind children (Thompson, 1941; Eibl-Eibesfeldt, 1972). Studies of the survival value of smiling (3) can start both from studies of its direct effects (eliciting smiling, talking, handling from mother according to Ambrose, 1966) and of its occurrence and causation in different species (Ambrose, 1966) where correlations are made between variation in smiling and variation in other features of the social situation of the infant. Thus Ambrose suggests that smiling functions to maintain contact with mother, to some extent substituting for the human baby's apparent inability to cling to its rather hairless mother. Other effects and survival values could well be proposed for this particular piece of behaviour. The phylogeny of smiling (4) has been investigated most thoroughly by van Hoof (1972) and Andrew (1963). Van Hoof traces its origins from morphologically similar expressions in other higher primates, in which the 'smiles' occur with slightly different behaviour and in different situations suggesting a gradual swing from a more 'fearful-plus-friendly' mix to a less ambivalently 'friendly' content. He is thus describing a quantitative historical change in the causal mechanism of the morphological pattern.

Among other advantages of this classification of questions is its emphasis on the distinction between causes of behaviour and results of behaviour. Distinction of causes and effects (or at least preceding and following events) can be extremely important, for instance in studying communication. Signals[1] are given as a result of various causal factors, which have effects on other individuals. A major question about communication is how the causal mechanisms behind the signal are organised to produce adaptive effects. A part of the answer will concern the kinds of effects of the signal on the ensuing signalling (does it stop, continue the same, increase, change to other signals, etc.?). It would be impossible to take any practical steps with this question without the initial distinction of causes and effects. The mechanisms of 'intention' can only be studied if the distinctions of input, output, feedback, feed-forward, are maintained. Many writings which use the word 'intention' use it as an explanation of an observed behaviour. Intention is not an explanation but it may be a phenomenon to be explained. MacKay (1972) gives a useful description of the role of cybernetics in providing frameworks for the study of complex aspects of communication such as 'intention to communicate'.

Thus in classical ethological studies of the 'meaning' of signalling behaviour two kinds of meaning are distinguished, (1) what the signal means in terms of how it reflects the motivational or causal situation of the signaller; (2) what the signal means to the reactors, what effects it has on their behaviour. In everyday language (1) is often the same as (2), the actor 'wants to make the reactor do' whatever is in (2). This ignores

---

[1]   In this usage 'signals' is really synonymous with 'behaviour'. No special meaning of the term 'signal' is required by this methodology. In practice most ethologists might think in terms of three classes of 'signal': (1) Behaviour which occurs in association with particular situations or subsequent behaviour by the 'signalling' animal and so could transmit useful information to a reactor. (2) Behaviour which in addition to the above features may be limited to social situations or adjusted according to the reactor's behaviour. (3) Behaviour which comparative evidence suggests has been specially modified in evolution to increase its effect on reactors.

the question of why he wants to, and conceals the question of what decides the behaviour used to influence the reactor, i.e. of the mechanism by which (1) is adapted to have the effects in (2). Any analysis of this problem relies entirely upon having descriptions of the signals which are independent of the causes or effects of the signals. These points are discussed more fully by Brannigan and Humphreys (1972), Grant (1969), Blurton Jones (1971), and Cullen (1972).

3. Operational definitions of large categories

Many studies of development of social behaviour simply assume the reality of categories such as 'aggression' or 'attachment' as motivational or causal or developmental unities and then proceed to attempt to 'measure' them by ratings on a predetermined scale of the category, or by observing incidents which are then 'coded' into the categories and counted. This procedure has for long seemed very alien to ethologists and recently, perhaps partly as a result of contact with ethology, there has been some move away from this in psychology particularly in the U.S.A. (e.g. Maccoby and Feldman, 1972). A basic point is that if there is such a 'thing' as 'aggression' or 'attachment' then all the possible measures of it should show signs of measuring the same thing, *for example* they may vary together. Otherwise there is little point in the category except to preserve confusion and established theories. There is no advantage in comparing studies of attachment which use different measures unless we know that the measures are measuring the same thing (are measures of each other). Yet if two such measures vary independently, investigation of the variation of some measure (or judgement) of both of them lumped together will obscure their relationships to causal variables rather than reveal them. Incredible as it may seem, there have been studies which go so far as to use behaviour of children towards other children as measures of dependency or attachment to mothers (in many observational situations there is a negative correlation between behaviour to children and to mother).

Such categories on the other hand may be intended to represent a cluster of behaviours having the same effects as each other (as in Bowlby's use of 'attachment'). Beer (1960–3), Rowell (1960) and Slotnick (1967) have shown how functional clusters need not imply any causal unity. No doubt, since many selection pressures act on any feature of behaviour, the functional categories are not so uniform either.

4. Comparative studies of man and animals

Although comparative studies are justly a part of ethology, they require much more caution than has been shown so far by ethologists writing about man and by psychologists drawing on animal comparisons. In common with Callan (1970) (considering ethology and social anthropology), I feel that the contribution of comparative studies to the main concerns of psychology (causation and development of behaviour and individual differences in behaviour) is more limited and is of a different kind than the contributions so far claimed. Even so, great problems of interdisciplinary communication remain. It seems clear for instance that few ethologists understand what sociologists are doing and few sociologists understand what ethologists are doing. Comparative accounts, such as that by Lorenz (1966) are widely taken to say that, for example, comparative evidence for the adaptiveness of aggression implies that aggression in man must have a certain kind of causation ('spontaneous' increasingly likely to be performed with increasing time from last performance, and seeking out appropriate stimuli) and certain kind of ontogeny ('innate', developing almost regardless of external factors). But this does not necessarily follow. So long as the adaptive criteria for the 'finished product' are met, the developmental history and causal organisation may vary under the influence of quite different selective pressures. The comparative method has valuable but very different contributions to make.

Besides these examples, there is a quite separate tradition of systematic study and experiment on animal behaviour intended to be relevant to human behaviour. The best-known examples are those of Harlow and Harlow (1965) on rhesus monkey babies. Other important series of studies are those of Hinde and Spencer-Booth (1968) and of Jensen, Bobbitt and Gordon (1967). There is also a large body of data on social organisation of wild primates (DeVore, 1965; Crook, 1970*a*), aimed at elucidating relationships between ecology and social structure, and with a usually covert interest in revealing the evolutionary history of human social behaviour and social organisation. The developmental studies continue in close liaison with and interest from some students of child behaviour who are sure of their relevance, and with total lack of interest from others who are equally sure of their irrelevance. The primate sociology studies (with some notable exceptions) seem more isolated from studies of human behaviour, no doubt partly from their origins among physical anthropologists. However, there can be few sociologists, and few British social anthropologists who are anything other than certain of the irrelevance of animal studies. They may have a point in so far as it is all too easy to make facile leaps from monkeys to people. However, some ways in which these studies have a bearing on human work are relatively uncontroversial. They may suggest hypotheses to test on humans (e.g. studies of 'peck orders' or dominance hierarchies in groups of children by McGrew, 1972*b*, Esser, 1968), they may exclude certain

269

uniquely human characteristics from the explanations of phenomena found in both man and animals, they may advance knowledge of developmental mechanisms in general, they may help solve difficult problems of methodology. Less safely animals may be used, as in physiology, for the experimental tests of theories built up from direct observational and correlational evidence on humans. It is worth noting that this practice is now being questioned in physiology, see for example Drew *et al.* (1970) on brain and behaviour studies in man, chimps and monkeys. These authors argue that there are many indications that the ways in which the rhesus monkey brain works are fundamentally different from the way in which the human and chimpanzee brain works. In this chapter I wish to concentrate on the more controversial subject of direct animal–man comparisons, the evolutionary perspective on behaviour, their interpretation and their role in research on human behaviour.

The comparative side of comparative ethology was originally very much a part of taxonomy (e.g. Lorenz' work on the Anatidae, 1941, 1953) and based on the methods of comparative anatomy; there should be no distinction between comparative ethology and comparative functional anatomy. But the application of comparative ethology to studies of man often differs from its orthodox role of explaining (by reference to survival value and evolutionary change) the characteristics which distinguish one animal from another, or of working out how one animal is related to another. This orthodox role is fulfilled when comparative studies are used to continue the explanation of why people behave as they do beyond explanation in terms of causation and development into the natural selection and phylogenetic reasons for such causal and developmental systems. This is a very respectable way of using comparative data but it is seldom used where man is the subject of study.

Thus the most academically respectable contribution of comparative method is to continue the hierarchy of explanations through 'the four whys'. In this task the comparative method follows on behind the discoveries of the psychologist and sociologist. The latter discover that people behave in certain ways and develop in certain ways and that societies are structured in certain ways. The biologist can then join in and attempt to explain why Homo sapiens evolved into an animal that responds and develops in these ways. He can try to assess the way selection pressures have modified any general primate or mammalian pattern into the human pattern. In other words he is attempting to determine the survival value and the evolutionary history of the behaviour described by the psychologist or sociologist. Many sociologists may be prepared to take it as given that man is a social animal (whatever that means). Biologists and a very thriving school of American anthropologists (e.g.

270

Washburn, 1964; DeVore, 1965; Lee and DeVore, 1968; Lancaster, 1968*a, b*, 1971; Trivers, 1971) would like to know (among other things) the precise role of predation and distribution of food sources, etc., in bringing about this particular social animal that is social in its particular ways. For example, in many animals grouping seems to have to do with protection against predators. Among the primates Crook and Gartlan (1966) suggest that an interaction between predation and food supply in different conditions of aridity determine both group size and proportions of males. Males are a luxury in arid regions to be afforded only for their value in defence against predators, in the absence of refuges. In the evolution of man it may have been the increased predation on a ground-living hominid that set the scene for the later evolution of increased food sharing and co-operative hunting (closely correlated with each other among the mammals as a whole). Co-operative hunting has been claimed by some to have been a situation giving great selective advantage to development of language (Lancaster, 1968*a*). Using the broader, and therefore, taxonomically safer, basis of the mammals as a whole Eisenberg (1966) has shown how social organisation, primarily a matter of spacing, functions to balance the selective pressures of predation and food supply.

The search for a 'human pattern' will appear to be a naïve aim to the psychologist and sociologist who may be surprised to think that a zoologist expects any limit to human variability. This is simply because the zoologist is familiar with the more dazzling variety found in the animal kingdom and the psychologist is not. The consequences of this for mutual misunderstanding are great. For example, it explains why the zoologist expects universal, cross-culturally constant features of man to be interesting. They will provide an intriguing set of similarities and differences from various other animals. This familiarity with a wider range of variability is a major part of what is meant by the 'zoological perspective'. Simple measures like group sizes and age and sex compositions of groups, and mobility of members are thus of great significance to a zoologist looking at human society because he sees no *a priori* reason for them to be as they are. To the sociologist these measures are trivial and boring, sometimes because we are all familiar with them and also because the sociologist is familiar with a range of more complex phenomena and is anyway primarily interested in differences between societies. Thus he tends to take these simple measures as 'givens' which do not need questioning. While I would agree with Callan's (1970) criticism of Morris' (1967) '90 per cent of copulations occur when the couple is in a pair bonded state' for its jargonist tone, vagueness of the term 'pair bonded state' and uncertainty about what the real percentage is, I cannot agree that this is a statement of the trivial or obvious. There

271

are surprisingly few other mammals of which this could be said. We all have our ideas about the reasons for this but they all permit further questioning of their starting point. The implications of questioning the reasons for this 'obvious' fact are profound, the reader who wishes to pursue them could make a useful start with Orians (1969) and Eisenberg (1966). Morris considerable achievements in breaking through the 'obvious' barrier should not be lost to sight among the faults in his arguments.

Other uses of a comparative approach to man are on much less safe ground but perhaps are of more potential use to the behavioural sciences. The simplest is the use of data on animal behaviour to suggest things to look for in human behaviour. For example, Esser *et al.* (1965), Esser (1968), and McGrew (1969, 1972*b*) followed the finding of territory and dominance orders in animal societies by examining some human groups for similar phenomena. This practice has heuristic value provided one does not then treat the existence of the behaviour in animals as explaining its occurrence in man, or implying certain processes or development of this behaviour in man (as sometimes appears to be done, for example in Morris 1969).

Two more general uses of comparative studies are in providing 'frameworks' and 'perspective'. Working out the survival value of a piece of behaviour may actually help, in a purely heuristic way, in studies of its causation and development. If one decides to study the causal control of behaviour which subserves a spacing function one may be saved from the theoretical blinkers imposed by deciding to study 'aggression and fear'. If nothing else, the oversimplications get transferred to the ecology rather than to the causation. (Thus there may actually be many other selection pressures favouring or opposing fighting.) Also the study can be directed towards a clear aim; understanding how the behaviour that serves this function develops and is controlled. Perhaps many difficulties arise in studying child development because we do not clearly know what childhood is for. Richards and Bernal (1972) and Konner (1972) are exceptional in paying attention to the survival value of behaviour in children, realising, like Bowlby (1969), that the child must survive while a child and is thus not simply a part-formed adult.

The evolutionary perspective may have its liberating effect by putting one in a position to step aside from existing theory and say for example: there must be a system to ensure protection of infants from predation, or there must be a spacing mechanism (kinship?), let us see what it is like, let us see how the organism solves the task of protection or spacing. Clearly such systems could cut across all existing categorisations of behaviour. The existence of a way of solving a problem of survival does not imply that there must be a unitary unvarying behaviour system

272

serving this function (Rowell, 1960; Beer, 1960–3; Slotnick, 1967) but it does impel us to try to find out how the particular organism solves the problem. The theoretical advances by Bowlby (1969) owe much to the liberating effect of considering the survival value of attachment. An evolutionary perspective may also highlight the differences between the present environment and the environment in which selection occurred and perhaps it can thereby suggest new features of the environment whose effects on behaviour are untested or neglected.

This use of the evolutionary perspective as exemplified by Bowlby (1957, 1969) is purely heuristic. It is undoubtedly good to stop assuming that clinging is a bad habit derived from the need to feed babies, and to start looking to see precisely how it develops and what role it plays in development of social behaviour. But this was not a change of view logically dependent on the adaptive values of attachment and of suckling. For instance, as described below, the adaptive role of suckling in attachment may have been underestimated by Bowlby, yet his new look at attachment remains an important contribution. Comparative studies of mammalian childrearing practice (Ben Shaul, 1962; Martin, 1968; Blurton Jones, 1972*d*) suggest that some features of suckling may be modified during evolution as adaptations to bring about close mother–infant contact (which in some ways strengthens Bowlby's position against the early 'dependency' thteory). The composition of milk, frequency of feeds and rates of suckling within a sucking bout (and possibly the duration of feeds) are closely adapted to different patterns of contact between mother and infant. (Statements relating milk composition solely to growth rate, e.g. Widdowson (1970), are usually based on very small samples of mainly domesticated species. Widdowson considered nine species whereas Ben Shaul considered 100.) The nutritional requirements of a variety of growth rates are met within each type of contact and contact types correlate with milk composition within groups that have similar growth rates. Thus the milk composition and feeding and suckling rates appear to be largely adaptations to a particular kind of contact. Human milk composition and sucking rates are those of a nearly continuous feeder in nearly continuous contact with the mother. (To argue that the human newborn was a spaced feeder would require it to have a growth rate very much lower on the grossest of scales than that of a chimpanzee, whereas its growth rate on any measure is higher than that of a chimpanzee.) It thus appears that some features of human newborn feeding are adaptations to close 'contact' between mother and young and may even be adaptations functioning to help develop attachments (e.g. Altman's (1963) description of the alternation of suckling and following in young cervids). Also, on quite different grounds Konner (1972) has argued that Bowlby may have too far de-emphasised

273

the importance of feeding in development of attachment. That suckling may in many ways be adapted to produce attachment does not decrease the validity of Bowlby's new perspective but it clearly also suggests (but does not in any way prove) that evolution may have exploited the reinforcement mechanism to produce attachment, perhaps with the help of the contrivance of face-to-face positions during suckling as suggested by Abercrombie (1971). Although whether suckling does this by reinforcement from feeding or calming (Kessen, Leutzendorff and Stoutsenberger, 1967), or by enforcing frequent interaction (as the evidence of Schaffer and Emerson, 1964, would suggest) is not answered by comparative evidence.

The most entertaining but least respectable (although some rationale can be worked out for its methodology, see Blurton Jones, 1972*d* and next section) use of comparative methods is to extrapolate 'missing data' about behaviour of man. The extrapolated 'data' may also then be used as a framework which gives a pattern to or suggests hypotheses for direct studies. Any degree of specificity of the extrapolations can only apply to man in the ecological niche in which most of his evolution occurred (i.e. the 90 per cent of Homo sapiens generations who came before the origin of agriculture). In this respect it may have a use as evidence about the representativeness of some aspects of behaviour of surviving hunter-gatherers. More general extrapolations, perhaps general enough to characterise the species (perhaps comparable with the cross-cultural generalisations by Murdoch, 1949) may be applicable also to post-agricultural man (e.g. rules about the ways primate or human societies change in relation to ecological pressures). If we are to use comparative evidence to support the representativeness of surviving hunter-gatherers then direct evidence to confirm the extrapolations largely waits on the ingenuity of archaeologists but otherwise, in the case of the more general extrapolations, direct human data is more readily available. Direct data are essential before any firm conclusions can be based on extrapolations to post-agricultural man. But it may be that the extrapolations have considerable heuristic value for those who are concerned with the more general traits of human behaviour – the rules of behaviour that are general to our species and shared with differing numbers of our animal relatives. Much of behavioural science is in a position analogous to the position of linguists in a world in which all animals use language. In such a world it is very hard to see the wood (or forest) for the trees. It is probably true that the hardest features of human behaviour for the scientist to notice are some of the most general. Among these may be some of the most important and dangerous, e.g. the combination of population density and social history that leads to justification of wars and other violence, the appeal of objects and acquisitions.

The usefulness of these extrapolations is certainly debatable. Some of the least useful are those that break the rules of comparative method, such as much of what Lorenz (1966) says about aggression. The 'perspective' use seems to consist mainly of taking us outside existing theory, and outside our own cultural suppositions (in the same way as can social anthropology) and perhaps even outside anthropocentric theories (the best-hidden assumptions in psychology). This function is claimed by Morris (1967) and whatever criticisms may be directed at other features of his book, it would be ungrateful to take exception to his willingness to attempt a broad overall look at the human species.

A recent and exciting example of the 'perspective' value of a consideration of the evolution of human behaviour is the paper by Trivers (1971) on the evolution of reciprocal altruism by natural selection. Under this heading he includes: helping in times of danger, sharing food, helping sick, wounded old or young, sharing implements, sharing knowledge. He considers in some detail the implications of the selective mechanism for various requirements to allow evolution of reciprocal altruism, such as long life-span, and lack of hierarchical social organisation. His considerations lead to detailed implications about detection of cheating, sanctions against cheating, including aggression, etc. This has considerable implications for the study of human aggression, including its development in which it is so clearly related to transfer of objects from one child to another, as too are some of the earliest non-aggressive interactions with peers. It is also an example of a framework drawing new and closer attention to a feature whose generality to human cultures has been neglected in favour of its great and intriguing variation from one culture to another. Trivers' conclusions about dominance hierarchies also make an interesting fit with the evidence from the correlation of sex differences in adult size with sex ratios and social structure in mammals. The relatively small (for higher primates) dimorphism of man (Tanner, 1962) fits with a less hierarchical, more balanced sex ratio kind of group structure.

Another reason for a biologist's thinking that there may be a value in both comparative extrapolations and in knowledge of survival value of behaviour is a hunch, an often hidden but well-supported assumption, that if you modify a system away from its evolved position you can expect 'no end of trouble'. This view is now well known and well substantiated in ecology. It may be no less true of behaviour and social organisation (if these three can indeed be separated: ecological problems of modern man are results of his social behaviour, the social behaviour of evolving man is a result of his ecology). But it is certainly true that changing part of the system *need not* have any far reaching consequences. It is just that biologists (ever since Darwin's (1859) discussion of the influence of the abundance of cats on the abundance of red clover) have become very used to seeing very long chains of consequences following a change in a natural system. If sufficient is known about the natural system and about the adaptive value of the piece of it that is being changed, then it should be possible to predict some of the consequences of the change. To do this for any feature of human behaviour requires much more extensive comparative work than has been done so far. Even if such work were done, I feel that comparative studies can still only act as guide lines and not as substitutes for direct data on what people do. But the expectation of a coherent system of behaviour, social organisation and ecology, characterising any species is what is behind the interest many biologists have in understanding the social, ecological and physical environment in which human social behaviour evolved (and in the context in which the developmental process in an individual was evolved to function). It should not be forgotten, as it sometimes is by both biologist and non-biologist, that all the most complex and human characteristics (conscience, language, ideals, beliefs, etc.) also have an evolutionary history, despite the popular (because ego-inflating) belief among non-anthropologists that the origin of these 'higher' characteristics of man was rooted in recent history rather than firmly in pre-agricultural prehistory.

Comparative studies have shown their usefulness to direct studies most clearly with respect of the newborn child. The most authentic account of this may be expected from Konner (in press) who besides being in touch with comparative studies and concerned to find the adaptive value of features of newborn and later behaviour (1972) has studied the newborn in a hunter-gatherer culture, the Zhun/twa (! Kung) bushmen, where the ecological pressures are basically the same as those on evolving man, this being the ecological niche in which man evolved. Indeed Washburn (1971) has pointed out that this environment is not very different even in geographical and faunal and floral characteristics from the habitat in which the bulk of human and proto-human populations lived, even quite late in the Paleolithic. One example from the newborn period to illustrate the kind of relationship that may be expected between comparative studies and direct studies must suffice here. It stems from the comparative data on milk composition and sucking rates described above, from which it was concluded that the human mother and newborn are adapted to suckle very frequently. Konner's observations (1972) confirm that Zhun/twa (! Kung) bushman mothers and infants indeed perform this way. (One may choose whether to take this as confirmation of the comparative story, or as evidence that bushmen are representative of pre-agricultural man in this respect.) In examining their data on the successes and failures of Cambridge mothers who attempted to breastfeed their babies, Richards and Bernal (personal communication) found that successful breast-feeders were feeding their baby at intervals of three hours as opposed to the bottlefeeders' four hours. Failed breastfeeders were those who per-sisted in trying to keep the four-hour schedule recommended by doctors, midwives and health visitors. Knowing the correlation among mammals of feeding interval and milk led Richards and Bernal to suggest that the difference between human milk and cow's milk was the cause of the short intervals of breast-fed babies, and its low fat and protein content as a reason for the failure of the babies and thus their mothers to tolerate four-hour intervals, rather than any more complex and obscure psycho-logical reason. Bernal and Richards (in press) also point out the im-portant fact that what determines whether a mother tries to persist with four-hour intervals or not is associated in present-day Cambridge with social class and is perhaps to do with her willingness to go against the advice of experts. However, these findings suggest, more strongly than had the comparative data itself, that one should look back at the physio-logy of the control of onset of lactation for correlations of this with frequency of feeds and kind of mother–child contact. The prediction would be that the recommended four-hour intervals are less effective in establishing a good milk supply than would be more frequent (two-hour or less) feeds.

The kind of comparative study which I have been describing is not the comparison of single species with man but the detection of overall correlations of behaviour with anatomy and/or ecology in the mammals as a whole. The rules derived from such studies could then be applied to any higher primate or great ape pattern that can be discerned, to give a picture of the likely modifications of this pattern that might have been involved in the evolution of man. Most studies comparing higher primates and man suffer from too little if any, reference to the rest of the mammals. But equally well these correlations can be applied to known data (e.g. anatomy and physiology) about man to extrapolate the behavioural or ecological correlates of such data (as was done in Blurton Jones, 1972*d*). The more direct one-to-one comparisons that are cur-rently made between chimpanzee and 'Western' man, with more or less clear indication of what these comparisons are held to mean, would be much more usefully made between 'Western' industrialised man and hunter-gatherer man, particularly while people do still survive in a hunter-gatherer way of life. (I do not wish to deny the importance and interest of recent studies of wild chimpanzees such as those by Van Lawick–Goodall (1965, 1968), Reynolds (1966), Sugiyama (1968),

Suzuki (1969), Nishida (1968, 1970) and Izawa (1970) but to point out another area for comparison with the 'biological'.) The ecological pressures (survival values) are much more clearly visible in such people, as the work of the Harvard group shows clearly (Lee, 1968; Konner, 1972; Lee, in press). There are none of the problems in comparing human versus non-human subjects, even though reviewers such as Drewe *et al.* (1970) produce good arguments that the chimpanzee brain and human brain are considerably more comparable with each other than are monkey brains with either chimp or human brains. Problems do arise in considering firstly how representative surviving hunter-gatherers are of the variation in pre-agricultural Homo sapiens, and second in filling in the picture of the pre-Homo sapiens period of human evolution. Here both archaeology and comparative animal studies can contribute to the anthropologist's evaluation of the position. Current evidence is that the well-studied African hunter-gatherer cultures are not living in refuge areas and while some of these are apparently areas of poor productivity these people may be far less specialised than has often been assumed. However, information about a wider range of surviving hunter-gatherers would be of great value.

AN EXAMPLE OF THE BEARING OF COMPARATIVE
STUDIES ON DIRECT STUDIES OF HUMAN
BEHAVIOUR

Does it tell us anything about development of social behaviour to decide whether nursery school is a 'natural' situation?

Obviously, the meaning of the word 'natural' is crucial here. Ethologists sometimes say they study naturally occurring behaviour, or behaviour in a natural setting, or they are described as making 'naturalistic' observations. Several different things are meant by these expressions: (1) description of observed behaviour, which then becomes the phenomenon to be explained; (2) exploitation of a wide range of un-elicited variation in behaviour from moment to moment, individual to individual, population to population, and situation to situation which helps to weed out the least likely hypotheses and suggest the most likely ones; (3) the argument that one should begin to understand the subject's 'uninterfered with' behaviour before trying to design tests like the 'fear of strangers' test procedure (responses to strangers are probably a complex of 'fear', 'curiosity' and 'sociability'); (4) in animal studies but much less in human studies, it is also implied that ethologists study behaviour in the setting in which it evolved and in which it has maximal survival value so that we may begin to identify and be guided by the survival value of the behaviour that we observe. This is the sense in which I use 'natural' below.[2] In man this would mean studying childhood in hunter–gatherer peoples as has been done by Konner (1972) and Draper (in press) on Zhun/twa (! Kung) bushmen, and to a lesser extent by Gould (1969) and others currently on Australian aboriginal children.

The sorts of evidence described above indicate the following about the 'naturalness' (in the fourth sense) of nursery school. The evidence on mother–child contact comes from comparative animal studies and studies of contemporary hunter-gatherers (shown by Lee (1968) and Woodburn (1968) to be less atypical than usually assumed). The evidence on child-child contact comes from palaeodemography and archaeology and contemporary hunter-gatherers. (Comparative evidence on this at present simply fills out the demographic considerations (length of childhood and rate of reproduction).)

The best bet is that throughout the evolution of man up to at least the beginnings of agriculture most children in the 0–5 year range have had nearly continuous access to both mother and to a few children of varied ages (but also to father and other adult relatives of assorted ages). Thus in the evolutionary sense nursery school is 'natural' in providing contact with peers but 'unnatural' in delaying this contact until three years old and in removing access to mother and other relatives and in failing to provide contact with children of widely differing ages (including babies) and in adding contact with the unrelated and unfamiliar teacher. But staying at home in 'Western' society is equally unnatural, restricting contact with peers, particularly in the 'middle' class and in high-rise flats to limited special occasions (except in large families and in a few exceptional housing layouts with adjoining or communal gardens, as may be found sometimes in the U.S.A. and very rarely in the U.K., and perhaps the back-alley of nineteenth-century workmen's buildings – the inter-face, to use a phoney word necessitated only by distinctions which are comparably phoney, between ecological psychology, anthropology, evolution and child development should be discernible to the least discerning here).

ARE THERE ANY DISADVANTAGES IN BEING UNNATURAL?

Disadvantages may be of several kinds ranging from aggravation or minor unhappiness, to extinction. Extinction is likely to come about

---

[2] This sense has nothing to do with being non-industrial or 'not like us'. There is no implication that industrial society is any more unnatural than agricultural society. Indeed in some respects such as wide dispersion of wealth (food, jobs) rather than a concentrated landlord system it may even be more natural than some agricultural societies.

only through the close match of childrearing to the economic and other natures of the society, though it would be hard to say which part of this match came first on a historical scale. It has long been thought that Western man, unlike his ancestors was free of the threat of extinction but it is now clear that a threat is imminent from any one of three features of social behaviour: nuclear, chemical or biological war (or accidents relating to the manufacture and distribution of such weapons), destruction of the habitat, or depletion of natural resources, each related to population size. The lesser disadvantages of various deficits of mothering have been the subject of most of developmental psychology in the last fifty years. Effects of mothering by one, more than one, constant figure, a succession of short-term figures, and of separation from a previously single consistent mother have been discussed by Bowlby (1951), Ainsworth *et al.* (1962) and Rutter (1971, 1972). It is important to remember that results of certain child-care patterns may be disadvantageous in some cultures but not in others. A person who could not part from his relatives would do badly in the professional classes of Europe and North America. A person who has no attachment to anyone might do very well in this context and clearly does better (for his material welfare, and by Western standards) than someone 'attached' to a whole village.

But it is probably not necessary to think so far to find limitations to the value of raising children in a situation that requires either separations from mother or from playmates. Either of these separations brings problems, problems with one probably produce problems with the other. Children who cry at separation from their mother seem when away from their mother to interact very little with other children and thus probably fail to benefit from increased exposure to children. Not much is known of children, who even at an early age do not cry on separation. Such children exist but we do not know how they differ later on from the others. There may also be disadvantages in lack of early contact with other children.

Hansen (1966) and Harlow and Harlow (1965) have shown important influences of exposure to peers on rhesus monkey babies. Hinde and Spencer-Booth (1967) and Jensen, Bobbitt and Gordon (1967, 1968*a, b*) have demonstrated effects of presence and absence of social companions and of complex or plain environments on macaque mother–infant interaction. Are there any indications that human families may suffer from these same effects: a tendency towards a critical period for the influence of peers on later social behaviour, a worsening of mother–infant relationships in the absence of playmates?

Observing children at nursery school I was struck by the presence of children, even over the age of three, who interacted very little with any

280

of the other children, though they talked and showed things to the teacher (while not following the teacher around in the manner of some of those children who cry when their mother leaves them and who may appear equally asocial in the absence of the mother). Leach (1972) studied in detail the mother–child and child–child interactions in a small number of under fives who were patients of a hospital psychiatry department. These children directed very few behaviour items towards other children (normal or abnormal), elicited disproportionately few responses from others, and responded disproportionately less to the initiations by other children. Most of her abnormal subjects had intense anxiety and refusal to leave their mother as their main presenting symptoms, so that one cannot be sure whether the absence of response to children was a result of anxiety engendered by an unsatisfactory relationship to the mother, or whether absence of adequate interaction with peers produced distortions of the one existing interaction with the mother. As Leach points out, whichever of these is the case, these children are trapped in a situation where neither peers nor mother provide very rewarding interactions. In a current study of simpler measures of behaviour in a much larger number and variety of normal and abnormal children, M. F. Hall (pers. comm.) finds that a notable feature of the majority of children who are psychiatric patients is a reduced proportion of behaviour directed towards other children rather than towards adults. It is still not possible in a cross-sectional study to say whether this deficit is a result or a cause of the disordered mother–child relationship that often brings the family to the psychiatrist. But the deficit in behaviour to peers in a wide range of kinds of disorder takes the argument a step further than Leach's study and suggests that it might be as well to bear in mind causal relationships in both directions rather than only concentrating on effects originating in the mother. Popular discussion of the problems of young families in tower flats, and comments from a social anthropologist's cross-cultural viewpoint by Leach (1968) on the problems arising from the restriction of the nuclear family in 'Western' society would also argue for something analogous to the situation in the monkey families deprived of neighbours and playthings in Hinde and Spencer-Booth and in Jensen's experiments.

The kinds of interaction that a child can have with other children differ markedly, particularly in a mixed age group, from those it can have with adults. In interactions with other children in mixed age groups no child is always smaller and weaker or always bigger and stronger than its companions (Konner, 1972), it can win fights and lose them, initiate activities and play more and rougher rough and tumble play, it can get to know newcomers who are its own size and not only adults twice its size, it can interact with smaller and more helpless children with a degree of 'nurturance' scarcely described in our culture of single-aged peer groups.

Another notable point which is often ignored (under the influence of Parten's (1933) categories of parallel and co-operative play) is that interactions with other children begin remarkably early in life. Blurton Jones (1972c) describes details of interactions between children of two and upwards. Anderson (1972a, b) has mentioned the common occurrence of interactions of one to two-year-olds with other children when out with their mothers in a park. Mueller (pers. comm.) and Bronson (1972) are investigating the considerable repertoire of interaction of one to two-year-olds in greater detail. Bridges (1932, 1933) and Maudry and Nekula (1939) describe numerous interactions between institutionalised children aged nine months to two years. Bridges describes a wide range of behaviour including holding objects out towards someone, and chasing with laughing, in children who could only stand by holding the edge of the playpen. Questioning mothers of children at our research playgroup suggested that these reports would be representative of the age of onset of behaviour to peers in family living children as well. Given the opportunity, one to two-year-olds interact with other children, so the possibility clearly exists that the one to three-year-old period is an important time for effects of experience on the development of interactions with peers. It is also a time during which minimal opportunity occurs in 'Western civilisation'. Numerous studies have commented on the greater incidence of emotional and social problems in first borns and they usually seek explanations in terms of the lack of experience or differing ideals of the mother. It would seem to me equally likely that the explanation would be found in the smaller amount of contact with other children during the years one to three.

If there are these effects of early access to children they may account for some of the difficulty in demonstrating consistent effects of nursery school. If children with ample early access to other children were separated from those without (e.g. middle-class or high-flat dwelling second borns versus middle-class or high-flat first borns) effects might be more clearly seen. An added complication is the self-recruiting of nursery school samples. Analysis of the applicants to our research playgroup indicate that the middle class bring those who most need the social contact (first borns) but least need the intellectual stimulation whereas the manual workers bring those who least need the social contact but most need the intellectual stimulation (second and later born children). This analysis however also pinpointed the reciprocal problem. The middle-class mothers brought their children younger than the working-class mothers, and so young that crying on separation from the mother was very common. Sending such a child to playgroup defeats the aim of letting it play with children, under two-and-a-half-year-olds who cry on separation seem to be often very inactive if left at the playgroup.

In view of this it is perhaps no longer surprising that it is found in studies which ignore the factors that determine which children go to nursery school such as did Raph *et al.* (1968) and Swift (1964), that there are minimal effects of experience at nursery school on social behaviour (although Moore (1969) finds marked and long-lasting later correlates of substitute care, which includes nursery school). This is not to say that there are no children for whom there may be effects, and it is also clear that the investigation of effects should use more careful data on interactions. That Ralph *et al.* found decreased 'negative' interactions resulting from experience suggests either that the changes on joining a new group described by McGrew (1972*a*) have an important effect on Raph's data, or that for instance the continuing changes in the organisation of aggression described by Blurton Jones (1972*c*) are indeed influenced by experience with children. The early developing individual differences in 'sociability' may turn out to be less modifiable than expected. But it is not known how far they are due to differences in early contact with other children. Too many factors affect the very gross scores of sociability that are used by Raph *et al.* Behaviour analysis should be more subtle, for example comparing children who watch others with children who play alone with objects rather than lumping them in contrast with those who show more obvious interactions.

These various lines of fragmentary evidence suggest to me that it is well worth investigating the proposition that Western society puts an exceptionally heavy burden on the mother–child relationship which leads to short-term unhappiness for mothers and to cumulative complications in the relationship, which may indeed then be one link in the aetiology of many emotional and personality disorders of children (perhaps also in their mothers, see Rutter (1970) on positive relationship of marriage to mental ill-health for women but not for men). The discovery by Schaffer and Emerson (1964), confirmed by Blurton Jones and Leach (1972), that children may be 'attached' to other children such as siblings (in the senses respectively of crying when left by them, and prevented from crying at departure of mother by their presence) suggests that ways of reducing this pressure on the mother–child interaction may not be hard to find in principle. But practice, like sending all twelve-year-old girls to school when they could at least part of the time be relieving hard-pressed mothers and learning to deal with babies and children to everyone's advantage (as they are increasingly in some progressive educational areas), and like segregating over and under five-year-olds at school, makes such solutions highly difficult without more extensive interference with the feedbacks between social organisation, personality and childrearing.

IS THERE SUCH A THING AS HUMAN ETHOLOGY?

Eibl-Eibesfeldt and Hass (1967) and Crook (1970*b*) both use the phrase human ethology; Eibl-Eibesfeldt's usage (more closely tied to modern 'comparative ethology') seems to cover a collection of existing studies and a limited range of likely future studies of e.g. facial expressions and other signals, and effects and functions of morphological signals. Crook (with the original usage of ethology much more in mind) finds this too limited and claims a larger canvas for human ethology, including in addition the whole field of person–person interaction and of social organisation and its relationship to population dynamics. Crook very rightly stresses the importance of social structure both in animal and human studies and illustrates the advances in studying social structure that have been made in work on primate and other non-human societies. Freedman (1967) stresses the ethologists' interest in universal patterns and in function, in an interesting exercise in evolutionary perspective. These writings might be taken by some to reflect a claim that human ethology was a definable field of subject matter, that there are some features of man to be called ethology, others to be called psychology and so on. Such a claim would be quite unacceptable unless one were radically to change the contemporary usage of these terms, for instance by limiting psychology to the psyche and excluding behaviour from its subject matter. This claim would be even less acceptable than the separation by subject matter of psychology, sociology, social anthropology, physical anthropology, human biology. These subjects have large areas of overlap and larger areas of inter-dependence, but human ethology would have to overlap all of them and is therefore clearly not concerned with distinctive subject matter. There is unlikely to be any such subject as human ethology. But this is not to deny a role to ethology as a school within or as an approach to the human behavioural sciences.

I and others have argued elsewhere (Blurton Jones, 1972*a*) that some aspects of ethological methods may help in studies of causation and ontogeny. I also submit that the approach and general outlook of ethology can be of great help to the achievement of a biology of behaviour, of a unified science of behaviour of the type called for by Bowlby (1969). I would claim that such a unified science virtually exists already in the work of researchers such as Bowlby (1969), Lee and DeVore (1968), DeVore and Konner (in press), Konner (1972), Lee (in press), Richards and Bernal (1970, 1972) and Crook (1970*b*, and previously). I think that the 'four whys' and their relationship in the process of evolution is the key to such a unification. Thus, it is not possible to study interactions between people without some reference to, for example, sexual dimorphism and age differences (e.g. Morris, 1967; Wickler, 1967; Freedman, 1967). The effects and survival value of age and sex differences indicate the role of these differences in social organisation. It is impossible to elucidate these without reference to work in human biology and physiology (e.g. Newman, 1970) or to population dynamics (e.g. Crook and Gartlan (1966) on proportion of males and with it degree of size dimorphism in relation to predation and seasonality of food supply). On this basis relationships exist between many parts of the behavioural and human sciences in many directions.

One theoretical contribution of ethology may be therefore in extending human biology to include the behavioural sciences in a mutual relationship (behaviour is anatomy and physiology functioning, and thus being exposed to natural selection). The interest in variability in human biology is reflected in ethology for example in Crook's emphasis of the extent and adaptive significance of variability in primate social organisation. Variability is of course the raw material of adaptive change, whether in evolutionary or shorter time scales. A major problem remains in finding out precisely how this variability is able to lead to and maintain adaptive social structure, i.e. in discovering the routes of feedback from survival value of a social system to the ontogeny of its new members.

SUMMARY

In this chapter I have attempted to summarise features of ethological method and illustrate the possible roles of evolutionary theory in the study of development of social behaviour.

Ethological methods can be characterised as being more commonly concerned than is usual in psychology with:

(1) exact descriptions of observable behaviour,

(2) concern with the natural history of behaviour as the proper source of hypotheses,

(3) distrust of untested major categorisations of behaviour,

(4) analyses of the 'meaning' of social behaviour into: (*a*) the causal factors and control systems behind the performance of the behaviour by the performing individual, and (*b*) the effects of the behaviour on other individuals,

(5) divisions of explanations of behaviour into four different kinds, concerning respectively: causation, development, survival value, evolutionary history.

Evolutionary theory lies behind several of the existing and proposed applications of ethology to human behaviour (besides forming the basis of the four kinds of explanation). Many published comparisons of human and animal behaviour fail either from ignoring available human data or from breaking with the normal procedures of comparative behaviour studies (basically the procedures of comparative anatomy). They especially ignore the archaeological data on the ecology of evolving man and anthropological data on contemporary hunter-gatherer peoples. On the other hand many criticisms of comparative studies suffer from ignorance of the animal data.

Even on zoological grounds it is not safe to assume that human behaviour is similar to that of non-human primates. Primates are no exception to the rule that the characteristics of an animal are a result of specialisations adapting the basic form of that animal's group to the ecological niche of that species. Primates species vary, in structure and behaviour. Within a species, cultural variations in behaviour are known to be important adaptations in non-human primates (Crook and Gartlan, 1966; Gartlan, 1968; Denham, 1971). Man is exceptional among primates for doing a substantially larger amount of predation than other primates. Comparative studies should look for predatory specialisations on a great-ape pattern. To do this, studies of predators (e.g. Kruuk, 1972) and their nearest non-predatory relatives are every bit as necessary as studies of primates (see also Eisenberg, 1966). It has also sometimes been forgotten that it is not only the environment in the sense of climate, vegetation, concealment that modifies an animal but also what it does for a living – the way it manages to use that environment without competing fatally with other species in the same environment. Here again one can see a limitation in contemporary studies of primate social behaviour. The ecology of a species is hard to understand without extensive knowledge of its neighbours, prey, predators and potential competitors. This is true of studies of the ecology of hunter-gatherer people as well. Does it really work out so well to be the super-omnivore of the tropics, and the super-predator of the cold temperate–arctic regions?

Comparative studies cannot substitute for direct data on man, but they are essential for an understanding of the last two ethological explanations – survival value and evolutionary history (different developmental mechanisms have different survival values in different ecological niches, and developmental mechanisms have evolutionary histories just like any other feature of an animal – not excluding man's most human features). Knowledge about survival value and evolution of human behaviour, and other outcomes of comparative studies, may be of value in directing studies of human behaviour, mainly by playing a framework role as in Bowlby's theory of attachment.

We now know enough about developmental processes to realise that the fact that behaviour has an evolutionary history does not imply that behaviour will not vary from culture to culture. None the less biologists may feel that 'universal' features of human behaviour are interesting and require explanation, whether they are at the level of small motor patterns described by Eibl-Eibesfeldt, the social context of these patterns as investigated by Eibl-Eibesfeldt (1972) and by Ekman, Sorenson and Friesen (1969), the more complex features of behaviour listed by Murdoch (1949), the extraordinarily generalised basic structures of Levi-Strauss or simple and 'obvious' features of group sizes, parental behaviour, gross sex ratios, lack of mating seasons, etc. This is probably because being familiar with the entire animal kingdom enables biologists to realise that these universals could be different in man and are different in many animals. It is not obvious or unimportant that all people are the same in some things. The explanations of these constants will be found not in studying variation within a universal (i.e. studying differences between cultures may enable one to explain differences between cultures but not to explain the things that do not vary) but in comparing cases where the feature itself is present or absent (usually cross-species comparisons).

In this chapter some examples of comparative studies are combined with archaeological and anthropological data to argue that access to other children of varied ages has been neglected too much in studies of child development. The possibility is discussed that we are set severe limitations on the childrearing arrangements available to us, by the timing of relationships and influences between mother and child. It is suggested that direct data still needs to be obtained to show how far these are incompatible with situations commonly found in the exceptionally non-communal life of industrial society (mother and child isolated at home for the child's first three years) and with situations currently advocated (day care for children below three years old). The literature on the striking correlations between childrearing practices and the nature of a culture is noted and its integration with the current approach would form an example of the closer relationships between traditionally separate branches of the behavioural sciences which this writer feels is required. Such an integration may be fostered by an interest in an evolutionary framework to behaviour and in a human biology that fully acknowledges that behaviour is genetics, anatomy and physiology being exposed to natural selection.

ACKNOWLEDGEMENTS

I am happy to acknowledge that this paper owes much to pleasant and enlightening discussions with M. J. Konner and John Pfeiffer. I wish to thank the Nuffield Foundation for financial support and the

N. G. Blurton Jones

Wenner-Gren Foundation and the Royal Society for support for fieldwork with the Zhun/twa Bushmen, whose extensive influence on many of the views expressed I gratefully acknowledge.

REFERENCES

Abercrombie, M. L. J. (1971). Face to face – Proximity and distance. *J. Psychosom. Res.* **15**, 395–402.

Ahrens, R. (1953). Beitrag zur Entwicklung des Physiognomie und Mimikerkennens. *Z. Exptl. Angew. Psychol.* **2**, 412–54, 599–633.

Ainsworth, M. D., Andrey, R. G., Harlow, R. G., Leibovici, S., Mead, M., Pough Dane, G. and Wootton, B. (1962). Deprivation of maternal care. A reassessment of its effects. *Public Health Paper* **14**, Geneva, W.H.O.

Altman, M. (1963). Naturalistic studies of maternal care in moose and elk. In Rheingold, H. L. (ed.). *Maternal Behavior in Mammals.* New York, Wiley.

Ambrose, J. A. (1966). Ritualization in the human infant–mother bond. *Phil. Trans. Roy. Soc. B.* **251**, 359–63.

Ambrose, J. A. (1968). The comparative approach to early child development: the data of ethology. In Miller, E. (ed.), *Foundations of Child Psychiatry*, London, Pergamon.

Anderson, J. W. (1972*a*) Attachment behaviour out of doors. In Blurton Jones, N. G. (ed.). *Ethological Studies of Child Behaviour.* London, Cambridge Univ. Press.

Anderson, J. W. (1972*b*). On the psychological attachment of infants to their mothers. *J. Biosoc. Sci.* **4**, 197–225.

Andrew, R. J. (1963). The origin and evolution of the calls and facial expressions of primates. *Behaviour*, **20**, 1–109.

Beer, C. G. (1960–3). Incubation and nest-building behaviour of black-headed gulls. *Behaviour*, **18**, 62–106; **19**, 283–304; **21**, 155–76.

Ben Shaul, D. M. (1962). The composition of the milk of wild animals. *Int. Zoo Year Book.* **4**, 333–42.

Bernal, J. F. and Richards, M. P. M. (1973). What can zoologists tell us about human development? In Barnett, S. A. (ed.). *Ethology and Development.* London, Spastics Society, Heinemann.

Blurton Jones, N. G. (1971). Criteria for use in describing facial expressions of children. *Human Biology*, **43**, 365–413.

Blurton Jones, N. G. (1972*a*) (ed.). *Ethological Studies of Child Behaviour.* London, Cambridge Univ. Press.

Blurton Jones, N. G. (1972*b*). Characteristics of ethological studies of human behaviour. In Blurton Jones, N. G. (ed.). *Ethological Studies of Child Behaviour*, London, Cambridge Univ. Press.

Blurton Jones, N. G. (1972*c*). Categories of child–child interaction. In Blurton Jones, N. G. (ed.). *Ethological Studies of Child Behaviour*, London, Cambridge Univ. Press.

Blurton Jones, N. G. (1972*d*). Comparative aspects of mother–child contact. In Blurton Jones, N. G. (ed.). *Ethological Studies of Child Behaviour*, London, Cambridge Univ. Press.

Blurton Jones, N. G. and Leach, G. M. (1972). Behaviour of children and their mothers at separation and greeting. In Blurton Jones, N. G. (ed.). *Ethological Studies of Child Behaviour*, London, Cambridge Univ. Press.

288

Bowlby, J. (1951). *Maternal Care and Mental Health*. Geneva, W.H.O.

Bowlby, J. (1957). An ethological approach to research in child development. *Brit. J. Med. Psychol.* **30**, 230–40.

Bowlby, J. (1969). *Attachment and Loss*, Vol. 1, *Attachment*, London, Hogarth Press.

Brackbill, Y. (1958). Extinction of the smiling response in infants as a function of reinforcement. *Child Development*, **29**, 115–24.

Brannigan, C. and Humphreys, D. (1972). Human non-verbal behaviour, a means of communication. In Blurton Jones, N. G. (ed.). *Ethological Studies of Child Behaviour*. London, Cambridge Univ. Press.

Bridges, K. B. M. (1932). Emotional development in early infancy. *Child Development*, **3**, 324–41.

Bridges, K. B. M. (1933). A study of social development in early infancy. *Child Development*, **4**, 36–49.

Bronson, W. C. (1972). Competence and the growth of personality. In Bruner, J. S., Connolly, K. J. (eds.). *The Early Growth of Competence*. London, Academic Press.

Callan, H. (1970). *Ethology and Society*, London, Oxford Univ. Press.

Crook, J. H. (1970*a*). (ed.). *Social Behaviour in Birds and Mammals*. London, Academic Press.

Crook, J. H. (1970*b*). Social organisation and the environment; aspects of contemporary social ethology. *Animal Behaviour*, **18**, 197–209.

Crook, J. H. and Gartlan, J. S. (1966). Evolution of primate societies. *Nature*, **210**, 1200–3.

Cullen, J. M. (1972). Some principles of animal communication. In Hinde, R. A. (ed.). *Non-Verbal Communication*. London, Cambridge Univ. Press.

Darwin, C. (1859). *The Origin of Species*. London, Murray.

Denham, W. (1971). Energy relations and some basic properties of Primate social organisations. *American Anthropologist*, **73**, 77–95.

DeVore, I. (1965). (ed.) *Primate Behavior*. New York, Holt, Rinehart and Winston.

DeVore, I. and Konner, M. J. (in press). Man as hunter; a preliminary reappraisal. In White, N. F. (ed.). *Application of Ethology to Human Growth and Development*, Hamilton, Ontario, McMaster Univ.

Draper, P. (in press). The cultural ecology of bushman childhood. In Lee, R. and DeVore, I. (ed.). *Studies of Bushmen Hunter-gatherers*. Cambridge, Mass., Harvard Univ. Press.

Drewe, E. A., Ettlinger, G., Milner, A. D. and Passingham, R. E. (1970). A comparative review of the result of neuro-psychological research on man and monkey. *Cortex*, **6**, 129–63.

Eibl-Eibesfeldt, I. and Hass, H. (1967). Film studies in human ethology. *Current Anthropology*, **8**, 477–9.

Eibl-Eibesfeldt, I. (1972). Similarities and difference between cultures in expressive movements. In Hinde, R. A. (ed.). *Non-Verbal Communication*, London, Cambridge Univ. Press.

Eisenberg, J. (1966). The social organisation of mammals. *Handbuch der Zoologie* **8**, (10/7) Liefering 39.

Ekman, P., Sorenson, E. R. and Friesen, W. V. (1969). Pan-cultural elements in facial displays of emotion. *Science*, **164**, 86–8.

Emde, R. N. and Konig, K. L. (1969). Neonatal smiling and R.E.M. states. *J. Amer. Acad. of Child Psychiatry*, **8**, 57–67.

Esser, A. H. (1968). Dominance hierarchy and clinical courses of psychiatrically hospitalised boys. *Child Development*, **39**, 147–57.

Esser, A. H., Chamberlain, A. S., Chapple, E. D. and Kline, N. S. (1965). Territoriality of patients on a research ward. In Wortis, J. (ed.). *Recent Advances in Biological Psychiatry*, **7**, New York, Plenum Press.

Fantz, R. L. (1967). Visual perception and experience in infancy. In Stevenson, A. W. (ed.). *Early Behavior*. New York, Wiley.

Freedman, D. G. (1967). A biological view of man's social behavior. In Etkin, W. (ed.). *Social Behavior from Fish to Man*. Chicago and London, Univ. Chicago Press.

Freedman, D. G. (in press). *Human Infancy in Evolutionary Perspective*. New York, Basic Books.

Freeman, D. (1966). Social anthropology and the scientific study of human behaviour. *Man* (n.s.), **1**, 330–42.

Gardner, B. T. and Gardner, A. A. (1971). Two-way communication with an infant chimpanzee. In Schrier, A. and Stollnitz, F. (eds.). *Behavior of Nonhuman Primates*, Vol. 4, New York and London, Academic Press.

Gartlan, J. S. (1968). Structure and function in primate society. *Folia Primat.* **8**, 89–120.

Gould, R. A. (1969). *Yiwara; foragers of the Australian desert*. London, Collins.

Grant, E. C. (1965). The contribution of ethology to child psychiatry. In Howells, J. B. (ed.). *Perspectives in Child Psychiatry*, Edinburgh, Oliver and Boyd.

Grant, E. C. (1969). Human facial expression. *Man*, **4**, 525–36.

Hansen, E. W. (1966). The development of maternal and infant behaviour in the rhesus monkey. *Behaviour*, **27**, 107–49.

Harlow, H. F. and Harlow, M. K. (1965). The affectional systems. In Schrier, A. M., Harlow, W. F. and Stollnitz, F. (eds.). *Behavior of Nonhuman Primates*, Vol. 2. New York, Academic Press.

Hinde, R. A. (1966). *Animal Behaviour* (2nd ed. 1970). London and New York, McGraw-Hill.

Hinde, R. A. and Spencer-Booth, Y. (1967). The effect of social companions on mother–infant relations in rhesus monkeys. In Morris, D. (ed.). *Primate Ethology*, London, Weidenfeld and Nicolson.

Hinde, R. A. and Spencer-Booth, Y. (1968). The study of mother–infant interactions in captive group-living rhesus monkeys. *Proc. Roy. Soc. B.* **169**, 177–201.

Hodos, W. (1970). Evolutionary interpretations of neural and behavioural studies of living vertebrates. In Schmitt, F. O. (ed.). *The Neurosciences: Second Study Program*. New York, Rockefeller Univ. Press.

Hutt, S. J. (1970). The role of behaviour studies in psychiatry; an ethological viewpoint. In Hutt, S. J. and Hutt, C. (eds.). *Behaviour Studies in Psychiatry*. Oxford, Pergamon.

Hutt, S. J. and Hutt, C. (1970a) (eds.). *Behaviour Studies in Psychiatry*. Oxford, Pergamon.

Hutt, S. J. and Hutt, C. (1970b). *Direct Observation and Measurement of Behaviour*. Springfield, Illinois, Thomas and Thomas.

Izawa, K. (1970). Unit groups of chimpanzees and their nomadism in the savanna woodland. *Primates*, **11**, 1–45.

Jensen, G. D., Bobbitt, R. A. and Gordon, B. N. (1967). Sex differences in social interaction between infant monkeys and their mothers. In Wortis, J. (ed.). *Recent Adv. Biol. Psychiat.* **9**. New York, Plenum Press.

Jensen, G. D., Bobbitt, R. A. and Gordon, B. N. (1968a). Effects of environment on the relationship between mother and infant pigtailed monkeys (*M. nemestrina*) *J. Comp. Physiol. Psych.* **66**, 259–63.

Jensen, G. D., Bobbitt, R. A. and Gordon, B. N. (1968b). Sex differences in the development of independence of infant monkeys. *Behaviour,* **30**, 1–14.

Kagan, J. (1971). *Change and Continuity in Infancy.* New York, Wiley.

Kessen, W., Leutzendorff, A. M. and Stoutsenberger, K. (1967). Age, food deprivation, non-nutritive sucking, and movement in the human newborn. *J. Comp. Physiol. Psychol.* **63**, 82–6.

Konner, M. J. (1972). Aspects of the developmental ethology of a foraging people. In Blurton Jones, N. G. (ed.). *Ethological Studies of Child Behaviour,* London, Cambridge Univ. Press.

Konner, M. J. (in press). Maternal care, infant behaviour and development among the Zhun/twa (!Kung) bushmen. In Lee, R. and DeVore, I. (ed..) *Studies of Bushmen Hunter-gatherers,* Cambridge, Mass., Harvard Univ. Press.

Kruuk, H. (1972). *The Spotted Hyena,* Chicago and London, Univ. of Chicago Press.

Lancaster, J. (1968a). Primate communication systems and the emergence of human language. In Jay, P. (ed.). *Primate Studies in Adaptation and Variability.* New York, Holt, Rinehart and Winston.

Lancaster, J. (1968b). On the evolution of tool-using behaviour. *Amer. Anthropol.* **50**, 56–66.

Lancaster, J. (1971). Play-mothering: the relations between juvenile females and young infants among free-ranging vervet monkeys (*Cercopithecus aethiops*). *Fol. Primatologia,* **16**, 313–35.

Lawick-Goodall, J. van (1965). Chimpanzees of the Gombe Stream Reserve. In DeVore, I. (ed.). *Primate Behavior,* New York, Holt, Rinehart and Winston.

Lawick-Goodall, J. van (1968). The behaviour of freeliving chimpanzees in the Gombe stream reserve. *Anim. Behav. Monog.* **1**, 165–311.

Leach, E. R. (1968). *A Runaway World?* London, B.B.C. Publications.

Leach, G. M. (1972). Comparison of social behaviour of anxious children and normal children in a playgroup setting. In Blurton Jones, N. G. (ed.). *Ethological Studies of Child Behaviour.* London, Cambridge Univ. Press.

Lee, R. B. (1968). What hunters do for a living, or, how to make out on scarce resources. In Lee, R. B. and DeVore, I. (eds.). *Man the Hunter,* Chicago, Aldine.

Lee, R. B. and DeVore, I. (ed.) (in press). *Studies of Bushmen hunter-gatherers.* Cambridge, Mass., Harvard Univ. Press.

Lee, R. B. and DeVore, I. (eds.) (1968). *Man the Hunter.* Chicago, Aldine.

Lorenz, K. (1941). Vergleichende Bewegungsstudien an Anatinen. *Supp. J. Ornith.* **89**, 194–294.

Lorenz, K. (1953). *Comparative Studies on the Behaviour of the Anatinae.* London, The Avicultural Society.

Lorenz, K. (1966). *On Aggression.* London, Methuen.

Lorenz, K. (1970). *Studies in Animal and Human Behaviour* Vol. 1 (trans. Martin, R.). London, Methuen.

Maccoby, E. and Feldman, S. S. (1972). Mother-attachment and stranger reactions in the third year of life. *Child Devel. Monogr.* **37**, 1–86.

MacKay, D. (1972). Formal analysis of communicative processes. In Hinde, R. A. (ed.). *Non-Verbal Communication.* London, Cambridge Univ. Press.

Manning, A. (1967). *An Introduction to Animal Behaviour.* New York, Wiley.

Marler, P. and Hamilton, W. J. (1967). *Mechanisms of Animal 'Behavior.* New York, Wiley.

Martin, R. D. (1968). Reproduction and Ontogeny of tree-shrews (*Tupaia belangeri*) with reference to their general behaviour and taxonomic relationships. *Z. Tierpsychol.* **25**, 409–95, 505–32.

Mason, W. A. (1965). Determinants of social behaviour in young chimpanzee. In Schrier, A. M., Harlow, H. F. and Stollnitz, F. (eds.). *Behaviour of Nonhuman Primates.* New York, Academic Press.

Maudry, M. and Nekula, M. (1939). Social relations between children of the same age during the first year of life. *J. genet. Psychol.* **54**, 193–215.

Moore, T. (1969). Stress in normal childhood. *Human Relations,* **22**, 235–50.

Morris, D. (1967). *The Naked Ape.* London, Cape.

Morris, D. (1969). *The Human Zoo.* London, Cape.

McGrew, W. C. (1969). An ethological study of agonistic behaviour in preschool children. In Carpenter, C. R. (ed.). *Proc. Second Int. Con. Primatology, Vol. I, Behaviour.* New York and Basel, Karger.

McGrew, W. C. (1972a). Aspects of social development in nursery school children, with emphasis on introduction to the group. In Blurton Jones, N. G. (ed.). *Ethological Studies of Child Behaviour.* London, Cambridge Univ. Press.

McGrew, W. C. (1972b) *An ethological study of children's behavior.* New York and London, Academic Press.

Murdoch, G. P. (1949). *Social Structure.* New York, Macmillan.

Newman, R. W. (1970). Why man is such a sweaty and thirsty naked animal. A speculative review. *Hum. Biol.* **42**, 12–27.

Nishida, T. (1968). The social group of wild chimpanzees in the Mahalia Mountains. *Primates,* **9**, 167–224.

Nishida, T. (1970). Social behaviour and relationship among wild chimpanzees of the Mahalia Mountains. *Primates,* **11**, 47–87.

Orians, G. (1969). On the evolution of mating systems in birds and mammals. *Amer. Naturalist,* **103**, 589–603.

Parten, M. B. (1933). Social play among preschool children. *J. abnorm. soc. Psychol.* **28**, 136–47.

Raph, J. B., Thomas, A., Chess, S. and Korn, S. J. (1968). The influence of nursery school on social interactions. *Amer. J. Orthopsychiat.* **38**, 144–52.

Reynolds, V. (1966). Open groups in hominid evolution. *Man* (n.s.), **1**, 441–52.

Richards, A. I. (1970). Socialization and contemporary British anthropology. In Mayer, R. (ed.). *Socialization, the approach from social anthropology.* London, Tavistock.

Richards, M. P. M. and Bernal, J. F. (1970). The effects of bottle and breast feeding on infant development. *J. Psychom. Res.* **14**, 247–52.

Richards, M. P. M. and Bernal, J. F. (1972). Observational study of mother–infant interaction. In Blurton Jones, N. G. (ed.). *Ethological Studies of Child Behaviour.* London, Cambridge Univ. Press.

Rowell, T. E. (1960). On the retrieving of young and other behaviour in lactating golden hamsters. *Proc. Zool. Soc. London,* **135**, 205–82.

Rutter, M. (1970). Sex differences in children's responses to family stress. In James, A. E. and Koupernick, C. (eds.). *The Child in His Family.* New York, Wiley.

Rutter, M. (1971). Parent–child separation; psychological effects on the children. *Child Psychol. Psychiat.* **12**, 233–60.

Rutter, M. (1972). *Maternal Deprivation Reassessed*. London, Penguin.

Schaffer, H. R. and Emerson, P. E. (1964). The development of social attachments in infancy. *Monogr. Soc. Res. Child Developm*. **29**, 1–77.

Slotnick, B. M. (1967). Intercorrelations of maternal activities in the rat. *Anim. Behav*. **15**, 267–9.

Sugiyama, Y. (1968). Social organisation of chimpanzees in the Budongo Forest, Uganda. *Primates*, **9**, 225–58.

Suzuki, A. (1969). An ecological study of chimpanzees in a savanna woodland. *Primates*, **10**, 103–48.

Swift, J. (1964). Effects of early group experience, the nursery school and day nursery. In Hoffman, M. L. and Hoffman, L. W. (eds.). *Review of Child Development Research*. New York, Russell Sage.

Tanner, J. M. (1962). *Growth at Adolescence*. Oxford, Blackwell.

Tiger, L. and Fox, J. R. (1966). The zoological perspective in social science. *Man* (n.s.), **1**, 75–81.

Thompson, J. (1941). Development of facial expressions in blind and seeing children, *Arch Psychol*. **37**, No. 264 (New York).

Tinbergen, N. (1951). *The Study of Instinct*. London, Oxford Univ. Press.

Tinbergen, N. (1963). On aims and methods of ethology. *Z. Tierpsychol*. **20**, 410–33.

Trivers, R. L. (1971). The evolution of reciprocal altruism. *Quart. Rev. Biol*. **46**, 35–37.

Washburn, S. L. (ed.) (1964). *Classification and Human Evolution*. London, Methuen.

Washburn, S. L. (1971). Introduction to symposium on Bushman hunter-gatherers. American Anthropologists Association, New York City.

Wickler, W. (1967). Socio-sexual signals and their intraspecific imitations among primates. In Morris, D. (ed.). *Primate Ethology*. London, Weidenfeld and Nicolson.

Widdowson, E. M. (1970). Harmony of growth. *Lancet* **1**, 901–5.

van Hoof, J. A. R. A. M. (1972). A comparative approach to the phylogeny of laughter and smiling. In Hinde, R. A. (ed.). *Non-Verbal Communication*. London, Cambridge Univ. Press.

Woodburn, J. (1968). An introduction to Hadza ecology. In Lee, R. B. and DeVore, I. (eds.). *Man the Hunter*. Chicago, Aldine.

Zegans, L. C. (1967). An appraisal of ethological contribution to psychiatric theory and research. *Amer. J. Psychiat*. **124**, 794–839.

14

The psychology of child psychology

David Ingleby

When St John the Divine writes, 'I was in the Spirit on the Lord's day', he seems to be letting us know that 'being in the Spirit' was a necessary condition for having the revelation he proceeds to unfold. In this paper I want to suggest that (although we are not told this, but have to find out for ourselves) the revelations of child psychology also require that one be in a certain spirit before they become convincing; that they are as much products of the mentality which is brought to bear on the evidence as of the evidence itself.

The mentality we are talking about is not, as in St John's case, a transitory state of the individual: it is the shared corpus of concepts, attitudes and methods of inquiry into which the 'fully trained' psychologist has been initiated. With the help of some of the papers in this volume, I shall try first of all to elucidate this mentality, and then to demonstrate that it can only be understood in terms of its place in (to borrow Laing's useful definition) 'the *political* order . . . the ways persons exercise control and power over one another' (Laing, 1967, p. 107).

In other words, I want to consider this mentality not just as a set of ideas viewed apart, but as an ideology; the essential difference being that an ideological critique takes into account the interests which a particular mentality is defending. As Mannheim states:

The concept 'ideology' reflects the one discovery which emerged from political conflict, namely, that ruling groups can in their thinking become so intensively interest-bound to a situation that they are simply no longer able to see certain facts which would undermine their sense of domination. There is implicit in the word 'ideology' the insight that in certain situations the collective unconscious of certain groups obscures the real condition of society both to itself and to others and thereby stabilises it. (1936, p. 36)

The 'psychology of child psychology' I am thus trying to sketch is an exercise quite different in spirit from child psychology itself; I shall be attempting to practise the kind of psychology which that profession does not apply, in order to show why it does not apply it. For – with a few deviant exceptions (e.g. Reich or Laing) – child psychology has not looked at its subject-matter in the light of the political system in which

295

David Ingleby

it is found: the political order is usually seen as a source of extraneous variance which must be partialled out of the data to make them truly 'psychological'. If this is how psychology is to be defined, indeed, then the present essay is not psychology at all: but its purpose is to demonstrate that the 'facts' produced by any psychology which attempts to ignore the political context of what it observes will be about as useful as, say, an analysis of a violin concerto which ignores what the orchestra is playing.

In an earlier paper (Ingleby, 1970) I collected some examples of the way in which the approach which has come to be regarded as 'scientific' psychology seemed to be shot through with ideological biases. In the light of these biases I went on to contend that the 'scientific' label is a device for throwing us, ideologically speaking, off the scent: for that which is 'scientific', by definition, does not depend for its authority on the political loyalties implicit in it. My contention was that the social function which determines the spirit of inquiry in psychology – whatever convictions psychologists may have about it – is the maintenance of the *status quo*: psychology borrows habits of thought from natural science and applies them to the human sphere in a manner which is logically quite inappropriate, but politically highly functional. This activity was referred to as 'reification', defined as 'the misrepresentation of praxis as process' – 'praxis' being the type of activity which characterises an agent, and has to be understood as projects or communications having meanings, and 'process' being the activity of things, which does not harbour meanings in the same sense, but can be completely understood in terms of its antecedent causes (the traditional scientific paradigm of explanation). The effect of the many reifications that occur in psychology is to dehumanise the individual in the same way that the political system dehumanises him, i.e. to represent as impersonal, thing-like processes those aspects of people which the political order itself needs to remove from their agency; either to eliminate them, as in the case of 'deviant' behaviour (and other attempts men make to build their own order of values and perceptions), or – by abolishing the very distinction between people and things – to facilitate the use of people as if they were things. Where reification assists in the elimination of deviance, it is also accompanied by a 'normative' component (for instance, in the 'disease model' of abnormal experience or behaviour): the logic of 'correct/incorrect' functioning is superimposed on the dimension 'socially desirable/ undesirable', via the use of metaphorical dichotomies like sickness/ health, disordered/well-ordered, adjusted/maladjusted, adaptive/maladaptive, and so on.

Thus, in the earlier paper, the ideological content of psychology was located in a single general concept – reification – instances of which

296

were described in theories of intelligence, personality and learning, and in psychiatry. The issues have been greatly clarified for us since then by Harré and Secord's (1972) analysis of the 'paradigm shift' which they claim to detect in the social sciences; their 'old' and 'new' paradigms overlap to a large extent with my 'process/praxis' distinction, though – in line with the current paradigm of 'philosophy of science' itself – they do not dwell on the political significance of these modes of explanation. In this essay I wish to return to the same theme, by showing how child psychology has wished out of existence the all-important political context of childhood, and how it is obliged to do this by virtue of the social function of the 'people professions' to which it belongs.

To summarise, then: I start from the belief that practically every act in relation to a child, from the moment of his birth and even before, reflects constraints dictated by that child's place in the political system. (From this point of view, we might say that the whole field of child development ought properly to be regarded as the study of socialisation.) In psychology, however, this determination is not simply ignored, but the evidence about it is suppressed by the very methodology of the profession: the end result of which is the illusion captured in Mary Ainsworth's phrase about the infant being 'social from the beginning (this volume, p. 99). I hope to show that this illusion which would appear inexplicable if one considered child psychology simply as a neutral, truth-finding enterprise, becomes intelligible if we examine the place in society occupied by the makers of it.

Now the most effective means which psychologists have devised for keeping the political context of childhood out of the picture was the creation of that venerable distinction between 'socialisation' and the rest of development, and the relegation of ideology to the waste-paper basket of 'cultural variables', which are supposed to enter only into the learning of explicit moral principles, allegiances, and social concepts. Having thus disposed of political factors, psychologists have moved increasingly towards areas where these influences are regarded as minimal, and towards a methodology which does not cater for them. The hope appears to be that if child development is studied sufficiently early on and in a sufficiently 'biological' way – which means, in the main, using concepts and observational methods borrowed from the study of animals, whose politics are less of a problem – if this is done, a picture of the process can be built up which will hold good regardless of the structure of the society in which the child develops. (One is reminded inevitably of the magical power to banish unpleasant impurities which is also ascribed to 'biological' detergents.) That such a picture is logically possible to achieve, I will not argue over here: but the fragments of the original garment which would survive such drastic laundering would, alas, be of little use to anyone. We shall see later, in fact, how usable conclusions may be drawn from such research only by the addition of unstated and untested assumptions. The political system is inextricably present in the most basic aspects of childrearing and (as Busfield shows in this volume) in the process of conception and gestation as well: its influence is manifest in the whole environment in which the child undergoes the first stages of his life.

This is true, first, in a practical and material sense. For example, the extent to which a mother can *afford* to meet her child's demands – how much food and attention she can give and when, how much crying she can permit or tolerate – must be strongly influenced by her position in the system of production and consumption; so that even the simplest 'time-and-motion study' approach is portraying the results of a given political system. Here, in fact, it might make sense to 'partial out social class' in order to study the effects of such environmental variables in their own right. On a different level of analysis, however, the influence of the child's environment cannot be disentangled from the socio-economic determinants of that environment. I am referring to the moulding of a child's mentality which starts with the first interactions, and which is all the more potent for being unconscious as well as unspoken: that is, the formation of his ideas about his own needs and propensities, and the response to them that can be expected from the world around him – about what he may take, own, reject, give, do or say; all of which boil down to expectations derived from early experience. These ideas are not so much expounded in the process of socialisation as embodied and enacted in it.

Psychology does not, in fact, provide us with a very adequate way of describing and measuring what I have called here the child's 'mentality': the topic spreads out untidily under several headings – concept formation, construct theory, motivation, language learning, attachment theory, object relations, psychodynamics. However vague it seems one must remain about its definition, this seems to me no drawback in asserting that it must be to a large extent a product of the political system – the totality of power relations – that the child grows up in. This, of course, is a truism in Marx (cf. 1910, p. 119: 'The same men who establish social relations conformably with their material productivity, produce also the principles, the ideas, the categories, conformably with their social relations'): but its application within the field of child psychology has been not only neglected, but quite strongly resisted.[1]

[1] Even Marcuse (1955) goes only part of the way in applying it. While observing how the 'reality principle' is a manifestation of the requirements of socio-economic organisation, Marcuse retains to state his argument Freud's own metapsychology of ego, super-ego and id – not realising that these concepts themselves embody demarcations dictated by those same requirements.

Thus, the aim of studying the child as if he and his family were living on a desert island is a futile one: they aren't – and even if they were, they would probably still behave as though they weren't. From the start, the responses which the child receives to his demands and activities are shaped by the fact that both his 'input' and his 'output' are destined for the slots which the social system will provide for them. In the type of society most psychology is written about, these slots will be highly specific ones, requiring the individual to adapt his demands obediently to market conditions (cf. Jules Henry's (1966) 'virtuoso consumer'), and to tailor his creative capacities to labour conditions, since – to the system that sustains him – his physical energy, sensory-motor skills, and imagination (should he be privileged enough to retain any) are all essentially *commodities*. Precisely how the prevailing relations of production and consumption will impinge on him will vary greatly with his class position, but it is those relations which are the most important factors in determining the mould in which 'socialisation' casts him. In Ainsworth's paper we find a reference to these factors which epitomises child psychology's endorsement of the *status quo*: she writes (p. 99) of the child learning 'rules, proscriptions, values and modes of behaviour which fit him to his *appropriate* role in a social group' (my italics), but leaves the question 'appropriate to what?' in convenient suspense. The answer we can expect to this question from most child psychologists, if they provide one at all, will usually be something like 'appropriate to his needs and talents', rather than (e.g.) 'appropriate to the position occupied by his racial, sexual and income group in the political system': an answer informed by something more than optimism, and something less than scientific evidence.

Ainsworth's contribution is worth studying in more detail to discover the covert assumptions which enable her to make, out of the evidence collected, such a politically evasive picture of socialisation. (I have not selected this example because it is an unrepresentative or, indeed, an undistinguished piece of work in its own field, but rather for the opposite reasons: it is the internalised professional stance, rather than any variations on it, which I wish to trace.) It is worth quoting one section of this article in full:

If an infant is reared in a social environment not too dissimilar from that in which the species evolved – an environment in which adults are responsive to the signals implicit in his behaviour – it seems likely to us that he will gradually acquire an acceptable repertoire of more 'mature' social behaviours without requiring heroic efforts on the part of his parents specifically to train him to adopt the rules, proscriptions and values they wish him to absorb. Because of these considerations we find the concept of 'socialisation' essentially alien to our approach. (This volume, p. 99)

First, there is no quicker way to appreciate the *attitude* to the mechanisms of socialisation implicit in this paragraph than by placing alongside it another statement on the same topic:

In fact, the world still seems to be inhabited by savages stupid enough to see reincarnated ancestors in their newborn children . . . What barbarism! Take a living child, sew him up in a dead man's skin, and he will stifle in such senile childhood with no occupation save to reproduce the avuncular gestures . . . These backward aborigines can be found in the Fiji Islands, in Tahiti, in Vienna, in Paris, in Rome, in New York – wherever there are men. They are called parents. (Sartre, 1960, pp. 14–15; quoted in Laing, 1967.)

Clearly, these two writers have not reached the same conclusion: but is there necessarily any difference in the data they have started from? The assumptions and values which Sartre has brought to the data are pretty obvious: Ainsworth's are better concealed, and it will be instructive to uncover them.

In this paragraph we encounter first an important non-sequitur, in the implicit argument that since socialisation does not require 'heroic efforts' on the part of the parents, their aims cannot be in conflict with the child's own dispositions – and hence socialisation, as it is usually understood, does not take place at all. We shall not dwell on the limitations of Ainsworth's own evidence as proof of this assertion, save to note that it covers only a small area of potential conflict between parents and children, and does not study parental behaviour closely enough to reveal the subtler, but no less effective, methods of 'gentle persuasion' that her middle-class mothers may be putting their energies into. Nor need we speculate too much about the – equally unobserved – efforts and sacrifices which the children in this study may have been making. For there is no reason why socialisation should not be performed in such a way as to fully deserve Sartre's strictures, without requiring the least heroism on the part of the parents. Consider, after all, the position they are in: relative to the child, they have total authority, and almost as much power. Regarding their authority (the nature of which we must discuss later), it need only be remarked here that even the professedly impartial scientific observer describes the child's crying as a 'nuisance' (above, p. 100), automatically adopting the parents' point of view, and ignoring the fact that the child would hardly be crying if he himself were not experiencing some 'nuisance'. Apropos of the power which parents have, it should be remembered that the infant over which they have this authority has the most advanced learning abilities of any known organism: had Shakespeare written 'What a piece of work is man . . . ' in this cybernetic age, he might have been able to adduce more pointedly than I can the fact this creature, in its pint of grey matter, can dwarf the computing power of I.B.M. itself. Add to this the fact that the pleasure and misery which motivate the infant to learn are unmitigated by any adult system of emotional defences, and it should be apparent that the Jesuits' claim to be able to make what they liked of a child, given a sufficiently early start, is (like Ainsworth's, to which it bears a family resemblance) not a particularly remarkable one. The sad fact is that the 'heroic efforts' which parenthood entails for most of us are a sign more often of incompetence than of anything else. If B. F. Skinner could train pigeons to guide missiles to their target with a brief, unheroic training programme, why should America's mothers, teachers and colonels achieve less in the twenty years they have to teach their progeny to do likewise?

In short, for Ainsworth to claim (p. 119) that the child 'does not need to be taught to be social', in view of its predisposition to obedience, is about as accurate as describing a wrist-watch as 'self-winding' by virtue of its having a knob to wind it with. Who 'winds up' the child, how, and with what in mind, are questions that are likely to tell us far more about the end-product than a description of the knob.

The reluctance of child psychologists to think too hard about these questions is well demonstrated in the notion that the 'rules, proscriptions, values and modes of behaviour' which a child must acquire to become 'social' are those which his *parents* require him to absorb. In the sense that parents may have wishes for the child that reflect their identification with interest-groups outside the family, this is partly true: but on the obvious interpretation, this notion seems a straightforward reversion to the 'desert island' school of socialisation. It turns a blind eye to the fact that parents are not simply acting in their own interests, or even in those of the child, in bringing him up: they are first and foremost *representatives* of a particular sector of a particular political system, and – ultimately – it is in the cause of the perpetuation of that system that efforts will be directed. This oversight achieves an important misrepresentation of the nature of parental authority. If Ainsworth's choice of words were correct, it would be open to parents to bring up children in any mould which pleased them: whereas a whole area of legislation exists to ensure that parents who do this are deprived of their parental authority the moment their aims come into conflict with those of the political order.

This disingenuousness about parental authority is curiously widespread amongst child psychologists. In another tradition, for instance, Maude Mannoni – a therapist whose method, following Lacan, is to make explicit to a child aspects of his situation to which he has been denied the verbal keys – offers to her young patients the following 'keys' to the nature of authority:

When a Mummy gets cross, there is a father inside her saying, 'Bring our daughter up well, take care of her'. (1969, p. 142)

Or:

Daddy is *the big boss*. Mummy and Paul take orders from Daddy. (*ibid.* p. 134, my italics)

Luckily, neither of these patients were so disturbed as to respond 'Why?' to these statements. One wonders how Mme Mannoni would have answered them: would a few words on the French family's relation to (capitalist) society, and the father's traditional role in mediating it, have let more cats out of the bag than she feels a therapist should, or more than she knows are inside it? This example could be paralleled – indeed, bettered – from many sources, but its peculiar irony demonstrates a feature of the therapeutic professions which deserves to be discussed later on: an analyst whose skills in revealing the structure of human relationships are among the highest that can be bought slips into the role of mystifier the moment an element of extra-familial structure comes into the picture.

In passing, we may note that the idea that parents bring up children on their own behalf reflects an important mystification practised not only by researchers but also – however unwittingly – by parents themselves: it is a technique for disguising control found in many different situations, which one might label 'phoney personalisation'. Learning to 'get into' the role of parent involves learning to affect a highly personal kind of pleasure or displeasure over matters which may not affect the parents' (or the child's) actual private interests at all: it would be naïve to call this 'acting', but it is recognisably the same tactic that one can discern in the hired actor who enthuses over spelling in 'Sesame Street', the house-wife interviewee in the margarine commercial, the crusading General, the tireless executive, or the Head of State addressing his public. Their job is made easier by the fact that its 'phoney personalisation' deflects any questions about who they might be working for: the more personal in-volvement is displayed, the fewer suspicions arise about absent parties whose interests might be being promoted. And parents, of course, are seldom aware that they are 'working for' anyone – or even working at all: only in, for instance, *Mein Kampf* do they earn their eulogies for service to the State. At times, of course – like many schoolmasters – they are in the unpleasant position of having to carry on imposing goals and values long after their ability to 'personalise' them has worn off, and before they have worked out any substitutes.[2]

---

[2] We may note, before leaving the subject, that an important function of the per-sonalisation of delegated roles is that any protest against their performance is ab-

Thus, both the psychologist's and the parent's pretence that primary socialisation serves only the interests of the primary group provides a vital line of defence for the interests it really serves. To modify the infant's propensities in such a way as to make coexistence with him possible will surely be agreed by everyone to be not only necessary but in the child's own interests. Hence – since no genuine conflict of interests exists – there can be no argument about whose side to take: we are all on the same side. Such a picture can only obscure the true reasons for 'failures of socialisation'. If the parents fail to produce a child adapted and reconciled to his allotted place in society, then on this model something is wrong with either the child or his parents (cf. the 'breakdown of family life' which is sometimes blamed for black unrest): for Science has shown that under normal conditions of family rearing, people will grow up adapted. It does not take much thought to see that what is masquerading here as a biological discovery is, in fact, nothing but a political preference for the *status quo*. In reality, children may also fail to acquire the 'right' values because they recognise the conflict between them and their actual interests, or because the parents do not fulfil their parental function (political rather than biological) and impose them. There are plenty of circumstances in which a family that produced, say, draft-evaders or transgressors of the law of property would not be in any sense biologically malfunctioning.

Faced with such an argument, the psychologist is likely to admit that the ethic into which a child is socialised does, after all, contain certain norms which subsume even the interests of the family to the smooth running of society as a whole. It is traditional to assume, at this point, that stating the need for some kind of 'social contract' sanctions whatever notion of 'social' or 'anti-social' behaviour is current in the situation being observed. It is not the purpose of this article to dispute whether some rule-based social structure – i.e. a political order – is necessary: but the argument that *some* version of the 'reality principle' must be instilled into a child cannot be used to justify the imposition of whichever happens to be around at the time. Such a presumption can only be based on the belief that the prevailing political system is the only possible or desirable one: an illusion which psychologists are not alone in holding.

Yet mere ethnocentricity is too simple an explanation of why psychologists present a view of socialisation which serves to protect the *status quo*. Their involvement with the power-structure within which they work has to be understood via a more careful examination of the exact role which they play in that structure: for this mentality does not arise in ivory towers. (Neither, one might add, does the so-called 'ivory-tower'

---

sorbed by their unfortunate performers – as soldiers, policemen, mental nurses, teachers and parents are always finding out.

mentality itself.) When we explore the channels through which psychological knowledge is made effective, we find first that those responsible for implementing it belong to what we might call the 'people professions' – those whose province is the regulation of human behaviour and the removal of 'social problems': that is, psychiatry, social work, the educational, penal and welfare systems. (I have deliberately avoided the widely used term 'helping professions' because I want to emphasise what the latter have in common with behaviour-regulating institutions such as the prison system, which nobody – as yet – speaks of as 'helping'.)

Now it is not within my competence or this paper's scope to offer a thorough analysis of the way these institutions work, but for the purposes of my argument several key features of them may be singled out; the point I want to make being that it is implicit in their role in the social system that their energies will be devoted to adapting men to that system, instead of helping to adapt the system to human needs. It is the job itself, rather than the people who do it or the theories they inherit, that is by nature conservative.

First, the 'people professions' are almost entirely financed and administered by public authorities. This is an inevitable – and in one obvious way, desirable – feature of a welfare system; but it does seem to have led to the consequence that the people the professions in practice cater to – who, incidentally, also represent for the most part the economically least privileged sector of society – have no say in the way they are organised, no access to their secrets, and no right to dispute their advice.

Secondly, their manner of functioning is primarily by way of 'confiscating' problems: either by institutionalising problem individuals, or by defining their difficulties in a specialised language which purports to remove them from the layman's province – for instance, the jargon of clinical psychiatry, psychodynamics, or educational psychology. (Thus, there is more than a grain of truth in the vulgar criticism that psychology says what everybody knows in a language nobody understands.) This, again, stems from the concept of 'welfare services' as a system set up *alongside* existing society, rather than part of it, whose task is to repair the damage done to human beings by the way of life the social system entails for them: its function thus being inevitably corrective, rather than preventive.

Thirdly, in consequence of this, the social expertise of the people professions must stop short abruptly at a certain level of the power structure; and the contradictions which these limits give rise to are responsible for much of the anguish among workers in these professions – whether they realise it or not. (See, e.g. Cannan, 1972.) The closer one works to the client, the more conspicuous the contradictions become. Consider, for example, the paradox of social workers and therapists who use 'object relations theory' to help their clients – an elaborate language for dealing with, among other things, the problems of having, getting, and giving, and the distinction between 'using' others as objects and relating to them as people. Their task is to raise their clients' consciousness of these issues, but somehow to stop short of the level where questions would start to arise about the same issues in relation to the larger structures of society. It is healthy for members of a family to become conscious of their envy, to resist being used, and so on – as long as they do it in the privacy of their own home; but what if they extend the process to their landlords, employers and rulers? One may make the same point by noting that the problems of having, getting, giving, and 'using' people are precisely what Marx wrote about (i.e. property, consumption, production and alienated labour); but no social worker is likely to be initiated into the analysis he offered.

In a sense, then (not a very nice one), the people professions treat their clients as if they were children, with very limited rights to knowledge about, and responsibility for, their own situations; but, of course, they are not children, and this state of affairs is not adequately explained by the nature of their problems. A certain degree of authority is proper to anyone in an advisory role, but the 'people professions' operate with a variety of paternalism that is quite incompatible with their claim to be 'helping people to lead better lives', and betrays the fact that their real duties lie altogether elsewhere. If such were really their aim, then we should expect their voice to be the most insistent in articulating and attacking the ways in which the political system itself systematically limits the quality of their clients' lives: moreover, it would be the latter to whom they would divulge their analyses of the situation, not to the others in authority over them. In practice, they apply their energies to ways of dealing with problems that offer the minimum disruption to the existing order – on peril of their jobs. For if the human wreckage produced by the way society is organised can be discreetly removed, processed, and returned in re-usable form by these social garbage-workers, then not only will the service avoid producing disruption itself: it will prevent the disturbance which might result if the evidence of the political system's failure to meet human needs were left in our midst.

These, then, are the trades to which psychology purveys the commodity of its knowledge, and to whose functions it thereby allies itself; just as the child's mentality is tailored to the social functions he will perform, so is that of the child psychologist. It is by virtue of the need to maintain the myth that the prevailing order is the only possible or desirable one that statements such as Ainsworth's 'the child is born social' gain approval: Reich, Laing, Henry, Sartre, or Marcuse can only offer the type of knowledge for which psychology – quite literally – has no use.

305

Here, then, we arrive back at the central theme of this paper: that how people are trained to act and think – whether they are children, parents, researchers, or practitioners with people – has to be understood in terms of their position in the political order: we cannot pretend any longer that it isn't there. Both science and the people professions still confuse themselves and the rest of society with a Victorian image of magnanimous neutrality – one which might, indeed, have had some relevance in the days when science was still within the technical and intellectual means of curious gentlefolk, and charitable activities were an individualistic free-for-all. Now, however, these activities have become industries, and those who staff these industries are a new proletariat, who (like the rest) must submit to being used in order to stay alive. We must therefore be extremely careful not to set up these mental and emotional workers as 'enemies of the people', as much so-called radical criticism tends to do: in reality, the scientist, psychiatrist or social worker (like the teacher, the policeman, or the parent) is as exploited as those whose exploitation he facilitates, as brainwashed as those he brainwashes. What species of prostitute is more pitiable than the person whose most highly developed thoughts and feelings are bought and put to uses he has no inkling of?

Finally, if it is true that the mentality informing most psychological research is inherently conservative, our most urgent task is to find a framework within which psychologists could work who do not share the conviction that the existing political order is the only possible or desirable one. My belief here is that a sufficiently thorough analysis of the existing framework will supply all the keys to the construction of a new one.

Following a line of thought suggested by Gabel (1970), we may consider the problem as analogous to the psychotherapy of psychoses. The analogy runs as follows: Ideologies are epistemological structures whose intrinsic rigidities preclude the perception of certain areas of reality which must be concealed for the security of the existing power-structure; in the same way, it has been argued by those who have studied psychosis in its familial context, that psychotic thought-patterns represent attempts to embrace reality without betraying the power-structure of the relationships an individual is entangled in. (Mme Mannoni's therapy, in these terms, consists in telling her patients the truths which the family finds unspeakable, in order that their experience may make sense again.) The limits a psychologist unwittingly imposes on his own awareness, by assimilating the 'spirit' of the profession, correspond to the paranoid individual's defences against reality-testing: any evidence which might threaten the overall picture is either systematically ignored or turned into evidence confirming it. And this is not to protect the psychologist's (or paranoiac's) own interests, but the interests of those who rely on his unawareness to maintain their own positions. Anyone who sets out to do therapy on such thought-structures must do so primarily by analysing their inherent contradictions. We must work in the same way as the therapist, who, for example, demonstrates to a person that their difficulty in finding a 'lovable' person to live with stems from their deeper need for the presence of an 'unlovable' person by contrast with whom *they* can feel lovable. The people professions have difficulty in 'helping people to lead better lives', and the human sciences in understanding man in his social matrix: both must be helped to see, for a start, the extent to which their role in society requires them to fail at these very tasks.

If, then, the object is to produce a psychology which is genuinely open to reality testing (which is, after all, what a 'scientific' psychology would be), what has to be done is to restore an open-mindedness to psychology which will allow the situations it studies to impress their own logic on the observer – rather than imposing on these situations the fetishised concepts which survived the test of ideological acceptability. This does not imply a return to some naïve theory of 'direct' perception, but ceasing to delimit in advance the concepts which will best serve to grasp a situation, and replacing the closed 'shop-talk' of psychologists with an open language that will admit all perceptions. This goal would seem to correspond to the phenomenologists' 'return to the things themselves' (see Merleau-Ponty, 1962): but if our earlier analysis is correct, this kind of objectivity cannot be achieved by intellectual thoroughness alone, but by withdrawal of one's allegiance to the interest groups defended by the existing framework. 'Divergent thinking' is not enough: in the human sciences, phenomenology is inescapably a political activity, in that it must involve the undermining of a major system of power and control – that is, intellectual orthodoxy.

In other words, the relationship of psychology to the 'people professions', and of these professions to the existing order, must change. I have tried to show that membership of the élite to which most of my readers will belong confers many powers, but entails – indeed, is conditional on – a systematic attenuation and distortion of one's awareness. To set right that 'false consciousness', it is not enough simply to set off in pursuit of a wider range of viewpoints – as if, by some ingenious system of mirrors, one could see what the world would look like from a different position in the political order: one doesn't escape so easily from the bemusement of one's own mentality, from the habits of thought and perception laid down during the many years spent socialising into a class and a profession. The only way is to analyse just what this mentality is: and the shortest route to an understanding of it, as I have tried to show, is by discovering the power-structure it props up.

David Ingleby

REFERENCES

Cannan, C. (1972). Social workers: training and professionalism. In Pateman, T. (ed.). *Counter Course*. London, Penguin.

Gabel, J. (1970). *Sociologie de l'Aliénation*. Paris, Presses Universitaires de France.

Harré, R. and Secord, P. F. (1972). *The Explanation of Social Behaviour*. Oxford, Blackwell.

Henry, J. (1966). *Culture against Man*. London, Tavistock.

Ingleby, J. D. (1970). Ideology and the human sciences. *Human Context*, **2**, 159–80. Reprinted in Pateman, T. (ed.). *Counter Course* (1972). London, Penguin.

Laing, R. D. (1967). *The Politics of Experience*. London, Penguin.

Mannheim, K. (1936). *Ideology and Utopia*. London, Routledge and Kegan Paul.

Mannoni, M. (1969). *The Child, his Illness, and the Family*. London, Tavistock.

Marcuse, H. (1955). *Eros and Civilisation*. Boston, Beacon Press.

Marx, K. (1910). *The Poverty of Philosophy* (trans. Quelch, H.), Chicago.

Merleau-Ponty, M. (1962). *Phenomenology of Perception* (trans. Smith, C.). London, Routledge and Kegan Paul.

Sartre, J.-P. (1960). Foreword to *The Traitor* by André Gorz. London, Calder.

Author Index

Subject Index

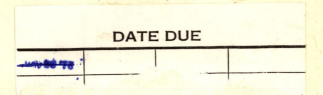

DATE DUE